SOCRATES

A SOURCE BOOK

COMPILED AND
IN PART TRANSLATED BY

John Ferguson
Dean and Director of Studies in Arts,
The Open University

Published by
Macmillan *for*
The Open University Press

First published 1970 by
MACMILLAN AND CO LTD
London and Basingstoke
Associated companies in Toronto Dublin
Melbourne Johannesburg and Madras

SBN 333 12146 5 (hard cover)

Printed in Great Britain by
RICHARD CLAY (THE CHAUCER
PRESS) LTD
Bungay, Suffolk

For Doreen and Robin

Contents

Preface

This is an attempt to present for the English-speaking reader the main source material about Socrates. R. Levin, *The Question of Socrates* (Harcourt, Brace & World, 1961) did something similar, but used only the more obvious sources. I have tried here to include some of the more out-of-the-way sources, though the result is by no means inclusive. I have in general not included later passages (*a*) when they merely reproduce something from Plato or Xenophon; (*b*) where the anecdote or *mot* recorded of Socrates is patently later; (*c*) where the passage appears in an almost identical form in more than one later writer (though I have not been consistent about this). For Plato and Xenophon I have had to be selective, and have assumed on the evidence of Aristotle (see the Introduction) that the Theory of Forms belongs to Plato, not to Socrates.

The exigencies of the Open University timetable have made the work more hurried than I would wish.

(*a*) I am sure that some passages are missing which ought to be included, though I trust that they are not many, and that there are none of vital importance.

(*b*) Where I have used the translations of others I have in general used out-of-copyright versions. I have not had the time to revise these in the interest either of accuracy or of contemporaneity.

(*c*) I am not a textual critic, and have not always been able to establish the best text, though I have drawn attention to some of the passages which raise major problems. I have in general used the Oxford text, Teubner or Loeb.

(*d*) Some of the passages have, so far as I can see, never been trans-

ated. In these and in most of the briefer extracts I have made my own version, and have no doubt error and infelicity will be found, though I hope nothing to lead others into major error.

I am most grateful to Mrs Gillian Salway for undertaking the translation of Libanius' *Apology*, which has never previously been translated into English.

Passages are taken from the following published translations. Unattributed translations are my own.

Anonymous, *Socrates* (London, 1887).

Anonymous (ed.), *The Complete Works of Xenophon*, trans. into English by Ashley, Spelman, Smith, Fielding, Welwood and others (London, 1877).

Carlill, H. F., *The Theaetetus and Philebus of Plato* (London, 1906).

Cary, H., Davis, H., and Burges, G., *The Works of Plato* (London, 1848–52).

Crosby, M., and Calder, W. M. III, 'Libanius: *On the Silence of Socrates*', *Greek, Roman and Byzantine Studies*, III (1960) 185 ff., quoted by kind permission of the editor and translator.

Davies, J. Ll., and Vaughan, J. D., *Plato's Republic* (London, 1866).

Jowett, B., *The Dialogues of Plato*, 3rd ed. (Oxford, 1892).

Prickard, A. O., *Selected Essays of Plutarch*, II (Oxford, 1918).

Shelley, P. B., *Essays, Letters from Abroad, Translations and Fragments* (London, 1840).

Shilleto, A. R., *Plutarch's Morals: Ethical Essays* (London, 1888).

Stanley, T., *Claudius Aelianus: His Various History* (London, 1665).

Taylor, T., *Dissertations of Maximus of Tyre*, 2 vols (London, 1804).

Taylor, T., and Sydenham, F., *The Works of Plato* (London, 1804).

Taylor, T., *Select Works of Porphyry* (London, 1823).

Tucker, T. G., *Selected Essays of Plutarch* (Oxford, 1913).

Wright, J., *The Phaedrus, Lysis and Protagoras of Plato* (London, 1888).

Yonge, C. D., *The Lives and Opinions of Eminent Philosophers by Diogenes Laertius* (London, 1853).

Finally, a deep debt of gratitude is due to my secretary, Doreen Lewis, and all her staff for co-operating in preparing the typescript from illegible scrawl under considerable pressure, to my mother, Dr Nesta Ferguson, and to Alison Gunn for their lynx-like scanning of the proofs, to my colleague, Leslie Lonsdale-Cooper, Director of Publishing in the Open University, for her friendly co-operation, and to Macmillan for their helpfulness in the production of the book.

J. F.

Introduction

The Sources

The main sources from which our knowledge of Socrates is drawn are Plato and Xenophon. Both knew him personally. Both wrote voluminously about him. Both depict him in dramatic situations. Both include a certain amount of biographical detail incidentally to their main purpose. Both record the defence Socrates is supposed to have made at his trial.

Unfortunately their evidence conflicts. It is not merely that the two defence speeches (**2.2**; **3.1**) are completely different. It is that in the pages of Xenophon Socrates appears as an eminently worthy but dull, prosy and sententious moralist ('the patron-saint of moral twaddle', said Hegel); in the pages of Plato he is witty and humorous, and a great metaphysical thinker as well. It is Socrates who propounds the Theory of Forms, the theory that the material world is unstable, fluctuating and unreal, and true reality exists in the stable, unchanging Forms which lie behind the material world, invisible and inaccessible to the senses, but accessible to the intellect. Thus all the beauty in this world is imperfect. Perfect beauty is the Form of beauty, and the objects we call beautiful are beautiful in so far as they imitate or participate in the Form of beauty: use what account of the relationship we may, it is by Beauty that beautiful things are beautiful (**2.4.7**).

About the year 1900 there was a general view that Xenophon's was the authentic portrait, and Plato had infused his own genius into his portrait of Socrates. In the year 1911 two British scholars, John Burnet in his still remarkable edition of *Plato's Phaedo*, and A. E. Taylor in *Varia Socratica*, 1 (a second volume was never in fact published), put forward the view that it was Xenophon who had imposed his own dullness on Socrates, and Plato's portrait was in all essential matters veridical: in particular, the Theory of Forms belonged to Socrates.

This extreme view cannot be sustained: a few scholars still hold it, but they are flying in the face of the evidence. The decisive points are as follows:

(*a*) We have the explicit evidence of Aristotle that Socrates did not separate the Forms (**6.3.2**). Socrates in Plato plainly does separate the Forms: the Forms are independent of material objects: in scholastic language they are *realia ante rem*, not *realia in re*, still less *nomina post rem*. Aristotle did not know Socrates, but he came to Athens within living memory of Socrates' death, and worked with Plato for twenty years. If, as Taylor asserts, the source of his information about Socrates was Plato (it need not have been), then the conclusion is not that the evidence of the dialogues overrides that of Aristotle but that Plato knew perfectly well that he was using Socrates as the mouthpiece for a developed doctrine which he regarded as following logically from Socrates' view but which Socrates never held. The evidence of Aristotle is decisive and cannot be scouted.

(*b*) However, internal evidence from Plato reinforces the conclusion.

(i) In the seventh *Letter*, which is generally though not universally accepted as genuine, Plato tells how as a result of his reflections on Socrates' death he came to the conclusion, some ten years later, that mankind would never be justly governed until philosophers became kings or kings philosophers (**2.7.2**). This conclusion he subsequently put into Socrates' mouth in *The Republic* (**2.5.3.3**). This is the clearest possible evidence that he is using the figure of Socrates in the dialogues as mouthpiece for his own views.

(ii) In *Phaedo*, which is a relatively early dialogue, as can be shown on stylistic grounds, Plato depicts Socrates on the day of his death, carefully unfolding the Theory of Forms as if for the first time (**2.4.7**).

In *Parmenides*, which is a relatively late dialogue, Plato depicts Socrates in his youth talking with Parmenides and hearing some of the details of the theory as propounded in *Phaedo* subjected to cogent and radical criticism (**2.6**). This makes no possible sense as part of the biography of Socrates. It would be a Looking-Glass world, to begin with criticisms in youth of a theory which you propound freshly and naïvely in old age. But it makes excellent sense as part of the biography of Plato: he began from Socrates' concern for definitions (**6.3.2**), and was at the same time wrestling with the views of Parmenides (who said that true reality could not change) and those of Heraclitus and his followers (who held that the material world was in a state of continual change) (**1.11.1**); through contact with the Pythagoreans in Sicily and South Italy in 388–387 he came to the Theory of Forms as a solution to all these problems, and propounded it in *Phaedo*; he elaborated it in *Phaedrus*, *The Banquet* and *The Republic*. Then, perhaps as a result of discussions in the Academy in which Aristotle participated, he found some of his presuppositions challenged. In *Theaetetus* he showed that no epistemology was possible without the Theory of Forms; in *Parmenides* he presented the criticisms but still asserted that without the Forms no discourse is possible; in *The Sophist* he presented the theory with considerable modifications.

In presenting these selections concerning Socrates I have assumed the above account as substantially true, and apart from the key-passages mentioned above, and passages which are clearly biographical in intent, I have not included anything from Plato's later works, as I regard these as pertaining to his thought, not to that of Socrates.

It is important to understand the view here taken. I assume that Plato began, perhaps before Socrates' death, recording the sort of conversations in which he shared. *Laches* or *Lysis* is a good example. In a typical conversation Socrates is searching for a definition: attempts at definition are made and refuted: Socrates refuses to offer an alternative himself; and the dialogue ends in *aporia*, an impasse. Then Plato became caught up in a pamphleteering controversy (see below) and was concerned to justify Socrates. As a result of his travels in the West and contact with the Pythagoreans he came to certain conclusions which seemed to him to follow logically from Socrates' concerns, and continued to put these into his mouth. Finally, his interests moved in a different direction, and Socrates drops out of the dialogues. But Plato was a skilful dramatist, and he feeds into his picture of Socrates authentic traits and biographical details. I have argued elsewhere that in *Protagoras* the views put forward by Protagoras are those of Democritus: but the dramatic portrait is of Protagoras not Democritus (*Bucknell Review*, xv, ii (1967) 49 ff.). So with Socrates. The views put forward are those of Plato; but the dramatic portrait is of Socrates not Plato himself. (See further **1.11.2**; **1.11.3**; **6.8.4**; **8.1.21**; **8.17.1**; **9.2.5**; **9.2.8**; **9.2.10**; **9.11.3**; **9.12.3**; **12.21.2**, and for the opposite view **8.1.31**; **8.12.4**; **8.24**; **12.21.3**.)

There is here a further point. We do well to be cautious about the evidence of Plato and Xenophon alike. Socrates was executed in 399 B.C., and there is no reason to doubt the words which Plato puts into his mouth, that he was about 70. Xenophon was born in about 430, Plato in 427. They can have known Socrates in any real sense only after he reached the age of 60 or thereabouts. There is no indication that either was among his close intimates: clearly they were not, in the sense that Crito was, or Alcibiades, or even Phaedo. Further, Xenophon was away from Athens during the last two years of Socrates' life, and Plato explicitly tells us that he was not present in the prison on the last day.

But they are, effectively, all we have: the object of this collection is to show the nature of the remaining evidence. Of these we may note the following:

(a) A gossiping biography written about A.D. 200 by Diogenes Laertius, drawing upon some early evidence, e.g. Socrates' older contemporary Ion of Chios. Of uneven worth, but not unimportant (**1.4**).

(b) The evidence of contemporary comic dramatists, and particularly Aristophanes' *The Clouds*. This is caricature and parody of course, but a caricature is an exaggeration of the truth, not an untruth. We may legitimately

assume that in the 420s Socrates was engaged in scientific exploration (**4.1.1**). This fits in with an autobiographical passage in *Phaedo* (**2.4.6**), where the science stops short in the 430s and therefore is more likely to apply to Socrates than to Plato.

(c) Some references in the fourth-century orators suggest that Socrates was regarded as a 'sophist', and that the charges against him were really political (**5.3**).

(d) It is clear that the case of Socrates was a *cause célèbre*. In the later 390s an orator named Polycrates circulated a pamphlet entitled *Speech in Prosecution of Socrates*, and some of Xenophon's work has been identified as an answer to this. It is possible that Plato's *Apology* was a similar answer, and therefore polemical and not historical. There is evidence that it was fashionable to write such Defences (**6.8.5**; **8.20**; **9.1.1.28**; **13.1.10**; **13.1.13**; **13.1.16**) and they continued to be a literary genre right through to the time of Libanius in the fourth century A.D. (**10.2**). It might seem right to dismiss such exercises as purely unhistorical, but the authors had access to documents lost to us, and they were trying to adduce new evidence and new arguments.

(e) Aeschines of Sphettus (**8.23**) would provide important evidence if we had more of him.

(f) Many anecdotes and impressions are preserved for us in later writers, Aelian, Athenaeus, Cicero, Plutarch, Maximus of Tyre, Stobaeus and others. Some of them can be traced back to reasonably respectable sources, such as the Peripatetic historians of philosophy. Others are commonplace anecdotes of the henpecked or impractical philosopher. Some are told, like most anecdotes, of different people in different generations. Some are commonplaces, and are handed down from one author to the next. We cannot rely on these anecdotes. The most we can say, as T. R. Glover once remarked, is that an anecdote may not be true, but to pass muster at all it must be *ben trovato*.

(g) The different schools of philosophy claimed Socrates as their father-figure. In the Hellenistic Age the Cynics, with their doctrine of non-attachment, developed the diatribe or sermon as a means of propagating their faith. Socrates, as we can see from Dio Chrysostom or Epictetus, and particularly from Stobaeus, who drew on Cynic sources, figured prominently in these sermons; and it was natural to attribute Cynic and ascetic sentiments to him. We should be particularly chary about the authenticity of these.

(h) To the Christians, Socrates may appear as the type of pagan philosophy which they reject, or he may be set among the precursors of Christ. I felt it useful to include a representative selection of Christian opinion, especially as they do sometimes draw on reliable sources.

Certainties are few: we are safest in the Socratic position: we know only that we know nothing.

Socrates the Educator

There is one very good reason why we should be wary of accepting without qualification the views of Plato or Xenophon or any other individual about Socrates. It is that Socrates' associates moved in such different directions. Socrates appears to have had the gift, which another great educator later claimed for himself, of being all things to all men. We are reminded of the old Hindu legend of the six blind men who went to 'see' an elephant. One felt the elephant's leg, and declared that the elephant was like a tree. The second passed his hand along the flank, and declared that the elephant was like a wall. The third pulled on the tail, and declared that the elephant was like a rope. The fourth encountered the squirming trunk, and declared that the elephant was like a snake. The fifth felt the ear, and declared that the elephant was like a fan. The sixth took the tusk between his hands and declared that the elephant was like a spear. So it was with Socrates (**8.1.4**; **8.2.1**; **8.3.9**; **8.4.8**; **8.9.2**; **8.10**; **8.13.7**; **12.6.3**; **12.16.5**; **13.1.28**).

Crito was his closest friend. We know nothing of him as a philosopher, save for a brief account in Diogenes Laertius, who records a curiously miscellaneous list of titles (**1.9**): if we pick out a single theme from the titles as more prominent than another we might call it culture. We note one title, *That men are not made good by education*.

Antisthenes appears to have followed Socrates with almost fanatical intensity. The Cynics were later to claim him as a link between Socrates and Diogenes. This was a fabrication, but it indicates well the nature of Antisthenes' own contribution to philosophy. He was a common-sense realist. To him reality lay in the solid materiality of this world, and he would have nothing to do with Plato's metaphysical construct. This is enough to show beyond much doubt that the Theory of Forms belonged to Plato not to Socrates. Antisthenes picked up Socrates' moralism, and turned it into a stern asceticism, evidenced by his well-known remark 'I'd rather be mad than enjoy myself'. It is interesting to note a contrast with Crito: one of Antisthenes' favourite themes was that virtue can be taught (**1.12.3**).

Aristippus stands in strong contrast to Antisthenes. He came from Cyrene in Africa, attracted to Athens, it seems, by Socrates' reputation. He is associated by tradition with the foundation of the Cyrenaic school of philosophy, which identified the end or goal of life with pleasure, particular pleasures being desirable for their own sake, and happiness or blessedness a life compounded of particular pleasures. Recent scholarship has argued cogently that the formal establishment of the Cyrenaic school was due not to Socrates' associate but to his grandson of the same name. None the less, all the evidence we have about the elder Aristippus suggests that he was a hedonist, and presumably found something in Socrates which appealed to his hedonism; if Socrates had been an ascetic in the Antisthenes mould he would hardly have exercised an appeal on Aristippus (**1.7**).

Aeschines of Sphettus is interesting. Our evidence suggests that he was a particularly close and valued associate of Socrates. He founded no school of philosophy. His Socratic dialogues do not appear to have presented any systematic viewpoint, but those who read them found that they had the stamp of authenticity beyond those of Plato, Xenophon and the others. This is significant (**1.6**; **8.23**).

Phaedo was another close associate, and Plato named his account of Socrates' death after him. We know little about his opinions: as far as we can see, his chief concern was ethics (**1.8**).

Euclides of Megara valued Socrates' company so greatly that he risked his life to visit Socrates during a period of conflict between Athens and Megara. He is listed by Plato as among those present at Socrates' death, and it was with him that Plato and others took refuge after the execution. Like Phaedo, Euclides founded his own school of philosophy. It is not easy in the light of our fragmentary information to reconstruct with certainty the tenets for which he stood. But it certainly seems that his prime interest was in logical analysis. He was opposed to the Theory of Forms, but drew together the One, which constituted Parmenides' picture of the universe, with the Good, which he perhaps derived from Socrates' interest in ethics (**1.11.1**; **9.6.4**).

Simon must be briefly mentioned, a cobbler who was fascinated by Socrates' conversation, jotted down notes of it and wrote them up, thus setting the fashion in Socratic dialogues for Aeschines, Plato and Xenophon. We have titles but not contents: if they are authentic, they may be taken as showing the range of Socrates' conversation. Like those of Crito, they are miscellaneous: they do not suggest any great concentration on one field or one approach. If we were to identify common points we might pick on three: they suggest a concern for definition; a number of them are ethical; and no less than four concern τὸ καλόν – conventionally 'beauty' but ranging over what we might call 'nobility' as well (**1.10**).

To these we must add **Xenophon**, with strong interests in ethics and education but no systematic philosophy, and **Plato**, with a sturdy metaphysical system, in addition to interests in epistemology, ethics, politics, literary criticism and other fields.

It is almost impossible that a single-minded dogmatist could have produced such complex reactions. 'How unlike our friend!' said Aristippus of a dogmatic assertion (**6.8.4**). We are driven to two conclusions, which are not mutually exclusive.

It is possible that Socrates was himself a person of some complexity.

Anatole France once said that there was never any great man who was not a blend of contradictions. Some such blend of contradictions stands out from the accounts in Plato and Xenophon. Thus we can see the hedonist and the ascetic. Greek society permitted homosexual relationships. It is evident that Socrates was intensely, physically, sensually attracted to handsome lads: his friends joke about it; it underlies his relation with Alcibiades; even at the last in prison he is stroking Phaedo's hair (**2.4.4**). But he had his body under complete control, and Alcibiades utterly fails to seduce him (**2.5.2.2**). There is a tradition which can be traced back as far as Aristoxenus, that he was a man of fierce temper, passionate lust and violent emotions, which he learned to keep under control. Similarly he enjoyed a banquet: Plato and Xenophon both depict him as sharing in the fun. But in Xenophon he moralises against extravagance in the use of scent (**3.4.2**) and in Plato at the last he has drunk everyone else under the table and is alone left sober (**2.5.2.1**). We can discern here the attraction he may have had for men as diverse as Aristippus and Antisthenes. Again we can see in him the rationalist and the mystic. Of all the aspects of Socrates portrayed in *Phaedo* none stands out more strongly than his determination to trust reason to the end, whether or not that end is bitter (**2.4**). But alongside this we have his divine voice, speaking to him in opposition to something he intends to do, a voice in which he equally has absolute confidence (**1.4**[**32**]; **2.1.4**; **2.2**[**40**]; **2.5.11**; **2.5.4.1**; **2.8.2**; **3.4.7**; **8.1.7**; **8.6.2**; **8.13.5**; **8.14.5**; **9.1.1.22–23**; **9.1.2.5**; **9.7.14**; **9.11.1.1**; **9.13**; **12.3.2**; **12.4.2**; **12.4.5**; **12.6.4**; **12.7.2**; **12.8**; **13.1.28**; **15.3.2**).

It is possible also that Socrates saw it as his mission to take people where they were and to respect them for what they were. His father was a sculptor; his mother a midwife. In a well-known passage in Plato's *Theaetetus* he proclaims his profession to be that of an intellectual midwife: he helps people to give birth to the thoughts that are in them; he naughtily adds that if they come to him with no thoughts ready to bring to birth he sends them off to Prodicus or one of the other sophists to be made pregnant (**2.5.4.1**). This is a positive assertion: it has a negative side. If he is following his mother's profession he is not following his father's: it is not his work to mould those whom he encounters into a form of his own choosing. There is here a philosophy of education. By this view education is not *educare*, cramming in, but *educere*, drawing out. It may be that at the last Socrates' claim on our attention is not his thought, but his personality as an educator.

The Historical Background

Socrates was executed in 399 B.C. There is no reason to doubt that he was about 70 when he died, which puts his birth to 469 B.C. He was thus born a little more than ten years after the repulse of the Persians at Salamis and Plataea. During those ten years an alliance led by Athens had harried the Persians across the Aegean, and about 467 won a triumphant naval victory at the Eurymedon. As he grew up Socrates watched a campaign of idealism and liberation turn into a new imperialism, and a free alliance turn into an Athenian empire.

Meantime at home the conservative leader Cimon was ousted, and the radical democrats broke the power of the traditional council of the Areopagus. Pericles began his long period of ascendancy in Athenian politics. He fostered nationalism by limitations on Athenian citizenship, and imperialism by his foreign policy; he fostered democracy by the principle and practice of state pay, subsidising the poorer classes and enabling them to participate in state affairs instead of leaving these to a class which could afford the leisure. For democracy did not mean representative government. No Greek would have called the Westminster system democracy; he would have called it elective aristocracy. Democracy in ancient Greece meant direct participation in government by all citizens (adult, male); and if our evidence shows that comparatively few spoke in the Assembly and took the lead in advocating policies, the vote was none the less with the people.

Athenian military power was based on her navy. The dominant land power in Greece was Sparta, and Sparta was jealous of Athens and her dramatic rise. Further, Sparta was an oligarchy, whose citizens went through an intensive discipline to train them in toughness and the military virtues. By retaining a clumsy currency of iron bars the Spartans avoided the corruption which was such a baneful feature of Athenian domestic politics, though it rendered them liable to temptation when they moved overseas. With two such different states a clash of power was likely. It was fostered by Corinth, an ally of Sparta, but a naval and commercial power, who disliked the Athenians 'fishing in their waters'. In 431 war broke out between Sparta and her allies and Athens and her allies. It dragged on, hot or cold, for twenty-seven years. In 415 Athens sent an expedition to Sicily: it was the sheerest aggression. Two years later she lost two armies there. Still, with extraordinary resilience she fought on for nearly ten years before the final disaster.

From about 419 a dominant influence in Athenian politics was exercised by Alcibiades, wealthy, noble, a ward of Pericles, a brilliant society playboy, yet

with something in him which could attract Socrates and be attracted by him (**2.5.2**; **9.1.2.6–10**). Other influences proved stronger. Alcibiades was a disaster. When attacked by his political enemies at home he ratted to Sparta, later staged a comeback at Athens, but failed and was dropped. This was a period of deep political suspicion, of plot and counterplot between left wing and right. In 406 the Athenians won their last great victory, at Arginusae, the 'Shining Islands'. The Athenian commanders, partly owing to a storm, failed to pick up their dead, or to rescue survivors from their disabled ships: the casualty list totalled 5000. Despite the victory, the politicians at Athens worked up public opinion against the commanders. A hysterical Assembly was for condemning them to death *en bloc*. Socrates happened to be in the chair – the office circulated by lot – and refused to put the motion as being illegal (**2.1.6.1**; **2.2**[32]; **8.16**; **9.4.3**; **9.7.8**).

In 404 Athens fell. The victorious Spartans put in power a small group of men favourable to them. They are known to history as the Thirty Tyrants or Thirty Dictators. Their leader, Critias, and one or two of the others had been associates of Socrates. They tried to involve Socrates in their régime by ordering him to arrest illegally a rich citizen of Salamis named Leon; he turned on his heel and walked away (**1.4**[24]; **2.2**[32]; **8.3.4**; **8.4.10**; **8.5.2**). In one story he tried to save Theramenes from execution (**7.1.1**).

The dictatorship fell before a coup. Democracy was restored, and with rare magnanimity proclaimed a political amnesty. It was during this period of amnesty that Socrates was condemned to death. The charges appear in slightly different forms. The indictment must have run something like 'Socrates is guilty of not recognising the gods worshipped by the state but introducing new divinities, and of corrupting the young men'.

The Intellectual Background

About the year 600 B.C. on the coast of Asia Minor, where different cultures met, where alphabetical writing had been developed and where the economic revolution created by coinage made early impact, a group of men began to ask new questions. We know their names – Thales, Anaximander, Anaximenes. The sort of questions they were asking were 'What is the universe made of? What is its basic constituent?' and 'How does a presumably simple basic constituent come to change into the complex and diverse world we know?' They were asking scientific questions. Their answers retained an element of religious myth, but they and their successors also used observation in drawing up their picture of the universe. Simple answers, suggesting a basic constituent of water or air, could not meet all the problems. About a century later two profound thinkers tangled the issues still further. Parmenides argued with devastating logic that change was impossible; the universe was one, single, continuous, ever-present whole. Heraclitus looked at the world and saw everything as being in a state of flux, though he acknowledged certain principles of stability, notably in the balance or tension of opposed forces, and in the Reason at the root of the universe. These views were in the long run dead-ends. If the basic constituent of the universe was not single it must be complex. This line of speculation led to the pluralism of Empedocles and Anaxagoras in the middle of the fifth century and eventually to the fully fledged atomism of Democritus, expounded in a book published in 405 B.C., though it is likely that the ideas

did not permeate to Athens till the next century after Socrates' death.

Although the tendency of such speculations was to replace religion and myth by rationalism, there remained a good deal of residual religion. Thales declared that 'Everything is full of gods'. Anaximander seems to have thought of the stuff of the universe, which he called 'the infinite', as divine, and our records assert that Anaximenes made air his god. Pythagoras stands in a line of his own, bringing together mysticism and mathematics. Empedocles, too, was a religious philosopher. The Reason which Heraclitus saw at the root of the universe, the Mind of which Anaxagoras spoke as having reduced chaos to order, are religious concepts, though not readily to be fitted into the pattern of Greek polytheism.

At the same time we can trace a certain amount which already by the mid-fifth century was making for scepticism. Xenophanes, who was associated with Parmenides by the later systematisers, wrote:

If horse and lions and oxen had hands
to draw and produce works of art as men
  do,
they'd draw and shape the bodies of gods,
horses like horses, oxen like oxen,
each in form like itself.

Parmenides and still more his subtle follower Zeno made for scepticism by their challenge to the common-sense world. When Zeno purported to show that it was impossible to cross a racecourse, that the fastest of runners could never catch up with the slowest of crawlers or that it was impossible for an arrow to move, people inevitably wondered what they could believe. Anaxagoras, too, appears as a rationalist. The Sun was to the Greeks a divinity: he declared it to be a red-hot stone as large as the Peloponnese: he was making a deduction from meteorites.

On another occasion a single-horned ram was regarded as an omen: Anaxagoras used dissection to show that the malformation was due to natural causes: the worthy Plutarch, who records the incident, anticipates an argument of modern theologians in wondering whether both might be true. By now the occasional atheist was found, a virtual impossibility in traditional society: Diagoras of Melos is the most famous. By the end of the century the cool scientific rationality of the Hippocratic doctors is pushing the gods still farther away. Epilepsy was called 'the sacred disease' and believed to be due to divine touch. The Hippocratic doctor who treats the subject says whimsically that we only call it divine because we do not understand it: really it has natural causes like other diseases.

In the middle of the fifth century two new factors were influencing the educational scene. The first was the advance in direct democracy. If a man wanted to make his mark in politics he needed eloquence. Only so could he persuade the Assembly to accept his policies. Equally important, only so could he persuade the jury to acquit him if his public conduct were challenged in the courts, since in Greece defendants were their own advocates. (Professionals might compose the speeches: the defendants delivered them.) Hence came a demand for training in oratory, which was met by the study and teaching of rhythm and cadence, fostered in Sicily by men like Tisias, Corax and Gorgias, and farther east by Thrasymachus, who is brilliantly though unflatteringly portrayed in Plato's *The Republic* (**2.5.3.1**). These men began to travel through the Greek world to purvey their skills. But the demands which these men were meeting with considerable integrity could also be met by logic-chopping. In Plato's *Euthydemus* we have a trivial argument: 'That dog is your father. He is a father. He is your

dog. Therefore he is your father.' Such logic, more subtly applied, must have found its place in the political Assembly. Moralists complained that these devices were used regardless of the ethics of the case advocated. It was a short step from making the weaker cause appear the stronger to making the worse cause appear the better, and it is a sign of the permeating power of the new logic that the moralists themselves pass ambiguously from one concept to the other.

Alongside this was increased leisure for the upper and middle classes. This in itself led to a demand for higher education, which was provided by the sophists. The word was not itself originally opprobrious. It meant expert or professor: a skilled cook can be called a sophist. These men offered courses of what we might call extra-mural lectures for a fee. The subjects which they professed ranged widely: rhetoric, of course, mathematics, language, literature, political history and political theory, fine art, dream-interpretations, athletics are only a few of those recorded. Some of the sophists were original scholars of genuine distinction. Hippias, for example, a polymath and practical craftsman, was a considerable mathematician who solved the problem of trisecting an angle by using the curve called the quadratrix. Plato and others were hostile to the sophists and their influence. Their charges against them boil down to two. First, their professionalism: they demanded fees. An unsympathetic modern interpreter has compared them to a clergyman demanding money for spiritual help. The comparison is inept. Plato's attitude is that of the Gentlemen to the Players: part social snobbery, and part the realisation that amateur enthusiasm has something to contribute which professionals seem to lose. Second, their combination of personal scepticism with dogmatic teaching. Thus

Gorgias is recorded as putting forward the proposition: 'Nothing exists. If it does exist it cannot be known. If it can be known, it cannot be communicated.' Protagoras, in a celebrated though ambiguous phrase, declared that 'Man is the measure of all things'. But if nothing can be communicated, why teach? And if my opinion is equally as true as yours, how can you teach me anything? What is subversive is not the honest intellectual doubt but the failure to reconcile that doubt with the profession of teaching: Protagoras' claim that his views are not truer but better is a mere quibble.

Mainly, the effect of sophistic education was to divert intellectual attention from the universe to men, from the macrocosm to the microcosm. It became a cliché later that Socrates brought philosophy down from the sky and planted her on earth (**8.1.15**), i.e. redirected attention from cosmology to man. But it was in fact the sophists who were responsible for this intellectual revolution: Socrates was a child of his time and their inheritor.

The Life of Socrates

The details of Socrates' life are scanty. He was born in 469, as we have seen, a citizen of Athens, of the deme Alopece. His father Sophroniscus was a sculptor, his mother Phaenarete a midwife. We can discount the mysterious Elmaglus who appears in a passage in Epiphanius (**12.12.2**), though it is a curious mystery. 'Sculptor' suggests to us a creative artist: 'stone-mason' might better indicate Sophroniscus' social standing and most of his work. No doubt Socrates was trained to follow his father as a stone-mason (as Jesus of Nazareth was trained to follow Joseph as a carpenter), and a group on the Acropolis representing the Graces were said to be his work (**8.3.6**; **9.3.3**; **9.5.2**; **9.10.1**; **9.10.3**;

12.21.2; **13.1.28**; **14.1.1.12**). The mordant satirist Timon, writing in the third century, called him a stone-worker (**1.4**[19]; **12.3.1**).

Of his life up to the outbreak of the Peloponnesian War we know little. Ion of Chios records him in Samos (probably during the Athenian campaign of 440), Aristotle in Delphi, Favorinus at the Isthmus of Corinth (**1.4**[23]); all these will have been before the war. The records about his marriages are confusing (**1.4**[26]; **9.1.2.2**; **9.2.11**; **9.3.8**). He seems to have been twice married, and as Xanthippe was his wife in his last years, we must suppose that he was married to Myrto, descendant of Aristides the Just (daughter or granddaughter or great-granddaughter) in middle life: marriages were arranged, and it seems a curious match, but Socrates may have appeared a bright young man, worth the attentions of the Establishment; there was in any case some family connection (**2.1.2.1**). Socrates cannot have been married when Aristophanes wrote *The Clouds* in 423; the dramatist could hardly have resisted some reference: we must assume that Myrto was by then dead, perhaps of the plague which struck Athens in the early years of the war. For the rest we see him studying with Archelaus, one of the advanced scientists of the period. It is less likely that he studied with Anaxagoras: in *Phaedo* his contact with Anaxagoras' thought is through a book. He also shared in the campaigns which preceded the war: we have a famous picture of him standing out 'contemplating' in the chill of the north day and night (**2.5.2.1**; cf. **1.4**[23]; **2.2**[28]; **8.12.6**; **9.1.2.10**; **9.7.8**). Socrates might be critical of Athenian democracy, but he was in some ways a conventional patriot, and performed his normal stints of military service when called upon. Iamblichus rebukes him for his loyalty to his tribe (**8.16**).

During the ten years of uninterrupted war which followed we see him again on campaign, at Delium in 424 (**1.4**[23]; **2.1.2.1**; **2.2**[28]; **2.5.21**; **9.1.2.10**; **9.2.5**; **9.7.8**; **9.9.1**). He was serving as a hoplite or heavy-armed infantryman, and this tells us that he was not living in the poverty to which he was later brought, since there was a property qualification for hoplites, who had indeed to raise the money for their own armour: this was the class of farmers and craftsmen, and this suggests that Socrates was in business as a stone-mason.

For the rest, our main evidence is Aristophanes' *The Clouds* (**4.1.1**). This shows that Socrates during the 420s was still predominantly, though not exclusively, engaged in scientific studies. In *Phaedo* Plato puts an autobiographical passage into Socrates' mouth (**2.4.6**). This tells how he studied with the scientists but moved increasingly from the scientific question 'How?' to the metaphysical question 'Why?' He thought that Anaxagoras' doctrine of Mind would answer this, but found that Anaxagoras was a Deist not Theist: Mind set the universe off but played no part relevant to Socrates' own life and surroundings. The latest science is that of Anaxagoras, Archelaus and Diogenes of Apollonia; this fits with the supposition that Plato is giving a picture of Socrates in the 420s.

In 421 an uneasy truce was patched up for the moment and travel was again possible. It must have been now that Chaerephon paid his visit to Delphi and asked if there was anyone in Greece wiser than Socrates (an improperly leading question), and was told that there was not (**1.4**[37]; **2.2**[21]; **9.2.6**). Socrates, at a loss already, was puzzled. This puzzlement led to a kind of conversion, a redirection of his life. According to Plato, he set himself to refute the oracle, by going to the men who claimed to have wisdom, and by pertinacious questioning showed that they did not have the wisdom they claimed. He himself disclaimed wisdom; he concluded that the oracle was right: everyone knew nothing; his wisdom consisted in knowing that he knew nothing. Hence the mission to expose false pretensions, and to this end to be always available in public, in the market-place, the city centre, the exercise-grounds, wherever plenty of people were to be found. And around him a knot of younger men, taking pleasure in the refutation of their elders, sometimes stopping there, sometimes ready to seek with Socrates a way forward. And with it all a neglect of his own professional and economic interests, and an increasing poverty lightened only by the generosity of his friends.

We can trace other aspects of his life and thought at this time. One is an increasing dissatisfaction with Athenian democracy. We are told that he opposed the disastrous expedition against Sicily (**9.1.2.5**). He evidently respected craftsmen as having knowledge or skill of a kind, and argued that politics was a craft, and required the expert. It was ridiculous to allow every Tom, Dick and Harry an equal voice, as the Athenians did, ridiculous to turn political representation into a lottery. If it required a specialist to pilot a ship through the Aegean, it equally required a specialist to pilot the ship of state through the stormy waters of history. These criticisms were absorbed by men like Alcibiades and Critias, who fancied themselves as the experts, but who lacked the moral integrity and self-discipline which Socrates saw as the first necessity in political craftsmanship. Socrates plainly was regarded as sympathetic to the Spartan way of life (**4.1.3.1**), though it never affected his own patriotism.

Liability to military service did not cease until the age of 60, but we have no record of Socrates serving after Amphipolis in 422 (**1.4**[22]; **2.2**[28]; **9.7.8**). Further, he avoided public participation in politics: his mystical voice forbade this, and he did not speak in the Assembly. But the executive Council was filled by lot from all the citizens (not just from those who put their names forward, as has been suggested, or Socrates would not be there). Socrates did not refuse this duty when it happened to fall his way, and, as we have seen, was in the president's chair in 406 when the motion was raised for the execution of the generals. The left-wing politicians will have seen his opposition as a piece of right-wing obstructionism.

Another outcome during this period was an almost complete redirection of his interests from science to ethics. Xenophon lists the sort of questions he asked: 'What is pious? What is impious? What is noble? What is shameful? What is just? What is unjust? What is self-control? What is lack of self-control? What is courage? What is cowardice? What is a state? What is a statesman? What is political leadership? What is a political leader? and so on' (**3.2.1**[16]). Xenophon has his own ethical bent, but Plato reflects the same interests.

His initial critique was negative. He was always spoiling for an argument (**2.5.4.2**). He loved remorselessly dragging someone round and round (**2.1.2.2**). He enjoyed the exposure of false pretensions (**2.2**[33]). All our sources agree upon his own self-control, his infuriatingly unruffled calm (**8.4.5**). One of his victims compared him to a torpedo-fish, a predator which numbs its victims with an electric charge before darting in to the kill (**2.1.7.2**; 'cramp-fish'). In Plato's *Apology* he compares himself to a gadfly, stinging the sluggish horse of Athens to life (**2.2**[30]). But his elenchus had its positive side in his intellectual midwifery: we have noted

this already and need say no more about it here.

One interesting result of his 'conversion' was his marriage to Xanthippe, which must have taken place shortly after. She has been handed down to posterity as the typical shrew – without overmuch justification. This is part of the legend of the philosopher who cannot run his own life.

After the war he stood as courageously against the dictators, friends though some of them had been, as he had against the democrats (**1.4**[24]; **2.2**[32]; **7.1.1**; **8.3.4**; **8.4.10**; **8.5.2**). Plato and others make a point of this in Socrates' defence, but they could hardly do so if it were not true. Socrates continued his criticisms of democracy under the restored democracy and the amnesty. Religious intolerance never became a major issue at Athens unless there were political issues in the background, rather as racial intolerance today seldom becomes a major issue unless there are economic issues in the background. George Grote showed decades ago that the respectable Meletus was only a façade for the left-wing politicians Anytus and Lycon: the overt issues in the prosecution were moral and religious, the covert ones political. Some later evidence suggests that Socrates (like Jesus before Pilate) did not make any defence (**7.2**; **8.14.3**; **9.16**). In this case Plato's and Xenophon's records of the defence are pamphlets like Libanius'. But Plato explicitly says that he was present, and it is perhaps best to regard his version as reasonably authentic. If so, we have the curious story of the 'assessment'. The verdict given, the prosecution proposed a penalty, the defence made a counter-proposition. In this instance the prosecution proposed death, expecting Socrates to propose exile, which was what they really wanted: his silence, not his blood. Socrates, regarding himself as a public benefactor, proposed free meals at state expense for the rest of his life: then, under pressure from his friends, compounded for a fine. The death sentence was confirmed. Socrates in prison had the chance of escape, and refused to take it. He accepted the verdict of laws when they favoured him; he must not flout them when they proved unfavourable (**2.3**). For this A. E. Taylor called him 'the one perfectly consistent conscientious objector in history'. Plato records his last day. He explicitly says that he was not present, and it seems that he puts his own views into Socrates' mouth, but we need not doubt that he gives a reliable picture of the way Socrates spent that day, of his versifications and of his last words.

Two words were evidently regarded as characteristic of his activity. One is the verb *phrontizein*, which is translated 'think' or 'contemplate'. It seems to have been used of Socrates from a fairly early stage. Plato shows him 'contemplating' at Potidaea before the war (**2.5.2.1**). The root of the Think-Tank in Aristophanes is the same (**4.1.1.1**) and other comedians use it (**4.2.2.1**; **4.2.3**). The same word appears in our later records (e.g. **8.15.3**; **10.2**[19]; **11.1.40.2**). The other word is *adoleschein*, which means 'talk a lot of nonsense'. Even in early Plato, where Socrates appears as a questioner, he talks a lot in the course of asking questions. The first word was presumably one applied by Socrates to his own activity; the other was applied to him by those who were opposed to his activities in later life (**3.3.1**).

In appearance, at least in later life, Socrates was striking and unmistakable, with stumping steps, bald-headed, bearded, snub-nosed, eyes *à fleur de tête* prominent and glaring; later authors speak of his pot-belly and bow-legs (**2.4.3**; **2.5.2.1**; **3.4.4**–5; **8.12.5**; **8.14.1**; **12.15.3**; **12.23.2**; **14.1.1.7**–8). The ancient statues portray him in the light of the literary description; they are for the most part vivid and consistent. The earliest type may go back to the 380s B.C. and represent a genuine memory.

Socrates the Sophist

Aeschines, the political orator, in the century after Socrates' death, records him as a sophist (**5.3**): so does Androtion (**9.11.2.6**; cf. **9.1.1.34**): in Aristophanes' comedy he has many of the features of the typical sophist. This is not wholly unjust.

In the first place, he shared in the revolution which made philosophy relevant to human life. It could even be said that he was concerned to make his associates more effective politicians. Cicero and the others were not wrong in saying that he brought philosophy down from the sky and planted her on earth; but he was not the only one, nor the first, to do so (**8.1.15**).

Secondly, he shared in the new interest in logic. The columnist 'Beachcomber' once said epigrammatically, 'Logic is an unfair means sometimes used to win an argument.' Some of Socrates' interlocutors must have felt just that. In *The Clouds* Aristophanes sees useless scientific investigation and hair-splitting logic as Socrates' main activities. Plato may put the most extreme quibbles into the mouth of Euthydemus and Dionysodorus, but some of the means which Socrates used to confute his interlocutors were not essentially different, and it matters little whether we are to suppose him blind to some of the fallacies, or deliberately playing on the blindness of others. F. J. E. Woodbridge in *The Son of Apollo* (Boston, 1929, p. 269) wrote of Socrates as he found him in Plato: 'Flattery, cajolery, insinuation, innuendo, sarcasm, feigned humility, personal idiosyncrasies, browbeating, insolence, anger, changing the subject when in difficulties, distracting attention, faulty analogies, the torturing of words, making adjectives do the work of nouns and nouns of adjectives, tacking on verbs to qualities which could never use them, glad of an interruption or a previous engagement, telling stories which make one forget what the subject of discussion was, hinting that he could say much more and would if his hearers were up to it, promising more tomorrow if they are really interested and want to go on – an accomplished sophist if ever there was one.' Overstated, of course – but without foundation?

Thirdly, it can be claimed that Socrates and the sophists were alike subversive of traditional principles. After all, Socrates' profession of ignorance cannot have seemed very different, and in itself was not very different, from the scepticism of a Protagoras or a Gorgias. And, more than Protagoras, Gorgias or any of the sophists, Socrates took positive pleasure in pulling to pieces the traditional wisdom of prominent men. There was in fact a generation gap not unlike that of the 1960s and 1970s A.D., and the young men went, perhaps indifferently, to Protagoras or Socrates, for a cleverness which was alien to the older generation.

Socrates' supporters made two claims to demonstrate the distinction between him and the sophists. Both were partial truths. The first and stronger claim was that he did not charge fees. This, in the obvious sense, was true. Still, we do well to remember that Roman advocates such as Cicero might not charge fees but were heavily dependent on the generosity and goodwill of their clients. Similarly in our own day we have been made in sport acutely aware of 'shamateurism'. Socrates might not charge fees, but it was the generosity of Crito and other associates that kept him going (**1.7.2**; **1.9**).

The second claim was that he taught nothing, because he had nothing to teach (**2.1.7.2**; **6.1**; **8.3.1**; **8.3.7**; **8.7.3**; **8.12.1**; **8.12.7**; **8.13.3**; **9.3.4**; **12.10.1**; **12.15.2**; **12.15.5**; **12.16.1**). This is the characteristic Socratic 'irony' – not irony in our sense, but a kind of self-depreciating mock-modesty – the profession of ignorance (**2.5.3.1**; **6.4.2**; **8.1.3**; **8.1.24**; **8.14.12**; **9.11.4.2**; **9.12.8**; **12.14.1**; **14.2.4**). Again, the claim is a partial truth only. Socrates might ask questions rather than make statements, but his questions were often leading questions and a form of concealed statement. I have suggested that Socrates cannot have been the dogmatic metaphysician he appears in Plato. But he had distinctive interests, attitudes and views which can be identified because they run through all our sources. We must finally try to spell these out.

Socrates' Contribution to Philosophy

We can isolate three distinctive contributions which Socrates made to philosophy.

The first is identified by Aristotle as inductive argument and definition by generalisation (**6.3.2**). It is excellently exemplified in the early dialogues of Plato. Thus in *Laches* (**2.1.2.3**) the question is asked 'What is courage?' Laches answers that courage is not running away in battle, and Socrates has no difficulty in showing that he is giving a particular example of courage, not an account of courage in general. What is it that is common to all courageous acts which makes us call them courageous? In other words, can we look at a variety of courageous acts, identify a common quality and arrive by induction at a generalised definition? Something similar happens in *Charmides* with self-discipline, in *Lysis* with friendship and in the first book of *The Republic* (which was probably written appreciably earlier than the rest and originally stood on its own) with justice.

The second is the use of dialogue as a means of approach to truth. It would be hard to overestimate the importance of this; it would be possible, for example, to draw a line directly from it to the dialectical philosophies of Hegel and Marx, or to link it intellectually with the American preference for discussion in education and the general hesitations now current about the formal lecture. Socrates' profession of ignorance is hardly more than a debater's trick, and a peg on which to hang a philosophy of education. That philosophy may be analysed somewhat as follows:

(a) Knowledge can be pursued and is worth pursuing.
(b) The search for knowledge is a co-operative enterprise.
(c) A question is a form of education: education is drawing out what is in a person rather than imposing on him a preselected view from outside.
(d) Knowledge, truth, must be pursued with a ruthless intellectual honesty.

Thirdly, Socrates shared in the revolution which diverted intellectual inquiry from scientific matters to questions germane to the way in which we live. At the centre of his thinking is the *psyche*. This word is conventionally translated 'soul', but it comprises, under a single head, the life-principle, the intellect and the moral personality. Socrates' concern is thus with ethics, but not with ethics in the narrow sense. The words which Plato puts into his mouth in self-defence can be amply justified: 'I spend my whole life going about persuading you all, old and young alike, not to bother about your persons or properties but first and foremost to concentrate on the greatest improvement of your souls' (**2.2**[30]). We can identify three important aspects of Socrates' ethical thinking:

(a) The first is the need for self-knowledge. In this he was only taking up a maxim associated with the oracle at Delphi, which is variously attributed to Thales, Phenomoe, Chilon and other of the traditional sages: 'Know yourself' (**9.14.2**; **12.5**). It remains important and salutary.

We seek to know the moving of each sphere,
And the strange cause of th' ebb and flow of Nile,
But of that clock within our breasts we bear,
The subtle motions we forget the while.

We that acquaint ourselves with every zone,
And pass both tropics and behold the poles,
When we come home, are to ourselves unknown,
And unacquainted still with our own souls.

So the Elizabethan Sir John Davies, and old Thomas Fuller asked with similar pertinence, 'Who hath sailed about the world of his own heart, sounded each creek, surveyed each corner, but that there still remains much *terra incognita* to himself?'

(b) The second aspect of Socratic ethics seems to have been the paradoxical assertion that virtue is knowledge (**6.4.1**; **6.4.3**; **6.5.1–2**; **6.5.4**; **6.6.1–2**; **6.6.4**). In Greek the assertion is not quite so paradoxical, as the word for virtue (*arete*) means 'goodness' or 'excellence' in the widest sense, and only among strictly ethical philosophers becomes the equivalent of our 'virtue'. It has been supposed, with some reason, that Socrates saw in this paradox a counterblast to the sophists who claimed to teach *arete*, but were sceptics in their theory of knowledge. But the paradox had one clear ethical consequence. Socrates does seem to have held that no one goes wrong deliberately: all wrongdoing is involuntary (**2.1.3; 2.1.5; 2.1.6.2; 2.1.7.1; 6.5.3; 6.5.6**). This is a surprising assertion on the face of it. We respond more readily to Paul's 'The good that I would I do not: the evil that I would not, that I do', or Ovid's Medea with her 'I see and applaud the better course, and follow the worse'. Yet Socrates' paradox is defensible. If I really and fully know that a course of action is the best, how can I fail to follow it? If I choose another course it is because for the moment I see it as better. It will be noted that there is in this argument an ambiguity over 'better' between a narrowly ethical sense and a more general sense. Still, it was not until Freud took the lid off the unconscious and demonstrated the limits of rationality that we had a clear answer to Socrates. Socrates is perhaps the leading exponent of an intellectualist or rational theory of ethics.

(c) Thirdly, both Xenophon and Plato, as well as minor sources, make clear that Socrates took a functional view of life and thought of excellence in terms of function (**2.5.3.2**). This in turn had a number of consequences. We may instance a tendency to equate the good with the useful, and the use of analogy from craftsmanship and other skills (**2.1.1; 2.1.2.3; 2.8.1; 6.6.1; 6.8.2; 8.3.2; 8.3.7;**

8.3.9; 8.23.1; 11.1.22; 11.1.92). It involved a teleological view of life (**6.8.6**). A knife is plainly designed for cutting, and Socrates seems to have seen the world of nature as designed for the service of man: the neck of the ox is designed for the yoke, rather than the yoke for the neck. But what is the function of man? This approach left open for later thinkers three broad possibilities. The first (Epictetus is a good example) saw man's function in religious terms. The second (Aristotle) saw man's intellect as his distinctive possession and his function in intellectual terms. The third (which was closest to Socrates himself) isolated the ethical function. All three could legitimately, and did, claim to be Socrates' heirs.

When all this is said, Socrates would be a footnote in the history of philosophy, were it not for his personality and influence. Alexander the Great was surrounded by staff-officers who seemed nonentities while he was alive, but after his death became emperors in their own right. Something similar is true of the intellectual emperors who surrounded Socrates. Or we may think of Samuel Johnson: when all his undoubted merits as writer and critic have been weighed to the full it is the impact of the personality that predominates. Or we may think of Jesus, who, like Socrates, left no writings, but the memory of a person, and an approach to life. One difference there was. C. F. Angus used to say that Socrates was one of the three most fascinating personalities who ever lived (the others being Gautama and Jesus), and the only one of the three who had never been worshipped as divine. One of the most charming tributes will be found in the pseudo-Platonic *Theages* (**2.8.2**), where the young man says, 'I never, at any time, learnt anything from you, as you know. I made progress, however, when I associated with you, even if I was only in the same house, though not in the same room; but more so when I was in the same room with you; and I seemed to myself to improve much more when, being in the same room, I looked at you, when you were speaking, than when I looked another way. But I made by far the greatest progress, when I sat near you and touched you.' Those who knew Socrates combine to say 'He was the best man I ever knew' (**2.4.8**; **3.2.24**). It is the impact of a richly human personality which at the last remains.

PART ONE

DIOGENES LAERTIUS

We know nothing about the author of *The Lives and Views of Eminent Philosophers*. We call him Diogenes Laertius, but the very name is uncertain. His date is uncertain: we may reasonably assume it to be the early third century A.D. His own standpoint is unclear, perhaps sceptical, perhaps Epicurean, perhaps eclectic. His work is gossipy, uncritical, a hotchpotch. But it remains our chief source for the lives of the philosophers, and preserves for us something of the labours of Sotion and Satyrus from four centuries earlier, and we notice other earlier authorities in the 'Life of Socrates', including an older contemporary of Socrates, Ion of Chios (**1.4**[23]).

1.1 Prologue

The succession passes from Thales to Anaximander, Anaximenes, Anaxagoras, Archelaus and Socrates, who introduced ethics. Then to the followers of Socrates, and Plato in particular, Speusippus and Xenocrates, Polemo, Crantor and Crates, and Arcesilaus, founder of the Middle Academy; then Lacydes, who took the New Academy view; then Carneades, Clitomachus. [15] This line of succession ends in Clitomachus. Another ends in Chrysippus. It passes from Socrates to Antisthenes, Diogenes the Dog, Crates of Thebes, Zeno of Citium, Cleanthes and Chrysippus. Another ends in Theophrastus. This is the end of Ionian philosophy.

. . . Some philosophers left written records behind them, others wrote no works at all, e.g. (according to some views) Socrates. (1, 14–16)

An important passage putting Socrates in his historical context, and showing how all the major later schools of thought, except the Epicurean, claimed to be his heirs.

1.2 Thales

Hermippus in his *Lives* attributes to Thales the story which others record about Socrates. They say that he used to express his gratitude to Fortune for three blessings, first because he was born a human being and not a wild animal, next because he was born a man and not a woman, third because he was born a Greek and not a foreigner. (1, 33)

Cf. **8.3.10**; **9.1.2.11**; **12.10.2**.

1.3 Archelaus

I. Archelaus was a citizen of either Athens or Miletus, and his father's name was Apollodorus; but, as some say, Mydon. He was a pupil of Anaxagoras, and the master of Socrates.

II. He was the first person who imported the study of natural philosophy from Ionia to Athens, and he was called the Natural Philosopher, because natural philosophy terminated with him, as Socrates introduced ethical philosophy. And it seems probable that Archelaus too meddled in some degree with moral philosophy; for in his philosophical speculations he discussed laws and what was honourable and just. And Socrates borrowed from him; and because he enlarged his principles, he was thought to be the inventor of them. (2, 16)

1.4 Socrates

I. [18] Socrates was the son of Sophroniscus, a statuary, and of Phaenarete, a midwife; as Plato records in his *Theaetetus*; he was a citizen of Athens, of the borough of Alopece.

II. Some people believed that he assisted Euripides in his poems; in reference to which idea, Mnesimachus speaks as follows:

The Phrygians are a new play of Euripides,
But Socrates has laid the main foundation.

And again he says:

Euripides: patched up by Socrates.

And Callias, in his *Captives*, says:

A: Are you so proud, giving yourself such
 airs?
B: And well I may, for Socrates is the
 cause.

And Aristophanes says, in his *Clouds*:

This is Euripides, who doth compose
Those argumentative wise tragedies.

III. [19] But, having been a pupil of
Anaxagoras, as some people say, but
of Damon as the other story goes,
related by Alexander in his *Successions*,
after the condemnation of Anaxagoras,
he became a disciple of Archelaus, the
natural philosopher. And, indeed, Aristoxenus says that he was very intimate
with him.

IV. But Duris says that he was a slave,
and employed in carving stones. And
some say that the Graces in the Acropolis are his work; and they are clothed
figures. And that it is in reference to
this that Timon says, in his *Silli*:

From them proceeded the stone polisher,
The reasoning legislator, the enchanter
Of all the Greeks, making them subtle
 arguers,
A cunning pedant, a shrewd Attic
 quibbler.

V. For he was very clever in all
rhetorical exercises, as Idomeneus also
assures us. But the thirty tyrants forbade him to give lessons in the art of
speaking and arguing, as Xenophon
tells us. [20] And Aristophanes turns
him into ridicule in his Comedies, as
making the worse appear the better
reason. For he was the first man, as
Favorinus says in his *Universal History*,
who, in conjunction with his disciple
Aeschines, taught men how to become
orators. And Idomeneus makes the same
assertion in his essay on the Socratic
School. He, likewise, was the first
person who conversed about human life;
and was also the first philosopher who

was condemned to death and executed.
And Aristoxenus, the son of Spintharus,
says that he lent money in usury;
and that he collected the interest and
principal together, and then, when
he had got the interest, he lent it out
again. And Demetrius, of Byzantium,
says that it was Criton who made him
leave his workshop and instruct men,
out of the admiration which he conceived for his abilities.

VI. [21] He then, perceiving that
natural philosophy had no immediate
bearing on our interests, began to enter
upon moral speculations, both in his
workshop and in the market-place.
And he said that the objects of his search
were –

Whatever good or harm can man befall
In his own house.

And very often, while arguing and
discussing points that arose, he was
treated with great violence and beaten,
and pulled about, and laughed at and
ridiculed by the multitude. But he bore
all this with great equanimity. So that
once, when he had been kicked and
buffeted about, and had borne it all
patiently, and someone expressed his
surprise, he said, 'Suppose an ass had
kicked me, would you have had me
bring an action against him?' And this
is the account of Demetrius.

VII. [22] But he had no need of
travelling (though most philosophers did
travel), except when he was bound to
serve in the army. But all the rest of his
life he remained in the same place, and
in an argumentative spirit he used to
dispute with all who would converse
with him, not with the purpose of taking
away their opinions from them, so
much as of learning the truth, as far as
he could do so, himself. And they say
that Euripides gave him a small work
of Heraclitus to read, and asked him
afterwards what he thought of it, and
he replied, 'What I have understood

is good; and so, I think, what I have not understood is; only the book requires a Delian diver to get at the meaning of it.' He paid great attention also to the training of the body, and was always in excellent condition himself. Accordingly, he joined in the expedition to Amphipolis, and he it was who took up and saved Xenophon in the battle of Delium, when he had fallen from his horse; [23] for when all the Athenians had fled, he retreated quietly, turning round slowly, and watching to repel anyone who attacked him. He also joined in the expedition to Potidaea, which was undertaken by sea; for it was impossible to get there by land, as the war impeded the communication. And they say that on this occasion he remained the whole night in one place; and that though he had deserved the prize of pre-eminent valour, he yielded it to Alcibiades, to whom Aristippus, in the fourth book of his treatise on the *Luxury of the Ancients*, says that he was greatly attached. But Ion, of Chios, says, that while he was a very young man he left Athens, and went to Samos with Archelaus. And Aristotle says that he went to Delphi; and Favorinus also, in the first book of his *Commentaries*, says that he went to the Isthmus.

VIII. [24] He was a man of great firmness of mind, and very much attached to the democracy, as was plain from his not submitting to Critias, when he ordered him to bring Leon of Salamis, a very rich man, before the thirty, for the purpose of being murdered. And he alone voted for the acquittal of the ten generals; and when it was in his power to escape out of prison he would not do it; and he reproved those who bewailed his fate, and even while in prison, he delivered those beautiful discourses which we still possess.

IX. He was a contented and venerable man. And once, as Pamphila says, in the seventh book of her *Commentaries*,

when Alcibiades offered him a large piece of ground to build a house upon, he said, 'But if I wanted shoes, and you had given me a piece of leather to make myself shoes, I should be laughed at if I took it.' [25] And often, when he beheld the multitude of things which were being sold, he would say to himself, 'How many things are there which I do not want.' And he was continually repeating these iambics:

For silver plate and purple useful are
For actors on the stage, but not for men.

And he showed his scorn of Archelaus the Macedonian, and Scopas the Crononian, and Eurylochus of Larissa, when he refused to accept their money, and to go and visit them. And he was so regular in his way of living that it happened more than once when there was a plague at Athens, that he was the only person who did not catch it.

X. [26] Aristotle says, that he had two wives. The first was Xanthippe, by whom he had a son named Lamprocles; the second was Myrto, the daughter of Aristides the Just; and he took her without any dowry, and by her he had two sons, Sophroniscus and Menexenus. But some say that Myrto was his first wife. And some, among whom are Satyrus, and Hieronymus, of Rhodes, say that he had them both at the same time. For they say that the Athenians, on account of the scarcity of men, passed a vote, with the view of increasing the population, that a man might marry one citizen, and might also have children by another who should be legitimate; on which account Socrates did so.

XI. [27] And he was a man able to look down upon any who mocked him. And he prided himself upon the simplicity of his way of life; and never exacted any pay from his pupils. And he used to say that the man who ate with the greatest appetite, had the least need of delicacies; and that he who drank with the greatest appetite was the least inclined to look for a draught which is not at hand; and that those who want fewest things are nearest to the Gods. And thus much, indeed, one may learn from the comic poets; who, without perceiving it, praise him in the very matters for which they ridicule him. Aristophanes speaks thus:

> Prudent man, who thus with justice long
>   for mighty wisdom,
> Happiness will be your lot in Athens, and
>   all Greece too;
> For you've a noble memory, and plenty
>   of invention,
> And patience dwells within your mind,
>   and you are never tired,
> Whether you're standing still or walking;
>   and you care not for cold,
> Nor do you long for breakfast time, nor
>   e'er give in to hunger;
> But wine and gluttony you shun, and all
>   such kind of follies.

[28] And Ameipsias introduces him on the stage in a cloak, and speaks thus of him:

> O Socrates, among few men the best,
> And among many vainest; here at last
> You come to us courageously – but where,
> Where did you get that cloak? so strange
>   a garment,
> Some leather cutter must have given you
> By way of joke: and yet this worthy man,
> Though ne'er so hungry, never flatters
>   any one.

Aristophanes, too, exposes his contemptuous and arrogant disposition, speaking thus:

> You strut along the streets, and look
>   around you proudly,
> And barefoot many ills endure, and hold
>   your head above us.

And yet, sometimes he adapted himself to the occasion and dressed handsomely. As, for instance, in the *Banquet* of Plato, where he is represented as going to find Agathon.

XII. [29] He was a man of great ability, both in exhorting men to, and dissuading them from, any course; as, for instance, having discoursed with Theaetetus on the subject of knowledge, he sent him away almost inspired, as Plato says. And when Euthyphron had commenced a prosecution against his father for having killed a foreigner he conversed with him on the subject of piety, and turned him from his purpose: and by his exhortations he made Lysis a most moral man. For he was very ingenious at deriving arguments from existing circumstances. And so he mollified his son Lamprocles when he was very angry with his mother, as Xenophon mentions somewhere in his works; and he wrought upon Glaucon, the brother of Plato, who was desirous to meddle with affairs of state, and induced him to abandon his purpose, because of his want of experience in such matters, as Xenophon relates. And, on the contrary, he persuaded Charmides to devote himself to politics, because he was a man very well calculated for such business. [30] He also inspired Iphicrates, the general, with courage, by showing him the gamecocks of Midias the barber, pluming themselves against those of Callias; and Glauconides said, that the state ought to keep him carefully, as if he were a pheasant or a peacock. He used also to say that it was a strange thing that everyone could easily tell what property he had, but was not able to name all his friends, or even to tell their number; so careless were men on that subject. Once when he saw Euclides exceedingly anxious about some dialectic arguments he said to him, 'O Euclides, you will acquire a power of managing sophists, but not of governing men.' For he thought, that subtle hair-splitting on those subjects was quite useless; as Plato also records in the *Euthydemus*.

XIII. [31] And when Charmides offered him some slaves, with the view to his making a profit of them, he would not have them; and, as some people say, he paid no regard to the beauty of Alcibiades.

XIV. He used to praise leisure as the most valuable of possessions, as Xenophon tells us in his *Banquet*. And it was a saying of his that there was one only good, namely, knowledge; and one only evil, namely ignorance; that riches and high birth had nothing estimable in them, but that, on the contrary, they were wholly evil. Accordingly, when someone told him that the mother of Antisthenes was a Thracian woman, 'Did you suppose,' said he, 'that so noble a man must be born of two Athenians?' And when Phaedo was reduced to a state of slavery he ordered Crito to ransom him, and taught him, and made him a philosopher.

XV. [32] And, moreover, he used to learn to play on the lyre when he had time, saying, that it was not absurd to learn anything that one did not know; and further, he used frequently to dance, thinking such an exercise good for the health of the body, as Xenophon relates in his *Banquet*.

XVI. He used also to say that the daemon foretold the future to him; and that to begin well was not a trifling thing, but yet not far from a trifling thing; and that he knew nothing, except the fact of his ignorance. Another saying of his was that those who bought things out of season, at an extravagant price, expected never to live till the proper season for them. Once, when he was asked what was the virtue of a young man, he said, 'To avoid excess in everything.' And he used to say that it was necessary to learn geometry only so far as might enable a man to measure land for the purposes of buying and selling. [33] And when Euripides, in his *Auge*, had spoken thus of virtue:

'Tis best to leave these subjects undisturbed;

he rose up and left the theatre, saying that it was an absurdity to think it right to seek for a slave if one could not find him, but to let virtue be altogether disregarded. The question was once put to him by a man whether he would advise him to marry or not? And he replied, 'Whichever you do, you will repent it.' He often said that he wondered at those who made stone statues, when he saw how careful they were that the stone should be like the man it was intended to represent, but how careless they were of themselves, as to guarding against being like the stone. He used also to recommend young men to be constantly looking in the glass, in order that if they were handsome they might be worthy of their beauty; and if they were ugly they might conceal their unsightly appearance by their accomplishments. [34] He once invited some rich men to dinner, and when Xanthippe was ashamed of their insufficient appointments he said, 'Be of good cheer; for if our guests are sensible men they will bear with us; and if they are not we need not care about them.' He used to say, 'That other men lived to eat, but that he ate to live.' Another saying of his was, 'That to have a regard for the worthless multitude was like the case of a man who refused to take one piece of money of four drachmas as if it were bad, and then took a heap of such coins and admitted them to be good.' When Aeschines said, 'I am a poor man, and have nothing else, but I give you myself'; 'Do you not', he replied, 'perceive that you are giving me what is of the greatest value?' He said to someone, who was expressing indignation at being overlooked when the thirty had seized on the supreme power, 'Do you, then, repent of not being a tyrant too?' [35] A man said to him, 'The Athenians have condemned you to death.' 'And nature', he replied, 'has condemned them.' But some attribute this answer to Anaxagoras. When his wife said to him, 'You die undeservedly'; 'Would you then,' he rejoined, 'have had me deserve death?' He thought once that someone appeared to him in a dream, and said:

On the third day you'll come to lovely Phthia.

And so he said to Aeschines, 'In three days I shall die.' And when he was about to drink the hemlock Apollodorus presented him with a handsome robe, that he might expire in it; and he said, 'Why was my own dress good enough to live in, and not good enough to die in?' When a person said to him, 'Such an one speaks ill of you;' 'To be sure,' said he, 'for he has never learnt to speak well.' [36] When Antisthenes turned the ragged side of his cloak to the light he said, 'I see your silly vanity through the holes in your cloak.' When someone said to him, 'Does not that man abuse you?' 'No,' said he, 'for that does not apply to me.' It was a saying of his, too, 'That it is a good thing for a man to offer himself cheerfully to the attacks of the comic writers; for then, if they say anything worth hearing, one will be able to mend; and if they do not, then all they say is unimportant.'

XVII. He said once to Xanthippe, who first abused him, and then threw water at him, 'Did I not say that Xanthippe was thundering now, and would soon rain?' When Alcibiades said to him, 'The abusive temper of Xanthippe is intolerable'; 'But I,' he rejoined, 'am used to it, just as I should be if I were always hearing the noise of a pulley; [37] and you yourself endure to hear geese cackling.' To which Alcibiades answered, 'Yes, but they bring me eggs and goslings.' 'Well,' rejoined Socrates, 'and Xanthippe brings me children.' Once she attacked him in the marketplace, and tore his cloak off; his friends

advised him to keep her off with his hands; 'Yes, by Jove,' said he, 'that while we are boxing you may all cry out, "Well done, Socrates, well done, Xanthippe".' And he used to say, that one ought to live with a restive woman, just as horsemen manage violent-tempered horses; 'and as they,' said he, 'when they have once mastered them, are easily able to manage all others; so I, after managing Xanthippe, can easily live with anyone else whatever.'

XVIII. And it was in consequence of such sayings and actions as these that the priestess at Delphi was witness in his favour, when she gave Chaerephon this answer, which is so universally known:

Socrates of all mortals is the wisest.

[38] In consequence of which answer, he incurred great envy; and he brought envy also on himself, by convicting men who gave themselves airs of folly and ignorance, as undoubtedly he did to Anytus; and as is shown in Plato's *Meno*. For he, not being able to bear Socrates' jesting, first of all set Aristophanes to attack him, and then persuaded Meletus to institute a prosecution against him, on the ground of impiety and of corrupting the youth of the city. Accordingly Meletus did institute the prosecution; and Polyeuctus pronounced the sentence, as Favorinus records in his *Universal History*. And Polycrates, the sophist, wrote the speech which was delivered, as Hermippus says, not Anytus, as others say. And Lycon, the demagogue, prepared everything necessary to support the impeachment; [39] but Antisthenes, in his *Successions of the Philosophers*, and Plato, in his *Apology*, say that these men brought the accusation: Anytus, and Lycon, and Meletus; Anytus, acting against him on behalf of the magistrates, and because of his political principles; Lycon, on behalf of the orators; and Meletus on

behalf of the poets, all of whom Socrates used to pull to pieces. But Favorinus, in the first book of his *Commentaries*, says that the speech of Polycrates against Socrates is not the genuine one; for in it there is mention made of the walls having been restored by Conon, which took place six years after the death of Socrates; and certainly this is true.

XIX. [40] But the sworn informations, on which the trial proceeded, were drawn up in this fashion; for they are preserved to this day, says Favorinus, in the temple of Cybele: 'Meletus, the son of Meletus, of Pittea, impeaches Socrates, the son of Sophroniscus, of Alopece: Socrates is guilty, inasmuch as he does not believe in the Gods whom the city worships, but introduces other strange deities; he is also guilty, inasmuch as he corrupts the young men, and the punishment he has incurred is death.'

XX. But the philosopher, after Lysias had prepared a defence for him, read it through, and said: 'It is a very fine speech, Lysias, but is not suitable for me; for it was manifestly the speech of a lawyer, rather than of a philosopher.' [41] And when Lysias·replied, 'How is it possible, that if it is a good speech, it should not be suitable to you?' he said, 'Just as fine clothes and handsome shoes would not be suitable to me.' And when the trial was proceeding Justus, of Tiberias, in his *Garland*, says that Plato ascended the tribune and said, 'I, men of Athens, being the youngest of all those who have mounted the tribune . . .' and that he was interrupted by the judges, who cried out κατάβα, κατάβα that is to say, 'Come down.'

XXI. So when he had been condemned by two hundred and eighty-one votes, being six more than were given in his favour, and when the judges were making an estimate of what punishment or fine should be inflicted on him, he said that he ought to be fined five

and twenty drachmas; but Eubulides says that he admitted that he deserved a fine of one hundred. And when the judges raised an outcry at this proposition he said, [42] 'My real opinion is, that as a return for what has been done by me, I deserve a maintenance in the Prytaneum for the rest of my life.' So they condemned him to death, by eighty votes more than they had originally found him guilty. And he was put into prison, and a few days afterwards he drank the hemlock, having held many admirable conversations in the meantime, which Plato has recorded in the *Phaedo*.

XXII. He also, according to some accounts, composed a paean, which begins –

> Hail Apollo, King of Delos,
> Hail Diana, Leto's child.

But Dionysodorus says that this paean is not his. He also composed a fable, in the style of Aesop, not very artistically, and it begins –

> Aesop one day did this sage counsel give
> To the Corinthian magistrates: not to trust
> The cause of virtue to the people's judgment.

XXIII. [43] So he died; but the Athenians immediately repented of their action, so that they closed all the palaestrae and gymnasia; and they banished his accusers, and condemned Meletus to death; but they honoured Socrates with a brazen statue, which they erected in the place where the sacred vessels are kept; and it was the work of Lysippus. But Anytus had already left Athens; and the people of Heraclea banished him from that city the day of his arrival. But Socrates was not the only person who met with this treatment at the hands of the Athenians, but many other men received the same: for as Heraclides says, they fined Homer fifty drachmas as a madman, and they said that Tyrtaeus was out of his wits.

But they honoured Astydamas, before Aeschylus, with a brazen statue. [44] And Euripides reproaches them for their conduct in his *Palamedes*, saying –

Ye have slain, ye have slain,
O Greeks, the all-wise nightingale,
The favourite of the Muses, guiltless all.

And enough has been said on this head.

But Philochorus says that Euripides died before Socrates; and he was born, as Apollodorus, in his *Chronicles*, asserts, in the archonship of Apsephion, in the fourth year of the seventy-seventh Olympiad, on the sixth day of the month Thargelion, when the Athenians purify their city, and when the citizens of Delos say that Diana was born. And he died in the first year of the ninety-fifth Olympiad, being seventy years of age. And this is the calculation of Demetrius Phalereus, for some say that he was but sixty years old when he died.

XXIV. [45] Both he and Euripides were pupils of Anaxagoras; and Euripides was born in the first year of the seventy-fifth Olympiad, in the archonship of Calliades. But Socrates appears to me to have also discussed occasionally subjects of natural philosophy, since he very often disputes about prudence and foresight, as Xenophon tells us; although he at the same time asserts that all his conversations were about moral philosophy. And Plato, in his *Apology*, mentions the principles of Anaxagoras and other natural philosophers, which Socrates denies; and he is in reality expressing his own sentiments about them, though he attributes them all to Socrates. And Aristotle tells us that a certain one of the Magi came from Syria to Athens, and blamed Socrates for many parts of his conduct, and also foretold that he would come to a violent death. [46] And we ourselves have written this epigram on him –

Drink now, O Socrates, in the realms of Jove,

For truly did the God pronounce you wise,
And he who said so is himself all wisdom:
You drank the poison which your country gave,
But they drank wisdom from your god-like voice.

XXV. He had, as Aristotle tells us in the third book of his *Poetics*, a contest with a man of the name of Antilochus of Lemnos, and with Antipho, an interpreter of prodigies, as Pythagoras had with Cylon of Croton; and Homer while alive with Syagrus, and after his death with Xenophanes the Colophonian: and Hesiod, too, in his lifetime with Cereops, and after his death with the same Xenophanes; and Pindar with Amphimenes of Cos; and Thales with Pherecydes; and Bias with Salarus of Priene; and Pittacus with Antimenides and Alcaeus; and Anaxagoras with Sosibius; and Simonides with Timocreon.

XXVI. [47] Of those who succeeded him, and who are called the Socratic school, the chiefs were Plato, Xenophon, and Antisthenes: and of the ten, as they are often called, the four most eminent were Aeschines, Phaedo, Euclides, and Aristippus. But we must first speak of Xenophon, and after him of Antisthenes among the Cynics. Then of the Socratic school, and so about Plato, since he is the chief of the ten sects, and the founder of the first Academy. And the regular series of them shall proceed in this manner.

XXVII. There was also another Socrates, a historian, who wrote a description of Argos; and another, a peripatetic philosopher, a native of Bithynia; and another a writer of epigrams; and another a native of Cos, who wrote invocations to the Gods.

(2, 18–47)

The story of 'the Delian diver' at 2, 22 comes from Ariston of Ceos, Life of Socrates; cf. 9, 11. I have corrected some names.

1.5 Xenophon

I. Xenophon, the son of Gryllus, a citizen of Athens, was of the borough of Erchia; and he was a man of great modesty, and as handsome as can be imagined.

II. They say that Socrates met him in a narrow lane, and put his stick across it, and prevented him from passing by, asking him where all kinds of necessary things were sold. And when he had answered him, he asked him again where men were made good and virtuous. And as he did not know, he said, 'Follow me, then, and learn.' And from this time forth, Xenophon became a follower of Socrates.

III. And he was the first person who took down conversations as they occurred, and published them among men, calling them *Memorabilia*. He was also the first man who wrote a history of philosophers. (2, 48) *Cf.* **II.1.14.**

1.6. Aeschines

1.6.1 Aeschines was son of Charinus, purveyor of sausages, or (in some views) of Lysanias. He was an Athenian, and used to hard work from his boyhood. This enabled him to keep up with Socrates, who said, ' Only the sausage-seller's son understands how to treat me with respect.' Idomeneus recorded that it was Aeschines not Crito who advised Socrates to escape from prison, and that Plato attributed the advice to Crito, because of Aeschines preferring Aristippus' friendship to his own. Menedemus of Eretria suggested without justification that Aeschines filched most of his dialogues from Xanthippe.

Some of them have been called 'headless'; they are very loosely constructed and lack Socrates' precision. (2, 60)

1.6.2 There is a story that Socrates, seeing Aeschines hard pressed by poverty, told him to borrow from himself by dieting. (2, 62)

1.7 Aristippus

1.7.1 Aristippus was by birth from Cyrene, and came to Athens, as Aeschines tells us, through Socrates' reputation. He became a professional lecturer (as Phanias of Eresus, the Peripatetic, records) and was the first of Socrates' followers to exact fees and send money to his master. He once sent twenty minas and had the money returned to him; Socrates said that his divine sign would not let him accept; he was in fact very annoyed about it. Xenophon was hostile to him; that is why he made Socrates direct his attack on pleasure to Aristippus. (2, 65)

1.7.2 Someone said accusingly, 'A disciple of Socrates taking fees?!' He replied, 'Of course. People sent Socrates corn and wine. He sent most of it back, but kept a little. His stewards were the leading men of Athens. I've only my slave Eutychides.' (2, 74)

1.7.3 When he was accused of deserting Socrates for Dionysius he replied, 'Ah but I went to Socrates for education, to Dionysius for fun.' He earned money by teaching. Socrates said, 'Where did you get that colossal sum?' He answered, 'Where did you get that tiny sum?' (2, 80)

1.8 Phaedo

Phaedo came from Elis. He was of upper-class family, but was a prisoner of war in his country's defeat, and forced into a brothel. By shutting the door he managed to get together with Socrates, and Socrates persuaded Alcibiades or Crito and their circle to buy his freedom. (2, 105)

1.9 Crito

Crito came from Athens. He was a close friend of Socrates, looked after him and saw that he was never in need. His sons Critobulus, Hermogenes, Epigenes and Ctesippus were students of Socrates. Crito wrote seventeen dialogues, which have been published in a single volume, as follows: *That men are not made good by education*; *On having more than enough*; *Expediency* or *The Statesman*; *Nobility*; *Crime*; *Neatness*; *Law*; *Divinity*; *The Sciences*; *Fellowship*; *Wisdom*; *Protagoras* or *The Statesman*; *Literary Studies*; *Creative Writing*; *Education*; *Knowledge* or *Science*; *What is Science?* (2, 121)

1.10 Simon

Simon was a cobbler by profession; he came from Athens. When Socrates came into his shop and started talking he used to make notes of all he could recall. That's why they call his dialogues hide-bound. . . . He was apparently the first to present Socrates' words in dialogue form. (2, 122)

1.11 Plato

1.11.1 The story goes that Socrates saw in a dream a cygnet on his lap, which in a flash grew its plumage and flew up with a musical call. Next day Plato was brought to him, and he exclaimed, 'That's my bird.' . . .

Plato was proposing to enter a tragedy, but he heard Socrates speaking in front of the Theatre of Dionysus, and threw his verses on the fire with the words:

> Hephaestus, come to my help: Plato needs you.

He was twenty at the time, and from this point he was a disciple of Socrates. When Socrates was gone, he attached himself to Cratylus, a follower of Heraclitus, and Hermogenes, who professed the philosophy of Parmenides. At the age of 28 (so Hermodorus records) he left Athens to join Euclides in Megara with other followers of Socrates. (3, 5)

For the first story, see **9.10.2**; **12.6.4**.

1.11.2 There is a story that Socrates heard Plato reading his *Lysis* and said, 'Heracles! What lies the young man is telling about me!' (3, 35)

1.11.3 Plato uses four mouthpieces to present his own views – Socrates, Timaeus, the Athenian stranger, the Eleatic stranger. (3, 52)

1.12 Antisthenes

1.12.1 Later he came up against Socrates, and profited so markedly from him that he advised his own pupils to join him as pupils of Socrates. He lived in Piraeus and walked five miles every day to listen to Socrates. He learned toughness from Socrates, rivalling his capacity for endurance, and in this way laid the foundations of Cynic philosophy. (6, 2)

1.12.2 He turned the torn part of his cloak so that it became obvious. Socrates noticed this and said, 'I can see your ambition through your cloak.' (6, 8)

Cf. **9.7.17.**

1.12.3 He claimed that virtue could be taught... and was sufficient for happiness; it required nothing except the strength of Socrates. (6, 11)

1.13 Sphaerus

Sphaerus was a pupil of Cleanthes after Zeno . . . . He was author of the following books: . . . *On Lycurgus and Socrates*, 3 vols. (7, 177)

PART TWO

PLATO (427–347 B.C.)

Socrates' most famous follower, but not his closest associate. A member of an upper-class family, he was embarking on a career in tragic drama when he met Socrates, who induced him to turn to philosophy. Politics seemed an obvious outlet, especially as some of his relatives were in power among the Thirty Dictators of 404. Their excesses, and the execution of Socrates by the democrats, put him off. After Socrates' death he took refuge in Megara for a time. At some point he studied with followers of Parmenides and of Heraclitus. Then in 388–387 contact with Pythagoreans in Sicily and South Italy focused his problems. He returned with the vision of a community dedicated to the training of statesmen, and a majestic view of the eternal Forms which underlie the imperfect perishable material world. He tried courageously but unavailingly to apply his principles in an unpromising situation in Sicily in 367 and again in 361. In his last years his politics moved farther to the right, and his interests became increasingly logical and mathematical. From 367 to his death Aristotle was his most prominent pupil.

He is one of our principal sources about Socrates, but increasingly used the figure of Socrates as mouthpiece for his own developed views: some of the problems are discussed in the Introduction. His portrait of the man remains vivid and compelling.

2.1 Socratic Dialogues

This term may be conveniently given to the dialogues which on stylistic grounds may be assigned to the earliest period of Plato's writing: probably before his visit to Sicily and Italy in 387 B.C. It is possible that he began writing even before Socrates' death. Many of them are short, entertaining and strongly characterised. The conclusion is usually negative: the dialogue ends in aporia *('no way forward') as Socrates protests his ignorance and his interlocutors' pretensions to knowledge have been refuted. Towards the end of the period the dialogues become more elaborate and Plato is beginning, it seems, to wrestle with the problems for himself.*

2.1.1 Charmides: *a dialogue on the meaning of moderation or self-discipline.*

'Medicine is the science of health?'

'Surely.'

'Now suppose you ask me "This science of health, what use is it? What good does it do?" I should reply that it is of considerable use. It produces health, a matter of some value, as you will admit.'

'Yes.'

'And if you ask me what good does architecture, or the science of building houses, do, I should reply that it produces buildings – similarly with all the other skilled professions. So it's your turn now. You claim that moderation is a science. Suppose someone asks you "Critias, moderation is the science of a man's self, what good does it do, worthy of its name?" It's for you to answer.' (165 C)

2.1.2 Laches: *a dialogue on the meaning of courage.*

2.1.2.1 LYSIMACHUS: But if, son of Sophroniscus, you have anything to advise for the good of this your fellow-wardsman, you ought to communicate it: and you are justified [in doing so]; for you happen to be a friend on your father's side; for I and your father were always associates and friends; and he ended his days before he had any difference with me: and some recollection came round me as these persons were speaking; for these lads, while talking with each other at home, made frequent mention of Socrates, and very much praised him; but I never have asked them whether they spoke of Socrates, the son of Sophroniscus. Tell me now, children, is this the Socrates of whom you so often made mention?

SONS: Yes, father, it is the same.

LYSIMACHUS: It is well, by Juno, Socrates, that you give a support to your father, who was the best of men, in other respects, and this too, that your interests shall be mine, and mine yours.

LACHES: And, moreover, Lysimachus, do not omit the acts of the man; for I have elsewhere beheld him, not only giving a support to his father but to his country likewise. For, in the flight from Delium, he retired along with me; and I tell you, that if the rest had been willing to be such [as he was], our city would have stood erect, nor would so great a disaster have befallen it. (180 D, tr. G. Burges)

2.1.2.2 NICIAS: You don't seem to realise that anyone who comes close to Socrates and starts a conversation with him, whatever subject he raises, will find himself remorselessly dragged round and round in argument till he ends up by giving a full account of himself and his life, past and present. (187 E)

2.1.2.3 SOCRATES: Let us then in the first place, Laches, endeavour to state what fortitude is; and in the next place we will consider by what means it can be present to young men so far as it is possible for it to be present by study and instruction. But do you endeavour to state what fortitude is.

LACHES: By Zeus, Socrates, it is not difficult to state. For if anyone is willing to remain in his place, and defend himself from the enemy, and does not fly, rest assured that he would be a brave man.

SOCRATES: You speak well, Laches; but perhaps from not speaking clearly myself, I am the cause of your not answering what I intended to ask, but something else.

LACHES: How say you this, Socrates?

[191] SOCRATES: I will tell you, if I am able. A brave man, as you say, is one who, remaining in his place, fights with the foe.

LACHES: So I say.

SOCRATES: And I also. But what, on the other hand, is he who, while flying, fights with the foe, and does not remain in his place?

LACHES: How flying?

SOCRATES: Just as the Scythians surely are said to fight, no less while flying than pursuing. And Homer somewhere, praising the horses of Aeneas, says, [*Il.* v 225,]

> Hither and thither swiftly to pursue
> And fly they know;

and for this very thing he praises Aeneas himself, and calls him, through his skill in flying, 'in flight expert'.

LACHES: And very properly, Socrates: for he is there speaking of chariots; but you are speaking about the Scythian cavalry; for so they fight; but the heavy-armed infantry of Greece [fight] as I say.

SOCRATES: Except perhaps the Lacedaemonians, Laches. For they say that the Lacedaemonians, when they engaged with the Gerrophori at Plataea, were not willing to remain and fight against them, but fled; but when the ranks of the Persians were broken, they rallied and fought like cavalry, and thus won the battle.

LACHES: You speak the truth.

SOCRATES: This then I meant [as the reason for saying], that I was the cause of your not answering correctly, because I did not put the question correctly. For wishing to ask you not only about those who are brave among the heavy-armed but also about those in the cavalry, and in every form of war, and not only about those brave in battle but also those in the dangers of the sea, and such as act a manly part in diseases, in poverty and in political affairs, and still further, not only such as bear themselves bravely up against pain or fear, but also bear themselves up against desires or pleasures, both by remaining, or turning their backs – for there are surely some men, Laches, brave in things of this kind likewise.

LACHES: And very much so, Socrates.

SOCRATES: All these, therefore, are brave; but some of them possess fortitude in pleasures, others in pains, others in desires and others in fears; and others, I think, possess timidity in these very same things.

LACHES: Entirely so.

SOCRATES: What, then, is each of these? This is what I was asking. Try, then, again to tell me, in the first place, what is that fortitude, which is the same in all these. Or do you not yet understand what I mean?

LACHES: Not very well.

[192] SOCRATES: But I will speak in this way; just as if I had asked, What is the swiftness, which happens to be present with us in running, in playing on the harp, and in speaking, and in learning, and in many other things, and we nearly possess that, about which it is worth while to say anything, in the acts of the hands or feet, or mouth or voice, or mind. Or do not you also say so?

LACHES: Entirely so.

SOCRATES: If, therefore, any one should ask me – What, Socrates, do you call that, which you denominate swiftness in all things? I should say to him, that I call by the name of swiftness that power, which accomplishes many things in a short time, as regards the voice, and running, and all other things.

LACHES: And you would say rightly.

SOCRATES: Do you, then, endeavour, Laches, in like manner, to define fortitude? What is that power, which is the same in pleasure and in pain, and in all the things in which we just now said it is, and is afterwards called fortitude?

LACHES: It appears, then, to me to be a certain endurance of the soul, if one must speak of that, which exists connected with fortitude taken universally.

SOCRATES: And this must be, if we are to reply to the question asked by ourselves. This, then, appears to me, that you do not consider every kind of endurance to be fortitude. And I, too, infer it from hence; for I nearly know, Laches, that you think fortitude to belong to the things which are very beautiful.

LACHES: Rest assured that it does belong to things the most beautiful.

SOCRATES: Is not, therefore, that endurance, which subsists in conjunction with prudence, beautiful and good?

LACHES: Entirely so.

SOCRATES: But what of that endurance, which subsists with folly? Is it not, on the contrary, hurtful and evil-working?

LACHES: Yes.

SOCRATES: Do you, then, say that a thing of this kind is beautiful, though it is evil-working and hurtful?

LACHES: This, Socrates, [would be] not just.

SOCRATES: You do not, then, acknowledge such an endurance as this to be fortitude, since it is not beautiful; but fortitude is beautiful.

LACHES: You say true.

SOCRATES: Prudent endurance therefore, according to your assertion, would be fortitude.

LACHES: So it seems.

SOCRATES: Let us see, then, in what it is prudent; or whether it is prudent in all things both great and small. Thus, for instance, if someone endures to spend his money prudently, knowing that, by thus spending it, he should obtain more, would you call him a brave man?

LACHES: By Zeus, not I.

SOCRATES: Or if someone, being a physician, while his son or anyone else is attacked with an inflammation in the lungs, and requests him to give something to eat or drink, should be inflexible and persist [in denying. Is this fortitude?]

[193] LACHES: Not even this at all.

SOCRATES: But in the case of war, where a man is enduring and willing to fight, and reasoning prudently with himself, through knowing that others will give him assistance, or that he shall fight against foes fewer and of less account than those on his own side, and, further still, that he has the advantage of the ground, would you say that this man, enduring with such-like prudence and preparation, is braver than him in the opposite army, who is willing to stand his ground and endure?

LACHES: The man in the opposing army seems to me, Socrates, to be the braver.

SOCRATES: And yet the endurance of the latter is more imprudent than that of the former.

LACHES: You say true.

SOCRATES: And will you say that the man, who endures in a cavalry engagement, with a knowledge of horses, is less brave than him, who endures without science?

LACHES: To me at least it appears that he is.

SOCRATES: And he too, who with the art of a slinger, or archer, or of any other kind, is enduring?

LACHES: Entirely so.

SOCRATES: And will you say, that such as are willing to descend into a tank, and there to endure swimming, although not skilled in that exercise, or in anything else of that kind, are braver than those who are skilled in them?

LACHES: What else, Socrates, could one say?

SOCRATES: Nothing, if indeed he think so.

LACHES: But I do indeed think so.

SOCRATES: And yet Laches, such persons encounter danger and endure more imprudently than those, who do this with art.

LACHES: So they appear.

SOCRATES: Did not then unseemly and imprudent boldness and endurance formerly appear to us to be hurtful likewise?

LACHES: Entirely so.

SOCRATES: But fortitude was acknowledged to be something beautiful.

LACHES: It was acknowledged.

SOCRATES: But now, on the other hand, we say that the unseemly thing, namely, imprudent endurance, is fortitude.

LACHES: We seem so.

SOCRATES: Do we, then, appear to you to speak well?

LACHES: By Zeus, Socrates, not to me.

SOCRATES: In your own language, then, Laches, you and I are not Dorically harmonised; for our works do not accord with our words. For some-one, as it seems, would say in deed that we have a share of fortitude; but he would not say in word, as I think, if he should hear us now discoursing.

LACHES: You speak most truly.

SOCRATES: What, then, does it appear to you to be beautiful for us to be in this condition?

LACHES: By no means.

SOCRATES: Are you willing, then, for us to yield to what we said, to this extent?

[194] LACHES: To what extent, and to what assertion?

SOCRATES: To that which orders us to endure. If then you are willing, let us persist in the inquiry, and endure, lest fortitude itself should deride us for not bravely searching it out; if, perchance, endurance itself is fortitude.

LACHES: I indeed, Socrates, am prepared not to previously stand aloof, although I am unaccustomed to such-like conversations. But a certain love of contention against what has been said has laid hold of me, and I am truly indignant that I am so unable to tell what I have in my mind. For I seem to myself to conceive what fortitude is; but I know not how it has just now escaped me, so that I cannot comprehend it in words and say what it is.

SOCRATES: But ought not a good huntsman, my friend, to keep running in pursuit, and not to give up?

LACHES: By all means.

SOCRATES: Are you, then, willing for us to invite Nicias also to the hunting, if perchance he is at all more ready to find a path than we are?

LACHES: I am willing; for how not?

SOCRATES: Come then, Nicias, and if you possess any power, assist your friends, tossed, as it were, in a storm of words and in doubt; for you see how pathless are our affairs. Do you then state what you think fortitude is, and free us from this doubt, and confirm by reason what you conceive it to be.

NICIAS: You appear to me, Socrates, for some time past, not to have well defined fortitude; for of that, which I have heard you correctly asserting, you make no use.

SOCRATES: What is that, Nicias?

NICIAS: I have often heard you asserting that each of us is good, as regards the things in which he is wise, but bad, as regards those of which he is ignorant.

SOCRATES: By Zeus, Nicias, you speak the truth.

NICIAS: If, therefore, the brave is a good man he is clearly a wise man.

SOCRATES: Do you hear, Laches?

LACHES: I do; but I do not very well understand what he means.

SOCRATES: But I seem to understand; and the man seems to me to call fortitude a certain wisdom.

LACHES: What kind of wisdom, Socrates?

SOCRATES: Why do you not ask this of him?

LACHES: I do.

SOCRATES: Come, then, Nicias, tell him what kind of wisdom fortitude would be according to your reasoning; for it is surely not that belonging to the hautboy.

NICIAS: By no means.

SOCRATES: Nor yet that belonging to the harp.

NICIAS: Certainly not.

SOCRATES: But what is it, then, or of what is it the science?

LACHES: You very rightly interrogate him, Socrates; and let him tell us what he says wisdom is.

[195] NICIAS: I say then, Laches, that it is the science relating to things of dread and daring, both in war and in all other things.

LACHES: How absurdly, Socrates, he talks!

SOCRATES: Looking to what do you say this, Laches?

LACHES: To what? Wisdom is surely separate from fortitude.

SOCRATES: Nicias does not say so.

LACHES: He does not, by Zeus; and therefore he is a trifler.

SOCRATES: Let us then teach, but not revile him.

NICIAS: It is not so. But Laches seems to me, Socrates, to be desirous for me likewise to appear to say nothing to the purpose, because he, too, appeared just now to be such a kind of person.

LACHES: Entirely so, Nicias; and I will endeavour to show this. For you do say nothing [to the purpose]; since, for example, in diseases do not physicians know things of dread? Or do brave men seem to you to know this? Or do you call physicians brave men?

NICIAS: By no means.

LACHES: Neither do you give that name, I think, to husbandmen, although they know things of dread in agriculture; and all other artificers know things of dread and daring in their own arts; and yet they are not in any respect the more brave for this.

SOCRATES: What, Nicias, does Laches appear to you to say? He appears, however, to say something.

NICIAS: He does indeed say something, and yet not what is true.

SOCRATES: How so?

NICIAS: Because he thinks that physicians know something more about the sick than the being able to say that a thing is healthful or unhealthful. Now they do know only so much as this. But whether to be well is a thing of dread to anyone rather than to be ill, think you, Laches, that physicians know this? Or do you not think that it is better for many not to recover from disease than to recover? For tell me this. Do you say that it is better for all men to live, and that it is not better for many to die?

LACHES: I think that the latter is the case.

NICIAS: To those, then, to whom it is an advantage to die, do you think the same things are dreadful, as to those it is [an advantage] to live?

LACHES: Not I.

NICIAS: But do you grant physicians to know this, or to any other artificer beside the man, who knows what are things of dread, and what are not, whom I call a brave man?

SOCRATES: Do you understand, Laches, what he says?

LACHES: I do; and I perceive that he calls prophets brave men: for who else knows to whom it is better to live than to die? And yet, Nicias, do you acknowledge yourself to be a prophet, or to be neither a prophet nor a brave man?

NICIAS: What then, do you think it belongs to a prophet to know things of dread and daring?

LACHES: I do; for to whom else does it?

NICIAS: Much more, thou best of men, to him of whom I was speaking; since it is necessary for a prophet to know merely the signs of future events, whether there will be to anyone death, or disease, or the loss of property, or victory, or defeat, either in battle or in any other contest. [196] But which of these things it is better for anyone to suffer or not to suffer, how does it belong to a prophet, more than to any other person, to judge of?

LACHES: I do not understand, Socrates, what he means to say. For he does not show whom he calls brave, either a prophet, or a physician, or any other person, unless he says that this brave person is a certain god. To me then Nicias appears to be unwilling to ingenuously confess that he is saying nothing to the purpose; but he turns himself upwards and downwards, concealing his perplexity; and both you and I would have been able to turn ourselves in this way, had we wished not to appear to contradict ourselves. If, indeed, our speeches had been in a court of justice he would have had some reason to act in this manner; but now in such a conference as this why should you vainly deck yourself with empty words?

SOCRATES: For no reason, as it appears to me, Laches. But let us see, lest Nicias thinks he is saying something to the purpose, and does not assert this merely for the sake of talking. Let us then inquire of him more clearly what he means; and if it shall appear that he says anything pertinent, let us assent to him; if not, we will teach him better.

LACHES: Do you, then, Socrates, if you will, question him; for I have questioned him enough.

SOCRATES: Nothing prevents me, for the questioning will be in common, both on my account and yours.

LACHES: Entirely so.

SOCRATES: Tell me then, Nicias – for I and Laches unite in the speech – do you say that fortitude is the science of things of dread and daring?

NICIAS: I do.

SOCRATES: But it does not belong to every man to know this; since neither a physician nor a prophet knows it, nor will a man be brave, unless he acquires this science. Did you not say so?

NICIAS: I do.

SOCRATES: According to the proverb then, in reality every sow would not know this, nor would it become valiant.

NICIAS: It does not seem to me it would.

SOCRATES: It is then evident, Nicias, that you do not believe that even the Cromyonian sow was brave. I do not say this in jest; but I think it is necessary for him who asserts this to admit that no wild beast is brave; or to grant that any wild beast, a lion, or a leopard, or any boar, is so wise as to be born to know what few men, through the difficulty of knowing, do. But he who lays down fortitude to be, what you lay it down, must necessarily say that a lion and a stag and a bull and an ape are similarly formed by nature with respect to fortitude.

[197] LACHES: By the gods, Socrates, you speak well; and do you, Nicias, truly answer us. Do you say that these wild beasts, which we all of us acknowledge to be brave, are wiser than we are? or, in opposition to all, dare you to call them not brave?

NICIAS: Indeed, Laches, I do not call either a wild beast or anything else brave, which through ignorance has no fear of things of dread, but [I call it] fearless and stupid. Or, do you think, that I call children brave, who through ignorance, fear nothing? But I am of opinion, 'the fearless' is not the same with 'the brave'. For, I think, that of fortitude and forethought very few have a share; but of confidence and boldness, and fearlessness, together with the want of forethought, very many men and women and boys and wild beasts have. Those acts therefore which you and the many call courageous, I call rash, but the brave are the prudent, about whom I am now speaking.

LACHES: Behold, Socrates, how well this man bedecks himself, as he thinks, with fine words; for those, whom all men acknowledge to be brave, he endeavours to deprive of this honour.

NICIAS: Not I indeed, Laches; but take courage. For I say that you and Lamachus are wise, if you are brave, and many others of the Athenians likewise.

LACHES: Against this I will say nothing; although I could say something, lest you should say that I am in reality an Aixonean.

SOCRATES: Say nothing, Laches; for you seem to me to have not at all perceived that Nicias here received this wisdom from our friend Damon; and Damon is very intimate with Prodicus, who appears indeed to distinguish the best of the sophists' such kind of terms.

LACHES: For it becomes a sophist, Socrates, to be ingenious on such kind of subjects, rather than the man, whom the city thinks fit to place in a post of pre-eminence.

SOCRATES: It does, thou blessed man, indeed become him, who presides over things of the greatest consequence, to have the greatest share of wisdom. But it appears to me a thing worthy of consideration, with a view to what does Nicias thus define fortitude.

LACHES: Consider, Socrates, this yourself.

SOCRATES: This I intend to do, thou best of men. Do not, however, imagine that I shall dismiss you from your share in the conversation; but do you apply your mind, and ponder with me upon what has been stated.

LACHES: Let it be so, if it seems to you to be necessary.

[198] SOCRATES: Nay, but it does seem. And do you, Nicias, tell us again from the beginning. You know that [at the beginning of our conference] we considered fortitude as a part of virtue.

NICIAS: Entirely so.

SOCRATES: Did not you answer also, that it was a part, there being likewise other parts, which, taken together, are called virtue?

NICIAS: How not?

SOCRATES: Are you, then, speaking of the same parts as I am? For in addition to fortitude, I call temperance, and justice, and certain other things of such kind [parts of virtue]. Do not you too?

NICIAS: Entirely so.

SOCRATES: Hold, then. For in these we agree. But let us consider about things of dread and daring, that you may not think some of them one thing, and we another. What, then, we consider such, we will state; and do you, if you do not agree with us, instruct us. We consider, then, those to be things of dread, which occasion fear; but those to be things of daring, which do not occasion fear. Now neither evils past, nor present, occasion fear; but those which are expected: for fear is the expectation of a future evil. Or does it not appear so to you, Laches, likewise?

LACHES: Very much so, Socrates.

SOCRATES: You hear, then, Nicias,

our assertions, that future evils are things of dread; but future things, either not evil or good, are things of daring. On these points say you in this way or in another?

NICIAS: In this.

SOCRATES: But do you call the science of these things fortitude?

NICIAS: I do.

SOCRATES: Let us then still further consider, whether, on the third point, you think with us.

NICIAS: What is that?

SOCRATES: I will tell you. For it appears to me, and to Laches here, that of whatever things there is a science, there is not one science of a thing past, [so as] to know how it has been, another of things present, [to know] how they are, and another [to know] how that, which has not yet been, may be and will be in the most beautiful manner; but the science is the same. For instance, with respect to healthiness at all times, there is no other than medical science, which, being one, sees what is, and has been, and will be healthy, and how it will be so. And with respect to things constantly growing out of the earth, agriculture is in a similar state. So too, in warlike concerns, you yourselves would testify that the science of a general thinks beforehand in the most beautiful manner of other things and of what is about to be; nor does it think it ought to be subservient to the prophet's art, [199] but to rule over it, as knowing better what does and will take place in war. And the law enjoins this; not that the prophet shall rule over the general, but the general over the prophet. Shall we say so, Laches?

LACHES: We will say so.

SOCRATES: What, then, do you agree with us, Nicias, that the same science has a knowledge of the same things, future, and present, and past?

NICIAS: I do; for so it appears to me, Socrates.

SOCRATES: Is not, then, fortitude, as thou, the best of men, sayest, the science of things of dread and daring?

NICIAS: It is.

SOCRATES: But things of dread and daring have been confessed to relate, the latter to future good, the former to future evil.

NICIAS. Entirely so.

SOCRATES: But the same science is existing to the same things, and to [those about to be], and existing in every way.

NICIAS: It is so.

SOCRATES: Fortitude, then, is not the science of things of dread and daring alone; for it not only has a knowledge of future good and evil but also of things present and past, [and existing in every way] like the other sciences.

NICIAS: So it seems.

SOCRATES: You have therefore, Nicias, given us in your answer some third part nearly of fortitude. And yet we asked you what the whole of fortitude is. And now, as it seems, according to your [former] assertion, fortitude is not only the science of things of dread and daring, but as your present reasoning, on the other hand, [shows] fortitude would be that which nearly relates to all things good and evil, and existing in every way. To change again thus, or how say you, Nicias?

NICIAS. To me, Socrates, it seems good.

SOCRATES: Does, then, such a person as this appear to you, blessed man, to be deficient at all in virtue, if he knows every good, and how in every point they are, and will be, and have been, and every evil in the same manner? And do you think that he is wanting in temperance, or justice, or holiness, to whom alone it belongs in matters relating to gods and men to practise caution touching the things of dread and not, and to obtain for himself what is good by knowing how to associate in a proper manner [with others]?

NICIAS: You appear to me, Socrates, to say something to the purpose.

SOCRATES: That, then, which is now, Nicias, adduced by you, would not be a part of virtue but virtue in general.

NICIAS: So it seems.

SOCRATES: And yet we said that fortitude is one of the parts of virtue.

NICIAS: We said so.

SOCRATES: But that which is now said, does not appear to be so.

NICIAS: It seems not.

SOCRATES: We have not therefore, Nicias, discovered what fortitude is.

NICIAS: We do not appear [to have done so].

[200] LACHES: And yet I thought, friend Nicias, that you would have discovered it, since you had a contempt for myself, when I answered Socrates; and I had very great hope that you would discover it by the wisdom, which has come from Damon.

NICIAS: It is an excellent thing indeed, Laches, for you to think it a matter of no moment, that just now you appeared to know nothing about fortitude, and that you are looking to this, whether I shall appear to be another such [ignorant person]; and it will be, as it seems, of no consequence for you together with myself to know nothing of things, which it is fitting for a man to have a knowledge of, who thinks himself something. You therefore appear to me to act in reality after the general manner of men, in looking not to yourself but to others. I think, however, on the points which we have spoken about, there has been said something in reason; and, if anything has not been stated sufficiently it shall be afterwards set to rights, with the assistance both of Damon, whom you somehow fancy you are ridiculing – and this too, although you have never seen him – and of others also; and, when I shall have fortified these assertions I will instruct you too with-

out grudging; for you appear to me to be in very great need of instruction.

LACHES: You are, Nicias, wise indeed; but, however, I advise Lysimachus here and Melesias to bid farewell to you and me concerning the education of youth; but not to dismiss this Socrates, as I said from the first: for I would do the very same thing, if my children were of a proper age.

NICIAS: I, too, agree with you in this, to seek no other person, if Socrates is willing to take the lads under his care; since most gladly would I intrust Niceratus to him, if he is willing; but when I put him in mind at all on this subject he recommends others to me, and is unwilling to [do aught] himself. But see, Lysimachus, whether Socrates will hearken more to you.

LYSIMACHUS: This at least, Nicias, is just; since I should be willing to do many things for him which I would not be very willing to do for many others. How say you, then, Socrates? Will you hearken to me and make an effort with us for these lads to become the very best?

SOCRATES: It would certainly be a dreadful thing, Lysimachus, not to be willing to make an effort for any to become the best. If, therefore, in the conversations just now held, I have appeared to know something, but these not to know, it would be just to invite me especially to this employment; but now [not]; for we are all similarly in a doubt. Why, then, should anyone select any of us? To me indeed it seems that [he should select] none. And since this is the case, consider whether I appear to advise you rightly. [201] Now, men, I say it is requisite – for there will be a carrying out into public of our discourse – that we should all of us in common inquire, in the first place, after the best master for ourselves – for we need one – and in the next place for these lads, sparing neither money nor anything else; but to let ourselves be in the condition we now are, I do not advise. And if anyone ridicules us, because at this time of life we think proper to frequent a school, it seems to me that it will be meet to bring forward Homer in our defence, who says, [in *Od.* XVII 34,]

Shame ill is present to a man in need.

We therefore, bidding a person go hang, if he says a word against us, let us take care in common of ourselves and the lads.

LYSIMACHUS: To me indeed, Socrates, what you say is very agreeable; and by how much the older I am, by so much the more willing am I to learn together with the youths. Do you, then, act in this way. Come tomorrow morning early to my house, and do not do otherwise, in order that we may consult about these very things. For the present let us break up the meeting.

SOCRATES: This, Lysimachus, I will do; and, god willing, I will come to you tomorrow morning. (190 E, N. G. Burges)

A good example of Socratic method, but with some apologetic purpose by Plato; the suggestion that Socrates is an ideal educator of youth runs counter to the view that he is a corrupter of youth.

2.1.3 Hippias Major:

SOCRATES: Say we not then of the whole body thus, that one part of it is beautiful for running, another for wrestling? and further, that all the animal kind, as a beautiful horse, and a cock, and a quail, and all utensils, and vehicles, for land and sea, ships and triremes, and all instruments both for music and the other arts, and pursuits and laws, and nearly every thing we call beautiful, are in the same position; and looking to each of them, in what way it has been born, made, or laid down, we speak of a thing which is useful, as being beautiful in what it is useful, and for what it is useful, and when it is useful; but another thing, which is entirely useless, we call not beautiful. Does it not so seem to you, Hippias?

HIPPIAS: To me it does.

SOCRATES: Correctly, then, do we now say that the useful happens to be more than all beautiful?

HIPPIAS: Correctly, Socrates.

SOCRATES: Now is not each thing, which is able to effect anything, useful, so far as it is able? but that, which is unable, useless?

HIPPIAS: Entirely so.

SOCRATES: Power, then, is beautiful, and want of power is not beautiful.

HIPPIAS: Very much so. And the rest of things, Socrates, testify in our favour that such is the case, [296] but particularly as regards matters of state. For of all things it is the most beautiful for a person to be powerful in state-affairs, and in his own city; but to be powerless, the least so.

SOCRATES: You say well. By the gods then, Hippias, is not wisdom on this account the most beautiful of all things, and ignorance the least so?

HIPPIAS: What else do you think, Socrates?

SOCRATES: Softly, my dear friend; since I have a fear about what I am saying.

HIPPIAS: What do you fear, Socrates? For your reasoning has proceeded very beautifully at present.

SOCRATES: I wish it had. But do you consider this with me. Could a person do anything, of which he knows nothing, and for which he has no power?

HIPPIAS: By no means. For how could he do that, for which he has no power?

SOCRATES: Are then they, who err, and act wrong, and do a thing unwillingly, other than those, who would not have so acted, unless they had possessed the power?

HIPPIAS: It is evident.

SOCRATES: But, however, they who are powerful are powerful through power; for assuredly it is not through want of power.

HIPPIAS: Certainly not.

SOCRATES: All then, who do anything, are able to do what they do.

HIPPIAS: Yes.

SOCRATES: And all men, beginning from boyhood, do many more evil things than good, and err unwillingly.

HIPPIAS: The fact is so.

SOCRATES: What, then, shall we say that this power and these means, however useful they may be for the doing evil, are beautiful? or do they want much of being so?

HIPPIAS: [They want] much, in my opinion, Socrates.

SOCRATES: The powerful then and the useful, Hippias, are not, it seems, the beautiful.

HIPPIAS: If indeed, Socrates, it has power to do good, or is useful for things of that kind.

SOCRATES: Away then has fled that thing, at once the powerful and the useful, as being without exception beautiful. Now this was that very thing, Hippias, which our soul meant to say, that the beautiful consists in utility and the power to produce some good.

HIPPIAS: So it seems to me.

SOCRATES: Now this is the advantageous. Is it not?

HIPPIAS: It is.

SOCRATES: Thus then beautiful bodies, and beautiful institutions, and wisdom, and all these things we just now mentioned, are beautiful, because advantageous.

HIPPIAS: Evidently so.

SOCRATES: The advantageous then appears to be, Hippias, to us, the beautiful.

HIPPIAS: Entirely so, Socrates. (295 C, tr. G. Burges)

An important passage for the view that wrongdoing is involuntary.

2.1.4 Euthydemus

SOCRATES: Providentially I happened to be seated on my own at the very spot in the changing room where you saw me. I was on the point of getting up to go, but as I was getting to my feet my familiar divine sign came to me. I sat down again. (272 E)

2.1.5 Protagoras

For Simonides was not so ill-informed as to express his admiration of those who committed no evil willingly, as though he imagined there were any in the world who did commit evil willingly. I had almost said, that no wise man ever entertained the opinion, that any mortal errs willingly, or commits base and wicked actions willingly. On the contrary, wise men well know that all who do base and evil deeds do them involuntarily. (345 D, tr. J. Wright)

2.1.6 Gorgias

2.1.6.1 SOCRATES: O Polus, I am not a public man, and only last year, when my tribe were serving as Prytanes, and it became my duty as their president to take the votes, there was a laugh at me, [474] because I was unable to take them. (473 E, tr. B. Jowett)

Seemingly a reference to the Arginusae episode (see the Introduction).

2.1.6.2 SOCRATES: For my position has always been that I myself am ignorant how these things are, but that I have never met anyone who could say otherwise, any more than you can, and not appear ridiculous. This is my position still, and if what I am saying is true, and injustice is the greatest of evils to the doer of injustice, and yet there is if possible a greater than this greatest of evils, in an unjust man not suffering retribution, what is that defence of which the want will make a man truly ridiculous? Must not the defence be one which will avert the greatest of human evils? And will not the worst of all defences be that with which a man is unable to defend himself or his family or his friends? – and next will come that which is unable to avert the next greatest evil; thirdly, that which is unable to avert the third greatest evil; and so of other evils. As is the greatness of evil so is the honour of being able to avert them in their several degrees, and the disgrace of not being able to avert them. Am I not right, Callicles?

CALLICLES: Yes, quite right.

SOCRATES: Seeing, then, that there are these two evils, the doing injustice and the suffering injustice – and we affirm that to do injustice is a greater, and to suffer an injustice a lesser evil – by what devices can a man succeed in obtaining the two advantages, the one of not doing and the other of not suffering injustice? must he have the power, or only the will to obtain them? I mean to ask whether a man will escape injustice if he has only the will to escape, or must he have provided himself with the power?

CALLICLES: He must have provided himself with the power; that is clear.

SOCRATES: And what do you say of doing injustice? Is the will only sufficient, and will that prevent him from doing injustice, or must he have provided himself with power and art; and if he have not studied and practised, will he be unjust still? Surely you might say, Callicles, whether you think that Polus and I were right in admitting the conclusion that no one does wrong voluntarily, but that all do wrong against their will?

CALLICLES: Granted, Socrates, if you will only have done. (509 A, tr. B. Jowett)

2.1.6.3 SOCRATES: Nay, I ask you, not from a love of contention but because I really want to know in what way you think that affairs should be administered among us – whether, when you come to the administration of them, you have any other aim but the improvement of the citizens? Have we not already admitted many times over that such is the duty of a public man? Nay, we have surely said so; for if you will not answer for yourself I must answer for you. But if this is what the good man ought to effect for the benefit of his own state, allow me to recall to you the names of those whom you were just now mentioning, Pericles, and Cimon, and Miltiades, and Themistocles, and ask whether you still think that they were good citizens.

CALLICLES: I do.

SOCRATES: But if they were good, then clearly each of them must have made the citizens better instead of worse?

CALLICLES: Yes.

SOCRATES: And, therefore, when Pericles first began to speak in the assembly the Athenians were not so good as when he spoke last?

CALLICLES: Very likely.

SOCRATES: Nay, my friend, 'likely' is not the word; for if he was a good citizen the inference is certain.

CALLICLES: And what difference does that make?

SOCRATES: None; only I should like further to know whether the Athenians are supposed to have been made better by Pericles or, on the contrary, to have been corrupted by him; for I hear that he was the first who gave the people pay, and made them idle and cowardly, and encouraged them in the love of talk and of money.

CALLICLES: You heard that, Socrates, from the laconising set who bruise their ears.

SOCRATES: But what I am going to tell you now is not mere hearsay, but well known both to you and me: that at first Pericles was glorious and his character unimpeached by any verdict of the Athenians – this was during the time when they were not so good – yet afterwards, when they had been made good and gentle by him, at the very end of his life they convicted him of theft, and almost put him to death, clearly under the notion that he was a malefactor.

CALLICLES: Well, but how does that prove Pericles' badness?

SOCRATES: Why, surely, you would say that he was a bad manager of asses or horses or oxen, who had received them originally neither kicking nor butting nor biting him, and implanted in them all these savage tricks? Would he not be a bad manager of any animals who received them gentle, and made them fiercer than they were when he received them? What do you say?

CALLICLES: I will do you the favour of saying 'yes'.

SOCRATES: And will you also do me the favour of saying whether man is an animal?

CALLICLES: Certainly he is.

SOCRATES: And was not Pericles a shepherd of men?

CALLICLES: Yes.

SOCRATES: And if he was a good political shepherd, ought not the animals who were his subjects, as we were just now acknowledging, to have become more just, and not more unjust?

CALLICLES: Quite true.

SOCRATES: And are not just men gentle, as Homer says? – or are you of another mind?

CALLICLES: I agree.

SOCRATES: And yet he really did make them more savage than he received them, and their savageness was shown towards himself; which he must have been very far from desiring.

CALLICLES: Do you want me to agree with you?

SOCRATES: Yes, if I seem to you to speak the truth.

CALLICLES: Granted then.

SOCRATES: And if they were more savage, must they not have been more unjust and inferior?

CALLICLES: Granted again.

SOCRATES: Then upon this view, Pericles was not a good statesman?

CALLICLES: That is, upon your view.

SOCRATES: Nay, the view is yours, after what you have admitted. Take the case of Cimon again. Did not the very persons whom he was serving ostracise him, in order that they might not hear his voice for ten years? and they did just the same to Themistocles, adding the penalty of exile; and they voted that Miltiades, the hero of Marathon, should be thrown into the pit of death, and he was only saved by the Prytanis. And yet, if they had been really good men, as you say, these things would never have happened to them. For the good charioteers are not those who at first keep their place, and then, when they have broken-in their horses, and themselves become better charioteers, are thrown out: that is not the way either in charioteering or in any profession. – What do you think?

CALLICLES: I should think not.

[517] SOCRATES: Well, but if so, the truth is as I have said already, that in the Athenian State no one has ever shown himself to be a good statesman – you admitted that this was true of our present statesmen, but not true of former ones, and you preferred them to the others; yet they have turned out to be no better than our present ones; and therefore, if they were rhetoricians, they did not use the true art of rhetoric or of flattery, or they would not have fallen out of favour.

CALLICLES: But surely, Socrates, no living man ever came near any one of them in his performances.

SOCRATES: O my dear friend, I say nothing against them regarded as the serving-men of the State; and I do think that they were certainly more serviceable than those who are living now, and better able to gratify the wishes of the State; but as to transforming those desires and not allowing them to have their way, and using the powers which they had, whether of persuasion or of force, in the improvement of their fellow-citizens, which is the prime object of the truly good citizen, I do not see that in these respects they were a whit superior to our present statesmen, although I do admit that they were more clever at providing ships and walls and docks, and all that. You and I have a ridiculous way, for during the whole time that we are arguing we are always going round and round to the same point, and constantly misunderstanding one another. If I am not mistaken, you have admitted and acknowledged more than once that there are two kinds of operations which have to do with the body, and two which have to do with the soul: one of the two is ministerial, and if our bodies are hungry provides food for them, and if they are thirsty gives them drink, or if they are cold supplies them with garments, blankets, shoes and all that they crave. I use the same images as before intentionally, in order that you may understand me the better. The purveyor of the articles may provide them either wholesale or retail, or he may be the maker of any of them – the baker, or the cook, or the weaver, or the shoemaker, or the currier; and in so doing, being such as he is, he is naturally supposed by himself and everyone to minister to the body. For none of them know that there is another art – an art of gymnastic and medicine which is the true minister of the body, and ought to be the mistress of all the rest, and to use their results according to the knowledge which she has and they have not, of the real good or bad effects of meats and drinks on the body. [518] All other arts which have to do with the body are servile and menial and illiberal; and gymnastic and medicine are, as they ought to be, their mistresses. Now, when I say that all this is equally true of the soul you seem at first to know and understand and assent to my words, and then a little while afterwards you come repeating, Has not the State had good and noble citizens? and when I ask you who they are, you reply, seemingly quite in earnest, as if I had asked, Who are or have been good trainers? – and you had replied, Thearion, the baker, Mithoecus, who wrote the Sicilian cookery-book, Sarambus, the vintner: these are ministers of the body, first-rate in their art; for the first makes admirable loaves, the second excellent dishes, and the third capital wine; to me these appear to be the exact parallel of the statesmen whom you mention. Now you would not be altogether pleased if I said to you, My friend, you know nothing of gymnastics; those of whom you are speaking to me are only the ministers and purveyors of luxury, who have no good or noble notions of their art, and may very likely be filling and fattening men's bodies and gaining their approval, although the result is that they lose their original flesh in the long run, and become thinner than they were before; and yet they, in their simplicity, will not attribute their diseases and loss of flesh to their entertainers; but when in after years the unhealthy surfeit brings the attendant penalty of disease he who happens to be near them at the time, and offers them advice, is accused and blamed by them, and if they could they would do him some harm; while they proceed to eulogise the men who have been the real authors of the mischief. And that, Callicles, is just what you are now doing. You praise the men who feasted the citizens and satisfied their desires, and people say that they have made the city great, not seeing that the swollen and ulcerated condition of the State is to be attributed to these elder statesmen; for they have filled the city full of harbours and docks and walls and revenues and all that, and have left no room for justice and temperance. [519] And when the crisis of the disorder comes, the people will blame the advisers of the hour, and applaud Themistocles and Cimon and Pericles, who are the real authors of their calamities; and if you are not careful they may assail you and my friend Alcibiades, when they are losing not only their new acquisitions but also their original possessions; not that you are the authors of these misfortunes of theirs, although you may perhaps be accessories to them. A great piece of work is always being made, as I see and am told, now as of old, about our statesmen. When the State treats any of them as malefactors I observe that there is a great uproar and indignation at the supposed wrong which is done to them; 'after all their many services to the State, that they should unjustly perish' – so the tale runs. But the cry is all a lie; for no statesman ever could be unjustly put to death by the city of which he is the head. The case of the professed statesman is, I believe, very much like that of the professed sophist; for the sophists, although they are wise men, are nevertheless guilty of a strange piece of folly; professing to be teachers of virtue, they will often accuse their disciples of wronging them, and defrauding them of their pay, and showing no gratitude for their services. Yet what can be more absurd than that men who have become just and good, and whose injustice has been taken away from them, and who have had justice implanted in them by their teachers, should act unjustly by reason of the injustice which is not in them? Can anything be more irrational, my friend, than this? You, Callicles, compel me

to be a mob-orator, because you will not answer.

CALLICLES: And you are the man who cannot speak unless there is some one to answer?

SOCRATES: I suppose that I can; just now, at any rate, the speeches which I am making are long enough because you refuse to answer me. (515 E, tr. B. Jowett)

2.1.7 Meno

2.1.7.1 SOCRATES: But those others, those who desire things which are evil, as you say, and who at the same time know that evil things are hurtful to the possessor, do they know that they themselves shall receive harm from those evil things in their having them?

[78] MENO: It is clear that they must know it.

SOCRATES: But know they not, that such as receive harm are in evil plight, so far as harm has befallen them?

MENO: This also must they know.

SOCRATES: And know they not besides, that such as are in evil plight are unhappy too?

MENO: I presume they do.

SOCRATES: Is there any man then, who chooses to be in evil plight, and to be unhappy?

MENO: I suppose there is not any, Socrates.

SOCRATES: No man, therefore, O Meno, wills or chooses anything evil; if it be true, that no man wills or chooses to be in evil plight, or to be unhappy. For indeed what else is it to be thoroughly unhappy than to desire things which are evil, and to have them our own?

MENO: I suspect that what you say, Socrates, is true. And no man wills or chooses anything evil. (77 E, tr. T. Taylor and F. Sydenham)

2.1.7.2 MENO: Socrates, I heard, before I had conversed with you, that the only part you take in conversation is this: [80] You pretend to be at a loss and doubtful yourself upon all subjects, and make others too no less to be at a loss what to think and say. You seem to be now playing the same conjurers' tricks upon me; you manifestly use incantations to bewitch me, and to fill me with such perplexity that I know not what to say. If you will allow me to joke a little I think you resemble exactly, not only in form but in other respects also, that broad sea-fish called the cramp-fish; for that, too, never fails to give a numbness to every person who either touches or approaches it. You seem to have done some such thing at present to me, and to have benumbed me. For I actually suffer a kind of numbness and stupidity, both in mind and body, and find myself disabled from giving you any answer; and yet have I a thousand times discoursed much about virtue, and to many persons, and extremely well too, as I thought; but I am now not in the least able to tell so much as what virtue is. I think that you have acted very prudently in never going out of your own country either by sea or land. For if you was to behave in this manner in any other city where you are a stranger you would run a risk of being driven thence as a magician or enchanter.

SOCRATES: You are full of craftiness, Meno; and I was very near being deceived by you.

MENO: Tell me how, Socrates, I pray you?

SOCRATES: I know with what design you brought a simile to which you likened me.

MENO: With what design now, do you imagine?

SOCRATES: That I, on my part, might bring some simile or resemblance of you. For this I know to be true of all handsome persons, they love to have images and pictures made of them. And indeed it is their interest; for of handsome persons the pictures are handsome too. But I shall forbear the drawing of your picture in return. And as to that which you have produced of me, if the cramp-fish be itself numb, and through its numbness benumb others also, then am I like to it, but otherwise I am not. For I do not lead others into doubtfulness on any subject, and make them be at a loss what to say; when at the same time I can easily explain the matter in hand, and have no doubts at all within my own mind; but as I am entirely distressed for true definitions of things myself; in this condition I involve in the same distresses those with whom I am conversing. Thus at present concerning the nature of virtue; what it is, I, for my part, know not: you indeed knew formerly, perhaps, before that you had touched me; but now you are like one who knows nothing of the matter. I am desirous, however, of considering it together with you, and of our searching out jointly what kind of a thing virtue is. (79 E, tr. T. Taylor and F. Sydenham)

2.2 Apology

[17] SOCRATES: I know not, O men of Athens, how you have been affected by my accusers, but I for my part, I assure you, scarcely recognised myself, so plausibly did they speak; and yet, not one word of truth, I may say, have they uttered. But among their many falsehoods, there was one at which I marvelled most of all: it was where they said that I was an eloquent speaker, and that you must therefore take care not to be led astray by me.

That they were not ashamed to make this assertion, when they knew that it was on the very point of being refuted by me, is, I think, the most shameless part of the whole thing; for it will soon be apparent that I am not in the least an eloquent speaker, unless perchance they call him eloquent who simply speaks the truth. If that indeed be what they mean, I should be willing to confess myself an orator, though not one after their fashion. These men, then, as I was saying, have spoken hardly one word of truth; but from me you shall hear the whole truth, yet not, by Zeus, O men of Athens, dressed up in finely worded speeches like their own, with figures and phrases and embellishments. No, indeed! you shall hear it plainly stated, in the first words that occur to me; and let none of you expect anything more than this from me, for I rely solely upon the justice of my cause. And certainly, citizens, it would ill become me, at my age, to appear before you like a boy with a carefully prepared speech. But this, above all, men of Athens, I beg and implore: if you hear me defend myself in the same words that I have been accustomed to use in the market-place, at the counters of the money-changers, where many of you have heard me, and in other places, do not be surprised, nor interrupt by raising a disturbance. For the matter stands thus. At the age of more than seventy years, I am now for the first time appearing before a court of justice, so that I am an utter stranger to the manner of speaking here. Therefore, just as you would doubtless pardon me, [18] if I were in reality a stranger, for speaking in that dialect and fashion which I had been brought up to use, even so now I ask this justice – for such it seems to me – at your hands: that you disregard my manner, whether it be better or worse, and consider this alone, and to this turn your whole attention, whether I speak what is just or not. For this is the virtue of a judge, and to speak the truth is that of an orator.

First then, men of Athens, I am bound to answer my former accusers and the first false charges which were brought against me, and then the later charges and the last accusers. For my accusers are many in number, and it is a long time now – many years, in fact – that they have been speaking falsely against me. These I fear more than Anytus and his friends, although they are formidable enough; but those, fellow-citizens, are more formidable, who, getting hold of you for the most part while you were yet children, have persuaded you to believe this false accusation, that there is a certain Socrates, a wise man, who speculates on things in the heavens, and searches into all things under the earth, and makes the worse appear the better reason. They, O Athenians, who have spread this report are my really formidable accusers, for their hearers suppose that men who search into such things as these do not believe even in Gods. Then, too, these accusers are many, and have been bringing charges against me for a long time, and presenting them to you moreover, at that age – either childhood or extreme youth – when you were most easy to be persuaded; appearing, in fact, like plaintiffs in court with no defendant present. But the most senseless thing about it all is that we are not able even to find out who they are, or to call them by name, unless someone among them happens to be a comic poet. All those who from envy and malice tried to mislead you, as well as those who urged upon you only what they themselves had been taught to believe – all these, I say, are very hard to deal with, for it is impossible to summon anyone of them here as a witness, or to question him. I must needs in defending myself fight, as it were, with shadows and question with no one to answer.

Assume with me, then, that, as I say, my accusers are of two classes, namely, those who of late have attacked me, and those old accusers of whom I have just spoken; and you will agree, I think, that I ought first to defend myself against the latter. For these you first heard accuse me, and much oftener too than those who came afterwards. This, then, is agreed. And so, Athenian citizens, I must needs make my defence, [19] and try to do away in so short a time with the bad opinion of me at which you have been arriving for so long a time. I could wish, indeed, if it were best for you as well as for me, that such might be the result, and that I might gain favour with you by my defence. But success, I think, will be difficult; how difficult, I do not conceal from myself. Let it so be, however, as God pleases; the law must be obeyed, and I must make my defence.

Let us therefore consider, from the beginning, what the charge is which gave rise to these slanders, and on which Meletus, you see, was relying when he brought this indictment against me, Well, then, in what words did my calumniators slander me? Let us read out their charge, as if it were a formal accusation made in court. 'Socrates is guilty of crime, in that he busies himself with prying into things under the earth and in the heavens, and making the worse appear the better reason, and teaching the same to others.'

This is the kind of charge; and this is what you yourselves have seen in the comedy of Aristophanes, where a certain Socrates appears wandering round, asserting that he walks the air, and babbling many other follies, about which I confess that I understand absolutely nothing at all. Now I do not mean to speak slightingly of this kind of knowledge, if anyone really possesses it; may I never be brought to trial by Meletus on so heavy a charge as that! But really, Athenians, I have nothing to do with these matters. As witnesses to this, I summon the greater part of you here present, and demand that all who have listened to my discourses shall speak out and inform one another. There must be many such persons here. If any of you, then, have ever heard me say either much or little about such matters, tell it now one to the other. The result of this experiment shows you that the other stories which are told about me are of the same stamp.

Nor is the report true, which you may have heard, that I undertake to teach men and charge fees for my instruction; there is not a word of truth in it. And yet this, I think, is a noble thing to do, if one is really capable of teaching men, like Gorgias of Leontini, and Prodicus of Ceos, and Hippias of Elis. For each one of these is able to go to any of our cities he pleases, and persuade our young men to forsake the society of their own fellow-citizens, [20] which they could have had without expense, and flock to him, and not only pay him money but feel grateful besides. And there is another philosopher, a Parian, of whose arrival here I heard in this way: I happened to meet a man who has spent more money on Sophists than have all others put together, Callias, the son of Hipponicus, and knowing that he had two sons, 'Callias,' said I, 'if your sons were colts or calves we should be able to find some master, probably some horse-trainer or farmer, whom we could hire to bring out and improve the good qualities of their nature. But now, seeing they are human beings, what master have you in view for them? Who understands those good qualities which belong to the man and citizen? I ask you, because I suppose that, having sons, you have considered the matter. Is there any such person,' I asked, 'or not?'

'Certainly there is,' he answered.

'Who is he?' I asked. 'Whence does

he come, and what is his fee for teaching?'

'Evenus, O Socrates,' he answered. ' He comes from Paros, and he charges five minas.' And I thought to myself that Evenus was a happy man, if he did in truth possess this art and teach it for so modest a fee. I assure you that if I had understood all this I should have prided myself upon it, and given myself airs. But I really do not understand it, O Athenians.

And here someone of you may turn upon me, and say, 'But, Socrates, what is it, then, that you are in the habit of doing? What is the origin of these slanders? For surely all this talk and this evil report about you did not arise while you, like the generality of people, were busying yourself about nothing unusual, and behaving in no wise differently from others. Tell us, then, what it is that we may not give a rash judgement about you.'

Now it seems to me that this is a very proper question, and I will try to show what it is that has brought this name and this evil report upon me. Listen, then. And although some of you may think that I am in jest, I shall tell you the whole truth: be assured of that. I have obtained this name, O Athenian citizens, by reason of nothing but a certain kind of wisdom. 'What kind?' do you ask? It is perhaps human wisdom, for in this I may, in reality, be said to be wise. The men, however, of whom I have just been speaking may turn out to have a kind of superhuman wisdom – I really do not know what else to call it, as I, for my part, do not pretend to understand it, and whoever says that I do, lies and seeks to slander me. And now, Athenians, do not interrupt, even if I seem to be talking extravagantly. The words which I am about to speak are not my own, but the speaker of them, to whom I shall refer you, is worthy of confidence. For to testify whether I have any wisdom, and

of what kind it is, I shall summon the God of Delphi. You know Chaerephon, I suppose. [21] He was a friend of mine from childhood, and was also one of the associates in your democracy, for he shared in the recent exile, and returned from it with you. So of course you know what sort of a man Chaerephon was, and how eager in whatever he undertook. Well, once he went to Delphi, and had the boldness to consult the oracle about this matter. He asked – I repeat, citizens, do not interrupt – he asked if anyone were wiser than I, and the Pythian priestess answered that there was no one wiser. To the truth of this his brother here will testify, as Chaerephon himself is dead.

Notice why I am telling you this. It is because I want to show you whence the calumny against me arose. Having heard the utterance of the oracle, I pondered in this wise: 'How shall I explain the God's answer, and what does his riddle mean? I am not conscious that in me is any wisdom, whether great or small. What, then, can he mean by saying that I am the wisest of all men? I cannot suppose that he is speaking falsely, for that is not in the law of his nature.' And for a long time I was at a loss as to what he meant, and then, after much hesitation, I set about my search in this way: I went to one of those who were reputed wise, thinking that there, if anywhere at all, I should be able to refute the oracle, and say to it, 'You said I was the wisest man, yet here is one wiser than I am.' But as I examined and conversed with him – there is no need of my calling him by name, but, Athenian citizens, it was one of our statesmen with whom I had this experience – it seemed to me that this man had the appearance of being wise in the eyes of many others, and most of all in his own, but in reality was not wise. Whereupon I tried to convince him that he only thought himself wise but was not really so, and consequently I became an object of hatred to him and to many of those who were present. And as I went away I reasoned thus within myself: 'I am wiser than this man; for it may well be that neither of us knows anything really beautiful and good, but he thinks that he knows something when he knows nothing, whereas I neither know nor think that I know anything. I do therefore seem to be wiser than he, at least in this small particular, that what I know not, I do not even think I know.' Thereupon I went to one of those who had the reputation of being even wiser than this man, and here it was the same thing over again. And so I incurred his hatred too, and that of many others.

After this, I went to many in turn, perceiving with grief and anxiety that I was making myself hated, but nevertheless under the necessity, so it seemed to me, of making the will of God my first object. Now, in order to find out the meaning of the oracle, I had to seek all those who had the reputation of knowing anything; and, by the Dog, Athenians! – for I must tell you the truth [22] – I swear to you that this was my experience. Those in best repute seemed to me, in my divinely appointed search, not far from the most deficient; while others, held to be inferior, were really superior, so far as wisdom was concerned. And now I must tell you the tale of my wanderings; for I went through what I may call real labours that the oracle might be proved beyond question true. From the statesmen, then, I went to the poets, the authors of tragedies and dithyrambics, and all the others, thinking that here I must detect myself in the very act of knowing less than they. Taking, therefore, such of their poems as seemed to me the most elaborated, I would ask what was their meaning, in the hope that together with this I might obtain from them some other knowledge. Now I am ashamed to tell you the truth,

citizens, and yet it must be declared; nearly all the bystanders, I may say, used to talk better than these very poets did about what they themselves had written. So much, then, about the poets I learnt in a short time: that what they did was done not by the help of wisdom but by a certain natural gift and inspiration, just as the soothsayers and diviners say many beautiful things, of which, however, they understand not a word. Under some such spell as this, it appeared to me, were the poets; and yet at the same time, because of their poetry, they thought themselves, I perceived, the wisest of men in regard to other things, as to which they were not at all wise. So I went away, thinking that I was superior to them also just as I was to the politicians.

Finally, I went to the artisans; for here I was conscious that I knew nothing, so to speak, while I was sure that I should find them versed in much that was beautiful. And herein I was not mistaken, for they knew what I did not know, and were in so far wiser than I. But it seemed to me, Athenian citizens, that the good artisans made just the same mistake as the poets. Each, because he worked well in his own art, thought himself wisest as to matters of another and a higher nature, and this error obscured the knowledge that he really possessed. So that when I asked myself, in the name of the oracle, whether I should be content to be as I am, neither wise with their wisdom nor ignorant with their ignorance, or else, like them, to possess both together, the answer which I made to myself and to the oracle was, 'It is better for me to be as I am.'

In consequence, Athenian citizens, of this investigation, [23] much hatred has been engendered against me, so fierce and bitter that it has given rise to many slanders; and through this I have also got the name of being a wise man. For the bystanders always think that I am wise about those subjects on which I expose the ignorance of another. But the truth probably is, citizens, that it is the God who is really wise, and that he means in this oracle to say that human wisdom is worth little or nothing. And although he seems to be speaking of Socrates, he is only making use of my name, and holding me up as an example, as if he were saying, 'He is wisest among you, O citizens, who, like Socrates, has come to know that he is in truth worth nothing as regards wisdom.' I, therefore, still go about according to the God's command, examining and questioning anyone who I think may be wise, whether citizen or stranger, and if it appears to me that he is not so, I make it known, and thus vindicate the oracle. And this occupation has left me leisure to do nothing worth speaking of, either in the state or for my own household, so that I am in very great poverty by reason of this my service to the God.

And yet again: those young men who have least to do, the sons of very wealthy persons follow me about without urging, and take pleasure in hearing these men cross-examined. They themselves, moreover, often imitate me, and undertake to examine others; finding indeed, I believe, no great scarcity of men who think they know something but really know little or nothing. Then those who have been cross-examined by them are angry with me, instead of being angry with themselves, and say that Socrates is a most pernicious fellow, and corrupts the young; but when they are asked in what way and by what teaching he does this, they have nothing to answer, because they do not know; that they may not appear, however, at a loss, they bring up the stock reproaches against all philosophers, that they tell of things in the heavens and under the earth, and teach men not to believe in Gods, and to make the worse appear the better reason. The truth, methinks, they would not wish to tell – that they have been convicted of pretending to knowledge when they really know nothing. Since then they are, as I believe, many in number and ambitious and violent, and have been speaking against me plausibly and after a concerted plan, they have been filling your ears for a long time with their violent calumnies. And this is why Meletus and Anytus and Lycon have attacked me: Meletus being incensed on behalf of the poets, Anytus on that of the artisans and politicians, [24] and Lycon on account of the orators; so that, as I said at first, I should be surprised if I were able, in this short time, to do away with a slander which has grown to be so great. This, O Athenian citizens, is the truth; and I tell it without concealing or suppressing anything, whether great or small. And yet I am well-nigh sure that it is this very frankness which makes me so hated; and this hatred, moreover, is a proof that I speak the truth, and that this is the cause of the calumny against me, and the ground of their prosecution; and if you will look into the matter, now or at any future time, you will find it to be so.

Let this, then, be a sufficient answer to the charges brought before you by my first accusers; I shall now try to defend myself against Meletus, the good man and the patriotic, as he calls himself, and against my later accusers. Let us next, therefore, take up the statement of their charge, as if they were a new set of accusers. It is, in substance, as follows: 'Socrates is guilty, first, of corrupting the young, and, secondly, of not believing in the Gods acknowledged by the state, but in other new divinities.' Such is the nature of the charge; and now let us examine each count in the indictment. It states, then, that I am guilty of corrupting the young: but I, O Athenians, state that Meletus himself is guilty; for he makes a jest of serious matters, bringing men lightly to trial, and pretending to be zealous and full of concern about matters to which he has never given a thought. That this is the real state of the case I will try to show you.

Come hither, Meletus, and tell me this. Have you not very much at heart that the young shall be as good as possible?

MELETUS: Certainly I have.

SOCRATES: Well, then, tell the court who it is that makes them better. This, of course, you must know; it is your business, for you it is who have discovered me, you say, to be their corrupter, and have brought me here, and accused me before this tribunal. Speak up, then, and tell us who it is that improves them. Do you not see, Meletus, that you are silent, and have nothing to say? And yet is not this silence shameful, and a sufficient proof, moreover, of just what I say, that you have never given a thought to these things? But tell us, my good friend, who does improve the young?

MELETUS: The laws.

SOCRATES: But, my excellent sir, what I asked was not this, but who the man is; and he of course, to begin with, must know these very laws of which you speak.

MELETUS: These judges here, Socrates.

SOCRATES: What do you mean, Meletus? Are they able to train up the young, and do they improve them?

MELETUS: Certainly.

SOCRATES: All of them, or only some and not others?

MELETUS: All.

[25] SOCRATES: By Hera this is good news that you bring us! We have no lack of benefactors, then. And who besides? Do these bystanders improve them, or not?

MELETUS: Yes, they also.

SOCRATES: And the senators?

MELETUS: The senators, as well.

SOCRATES: But is it possible, Meletus, that those who sit in the public assembly corrupt the young, or do not they all too improve them?

MELETUS: They too improve them.

SOCRATES: It seems, then, that all Athenians, except myself, make the young good and virtuous, and that I alone corrupt them. Is this what you assert?

MELETUS: I assert it most emphatically.

SOCRATES: You are laying a great misfortune at my door! But answer me this: do you think it true in regard to horses also, that all men improve and only one injures them? Or is it not rather, on the contrary, some one person, or at the most very few – namely, horse-trainers – who can improve horses, while most people, if they attempt to handle and break them into use, only do them harm? Is it not so, Meletus, in regard to horses and all other animals? It is, most assuredly, whether you and Anytus deny it or not. The young must be fortunate indeed, if only one person corrupts, while everyone else improves them! But, Meletus, you have sufficiently proved that you never troubled yourself about the young; a sure sign of your indifference is that you care nothing about the matter for which you are prosecuting me.

Tell us further, Meletus, in the name of Zeus, whether it is better to live among good or bad citizens. Answer, my good friend, for it is no hard question that I am asking. Do not the bad always work harm against their neighbours, while the good work good?

MELETUS: Certainly.

SOCRATES: And is there anyone who prefers to be injured rather than benefited by those with whom he lives? Answer, my good sir, for the law requires you to answer. Is there anyone who prefers being injured?

MELETUS: Certainly not.

SOCRATES: Come, then, do you bring me here on the charge of intentionally or unintentionally corrupting the young and making them worse?

MELETUS: Intentionally, I say.

SOCRATES: Why, how is this, Meletus? Are you at your age so much wiser than I at mine as to have already found out that the bad always work harm against those who are nearest them and the good work good, while I, on the other hand, have reached such depth of ignorance as not to know that, if through me one of my fellow-citizens becomes a knave I am in danger of receiving some harm at his hands? Do you maintain that I voluntarily commit so great an injury? Of this, Meletus, you have convinced neither me nor, I think, any other human being. [26] Either I do not corrupt men at all or else I corrupt them involuntarily, so that in either case you lie. Now, if I do it involuntarily it is not lawful to summon me here for involuntary offences of this kind, but you should take me apart to admonish and instruct me; since it is plain enough that if I learn better I shall leave off doing what I now do involuntarily. But you were unwilling to proceed thus, and, having shirked the duty of associating with me and instructing me, have brought me before this court, whither it is lawful to summon only those who need punishment, not those who need instruction.

But really, Athenian citizens, as I said before, it is clear enough that Meletus has never cared either much or little about these matters. Tell us, however, Meletus, in what way do you say that I corrupt the young? Is it, as stated in the indictment which you brought against me, by teaching them not to believe in the Gods in whom the city believes, but in other new divinities? Is this the teaching by which you say I corrupt them?

MELETUS: Most emphatically I say it is this.

SOCRATES: Then, Meletus, in the name of these very Gods of whom we are now speaking, tell me and these others here still more plainly what you mean. For I cannot make out whether it is that I teach men to believe in certain Gods – in which case I myself also must believe, and so do not offend by being an utter atheist, but only by believing in different Gods from those in which the state believes – or whether you charge me with not believing in any Gods at all, and teaching the same to others.

MELETUS: That is what I say, that you do not believe in any Gods at all.

SOCRATES: To what end, O wonderful Meletus, do you say this? Do I then not hold, with the rest of mankind, that the sun and moon are Gods?

MELETUS: No, by Zeus, judges, he does not, for he says that the sun is stone, and the moon earth.

SOCRATES: Do you forget, friend Meletus, and imagine that it is Anaxagoras you are accusing; or do you hold these persons here present to be so stupid and so unversed in letters as not to know that these doctrines which you ascribe to me belong to Anaxagoras of Clazomenae, whose books are loaded with them? And the young men learn them from me, forsooth, when they can often hear them at the theatre, for the sum of a drachma at most, and can then laugh Socrates to scorn if he pretends that they are his own – such singular doctrines too as these are! But tell me, in the name of Zeus, do you really think that I believe there is no God?

MELETUS: By Zeus I swear that you believe there is no God at all.

SOCRATES: Nobody will believe that, Meletus, and I doubt whether you do yourself. It seems to me, Athenians, that this man is exceedingly insolent and unrestrained, and that he has framed this indictment in a spirit of sheer wantonness and youthful intemperance. He is like a man who has made a mock-riddle, [27] and is putting this question to himself: 'Will the wise Socrates discover that I am jesting and contradicting myself in my words, or shall I be able to deceive him and my other hearers?' For it seems to me that he flatly contradicts himself in the indictment, very much as if he were to say, 'Socrates is guilty of not believing in Gods, but of believing in Gods.' And this is behaving like a person who is in jest.

Let us now examine together, citizens, what seems to me to be the absurdity in his statement. And do you, Meletus, answer me; and do you, Athenians, I pray, bear in mind what I asked of you in the beginning – not to interrupt me if I speak after my accustomed fashion. Can anyone, Meletus, believe in things relating to humanity, without believing in the existence of human beings? I wish he would answer, citizens, and not keep interrupting. Does anyone believe that there can be things relating to horses, and yet no horses? or things relating to flute-playing, and yet no flute-players? No one does, O best of men; since you do not choose to answer, I myself will tell both you and all the others here present. But this you *must* answer. Is there anyone who believes that there are things relating to divine beings and yet no divine beings?

MELETUS: There is no one.

SOCRATES: You delight me by giving an answer, albeit reluctantly, and only because you were compelled by the court. You confess, then, that I believe and teach that there are divine things; whether new or old, at all events in divine things I do believe, according to your own assertion, for to this you have sworn in your accusation. Now if I believe in divine things it surely follows of necessity that I believe

in divine beings. Is not this so? It is, indeed; for, as you do not answer, I assume you to have assented. Do we not regard divine beings (or demigods) as either Gods or the sons of Gods? Do you agree to this, or not?

MELETUS: Of course I do.

SOCRATES: Well, as you admit that I believe in demigods, then, if demigods are in some sense Gods, here is my proof that you jest and speak in riddles: for you say, first, that I do not believe in Gods, and then that I do, since I believe in demigods. For if the demigods are the illegitimate children of Gods, either by nymphs or by other mothers, as you know they do say is the case, what man could believe in the existence of the children of Gods without believing in the existence of Gods? It would be just as absurd as to believe that mules are the offspring of horses and asses, and yet not believe in the existence of horses and asses. Surely, Meletus, you can have framed such an indictment with no other motive than that of seeing how far you could venture with us, or else because you were at a loss for any true charge to prefer against me. But that you can persuade any human being who possesses the smallest grain of sense that the same person may believe in things pertaining to demigods and Gods, and yet at the same time in neither demigods nor Gods nor heroes, [28] of this there is no possibility.

But really, Athenian citizens, it seems to me that I do not need an elaborate defence to prove myself not guilty on the indictment brought against me by Meletus; what I have said may suffice. But the statement I made before – that I am very much hated by many people – this, you must know, is quite true, and this it is which will condemn me, if condemned I am, not Meletus, nor yet Anytus, but the malice and slander of the multitude. For this has destroyed many other good men, and will, I think, destroy many still; there is no danger that it will stop with me.

'But,' someone perhaps may say, 'are you not ashamed, Socrates, of having followed a pursuit on account of which you are now in danger of being put to death?' To such an one I might with good reason reply: 'You say not well, my friend, if you think that a man who is good for anything at all ought to take into account the chances of living or dying, and not rather, when undertaking anything, to consider only whether it be right or wrong, and whether the work of a good or of a bad man. Why, according to your opinion, all the heroes who fell at Troy would be but sorry fellows, and especially the son of Thetis, who set danger at naught in comparison with enduring any disgrace; so that when his mother, who was a goddess, addressed him, all eager to slay Hector, in words, I think, somewhat to this effect: "If thou, my son, avenge the death of thy companion Patroclus, and slay Hector, thou thyself must die; for thy own fate," said she, "awaits thee straightway after Hector," he, having heard the prophecy, made light of death and danger, dreading far more than these the disgrace of living as a coward who had not avenged his friend. "Let death come straightway," he said, "after I have punished the wrong-doer, so that I remain not here by the beaked ships, a laughing-stock and a useless burden of the earth." Do you suppose that he thought of death and danger?'

Now, Athenians, this is the very truth. Wherever anyone either stations himself because he thinks it right to be there or is stationed by his commander, there, I think, ought he to remain and face danger, taking into account neither death nor anything else in comparison with disgrace.

It would be a strange act indeed on my part, O men of Athens, after my remaining in whatever post I was stationed by the leaders whom you had appointed over me, at Potidaca, Amphipolis, and Delium, and facing death like any other man, if, now that I am, as I think and believe, under orders from the God to pass my life in the pursuit of wisdom and in examining myself and others – if now, I say, through fear of death or any other evil, [29] I were to desert my post! That would be strange conduct indeed, and then might I in truth be justly arraigned in court for not believing in the existence of Gods; for then should I be disobeying the oracle, and fearing death, and thinking myself wise when I was not. For to fear death, citizens, is nothing at all but to think you are wise when you are not wise – to think you know what you do not know. For no one knows what death is, or whether it may not be the greatest of all goods to men; yet do they fear it, as if they knew it to be the greatest of evils; and what is this but the same old disgraceful ignorance – that of thinking you know what you do not know? Now I, citizens, do perhaps differ from most men in this respect, and if I might claim to be wiser than anyone else it would be in this: that, not knowing much about the things of the world below, I am convinced that I do not know; but that it is wicked and shameful to do wrong and to disobey anyone, whether God or man, who is better than yourself, this I do know. From fear, then, of those evils which I know to be evils, I would neither fear nor flee that which for aught I know may be a good. So that, if you were now to acquit me, in despite of Anytus, who has urged that either I ought not to have appeared here at all, or that, having appeared, I ought not by any possibility to escape death, and who has, moreover, assured you that, if I am let off now, your sons will all be utterly ruined by the practice of what Socrates teaches; and if, in acquitting me, you should say: 'We will not put faith this time, O Socrates, in Anytus, but will let you go, on the condition, however, that you no longer spend your time in this search nor in the pursuit of wisdom, and that if you are caught doing either again you shall die' – if, I say, you were to release me on these conditions I should say to you, 'Athenians, I love and cherish you, but I shall obey the God rather than you; and as long as I draw breath and have the strength, I shall never cease to follow philosophy, and to exhort and persuade anyone of you whom I happen to meet, saying, as is my wont: "How is it, friend, that you, an Athenian, of the city greatest and of most repute for wisdom and power, are not ashamed to be taking thought for glory and honour, and for your possessions that they may become as great as possible, while you take neither thought nor heed for wisdom and truth and for your soul that it may become as good as possible?"' And if anyone of you questions my word, and says that he does take heed for these things I shall not at once send him away nor turn from him, but shall question, examine and test him; and if it appears to me that he does not possess virtue, but only says that he does, I shall upbraid him for making least of what is worth most, and much more of what is of less account. [30] And this I shall do to whomsoever I come across, be he young or old, stranger or citizen; but especially to you, citizens, as ye are nearer of kin to me. For this, be assured, the God commands; and I believe that there has never yet been a greater good in the state than this my service to the God. For I do nothing but go about persuading you, both young and old, not to let your first thought be for your body or your possessions, nor to care for anything so earnestly as for your soul, that it may attain to the highest virtue; and maintaining that not from possessions does virtue come but that from virtue do possessions and all other good things, both private and public, come to man. If by such discourse I corrupt the young, then this doctrine of mine must be harmful; and if anyone asserts that I say anything else than this he is talking nonsense. 'And, Athenians,' I should go on to say, 'either hearken to Anytus or not, and either acquit me or not; but understand that I shall never act differently, even if I have to die for it many times.'

Do not interrupt, Athenians, but keep that promise which I asked of you – not to interrupt, no matter what I say, but to listen; for I think that you will gain by listening. I am now going to tell you other things at which you will very likely raise a clamour; but do not so, I beg of you. You may be very sure that if you put to death such an one as I have just said I am you will not injure me more than your own selves. Neither Meletus nor Anytus could injure me in the least: they have not the power; for it is not, I think, allowed by the law of God that a bad man should injure one better than himself. He may indeed put him to death or send him into exile or deprive him of civil rights, and these he, and perhaps some others, may think to be great evils. I myself do not think so, but I hold to be a much greater evil that which Anytus is now doing – endeavouring to put a man to death unjustly. Wherefore, O men of Athens, I am far from defending myself for my own sake, as might be expected; but for your sake I do it, lest in condemning me you err, by rejecting the gift which God offers you. For if you kill me you will not readily find another such as I, who am, as it were, although the comparison may sound somewhat ridiculous, fastened upon the state by God like some gadfly upon a powerful, high-bred steed who has become sluggish by reason of his very size and needs to be aroused. And as such a gadfly does God seem to have fastened me upon the state; wherefore, besetting you everywhere the whole day long, [31] I arouse and stir up and reproach each one of you. Such a man, citizens, you will not easily find again, and if you take my advice you will spare me. But perhaps, being irritated, as sleepy persons are when suddenly aroused, you may strike out at me, and, persuaded by Anytus, hastily put me to death; and then slumber tranquilly on for the rest of your days, unless, indeed, God should in his care for you send someone else to rouse you. And that I am such a gift of God to the State you can see from this my conduct; for it is not in the ordinary course of human nature that I should have been thus neglectful of my own affairs, and have suffered my household interests to be uncared for these many years, while I was continually busying myself with yours, going about to each one of you individually, like a father or an elder brother, and trying to persuade you to take thought for virtue. If, indeed, I had gained anything by this, and had received pay for thus exhorting, I should have had some reason for it; but now you yourselves see that, although my accusers have so shamelessly made all these other charges against me, they have not reached such a height of impudence as to bring forward one witness to testify that I ever either received pay or asked for it. But I can bring forward, I think, a very sufficient witness that I am speaking the truth, namely, my poverty.

Perhaps, however, it may seem absurd that I go about in private, giving advice and busying myself about people's affairs in this way, and yet do not venture to come forward in your public assemblies and advise the State. But the reason is the one which you have often times and in many places heard me give – that there comes to me a something divine and spiritual, which Meletus indeed, by way of joke, has included in his indictment; and this is a voice which from childhood has frequently come to me, and which makes itself heard only to turn me back from what I am about to do, but never to impel me forward. This it is which stands in the way of my having anything to do with public affairs, and wisely, it seems to me, does it stand in the way; for you must know, O men of Athens, that if I had ever attempted to take part in the affairs of the State I should long ago have perished, and thus have done no good either to you or to myself. Now do not be angry with me for telling you the truth; there lives not the man who would be safe in honestly opposing you or any other populace, [32] and in trying to prevent many unjust and unlawful things from taking place in the State; he therefore who is really fighting for the right must, if he would be safe even for a short time, lead a private life, not a public one.

I will give you full proof of this, not in words, but in deeds, which you value more. Listen, then, to what has happened in my life, that you may know that to no man would I ever yield, through fear of death, against my sense of justice, even though by not yielding I might instantly perish. The story I am going to tell you is tedious, and in the style so often heard in courts of law, but it is nevertheless true.

I have never, Athenians, held any office in the State, except that I was once in the senate, and it so happened that our tribe (the Antiochian) had chief direction of state affairs on that occasion when the ten generals who had not picked up the men after the naval combat were brought to trial. You wished to try them all in a body, which was contrary to law, as you all afterwards admitted; but I then alone, out of the whole body of fifty Prytanes, was opposed to doing anything against the laws, and voted in the opposition. And though the speakers were all ready to lay an information against me or to arrest me summarily, and though you were all urging them on with shouts, I felt it my duty to brave the danger, with law and justice on my side, rather than to take part with you in counselling what was unjust, through fear of prison or death. And this happened when the city was still ruled by the democracy. But once, when the oligarchy was in power, the Thirty sent for me to the Rotunda, and commanded me to go with four others to Salamis, and bring Leon the Salaminian that he might be put to death. They had given many like commands to others, wishing to involve as many as possible in guilt. Then again, not by word but by deed, did I show that for death I cared not a whit – if this expression be not too unmannerly – but that not committing an unjust or unholy deed was what I cared for beyond all things else. That government, strong though it was, could not frighten me into doing anything unjust; and so, when we came out of the Rotunda, and the other four went to Salamis to bring Leon, I went back to my home. And on account of this I should perhaps have been put to death, had not the government of the Thirty soon afterwards been broken up. To the truth of all this many will testify.

Do you really think, then, that I could have lived so many years if I had led a public life, and, acting as an honest man, had stood by the right and held this, as I ought, above every other consideration? Far from it, O Athenian citizens; nor could any other man. But you [33] will find that I have always been the same my whole life long, in public affairs, if I ever took any part in them, as well as in private, never making concessions to injustice to please anyone at all, whether one of those whom my accusers call my disciples

or anybody else. Now I have never been a teacher to any man, but if anyone, whether young or old, wished to hear me speak while carrying out my mission I never grudged him the opportunity. Nor is it my habit to discourse when I am paid, and refuse to discourse when I am not; but I hold myself ready to be questioned alike by rich and poor, or if anyone prefers that I should question him, I let him first answer me and then hear what I have to say. And whether any of my hearers become better or worse, for that I cannot justly be made answerable, for I never promised any instruction whatever, neither have I ever taught in any way. If anyone, therefore, says that he has ever learned or heard from me in private what I have not said before all other men you may be sure that he is not speaking the truth.

But why is it, then, that certain people like to spend so much time in my company? You have heard already, O men of Athens – I have told you the whole truth – that they like to hear me examine those who think themselves wise and are not; for this, after all, is far from unpleasing. But on me, as I have said, it has been enjoined by God thus to act, both by signs and dreams, and in every way in which the divine will ever imposed any duty at all upon man. This, O Athenians, is the truth, and it is easy to prove. For if I am corrupting some of the young men, and have corrupted others, surely some of those who are now grown up, and have come to know that when young they received bad advice from me, ought now to appear in court, in order to accuse me and have me punished. Or if they themselves were unwilling to do this, some of their kinsfolk, fathers, or brothers, or others belonging to them, should, if members of their family had received any harm at my hands, remember it now against me, and seek my punishment. Many such, I doubt not, are here present; indeed, I see some of them at this moment. First, here is Crito, a man of my own time of life and from my own district, father of Critobulus here. Then Lysanias the Sphettian, father of Aeschines; and Antiphon the Cephisian, father of Epigenes. And I see others whose brothers have been much in my company: Nicostratus, son of Theosdotides and brother of Theodotus – now Theodotus himself is dead, so that he cannot seek to stop him; and Paralus, son of Demodocus, whose brother was Theages. I see also Adimantus, the son of Ariston, [34] whose brother Plato is present; and Aeantodorus, brother to Apollodorus here. And many others I might name to you, some one of whom Meletus ought by all means, in the course of his own argument, to have brought forward as witness against me; or, if he forgot it then, let him bring one forward now. I will give way. Let him speak out, if he have any such testimony. But you will find, citizens, that quite the contrary of this is true: all are ready to help me, the corrupter, the man who works evil to their kinsfolk, as say Meletus and Anytus. Now they who themselves have been corrupted, might have some motive for coming to my assistance; but their relatives who have not been corrupted and are now elderly men – what other motive have they for helping me than the good and true one, that they know Meletus is lying, while I am speaking the truth?

Well, citizens, these facts and perhaps others of the same nature make up about all the defence which I can offer. But someone among you may be indignant with me when he calls to remembrance how he himself, when engaged in some trial of far less importance than this, has prayed and besought the judges with many tears, and tried to move them to pity by bringing into court his children and others of his kinsfolk, with friends in great numbers; whereas I shall do none of these things, and that too when I am, it would seem, in danger of the last penalty. Very likely some judge who calls this to mind may harden himself against me, and so, goaded by the recollection, may cast his vote in anger. Now if this be the case with any of you – I do not assert that it is, but if it be – it seems to me that I can say with reason to such an one: 'My friend, I too have kinsfolk, for even as Homer says, "Not of wood nor of stone was I born, but of man."' Thus I have kinsfolk, and moreover, O men of Athens, I have three sons, one already a youth, two who are yet children. Not one of these, nevertheless, shall I bring here to implore you for my acquittal. And why will I do none of these things? It is not that I am self-willed, O men of Athens, or that I am wanting in respect to you, and whether I am courageous or not in facing death is another question; but as regards my own credit and yours, and that of the State, it does not seem honourable for me to do anything of the kind, especially at my age, and with the sort of reputation – whether true or false – that I have. For the world, at all events, has made up its mind that Socrates surpasses, in some way, most other men. [35] Now it would be a shame if those among you who are held to surpass others, either in wisdom or in manliness or in any other virtue, were to behave so unworthily. I have often seen men of good reputation behave strangely enough when brought to trial. They seemed to think that in dying they were to suffer something strange and terrible, as though they expected to be immortal if not put to death by you. Such men, methinks, fasten disgrace upon the State, in so much that any stranger would assume that the most virtuous of the Athenians, those who are picked out by their own fellow-citizens for posts of command and other honours, are in no wise better than women. But you, O men of Athens, those of you who have any reputation at all to lose, ought not thus to behave, nor should you suffer such behaviour in us. You ought to show that you will condemn the man who makes the city ridiculous by enacting such pitiable scenes, rather than him who keeps a quiet mind.

But putting aside, citizens, the discredit of the thing, it does not seem to me right either to owe one's escape to entreaties, or to supplicate a judge rather than to enlighten and convince him. For the judge sits in court to give judgement, not to award justice by favour; and he has not sworn to grant favours to whomsoever he pleases, but to judge according to the laws. It behooves us therefore not to accustom you to swear falsely, nor should you accustom yourselves to this, for in so doing we should neither of us be acting with piety. Do not therefore claim, O men of Athens, that where you are concerned I ought to act in a way which I believe to be neither good nor just nor holy, above all, by Zeus, at the very time that I am under a charge of impiety made by this man, Meletus. For if I were to persuade you and by force of entreaties overpower your oaths I should clearly be teaching you not to believe in Gods; and accusing myself of not believing in them while in the very act of defending myself against this accusation. But far from this, O men of Athens, I do believe in them as does not one of my accusers; and to you and to God I leave it to judge my case as shall be best for me as well as for yourselves.

[Here follows an interval, in which the judges retire to vote upon the question of the guilt of Socrates. They announce, upon their return, a majority of about sixty votes against him; the penalty of death is proposed by his adversary Meletus, and it is now the turn of Socrates to propose a counter-penalty. He proceeds thus:]

I do not feel aggrieved, O men of Athens, at the sentence you have just pronounced against me, and for this there are many reasons. [36] The result was not at all unexpected, and I wonder only at the relative numbers of the votes. For I had thought that the majority against me would be not small, but very large; and now, as it appears, if only thirty of the votes had been changed to the other side I should have been acquitted. And even now I may say that I have been acquitted, so far as Meletus is concerned; and not only this, but it must be evident to all that if Anytus and Lycon had not joined him in accusing me he would have failed to receive a fifth part of the votes, and so been fined a thousand drachmas.

The man, then, proposes for me the penalty of death. So be it. And what counter-penalty, O men of Athens, shall I propose to you for myself? Clearly one according to my deserts, must I not? What, then, shall it be? What do I deserve to suffer or to pay for my offence? You know what this is. My life throughout, I allowed myself no rest, but neglected what most men prize, money-making, family interests, military commands, public speaking and all offices of the State, as well as plots and factions, deeming myself in truth too good a man to be safe if I entered into such things. I did not go where I could be of no use either to you or to myself, but wherever I thought I could do most good to each one of you in private, thither I went, and tried to persuade each one of you not to take thought for his interests before he had taken thought how he might improve himself to the utmost in virtue and in wisdom; nor for the interests of the State before taking thought for the

State itself; and in all other concerns to proceed in the same way. What, then, do I, such a man as I have told you I am, deserve to receive? Some good, O men of Athens, at least if the penalty be fixed according to my real desert; and it should be a good, moreover, that strictly befits me. What, then, does befit a man – poor indeed, but your benefactor – who needs leisure that he may use it in exhorting you? Nothing better befits such a man, O Athenians, than to be maintained in the Prytaneum at public expense. He deserves this surely far more than does one who has gained a prize at Olympia in a horse or chariot race. For he may cause you to appear happy, but I cause you to be happy; he needs not to be maintained, but I do need it. If, then, I am to propose a penalty according to my just deserts, it shall be this [37] – maintenance in the Prytaneum.

Perhaps in saying this I may seem to be speaking defiantly, just as in what I said about the weeping and supplication. But this is not so, O Athenians. I speak thus, because I am fully persuaded that I have intentionally injured no man. You, however, I cannot convince of this, for it is but a short time that we have had to talk together. I think, indeed, that were it the law here, as in other countries, that capital trials should occupy not one day only but several, I should have been able to convince you; but it is not easy in a short time to do away with great slanders. Being fully persuaded, however, that I have done no injury to anyone else, far be it from me to do myself the injury of declaring that I deserve any evil, and of proposing any such penalty. What fear should induce me to do it? The fear lest I may suffer the penalty proposed for me by Meletus, of which I declare that I do not know whether it be a good or an evil? Shall I choose instead something which I know certainly to be an evil, and propose this

for my penalty? Imprisonment? And why should I wish to live in prison, a slave to the magistrates who may happen to be in authority? Or a fine, and imprisonment until I shall have paid it? But in my case that would be neither more nor less than imprisonment, for I have no money to pay it. Shall I say exile, then? – for likely enough you would accept this penalty. I must be fond of life indeed, if I am so blind to reason as not to foresee that, since you, my own fellow-citizens, have not been able to bear my discourses and arguments, which have become so burdensome and hateful to you that you are now seeking to get rid of them, it is not likely that others will bear them more readily. Far from it, Athenians! Truly my life would be a pleasant one, if I should go into exile at my age, and be compelled to perpetually change my abode and flee from one city to another. For I know full well that, wherever I go, the young men will hearken to me, as they do here; and if I repel them they themselves will persuade their elders to send me away, while if I do not repel them their fathers and kinsfolk will send me away on their account.

'But, Socrates,' someone may say, 'if you will only keep quiet and hold your peace, can you not take yourself off and live somewhere else?' Now, to make certain among you understand this, is hardest of all; for if I tell you that it would be disobeying the God, and that for this reason it is impossible for me to keep quiet, you will think that I am not in earnest, and will not believe me. [38] Or, again, if I say that the greatest good to man is to discourse daily about virtue and those other matters about which you have heard me speak and examine both myself and others, and that a life without examination is not worth living, you will be still less likely to believe me. Yet, citizens, I tell you that these are truths, hard though it be to convince you of it. Furthermore, I am not accustomed to think that I deserve any punishment at all. If, indeed, I had the money, I might have proposed such a fine as I could have paid, for this would not have harmed me. But as it is, that is out of the question, unless, indeed, you are willing to make my fine so small that I shall be able to pay it. I might possibly pay one mina of silver; therefore I propose that amount. But Plato here, O men of Athens, and Crito and Critobulus and Apollodorus bid me say thirty minas, and offer to be my sureties. This, then, I propose; and for the payment of the money they will be ample security to you.

[The vote of the judges is now taken upon the two penalties proposed by accuser and accused, and a majority is found to be in favour of the former. The trial is now ended, but Socrates avails himself of the short pause which elapses before his removal to prison to address his judges as follows:]

It is not much time, O men of Athens, that you will gain by shortening my life, in return for the evil name and the charge of having put to death Socrates, a wise man, which those who wish to speak ill of the city will fasten upon you. For those who wish to upbraid you will call me wise, even though I be not so. Now, if you had waited but a little while, what you wish would have happened in the natural course of events; for you see my time of life, how far on in years I am, how near to death! I say this not to all of you but only to those who have cast their votes for my death. And this also I wish to say to these same men: You probably think, O citizens, that I have been convicted for the lack of such arguments as might have persuaded you, if I had thought it right to do or say every kind of thing in order to escape

this sentence. Far from it. I have been convicted by a lack not of arguments but of audacity and of shamelessness, and of willingness to say such things as you would have liked to hear; because I would not weep and lament, and do and say many other things to which, indeed, you are accustomed in others, but which, as I have told you, would be unworthy of me. But I did not then think that, on account of danger, I ought to do anything unmanly, nor do I now repent the manner of my defence. I would much rather die, having thus defended myself, than live on such terms as those. For neither in a court of justice nor in war ought I or any other [39] man to use every possible device whereby to escape death. In battle it often happens that a man may save his life by throwing down his arms and turning in supplication to his pursuers; and in all kinds of dangers there are many like devices whereby death may be avoided, if a man be willing to do and say anything whatsoever to that end. But I suspect, ye citizens, that the difficulty is not in escaping death, but much rather in escaping evil, for this runs faster than death. Now I, being slow and old, am overtaken by death, the slower; and my accusers, being swift and skilful, by evil, the swifter of the two. And now I go away condemned by you to receive the penalty of death; but they go condemned by truth to receive the penalty of wickedness and wrong. I must abide by my sentence, they by theirs. These things, peradventure, were destined so to be, and I believe they are for the best.

And now, O ye who have voted against me, to you I desire to prophesy concerning the future. For I have now reached that moment wherein men are most gifted with prophetic power – the moment when they are about to die. I tell you, O ye citizens who have condemned me, that immediately after my death a punishment shall come upon you much severer, by Zeus, than that to which you have sentenced me. You have acted thus, thinking to be set free for the future from rendering any account of your lives; but I declare to you that the reverse of this will come to pass. Greater still will be the number of men who will cross-examine you – men whom I have thus far held back, so that you have not perceived their existence; and the younger they are, the more severe they will be and the more you will be harassed by them. For if you think that by putting men to death you will hinder anybody from casting reproaches upon you for not living righteously you are mistaken. That way of escape is by no means a possible or an honourable one; but this one is not only most honourable but most easy, not to restrain others, but to endeavour yourselves to grow in all virtue. Thus having prophesied to you who have condemned me, my part with you is done.

And now I turn to you who have voted in favour of my acquittal, for I would gladly talk with you of this thing that has just happened, while the officers are otherwise busied, and before I go to the place where I am to die. I pray you, then, my friends, stay with me yet this space of time, for nothing prevents our talking with one another as long as we are permitted. [40] To you, knowing that you are my friends, I wish to unfold the meaning of this which has now befallen me. For to me, O my judges – and in calling *you* judges, I name you indeed rightly – a wonderful thing has happened. The accustomed prophetic sign of my divine monitor has hitherto ever constantly opposed me even in the merest trifles, if I were about to make a mistake. And now that which you yourselves have witnessed – the greatest of evils, as it might be and indeed is considered – has come upon me; yet not once, either as I left my house this morning or on my way here to the court, or at any point in my argument, has the divine sign opposed me. And although on other occasions it has often cut me short in the midst of what I was saying, yet in this affair it has opposed me neither in my actions nor in my words. What do I take to be the reason of this? I will tell you. It must be that what has happened is for my good, and it is not possible that those of us who think death to be an evil are judging rightly. Of this what has happened seems to me a strong proof, for it is certain that the accustomed sign would have opposed me if I had not been on my way to my own good.

And now let us reason in this way, and we shall see what great hope there is that death is a good. For death must be one of two things: either he who is dead becomes as naught, and has no consciousness of anything; or else, as men say, there is a certain change and a removal of the soul from this place to some other. Now if there be no consciousness, and death be like a sleep in which the sleeper has no dreams, then were it a wonderful gain indeed. For I think that if anyone were called upon to single out that night in which he had slept so soundly as to have had no dreams at all, and, setting against it all the other nights and days of his life, to declare, after due thought, how many had been better and sweeter than that one – I think, I say, that even the great King himself, not to speak of any private person, would find these so few in number that they might easily be counted in comparison with all the other days and nights of his life. If death, therefore, be such as this, I call it a gain; for all eternity, indeed, would thus appear no longer than a single night. But if, on the other hand, death be a transition to another place, and if it be true, as has been said, that all who have died are there, what, O judges, could be a greater good than this? [41]

For if a man, being set free from those who call themselves judges here, is to find, on arriving in Hades, those true judges who are said to administer judgement in the unseen world – Minos and Rhadamanthus and Aeacus and Triptolemus, and those other demigods who were just in this life – will his transition thither be for the worse? What would not any one of you give to converse with Orpheus and Musaeus and Hesiod and Homer? I, at least, would gladly die many times, if this be true; for to my thinking that state of being would be wonderful indeed, if in it I might have the chance of meeting with Palamedes and Ajax, the son of Telamon, and other heroes of the olden time who died through unrighteous judgement. To compare my own suffering with theirs were, methinks, no unpleasing task; but best of all would it be to examine and question there, as I have done here, and discover who is really wise, and who thinks himself so but is not. What, O judges, would a man not give to question him who led the great army against Troy or Ulysses or Sisyphus or the thousand others, both men and women, whom one might mention? To dwell and converse with them and to question them would indeed be happiness unspeakable! For assuredly, in that world, at all events they do not put you to death for doing this; and not only in other things are they far happier than we here below but, if what is said be true, they are there immortal for the rest of time.

But you too, O judges, it behooves to be of good hope about death, and to believe that this at least is true – there can no evil befall a good man, whether he be alive or dead, nor are his affairs uncared for by the Gods. Neither has this thing happened to me by chance, for I am persuaded that to die now and be released from worldly affairs is best for me, and that this is

why the sign did not turn me back. Wherefore I bear no malice at all against my accusers or against those who have condemned me; but as it was not with this idea, but rather with the intent to do me injury, that they accused and voted against me, it is right that they should be blamed. This favour nevertheless I ask of them: When my sons are grown up, avenge yourselves, fellow-citizens, upon them, by tormenting them just as I have tormented you, if they appear to care for riches or for anything else above virtue; and if they pretend to be something when they are really nothing, then reproach them, as I have reproached you, with not caring for what they ought, and with thinking themselves to be something when they are worth nothing at all. [42] If you do this I shall have received justice at your hands – I, as well as my sons. But now it is time for us to go away, I to die, you to live. Which of us is going to the better fate is unknown to all save God. (tr. Anon.)

2.3. Crito

[43] SOCRATES: Why have you come at this time of day, Crito? Is it not still quite early?

CRITO: It is early indeed.

SOCRATES: About what time is it?

CRITO: Day is just beginning to dawn.

SOCRATES: I wonder that the keeper of the prison was willing to answer your knock.

CRITO: He is used to me now, Socrates, I have been here so often; and besides, he has received some kindness at my hands.

SOCRATES: Have you just come, or have you been here some time?

CRITO: Some little time.

SOCRATES: Then why did you not wake me up at once, instead of sitting by in silence?

CRITO: By Zeus, O Socrates, I for my part should not have wished to be awakened to such a state of sleeplessness and sorrow. But I have for some time been looking at you with wonder to see you sleep so serenely; and I purposely did not awaken you, that you might pass the remainder of your time as peacefully as possible. Often before in the course of your life have I esteemed you fortunate in having such a nature, but never so much as now, in this present misfortune, seeing how easily and calmly you bear it.

SOCRATES: But do you not see, Crito, that it would be quite inconsistent in one of my age to be disturbed at having to die now?

CRITO: But when others, Socrates, of the same age are overtaken by like misfortunes, their age does not prevent their being distressed at the fate before them.

SOCRATES: That is true. But why have you come so early?

CRITO: To bring bad news, Socrates; though not for you, it seems. But for myself and for all your friends it is indeed bitter and grievous; and I, above all others, shall find it most hard to bear.

SOCRATES: What is it? Has the ship come from Delos, on whose arrival I am to die?

CRITO: She has not actually arrived, but I suppose she will be here today, to judge from tidings brought by certain persons who have just come from Sunium and report that they left her there. It is evident, from what they say, that she will be here today, and thus tomorrow, Socrates, your life must needs end.

SOCRATES: But this, Crito, is for the best. If it please the Gods, so be it. I do not think, however, that the ship will arrive today.

[44] CRITO: Whence do you infer this?

SOCRATES: I will tell you. I am to die on the morrow of the day on which the ship arrives.

CRITO: So say they who order these things, you know.

SOCRATES: Well, then, I do not think she will arrive on this coming day, but on the following one. I infer this from a certain dream which I had this very night, only a little while ago. It was by some lucky chance that you did not awaken me earlier.

CRITO: What was your dream?

SOCRATES: It seemed to me that a woman in white raiment, graceful and fair to look upon, came towards me, and, calling me by name, said:

'On the third day, Socrates, thou shalt reach the coast of fertile Phthia.'

CRITO: What a strange dream, Socrates!

SOCRATES: But clear withal, Crito, it seems to me.

CRITO: Only too clear. But, O beloved Socrates, be persuaded by me while there is yet time, and save yourself. For if you die, it will not be simply a misfortune to me, but, apart from my being deprived of such a friend as I shall never find again, it will appear to many, who know neither you nor me very well, that, although it was in my power to save you had I been willing to spend money, I did not care to do so. And what imputation could be more shameful than that of valuing money more than friends? For the multitude will never believe that you were not willing to escape hence when we were eager to have you do so.

SOCRATES: But why, dear Crito, do we care so much about the opinion of the multitude? Surely the most reasonable, those who are most worth considering, will believe that all has happened as it really has happened.

CRITO: But do you not see that we must care about the opinion of the multitude? These very events now before us make it manifest that they are able to bring about not only the smallest evils but the greatest, perhaps, of all, if anyone is misrepresented to them by calumny.

SOCRATES: Would that they were really capable, Crito, of bringing about the greatest evils, for then would they be capable of the greatest blessings also, and that were well indeed. But as it is, neither of these can they bring about; they are not able to make men either wise or foolish: whatever they do happens by chance.

CRITO: This may be as you say. But tell me, Socrates; you are not concerned, are you, with regard to me and your other friends, lest, if you escape, the informers may make trouble for us as having stolen you away, and we be made to forfeit all our property, or at least a great deal of it, and perhaps suffer some other evil besides? [45] If it is, indeed, something of that kind which you fear, make yourself easy, for we should certainly do right in running this risk, were it even greater than it is, in order to save you. So do not refuse to take my advice.

SOCRATES: I am concerned about this, and about many other things besides.

CRITO: Now do not fear this, I beg of you; for the sum is not a large one, for the sake of which certain persons are willing to free you and conduct you hence. And do you not see how easily the informers are bought over? — so that we shall not need to spend much money on them. My own property is at your command, and is, I think, sufficient. But if, in your concern for me, you do not deem it right to make use of my property, here are friends from foreign parts, all ready to spend theirs. One indeed, Simmias the Theban, has brought for this very purpose a sufficient sum, and Cebes also and many others are holding themselves in readiness; so that, as I say, you must not refrain from saving yourself for fear of this. Nor let that of which you spoke in court be a difficulty to you — that after leaving here you would not know what to do with yourself. For assuredly, wherever you go, there you will be beloved. If you wish to go to Thessaly I have friends there who will make much of you, and afford you such security that none of the Thessalians shall in any way annoy you.

And, moreover, Socrates, it does not seem to me that you are even acting justly, in giving yourself up when it is in your power to be saved, for you are trying to bring the very thing upon yourself for which your enemies would strive, and for which they actually did strive in their desire to ruin you. And besides this, it seems to me that you are betraying your own sons, by forsaking them when it is in your power to bring them up and educate them; so that, as far as your help goes, their fate will be left to chance, and it will in all probability be that which usually befalls orphans in their bereavement. Either you ought not to have children or, having them, you ought to endure the trouble of caring for and educating them to the end. You seem to me to have chosen what is easiest; whereas you ought to choose as would a good man and brave, especially one who had professed his whole life long to make virtue his chief care. For my part, I really am ashamed for you, and for ourselves, your friends, when I reflect that this whole case of yours may appear to have taken the turn it has by reason of some unmanly weakness on our part, which allowed the trial to come on when it might have been prevented, and to be conducted as it was in court; and the crowning absurdity of the whole is that now at the end, in our baseness and cowardice, we seem to have merely sought our own safety, taking no more pains to save you [46] than you did to save yourself, when we might easily have done so if we had been good for anything at all. See to it, therefore, Socrates, that with this calamity disgrace do not come upon us as well as upon you. Think it over; or rather there is no longer time for thinking, but your mind must be already made up. There is but one step to take. On this coming night all must be accomplished. If we delay in the least it will be no longer possible. I beseech you, Socrates, be persuaded by me, and on no account refuse.

SOCRATES: Your zeal, dear Crito, is worth much, if it be well directed; but otherwise the greater it is, the more dangerous. It behooves us then to consider whether this ought to be done or not. For I am now, as ever before, ready to be convinced by that argument alone which to my sober reason appears the most convincing. And now that this fate has come upon me I cannot cast away the reasons which I gave in former times, for they still appear to me as good as ever, and I honour and reverence them just as I did before. Unless we can now find better ones, do not expect that I shall go over to your way of thinking, not even if the power of the multitude were to find still more bugbear terrors like the present ones – imprisonment and death and loss of possessions – wherewith to frighten us like children. How, then, may we most fairly look into the question? By taking up again that old argument about the opinions of men, to which you have just referred, and seeing whether it is still true, as we used to maintain, that we ought to pay attention to some and not to others; or whether, although this was true before my death was decreed, it has now become evident that it was a mere random saying, uttered only for the sake of talking, and was in reality mere childish nonsense. I wish to examine, Crito, together with you, whether the argument appears to me in a different light now that I am in this case, or whether it is still the same; and then we can either let it go or else abide by it. It has always been held, I believe, by those who profess to know anything, that, as I have just said, some men's opinions are to be had in honour, others' not. Tell me, by the Gods, Crito, does not this seem to you well said? [47] You, in all human probability, are not under the necessity of dying tomorrow, so that this present misfortune should not mislead you. Consider, then; does not this seem to you a satisfactory statement: that we are not to value all the opinions of men, but only some of them; and not those of all men either, but those of some only? Is not this well said?

CRITO: It is.

SOCRATES: And is it not the sound opinions we should value, rather than the worthless?

CRITO: Yes.

SOCRATES: And are not the opinions of the wise sound, and those of the foolish worthless?

CRITO: How could it be otherwise?

SOCRATES: Very well, and what was said before in regard to a like matter? Does a man, in training for the profession of gymnastics, pay attention to the praise and blame and opinion of all other men, or of the one only who happens to be his physician or trainer?

CRITO: Of the one only.

SOCRATES: He ought therefore to fear the censures and welcome the praises of this one person, and not those of the many.

CRITO: That is plain enough.

SOCRATES: Then he ought to act and exercise and eat and drink in the way which seems good to the one who understands and is a proficient, rather than in that approved of by all other men.

CRITO: That is true.

SOCRATES: Very good. If then, disobedient to the one, and dishonouring his opinion and approval, he honour that of the many who have no experience, will not harm come to him?

CRITO: How could it be otherwise?

SOCRATES: And what is the nature of this harm? Whither does it tend, and what part of the disobedient person does it affect?

CRITO: Clearly it affects the body; for that is what it destroys.

SOCRATES: True enough. Well, then, Crito, in regard to other things – not to go through with them all, in regard to the just and the unjust, the base and the beautiful, the good and the evil, on which we are now deliberating – are we to fear and follow the opinion of the many, or that of the one man (if indeed there be such an one) who is wise as to these matters, and whom we ought to fear and reverence more than all the others put together, while, if we be not led by him, we shall corrupt and degrade that part of us which is made better by justice, but ruined by injustice? Is there not such a part?

CRITO: I think there is, Socrates.

SOCRATES: Well, then, supposing, by not yielding to the opinion of the wise, we destroy utterly that part of us which is made better by health but corrupted by disease; is life worth living after this corruption has taken place? And that part is the body, is it not?

CRITO: Yes.

SOCRATES: And would life be worth living, with a miserable and corrupted body?

CRITO: By no means.

SOCRATES: But would it then be worth living, if that part of us were corrupted which injustice degrades and justice benefits? Or do we indeed hold that part, whatever it is, with which injustice and justice have to do, [48] of less account than the body?

CRITO: By no means.

SOCRATES: Of more importance then?

CRITO: Of much more.

SOCRATES: Then indeed, my friend, we ought not to heed at all what the multitude say of us, but only what the one man who understands about the just and the unjust, and what truth herself will say. So that, to start with, you do not state the case rightly in saying that we ought to give heed to the opinion of the multitude concerning the just and the honourable and the good and their opposites. 'But,' some-one may say, 'the multitude have power to put us to death.'

CRITO: Yes, and this is true enough. It might indeed be said, Socrates.

SOCRATES: You speak truly; and yet, my excellent friend, this argument which we have been following out appears to me the same as ever. Now consider also whether we still hold that it is not mere living which should be valued above everything else, but living a good life.

CRITO: Certainly we hold it.

SOCRATES: And that living a good life is the same as living an honourable and a just life; do we still hold that or not?

CRITO: We do.

SOCRATES: Then, starting from these admissions, we must consider whether I should be acting justly or not in trying to escape when the Athenians refuse to release me; and if it appears that I should be acting justly, we will make the attempt; if not, we will renounce it. Those considerations of which you speak, concerning the loss of possessions and reputation, and the bringing up of children, belong in truth, Crito, I fear, to those who thoughtlessly put men to death, and would as thoughtlessly bring them to life again if they could, with no reflection in either case; I mean that very multitude of which we have been speaking. But we, since our argument leaves us no escape, have, I think, no other question to consider than the one which we just now mentioned – whether we shall be acting justly in bestowing money and thanks upon those who will get me out of this place, thus aiding and abetting our own escape, or whether in truth both we and they shall thus be doing anything unjust; and if it does appear that we shall thus be acting unjustly we must not take into account the prospect of death if we remain quietly here, or of any other evil, in comparison with doing what is unjust.

CRITO: What you say, Socrates, seems to me admirable; but what shall we do then?

SOCRATES: Let us take counsel together, my friend, and if you have any objections to make to what I say, speak out, and you will find me ready to be convinced by you; but if you have not, pray, my good friend, no longer keep repeating this same thing – that I ought to depart hence against the will of the Athenians, for I hold it of great moment to act in this matter with your approval and not without your consent. Look, then, at the first step of our investigation, and see if it has been satisfactorily stated, and then try to answer my question [49] according to your real convictions.

CRITO: I will certainly try.

SOCRATES: Do we then hold that we ought in no way intentionally to commit injustice, or that we may commit it in one way, and not in another; or do we still, as in former times, admit that to act unjustly is in no case good and honourable? Are all the principles which we have acknowledged within these last few days to be now thrown away, and have we, Crito, at our age, been thus long and earnestly reasoning among ourselves, unconscious all the while that we were no better than children? Or rather, whether the mass of men acknowledge it or not, and whether a sterner or a milder fate is in store for us, is not what we said before still true, that to do injustice is in every way a disgrace and an evil to the doer of it? Do we admit this or not?

CRITO: We do.

SOCRATES: Then we ought not to do wrong at all.

CRITO: Certainly not.

SOCRATES: Nor should we, as the mass of men think, retaliate when unjustly treated, seeing that we ought never to commit any injustice at all.

CRITO: So it appears.

SOCRATES: How stands it, then? Ought we to do harm to any man?

CRITO: Of course we ought not, Socrates.

SOCRATES: How, then? Is it right, as the mass of men assert, to render evil for evil, or is it not?

CRITO: By no means.

SOCRATES: Because doing harm to others is in no wise different from committing injustice.

CRITO: You speak truly.

SOCRATES: So that we ought neither to retaliate nor to harm any man, no matter what we may suffer at his hands. But look, Crito, at what you are hereby acknowledging, lest you unadvisedly admit something contrary to your real opinion; for this I know is believed and will be believed by very few, and they who do hold it and they who do not have no common ground, but must of necessity despise each other, on account of their contrary opinions. Consider well, therefore, whether you agree with me and are of my mind; and then let us start with this conclusion, that it can never be right to commit injustice or to retaliate or to defend ourselves by rendering evil for evil. Or do you not agree to this first step, and will you give it up? To me it has always seemed and still seems true; but if you think otherwise, say so and instruct me. If, however, you do abide by it, listen to what follows.

CRITO: I do accept it and abide by it. Say on.

SOCRATES: I proceed, then, to tell you what follows from it; or rather, I will ask you to tell me. Ought a man to do what he acknowledges to be right, or ought he to betray the right?

CRITO: He ought to do what is right.

SOCRATES: Then notice how this applies. By going away without the consent of the state, shall we or shall we not be wronging those whom least of all we ought to wrong? And are we [50] thus abiding by what we acknowledge to be right, or not?

CRITO: I have nothing to answer, Socrates, to what you ask, for I do not know.

SOCRATES: Well, consider it thus. Suppose, as we were on the point of running away, or whatever else you may call it, the laws and the state should come and say: 'Tell us, Socrates, what is this that you think of doing? Are you not, by the deed which you are about to undertake, thinking to destroy, so far as in you lies, the laws and the whole state? For you do not deem it possible, do you, that that state can survive and not be overthrown in which the decisions of the courts do not prevail, but are by private individuals set aside and brought to naught?' How shall we reply, Crito, to this, and to other like questions? Anyone, above all an orator, might have much to say in behalf of the law we are breaking, which commands that judgements once decreed shall be decisive. Or shall we make answer that the State has injured us and not given righteous judgement? Shall we say this, or what shall we say?

CRITO: This, by Zeus, O Socrates.

SOCRATES: What, then, if the laws answer: 'And is this what was agreed between us, Socrates, or was it not rather that you should abide by the judgements decreed by the state?' And were we to express surprise at their speaking thus, they would very likely reply: 'Do not be surprised, O Socrates, at what we say, but answer, since you are in the habit of asking and answering questions. Come, then, what charge is it upon which you are trying to destroy us and the State? Did we not in the first place bring you into existence, and was it not by our authority that your father received your mother in marriage and gave you life? Tell us, therefore, is it those among us relating to marriage that you blame as not being right!' 'I do not blame these,' I should reply. 'Is it, then, those relating to the nurture and training of children, under which you yourself were brought up? Are those laws among us, pray, not well ordered which enjoined upon your father to instruct you in music and gymnastics?' 'They are well ordered,' I should reply. 'Very good. Having, therefore, been thus brought into existence and nurtured and educated, can you pretend to say that you are not our offspring and slave, you, even as were your fathers before you? And if this be so, do you think that your rights are equal with ours, and that whatever we undertake to do to you it is right for you to do to us in return? As regards your father or your master, if you chance to have one, your rights are surely not equal. You would have no right to pay him back what he had made you suffer, whether by retaliating if he had abused you or by striking him if he had beaten you, [51] or by doing anything else of the kind; and yet when it comes to us, your country and its laws, all this is allowable, forsooth, so that, if we have thought it right to undertake your ruin, you think yourself justified in doing in your turn all you can to bring about our destruction! And is this what you call acting justly, you who in very truth have made justice your special study? Are you so wise, pray, as to have missed the discovery that above your mother and father and all your other ancestors your country should be held in honour and reverence and holy awe, and is so held in the eyes of the Gods and of all reasonable men; that you must revere her and submit yourself to her, and soothe her in her anger more than if it were your father; that you must either induce her by persuasion to reverse her judgements, or else do whatever she commands; that you must suffer without resistance if she assigns to you suffering; and if she orders you to be scourged or imprisoned, or leads you into battle, there to be wounded or killed, that all this is right and must be done; that we must never give way nor retreat nor leave the ranks, but whether in battle or in a court of justice or anywhere else, we must either do what our city and our country command or else convince them of the true nature of justice? For it is impious to offer violence to your father or your mother; how much more, then, to your country!' What shall we say to this, Crito? Do the laws speak truly or not?

CRITO: It seems to me that they do.

SOCRATES: 'Consider then, Socrates,' the laws might continue, 'whether we speak the truth in declaring that you are not treating us justly in attempting to do this thing. For we, having brought you into existence, nurtured, educated you, given you, as well as every other citizen, a share in all our good things, have, moreover, proclaimed to every Athenian that after he has come of age, and examined our management of the city and ourselves, the laws, he has our permission, if he find that we do not please him, to take what belongs to him, and go wherever he wishes. And not one of us, the laws, hinders or dissuades any one of you, if we or the city do not please him, from taking his departure, if he wish, for one of our colonies, or from going to live in any foreign country that he may prefer, carrying with him all his possessions. But he among you who, having seen in what way we give judgement and manage the other affairs of the city, chooses to remain has, we assert, pledged himself, in very deed, to perform whatsoever we command; and him, if he does not obey us, we pronounce to be thrice guilty: first, as

disobedient to those who gave him being; secondly, as disobedient to those who brought him up; and thirdly, as neither obeying us when he has promised so to do [52] nor trying to convince us if so be that we are in the wrong. And we do not harshly require obedience to our orders, but we lay open all questions for consideration; yet while we give him the choice of either convincing us or obeying us, he does neither of the two.

'To these charges, Socrates, we declare you liable, if you do what is now in your mind; and that not less but more than all the other Athenians.' And if I were to ask why, they might retaliate, justly enough, by reminding me that I, of all the Athenians, had most pledged myself to this promise. 'We have strong proofs, Socrates,' they would say, 'that we and the city itself have pleased you, for you would not have dwelt here more constantly than have all the other Athenians if you had not been especially content. You never went out of the city at all, even to be a spectator at the games, except once to see the Isthmian; and you never went anywhere else unless you happened to be serving in the army. Nor did you ever, like other men, travel abroad, nor desire to know about other cities or other laws, for we and our city satisfied you. Thus heartily did you prefer us, and pledge yourself to be governed by us; and besides, the fact that your children were born here is a proof that the city satisfies you. Moreover, in this very trial you were at liberty, if you had wished, to propose the penalty of exile, so that what you are now attempting to do against the will of the city you could then have done with her consent. You boasted at that time that if you had to die you would not be distressed, for you preferred, as you said, death to exile. But now you feel no shame at the recollection of your own words, nor have you any reverence for us, the laws, since you are trying to destroy us, and are acting as would the meanest slave, trying to run away in defiance of the covenants and agreements according to which you had pledged yourself to be governed as a citizen. Now, then, answer us this. Do we speak the truth in saying that you have pledged yourself to be governed by us, not in word, but in deed?' What shall we say to this, Crito? Can we do otherwise than acknowledge it?

CRITO: We must needs do so, Socrates.

SOCRATES: 'Are you not then,' they may say, 'transgressing the covenants and agreements which were made with us, not by means of force or deception, nor yet because you were compelled to decide within a short time, for throughout the space of seventy years you were at liberty to go away if we did not please you, or if the agreements did not appear to you just. But you preferred neither Lacedaemon nor Crete, which you often speak of as well governed states, [53] nor any other of the Greek or foreign cities, and left Athens less frequently than do even the halt and the blind and the maimed; so much more than all other Athenians were you satisfied with her, and, as naturally follows, no less with us, her laws; for where is the man whom a city without laws would please? And now do you not intend to abide by your agreement? If you follow our advice, Socrates, you will, and not make yourself ridiculous by taking flight from the city.

'For just consider what good you will do yourself and your friends by setting at naught and violating these agreements. That your friends will be in danger of being exiled and deprived of their country and their property is well nigh certain; and as to yourself, if you go to one of the nearest cities – say Thebes or Megara, which are both well governed – you will go as an enemy to its constitution, and those of its citizens who care for the State will look upon you with suspicion, as a subverter of the laws; and thus you will confirm the opinion of your judges, so that your sentence will appear to have been justly awarded. For whosoever is a corrupter of the laws is very sure to appear also as a corrupter of young and thoughtless men. Will you, then, flee from well-governed cities, and from the men who are the most law-abiding? And if you must do this, is it worth your while to live? Or if you can without shame associate with them, what language will you use, O Socrates? Will you affirm, as you have done here, that virtue and justice and institutions and laws are the things most precious to men? And do you not think that this deed committed by Socrates will appear unseemly? You must think so. But suppose you leave these cities, and go to the friends of Crito in Thessaly; for there reigns the greatest disorder and licence, and they will very likely be glad to hear how ridiculously you ran away from prison in some disguise, perhaps clad in a leathern jerkin, or some other garment such as runaways are apt to wear, so that your whole semblance was changed. But do you imagine there will be nobody to relate how an old man, who has, in all probability, such a brief time remaining to live, was so greedy of life as to dare set at naught the highest laws? Perhaps not, if you do not offend anyone; but if you do, you will be sure, O Socrates, to hear many disgraceful things said about yourself. You will live a slave and a mean flatterer to all sorts of men; and to what end withal, but to fare sumptuously, just as if you had taken your flight into Thessaly merely to get a dinner? And all those discourses concerning justice and other virtue – what is to become of them? Or is it perhaps on account of your children that you wish to live, [54] so that you may bring them up and educate them? But what then? Will you take them to Thessaly, and there bring them up and educate them, making them aliens to their country, that this also they may have to thank you for? Or perhaps you think that they will be better cared for and educated here in Athens for your being alive, even if you are not living with them? Your friends, you say, will look after them. But do you suppose that, while they will do this if you depart for Thessaly, they will not if you depart for Hades? Assuredly, if they who call themselves your friends are good for anything you must believe that they will.

'But, Socrates, be persuaded by us who have brought you up, and do not place your children or your life or anything else above the right; that, when you have arrived in Hades, you may have all these things to urge in your defence before those who reign there. For neither in this life does it appear better or more just or more holy for you or for anyone belonging to you thus to act, nor when you shall have arrived in the other world will it be to your advantage. As it is now, if you depart hence you go as one wronged, not by us, the laws, but by men; but if you take to flight, thus disgracefully rendering back injustice and injury by breaking the covenants and agreements which you yourself made with us, and working evil against those whom least of all you ought to injure – your own self as well as your friends, your country, and ourselves – we shall be angry with you here while you are yet alive, and our brothers, the laws in Hades, will not receive you kindly, knowing that you sought, so far as in you lay, to destroy us. So do not, we beg you, let Crito persuade you to follow his advice rather than ours.'

These, you must know, my dear friend Crito, are the words which I seem to hear, even as the Corybantes imagine that they hear the sound of the flutes; and their echo resounding within me makes me unable to hear aught beside. Know, therefore, that if you say anything contrary to this you will but speak in vain. Nevertheless, if you think that anything will be gained thereby, say on.

CRITO: No, Socrates, I have nothing more to say.

SOCRATES: Then so let it rest, Crito; and let us follow in this way, since in this way it is that God leads. (tr. Anon.)

2.4. Phaedo

Plato's account of Socrates' last day has made an impact upon the imagination of later generations. None the less, he was not present himself, and says as much, though he had a good informant in Euclides. In the course of the dialogue Socrates argues with a calm certainty for the immortality of the soul: there is an overt contrast with the expressed agnosticism of The Apology, *but it need be no more than the difference between a public statement and a private confession of faith to friends. But the exposition of the Theory of Forms can hardly be authentic (see the Introduction). The picture of Socrates' calmness in the face of death has the ring of truth.*

2.4.1 [57] ECHECRATES: Were you personally present, Phaedo, with Socrates on that day when he drank the poison in prison? or did you hear an account of it from someone else?

PHAEDO: I was there myself, Echecrates.

ECHECRATES: What, then, did he say before his death? and how did he die? for I should be glad to hear: for scarcely any citizen of Phlius ever visits Athens now, nor has any stranger for a long time come from thence, who was able to give us a clear account of the particulars, except that he died from drinking poison; but he was unable to tell us anything more.

[58] PHAEDO: And did you not hear about the trial how it went off?

ECHECRATES: Yes; someone told me this; and I wondered, that as it took place so long ago, he appears to have died longer afterwards. What was the reason of this, Phaedo?

PHAEDO: An accidental circumstance happened in his favour, Echecrates: for the poop of the ship which the Athenians send to Delos chanced to be crowned on the day before the trial.

ECHECRATES: But what is this ship?

PHAEDO: It is the ship, as the Athenians say, in which Theseus formerly conveyed the fourteen boys and girls to Crete, and saved both them and himself. They, therefore, made a vow to Apollo on that occasion, as it is said, that if they were saved they would every year dispatch a solemn embassy to Delos; which from that time to the present they send yearly to the god. When they begin the preparations for this solemn embassy they have a law that the city shall be purified during this period, and that no public execution shall take place until the ship has reached Delos and returned to Athens: and this occasionally takes a long time when the winds happen to impede their passage. The commencement of the embassy is when the priest of Apollo has crowned the poop of the ship. And this was done, as I said, on the day before the trial: on this account Socrates had a long interval in prison between the trial and his death.

ECHECRATES: And what, Phaedo, were the circumstances of his death? what was said and done? and who of his friends were with him? or would not the magistrates allow them to be present, but did he die destitute of friends?

PHAEDO: By no means; but some, indeed several, were present.

ECHECRATES: Take the trouble, then, to relate to me all the particulars as clearly as you can, unless you have any pressing business.

PHAEDO: I am at leisure, and will endeavour to give you a full account: for to call Socrates to mind, whether speaking myself or listening to someone else, is always most delightful to me.

ECHECRATES: And indeed, Phaedo, you have others to listen to you who are of the same mind. However, endeavour to relate everything as accurately as you can.

PHAEDO: I was indeed wonderfully affected by being present, for I was not impressed with a feeling of pity, like one present at the death of a friend; for the man appeared to me to be happy, Echecrates, both from his manner and discourse, so fearlessly and nobly did he meet his death: so much so, that it occurred to me, that in going to Hades he was not going without a divine destiny, but that when he arrived there he would be happy, if any one ever was. [59] For this reason I was entirely uninfluenced by any feeling of pity, as would seem likely to be the case with one present on so mournful an occasion; nor was I affected by pleasure from being engaged in philosophical discussions, as was our custom; for our conversation was of that kind. But an altogether unaccountable feeling possessed me, a kind of unusual mixture compounded of pleasure and pain together, when I considered that he was immediately about to die. And all of us who were present were affected in much the same manner, at one time laughing, at another weeping, one of us especially, Apollodorus, for you know the man and his manner.

ECHECRATES: How should I not?

PHAEDO: He, then, was entirely overcome by these emotions; and I, too, was troubled, as well as the others.

ECHECRATES: But who were present, Phaedo?

PHAEDO: Of his fellow-countrymen, this Apollodorus was present, and Critobulus, and his father Crito, moreover Hermogenes, Epigenes, Aeschines, and Antisthenes; Ctesippus the Paeanian, Menexenus, and some other of his countrymen were also there: Plato I think was sick.

ECHECRATES: Were any strangers present?

PHAEDO: Yes: Simmias the Theban, Cebes and Phaedondes: and from Megara, Euclides and Terpsion.

ECHECRATES: But what! were not Aristippus and Cleombrotus present?

PHAEDO: No: for they were said to be at Aegina.

ECHECRATES: Was anyone else there?

PHAEDO: I think that these were nearly all who were present.

ECHECRATES: Well now: what do you say was the subject of conversation?

PHAEDO: I will endeavour to relate the whole to you from the beginning. On the preceding days I and the others were constantly in the habit of visiting Socrates, meeting early in the morning at the court-house where the trial took place, for it was near the prison. Here then we waited every day till the prison was opened, conversing with each other; it was not opened very early, but as soon as it was opened we went in to Socrates, and usually spent the day with him. On that occasion, however, we met earlier than usual; for on the preceding day, when we left the prison in the evening, we heard that the ship had arrived from Delos. We therefore urged each other to come as early as possible to the accustomed place; accordingly we came, and the porter, who used to admit us, coming out, told us to wait, and not enter until he called us. 'For,' he said, 'the Eleven are now freeing Socrates from his bonds, and announcing to him that he must die to-day.' But in no long time he returned, and bade us enter.

When we entered, we found Socrates just freed from his bonds, [60] and Xanthippe, you know her, holding his little boy and sitting by him. As soon as Xanthippe saw us, she wept aloud and said such things as women usually do on such occasions, as 'Socrates, your friends will now converse with you for the last time and you with them'. But Socrates, looking towards Crito, said, 'Crito, let someone take her home.' Upon which some of Crito's attendants led her away, wailing and beating herself.

But Socrates, sitting up in bed, drew up his leg, and rubbed it with his hand, and as he rubbed it, said, 'What an unaccountable thing, my friends, that seems to be, which men call pleasure; and how wonderfully is it related towards that which appears to be its contrary, pain; in that they will not both be present to a man at the same time, yet, if anyone pursues and attains the one he is almost always compelled to receive the other, as if they were both united together from one head.

'And it seems to me,' he said, 'that if Aesop had observed this he would have made a fable from it, how the deity, wishing to reconcile these warring principles, when he could not do so, united their heads together, and from hence whomsoever the one visits the other attends immediately after; as appears to be the case with me, since I suffered pain in my leg before from the chain, but now pleasure seems to have succeeded.'

Hereupon Cebes, interrupting him, said, 'By Jupiter, Socrates, you have done well in reminding me: with respect to the poems which you made, by putting into metre those fables of Aesop and the hymn to Apollo, several other persons asked me, and especially Evenus recently, with what design you made them after you came here, whereas before you had never made any. If, therefore, you care at all that I should be able to answer Evenus, when he asks me again, for I am sure he will do so, tell me what I must say to him.'

'Tell him the truth then, Cebes,' he replied, 'that I did not make them from a wish to compete with him, or his poems, for I knew that this would be no easy matter; but that I might discover the meaning of certain dreams, and discharge my conscience, if this should happen to be the music which they have often ordered me to apply myself to. For they were to the following purport; often in my past life the same dream visited me, appearing at different times in different forms, yet always saying the same things, "Socrates," it said, "apply yourself to and practise music." And I formerly supposed that it exhorted and encouraged me to continue the pursuit I was engaged in, [61] as those who cheer on racers, so that the dream encouraged me to continue the pursuit I was engaged in, namely, to apply myself to music, since philosophy is the highest music, and I was devoted to it. But now since my trial took place, and the festival of the god retarded my death, it appeared to me that, if by chance the dream so frequently enjoined me to apply myself to popular music I ought not to disobey it but do so, for that it would be safer for me not to depart hence before I had discharged my conscience by making some poems in obedience to the dream. Thus, then, I first of all composed a hymn to the god whose festival was present, and after the god, considering that a poet, if he means to be a poet, ought to make fables and not discourses, and knowing that I was not skilled in making fables, I therefore put into verse those fables of Aesop, which were at hand, and were known to me, and which first occurred to me.

'Tell this then to Evenus, Cebes, and bid him farewell, and, if he is wise, to follow me as soon as he can. But I depart, as it seems, today; for so the Athenians order.'

To this Simmias said, 'What is this, Socrates, which you exhort Evenus to do? for I often meet with him; and from what I know of him I am pretty certain that he will not at all be willing to comply with your advice.'

'What then,' said he, 'is not Evenus a philosopher?'

'To me he seems to be so,' said Simmias.

'Then he will be willing,' rejoined Socrates, 'and so will everyone who worthily engages in this study; perhaps indeed he will not commit violence on himself, for that they say is not allowable.' And as he said this he let down his leg from the bed on the ground, and in this posture continued during the remainder of the discussion.

Cebes then asked him, 'What do you mean, Socrates, by saying that it is not lawful to commit violence on one's-self, but that a philosopher should be willing to follow one who is dying?'

'What, Cebes, have not you and Simmias, who have conversed familiarly with Philolaus on this subject, heard?'

'Nothing very clearly, Socrates.'

'I, however, speak only from hearsay; what, then, I have heard I have no scruple in telling. And perhaps it is most becoming for one who is about to travel there, to inquire and speculate about the journey thither, what kind we think it is. What else can one do in the interval before sunset?'

'Why, then, Socrates, do they say that it is not allowable to kill one's-self? for I, as you asked just now, have heard both Philolaus, when he lived with us, and several others say that it was not right to do this; but I never heard anything clear upon the subject from anyone.'

[62] 'Then you should consider it attentively,' said Socrates, 'for perhaps

you may hear: probably, however, it will appear wonderful to you, if this alone of all other things is an universal truth, and it never happens to a man, as is the case in all other things, that at some times and to some persons only it is better to die than to live; yet that these men for whom it is better to die – this probably will appear wonderful to you – may not without impiety do this good to themselves, but must await another benefactor.'

Then Cebes, gently smiling, said, speaking in his own dialect, 'Jove be witness.'

'And indeed,' said Socrates, 'it would appear to be unreasonable, yet still perhaps it has some reason on its side. The maxim indeed given on this subject in the mystical doctrines, that we men are in a kind of prison, and that we ought not to free ourselves from it and escape, appears to me difficult to be understood, and not easy to penetrate. This, however, appears to me, Cebes, to be well said, that the gods take care of us, and that we men are one of their possessions. Does it not seem so to you?'

'It does,' replied Cebes.

'Therefore,' said he, 'if one of your slaves were to kill himself, without your having intimated that you wished him to die, should you not be angry with him, and should you not punish him if you could?'

'Certainly,' he replied.

'Perhaps then in this point of view, it is not unreasonable to assert, that a man ought not to kill himself before the deity lays him under a necessity of doing so, such as that now laid on me.'

'This, indeed,' said Cebes, 'appears to be probable. But what you said just now, Socrates, that philosophers should be very willing to die, appears to be an absurdity, if what we said just now is agreeable to reason, that it is God who takes care of us, and that we are his property. For that the wisest men should not be grieved at leaving that service in which they who govern them are the best of all masters, namely the gods, is not consistent with reason. For surely he cannot think that he will take better care of himself when he has become free; but a foolish man might perhaps think thus, that he should fly from his master, and would not reflect that he ought not to fly from a good one, but should cling to him as much as possible, therefore he would fly against all reason; but a man of sense would desire to be constantly with one better than himself. Thus, Socrates, the contrary of what you just now said is likely to be the case; for it becomes the wise to be grieved at dying, but the foolish to rejoice.'

Socrates, on hearing this, appeared to me to be pleased with the pertinacity of Cebes, [63] and looking towards us, said, 'Cebes, you see, always searches out arguments, and is not at all willing to admit at once anything one has said.'

Whereupon Simmias replied, 'But indeed, Socrates, Cebes appears to me, now, to say something to the purpose: for with what design should men really wise fly from masters who are better than themselves, and so readily leave them? And Cebes appears to me to direct his argument against you, because you so easily endure to abandon both us, and those good rulers, as you yourself confess, the gods.'

'You speak justly,' said Socrates, 'for I think you mean that I ought to make my defence to this charge, as if I were in a court of justice.'

'Certainly,' replied Simmias.

'Come then,' said he, 'I will endeavour to defend myself more successfully before you than before the judges. For,' he proceeded, 'Simmias and Cebes, if I did not think that I should go first of all among other deities who are both wise and good, and, next, among men who have departed this life, better than any here, I should be wrong in not grieving at death: but now be assured, I hope to go among good men, though I would not positively assert it, that, however, I shall go among gods who are perfectly good masters, be assured I can positively assert this, if I can anything of the kind. So that, on this account, I am not so much troubled, but I entertain a good hope that something awaits those who die, and that, as was said long since, it will be far better for the good than the evil.'

'What then, Socrates,' said Simmias, 'would you go away keeping this persuasion to yourself, or would you impart it to us? For this good appears to me to be also common to us; and at the same time it will be an apology for you, if you can persuade us to believe what you say.'

'I will endeavour to do so,' he said. 'But first let us attend to Crito here, and see what it is he seems to have for some time wished to say.'

'What else, Socrates,' said Crito, 'but what he who is to give you the poison told me some time ago, that I should tell you to speak as little as possible? For he says that men become too much heated by speaking, and that nothing of this kind ought to interfere with the poison, and that otherwise those who did so were sometimes compelled to drink two or three times.'

To which Socrates replied, 'Let him alone, and let him attend to his own business, and prepare to give it me twice, or, if occasion requires, even thrice.'

'I was almost certain what you would say,' answered Crito, 'but he has been some time pestering me.'

'Never mind him,' he rejoined.

'But now I wish to render an account to you, my judges, of the reason why a man who has really devoted his life to philosophy, when he is about to die, appears to me, on good grounds, to have confidence, and to entertain a firm hope [64] that the greatest good will befall him in the other world, when he has departed this life. How, then, this comes to pass, Simmias and Cebes, I will endeavour to explain.

'For as many as rightly apply themselves to philosophy seem to have left all others in ignorance, that they aim at nothing else than to die and be dead. If this, then, is true, it would surely be absurd to be anxious about nothing else than this during their whole life, but, when it arrives, to be grieved at what they have been long anxious about and aimed at.'

Upon this, Simmias, smiling, said, 'By Jupiter, Socrates, though I am not now at all inclined to smile, you have made me do so; for I think that the multitude, if they heard this, would think it was very well said in reference to philosophers, and that our countrymen particularly would agree with you, that true philosophers do desire death, and that they are by no means ignorant that they deserve to suffer it.'

'And indeed, Simmias, they would speak the truth, except in asserting that they are not ignorant; for they are ignorant of the sense in which true philosophers desire to die, and in what sense they deserve death, and what kind of death. But,' he said, 'let us take leave of them, and speak to one another.' (57A–64C, tr. H. Cary and H. Davis)

2.4.2 When Socrates had thus spoken, a long silence ensued; and Socrates himself was pondering upon what had been said, as he appeared, and so did most of us; but Cebes and Simmias were conversing a little while with each other. At length Socrates, perceiving them, said, 'What think you of what has been said? does it appear to you to have been proved sufficiently? for many doubts and objections still remain if anyone will examine them thoroughly. If, then, you are considering some other subject I have nothing to say; but if you are doubting about this do not hesitate both yourselves to speak and express your opinion if it appears to you in any respect that it might have been argued better, and to call me in again to your assistance if you think you can be at all benefited by my help.'

Upon this Simmias said, 'Indeed, Socrates, I will tell you the truth: for some time each of us, being in doubt, has been urging and exhorting the other to question you, from a desire to hear our doubts solved, but we were afraid of giving you trouble, lest it should be disagreeable to you in your present circumstances.'

But he, upon hearing this, gently smiled, and said, 'Bless me, Simmias; with difficulty indeed, could I persuade other men that I do not consider my present condition a calamity, since I am not able to persuade even you; but you are afraid lest I should be more morose now than during the former part of my life. And, as it seems, I appear to you to be inferior to swans with respect to divination, who, when they perceive that they must needs die, though they have been used to sing before, sing then more than ever, [85] rejoicing that they are about to depart to that deity whose servants they are. But men, through their own fear of death, belie the swans too, and say that they, lamenting their death, sing their last song through grief, and they do not consider that no bird sings when it is hungry or cold, or is afflicted with any other pain, not even the nightingale, or swallow, or the hoopoes, which they say sing lamenting through grief. But neither do these birds appear to me to sing through sorrow, nor yet do swans; but in my opinion, belonging to Apollo, they are prophetic, and foreseeing the blessings of Hades, they sing and rejoice on that day more excellently than at any preceding time. But I, too, consider myself to be a fellow-servant of the swans, and sacred to the same god, and that I have received the power of divination from our common master no less than they, and that I do not depart from this life with less spirits than they. On this account, therefore, it is right that you should both speak and ask whatever you please, as long as the Athenian Eleven permit.' (84C–85B, tr. H. Cary and H. Davis)

2.4.3 Socrates, therefore, looking steadfastly at us, as he was generally accustomed to do, and smiling, said, 'Simmias indeed speaks justly. If, then, anyone of you is more prompt than I am, why does he not answer? for he seems to have handled my argument not badly. It appears to me, however, that before we make our reply we should first hear from Cebes, what he, too, objects to our argument, in order that, some time intervening, we may consider what we shall say, and then when we have heard them we may give up to them, if they appear to speak agreeably to truth, or if not, we may then uphold our own argument. Come then, Cebes,' he continued, 'say what it is that disturbs you, so as to cause your unbelief.' (86D–E, tr. H. Cary and H. Davis)

2.4.4 PHAEDO: Indeed, Echecrátes, though I have often admired Socrates, I was never more delighted than at being with him on that occasion. That he should be able to say something is perhaps not at all surprising; [89] but I especially admired this in him, first of all that he listened to the argument of the young men so sweetly, affably and approvingly; in the next place, that he so quickly perceived how we were affected by their arguments; and lastly, that he cured us so well and recalled us, when we were put to flight as it were and vanquished, and encouraged us to accompany him, and consider the argument with him.

ECHECRATES: How was that?

PHAEDO: I will tell you: I happened

to be sitting at his right hand, near the bed, upon a low seat, but he himself sat much higher than I. Stroking my head, then, and laying hold of the hair that hung on my neck, for he used, often, to play with my hairs, 'To-morrow,' he said, 'perhaps, Phaedo, you will cut off these beautiful locks?'

'It seems likely, Socrates,' said I.

'Not if you are persuaded by me.'

'Why so?' I asked.

'Today,' he replied, 'both I ought to cut off mine and you yours, if our argument must die, and we are unable to revive it. And I, if I were you, and the arguments were to escape me, would take an oath, as the Argives do, not to suffer my hair to grow until I had renewed the contest, and vanquished the arguments of Simmias and Cebes.'

'But,' I said, 'even Hercules himself is said not to have been a match for two.'

'Call upon me, then,' he said, 'as your Iolaus, while it is yet day.'

'I do call on you, then,' I said, 'not as Hercules upon Iolaus, but as Iolaus upon Hercules.'

'It will make no difference,' he replied. 'But first of all we must beware lest we meet with some mischance.'

'What?' I asked.

'That we do not become,' he answered, 'haters of reasoning as some become haters of men; for no greater evil can happen to anyone than to hate reasoning.' (88E–89C, tr. H. Cary and H. Davis)

2.4.5 'And I seem to myself on the present occasion to differ from them only in this respect; for I shall not be anxious to make what I say appear true to those who are present, except that may happen by the way, but that it may appear certainly to be so to myself. For I thus reason, my dear friend, and observe how interestedly, if what I say be true, it is well to be persuaded of it; but if nothing remains to one that is dead I shall at least during the interval before death be less disagreeable to those present by my lamentations. But this ignorance of mine will not continue long, for that would be bad, but will shortly be put an end to. Thus prepared then, Simmias and Cebes,' he continued, 'I now proceed to my argument. Do you, however, if you will be persuaded by me, pay little attention to Socrates, but much more to the truth, and if I appear to you to say anything true, assent to it, but if not, oppose me with all your might, taking good care that in my zeal I do not deceive both myself and you, and like a bee depart leaving my sting behind.' (91B–C, tr. H. Cary and H. Davis)

2.4.6 'When I was a young man, Cebes, I was wonderfully desirous of that wisdom which they call a history of nature: for it appeared to me to be a very sublime thing to know the causes of everything, why each thing is generated, why it perishes and why it exists. And I often tossed myself upwards and downwards, considering first such things as these, whether when heat and cold have undergone a certain corruption, as some say, then animals are formed; and whether the blood is that by means of which we think, or air, or fire, or none of these, but that it is the brain that produces the perceptions of hearing, seeing and smelling, and that from these come memory and opinion, and from memory and opinion, when in a state of rest, in the same way knowledge is produced. And again considering the corruptions of these, and the affections incidental to the heavens and the earth, I at length appeared to myself so unskilful in these speculations that nothing could be more so. But I will give you a sufficient proof of this: for I then became, by these very speculations, so very blind with respect to things which I knew clearly before, as it appeared to myself and others, that I unlearnt even the things which I thought I knew before, both on many other subjects and also this, why a man grows. For before I thought this was evident to everyone, that it proceeds from eating and drinking; for that, when, from the food, flesh is added to flesh, bone to bone and so on in the same proportion, what is proper to them is added to the several other parts, then the bulk which was small becomes afterwards large, and thus that a little man becomes a big one. Such was my opinion at that time: does it appear to you correct?'

'To me it does,' said Cebes.

'Consider this further. I thought that I had formed a right opinion, when on seeing a tall man standing by a short one I judged that he was taller by the head, and in like manner one horse than another: and still more clearly than this, ten appeared to me to be more than eight, by two being added to them, and that two cubits are greater than one cubit, by exceeding it a half.'

'But now,' said Cebes, 'what think you of these matters?'

'By Jupiter,' said he, 'I am far from thinking that I know the cause of these, for that I cannot even persuade myself of this, when a person has added one to one, whether the one to which the addition has been made has become two or whether that which has been added, and that to which the addition has been made, [97] have become two by the addition of the one to the other. For I wonder, if when each of these was separate from the other, each was one, and they were not yet two, but when they have approached nearer each other this should be the cause of their becoming two, namely, the union by which they have been placed nearer one another. Nor yet, if any person should divide one, am I able to persuade myself that this, their division, is the cause of its becoming two. For this cause is the contrary to the former one of their becoming two; for then it was because they were brought nearer to each other, and the one was added to the other; but now it is, because one is removed and separated from the other. Nor do I yet persuade myself that I know why one is one nor, in a word, why anything else is produced or perishes, or exists, according to this method of proceeding; but I mix up another method of my own at random, for this I can on no account give in to.

'But having once heard a person reading from a book written, as he said, by Anaxagoras, and which said that it is intelligence that sets in order and is the cause of all things, I was delighted with this cause, and it appeared to me in a manner to be well that intelligence should be the cause of all things, and I considered with myself, if this is so, that the regulating intelligence orders all things, and disposes each in such way as will be best for it. If anyone, then, should desire to discover the cause of everything, in what way it is produced, or perishes, or exists, he must discover this respecting it, in what way it is best for it either to exist, or to suffer, or do anything else; from this mode of reasoning, then, it is proper that a man should consider nothing else, both with respect to himself and others, than what is most excellent and best; and it necessarily follows that this same person must also know that which is worst, for that the knowledge of both of them is the same. Thus reasoning with myself, I was delighted to think I had found in Anaxagoras a preceptor who would instruct me in the causes of things, agreeably to my own mind, and that he would inform me, first, whether the earth is flat or round, and when he had informed me would, moreover, explain the cause and necessity of its being so, arguing on the principle of the better, and showing that it is better for it to be such as it is, and if he should say that it is in the middle, that he would, moreover, explain how it is better for it to be in the middle; and if he should make all this clear to me I was prepared no longer to require any other species of cause. I was in like manner prepared to inquire respecting the sun, [98] and moon, and the other stars, with respect to their velocities in reference to each other and their revolutions, and other conditions, in what way it is better for both to act and be affected as it does and is. For I never thought that after he had said that these things were set in order by intelligence he would introduce any other cause for them than that it is best for them to be as they are: hence, I thought, that in assigning the cause to each of them, and to all in common, he would explain that which is best for each, and the common good of all. And I would not have given up my hopes for a good deal, but having taken up his books with great eagerness, I read through them as quickly as I could, that I might as soon as possible know the best, and the worst.

'From this wonderful hope, however, my friend, I was speedily thrown down, when, as I advance and read over his works, I meet with a man who makes no use of intelligence, nor assigns any causes for the ordering of all things, but makes the causes to consist of air, ether and water, and many other things equally absurd. And he appeared to me to be very like one who should say that whatever Socrates does he does by intelligence, and then, attempting to describe the causes of each particular action, should say, first of all, that for this reason I am now sitting here, because my body is composed of bones and sinews, and that the bones are hard, and have joints separate from each other, but that the sinews, being capable of tension and contraction, cover the bones, together with the flesh and skin which contains them. The bones, therefore, being suspended in their sockets, the nerves relaxing and

tightening enable me to bend my limbs as I now do, and from this cause I sit here bent up. And if again he should assign other similar causes for my conversing with you, assigning as causes voice, and air, and hearing, and ten thousand other things of the kind, omitting to mention the real causes, that since it appeared better to the Athenians to condemn me, I therefore thought it better to sit here, and more just to remain and submit to the punishment which they have ordered; for, by the dog, I think these sinews and bones would have been long ago either in Megara or Boeotia, [99] borne thither by an opinion of that which is best, if I had not thought it more just and honourable to submit to whatever sentence the city might order than to flee and run stealthily away. But to call such things causes is too absurd. But if anyone should say that without possessing such things as bones and sinews, and whatever else I have, I could not do what I pleased he would speak the truth; but to say that I do as I do through them, and that I act thus by intelligence, and not from the choice of what is best, would be a great and extreme disregard of reason. For this would be not to be able to distinguish that the real cause is one thing, and that another without which a cause could not be a cause: which indeed the generality of men appear to me to do, fumbling as it were in the dark, and making use of strange names, so as to denominate them as the very cause. Wherefore one encompassing the earth with a vortex from heaven makes the earth remain fixed; but another, as if it were a broad trough, rests it upon the air as its base; but the power by which these things are now so disposed that they may be placed in the best manner possible, this they neither inquire into nor do they think that it requires any superhuman strength; but they think they will some time or other find out an

Atlas stronger and more immortal than this, and more capable of containing all things, and in reality, the good, and that which ought to hold them together and contain them, they take no account of at all. I then should most gladly have become the disciple of anyone who would teach me of such a cause, in what way it is.' (96A–99C, tr. H. Cary and H. Davis)

The scientific details suggest that this is an authentic account of Socrates' intellectual development up to the 420s.

2.4.7 'But consider,' he said, 'what follows from thence, and see if you can agree with me. For it appears to me that if there be anything else beautiful, besides beauty itself, it is not beautiful for any other reason than because it partakes of that abstract beauty; and I say the same of everything. Do you admit such a cause?'

'I do admit it,' he replied.

'I do not yet understand,' he continued, 'nor am I able to conceive, those other wise causes; but if anyone should tell me why anything is beautiful, either because it has a blooming florid colour, or figure, or anything else of the kind, I dismiss all other reasons, for I am confounded by them all; but I simply, wholly, and perhaps foolishly, confine myself to this, that nothing else causes it to be beautiful, except either the presence or communication of that abstract beauty, by whatever means and in whatever way communicated: for I cannot yet affirm this with certainty, but only that by means of beauty all beautiful things become beautiful. For this appears to me the safest answer to give both to myself and others, and adhering to this, I think that I shall never fall, but that it is a safe answer both for me and anyone else to give, that by means of beauty beautiful things become beautiful. Does it not also seem so to you?' (100C–E, tr. H. Cary and H. Davis)

This is the culminating passage in the exposition of the Theory of Forms.

2.4.8 'To affirm positively, indeed, that these things are exactly as I have described them does not become a man of sense; that, however, either this or something of the kind takes place with respect to our souls and their habitations – since our soul is certainly immortal – this appears to me most fitting to be believed, and worthy the hazard for one who trusts in its reality; for the hazard is noble, and it is right to allure ourselves with such things, as with enchantments; for which reason I have prolonged my story to such a length. On account of these things, then, a man ought to be confident about his soul, who during this life has disregarded all the pleasures and ornaments of the body as foreign from his nature, and who, having thought that they do more harm than good has zealously applied himself to the acquirement of knowledge, and who having adorned his soul not with a foreign but its own proper ornament, [115] temperance, justice, fortitude, freedom and truth, thus waits for his passage to Hades, as one who is ready to depart whenever destiny shall summon him. You then,' he continued, 'Simmias and Cebes, and the rest, will each of you depart at some future time; but now destiny summons me, as a tragic writer would say, and it is nearly time for me to betake myself to the bath; for it appears to me to be better to drink the poison after I have bathed myself, and not to trouble the women with washing my dead body.'

When he had thus spoken Crito said, 'So be it, Socrates, but what commands have you to give to these or to me, either respecting your children or any other matter, in attending to which we can most oblige you?'

'What I always say, Crito,' he replied, 'nothing new; that by taking care of yourselves you will oblige both me and mine, and yourselves, whatever you do, though you should not now promise it; but if you neglect yourselves, and will not live as it were in the footsteps of what has been now and formerly said, even though you should promise much at present, and that earnestly, you will do no good at all.'

'We will endeavour then so to do,' he said; 'but how shall we bury you?'

'Just as you please,' he said, 'if only you can catch me, and I do not escape from you.' And at the same time, smiling gently and looking round on us, he said, 'I cannot persuade Crito, my friends, that I am that Socrates who is now conversing with you, and who methodises each part of the discourse; but he thinks that I am he whom he will shortly behold dead, and asks how he should bury me. But that which I some time since argued at length, that when I have drunk the poison I shall no longer remain with you, but shall depart to some happy state of the blessed, this I seem to have urged to him in vain, though I meant at the same time to console both you and myself. Be ye then my sureties to Crito,' he said, 'in an obligation contrary to that which he made to the judges; for he undertook that I should remain; but do you be sureties that, when I die, I shall not remain, but shall depart, that Crito may more easily bear it, and when he sees my body either burnt or buried, may not be afflicted for me, as if I suffered some dreadful thing, nor say at my interment that Socrates is laid out, or is carried out, or is buried. For be well assured,' he said, 'most excellent Crito, that to speak improperly is not only culpable as to the thing itself but likewise occasions some injury to our souls. You must have a good courage then, and say that you bury my body, [116] and bury it in such a manner as is pleasing to you, and as you think is most agreeable to our laws.'

When he had said thus he rose, and went into a chamber to bathe, and Crito followed him, but he directed us to wait for him. We waited, therefore, conversing among ourselves about what had been said, and considering it again, and sometimes speaking about our calamity, how severe it would be to us, sincerely thinking that, like those who are deprived of a father, we should pass the rest of our life as orphans. When he had bathed, and his children were brought to him, for he had two little sons and one grown up, and the women belonging to his family were come, having conversed with them in the presence of Crito, and given them such injunctions as he wished, he directed the women and children to go away, and then returned to us. And it was now near sunset; for he spent a considerable time within. But when he came from bathing he sat down, and did not speak much afterwards; then the officer of the Eleven came in, and standing near him, said, 'Socrates, I shall not have to find that fault with you that I do with others, that they are angry with me, and curse me, when, by order of the archons, I bid them drink the poison. But you, on all other occasions during the time you have been here, I have found to be the most noble, meek and excellent man of all that ever came into this place: and therefore I am now well convinced that you will not be angry with me, for you know who are to blame, but with them. Now, then, for you know what I came to announce to you, farewell, and endeavour to bear what is inevitable as easily as possible.' And at the same time, bursting into tears, he turned away and withdrew.

And Socrates, looking after him, said, 'And thou, too, farewell, we will do as you direct.' At the same time turning to us, he said, 'How courteous the man is; during the whole time I have been here he has visited me, and conversed with me sometimes, and proved the worthiest of men; and now how generously he weeps for me. But come, Crito, let us obey him, and let someone bring the poison, if it is ready pounded, but if not, let the man pound it.'

Then Crito said, 'But I think, Socrates, that the sun is still on the mountains, and has not yet set. Besides, I know that others have drunk the poison very late, after it had been announced to them, and have supped and drunk freely, and some even have enjoyed the objects of their love. Do not hasten then, for there is yet time.'

Upon this Socrates replied, 'These men whom you mention, Crito, do these things with good reason, for they think they shall gain by so doing, and I, too, with good reason shall not do so; for I think I shall gain nothing by drinking a little later, except to become ridiculous to myself, [117] in being so fond of life, and sparing of it when none any longer remains. Go then,' he said, 'obey, and do not resist.'

Crito, having heard this, nodded to the boy that stood near. And the boy, having gone out, and staid for some time, came, bringing with him the man that was to administer the poison, who brought it ready pounded in a cup. And Socrates, on seeing the man, said, 'Well, my good friend, as you are skilled in these matters, what must I do?'

'Nothing else,' he replied, 'than when you have drunk it walk about, until there is a heaviness in your legs, then lie down; thus it will do its purpose.' And at the same time he held out the cup to Socrates. And he having received it very cheerfully, Echecrates, neither trembling nor changing at all in colour or countenance, but, as he was wont, looking steadfastly at the man, said, 'What say you of this potion, with respect to making a libation to anyone, is it lawful or not?'

'We only pound so much, Socrates,' he said, 'as we think sufficient to drink.'

'I understand you,' he said, 'but it is certainly both lawful and right to pray to the gods, that my departure hence thither may be happy; which therefore I pray, and so may it be.' And as he said this he drank it off readily and calmly. Thus far, most of us were with difficulty able to restrain ourselves from weeping, but when we saw him drinking, and having finished the draught, we could do so no longer; but in spite of myself, the tears came in full torrent, so that, covering my face, I wept for myself, for I did not weep for him, but for my own fortune, in being deprived of such a friend. But Crito, even before me, when he could not restrain his tears, had risen up. But Apollodorus even before this had not ceased weeping, and then bursting into an agony of grief, weeping and lamenting, he pierced the heart of everyone present, except Socrates himself. But he said, 'What are you doing, my admirable friends? I indeed, for this reason chiefly, sent away the women, that they might not commit any folly of this kind. For I have heard that it is right to die with good omens. Be quiet, therefore, and bear up.'

When we heard this we were ashamed, and restrained our tears. But he, having walked about, when he said that his legs were growing heavy, laid down on his back; for the man so directed him. And at the same time he who gave him the poison, taking hold of him, after a short interval examined his feet and legs; and then having pressed his foot hard, he asked if he felt it: [118] he said that he did not. And after this he pressed his thighs; and thus going higher, he showed us that he was growing cold and stiff. Then Socrates touched himself, and said that when the poison reached his heart he should then depart. But now the parts around the lower belly were almost cold; when uncovering himself, for he had been covered over, he said, and they were his last words, 'Crito, we owe a cock to Aesculapius; pay it, therefore, and do not neglect it.'

'It shall be done,' said Crito, 'but consider whether you have anything else to say.'

To this question he gave no reply; but shortly after he gave a convulsive movement, and the man covered him, and his eyes were fixed; and Crito, perceiving it, closed his mouth and eyes.

This, Echecrates, was the end of our friend, a man, as we may say, the best of all of his time that we have known, and moreover, the most wise and just. (114 D–118 A, tr. H. Cary and H. Davis)

2.5 Dialogues of the Middle Period

2.5.1 Phaedrus

2.5.1.1 SOCRATES: Just as I was about to cross the river, I was made aware of my divine monitor's wonted sign – now it never occurs save to deter me from something or other I am intending to do – and methought therefrom I heard a voice from this very spot, forbidding me to depart hence till I had purified myself, as though I had been guilty of some offence against Heaven. (242 B, tr. J. Wright)

2.5.1.2 SOCRATES: Beloved Pan, and all ye other gods who here abide, grant me to be beautiful in the inner man, and all I have of outer things to be at peace with those within. May I count the wise man only rich. And may my store of gold be such as none but the good can bear. (279 B, tr. J. Wright)

2.5.2 The Banquet

2.5.2.1 The whole assembly praised his discourse, and Aristophanes was on the point of making some remarks on the allusion made by Socrates to him in a part of his discourse, when suddenly they heard a loud knocking at the door of the vestibule, and a clamour as of revellers, attended by a flute-player. – 'Go, boys,' said Agathon, 'and see who is there: if they are any of our friends call them in; if not, say that we have already done drinking.' – A minute afterwards they heard the voice of Alcibiades in the vestibule excessively drunk and roaring out: 'Where is Agathon? Lead me to Agathon!' – The flute-player, and some of his companions then led him in, and placed him against the door-post, crowned with a thick crown of ivy and violets, and having a quantity of fillets on his head. – 'My friends,' he cried out, 'hail! I am excessively drunk already, but I'll drink with you, if you will. If not, we will go away after having crowned Agathon, for which purpose I came. I assure you that I could not come yesterday, but I am now here with these fillets round my temples, that from my own head I may crown his who, with your leave, is the most beautiful and wisest of men. Are you laughing at me because I am drunk? [213] Ay, I know what I say is true, whether you laugh or not. But tell me at once whether I shall come in, or no. Will you drink with me?'

Agathon and the whole party desired him to come in, and recline among them; so he came in, led by his companions. He then unbound his fillets and he might crown Agathon, and though Socrates was just before his eyes, he did not see him, but sat down by Agathon, between Socrates and him, for Socrates moved out of the way to make room for him. When he sat down he embraced Agathon and crowned him; and Agathon desired the slaves to untie his sandals, that he might make a third, and recline on the same couch. 'By all means,' said Alcibiades, 'but what third companion have we here?' And at the same time turning round, and seeing Socrates, he leaped up and cried out: 'Oh Hercules! what have we here? You, Socrates, lying in ambush for me wherever I go! and meeting me just as you always do, when I least expected to see you! And, now, what are you come here for? Why have you chosen to recline exactly in this place, and not near Aristophanes, or anyone else who is, or wishes to be, ridiculous, but have contrived to take your place beside the most delightful person of the whole party?' – 'Agathon,' said Socrates, 'see if you cannot defend me. I declare my friendship for this man is a bad business: from the moment that I first began to know him I have never been permitted to converse with, or so much as look upon, anyone else. If I do, he is so jealous and suspicious that he does the most extravagant things, and hardly refrains from beating me. I entreat you to prevent him from doing anything of that kind at present. Procure a reconciliation: or, if he perseveres in attempting any violence, I entreat you to defend me.' – 'Indeed,' said Alcibiades, 'I will not be reconciled to you; I shall find another opportunity to punish you for this. But now,' said he, addressing Agathon, 'lend me some of those fillets, that I may crown the wonderful head of this fellow, lest I incur the blame that, having crowned you, I neglected to crown him who conquers all men with his discourses, not yesterday alone as you did, but ever.'

Saying this, he took the fillets, and having bound the head of Socrates, and again having reclined, said: 'Come, my friends, you seem to be sober enough. You must not flinch, but drink, for that was your agreement with me before I came in. I choose as president, until you have drunk enough – myself. Come, Agathon, if you have got a great goblet, fetch it out. But no matter, that wine-cooler will do; bring it, boy!' And observing that it held more than eight cups, [214] he first drank it off, and then ordered it to be filled for Socrates, and said: 'Observe, my friends, I cannot invent any scheme against Socrates, for he will drink as much as anyone desires him, and not be in the least drunk.' Socrates, after the boy had filled up, drank it off; and Eryximachus said: 'Shall we then have no conversation or singing over our cups, but drink down stupidly, just as if we were thirsty?' And Alcibiades said: 'Ah, Eryximachus, I did not see you before; hail, you excellent son of a wise and excellent father!' – 'Hail to you also,' replied Eryximachus, 'but what shall we do?' – 'Whatever you command, for we ought to submit to your directions; a physician is worth a hundred common men. Command us as you please.' – 'Listen then,' said Eryximachus, 'before you came in each of us had agreed to deliver as eloquent a discourse as he could in praise of Love, beginning at the right hand; all the rest of us have fulfilled our engagement; you have not spoken, and yet have drunk with us: you ought to bear your part in the discussion; and having done so, command what you please to Socrates, who shall have the privilege of doing so to his right-hand neighbour, and so on to the others.' – 'Indeed, there appears some justice in your proposal, Eryximachus, though it is rather unfair to induce a drunken man to set his discourse in competition with that of those who are sober. And, besides, did Socrates really persuade you that what he just said about me was true, or do you not know that matters are in fact exactly the reverse of his representation? For I seriously believe that, should I praise in his presence, be he god or man, any other beside himself, he would not keep his hands off me. But I assure you, Socrates, I will praise no one beside yourself in your presence.'

'Do so, then,' said Eryximachus, 'praise Socrates if you please.' – 'What,' said Alcibiades, 'shall I attack him, and punish him before you all?' – 'What have you got into your head now,' said Socrates, 'are you going to expose me to ridicule, and to misrepresent me? Or what are you going to do?' – 'I will only speak the truth; will you permit me on this condition?' – 'I not only permit, but exhort you to say all the truth you know,' replied Socrates. – 'I obey you willingly,' said Alcibiades, 'and if I advance anything untrue, do you, if you please, interrupt me, and convict me of misrepresentation, for I would never willingly speak falsely. [215] And bear with me if I do not relate things in their order, but just as I remember them, for it is not easy for a man in my present condition to enumerate systematically all your singularities.

'I will begin the praise of Socrates by comparing him to a certain statue. Perhaps he will think that this statue is introduced for the sake of ridicule, but I assure you that it is necessary for the illustration of truth. I assert, then, that Socrates is exactly like those Silenuses that sit in the sculptors' shops, and which are carved holding flutes or pipes, but which, when divided in two, are found to contain withinside the images of the gods. I assert that Socrates is like the satyr Marsyas. That your form and appearance are like these satyrs', I think that even you will not venture to deny; and how like you are to them in all other things, now hear. Are you not scornful and petulant? If you deny this I will bring witnesses. Are you not a piper, and far more wonderful a one than he? For Marsyas, and whoever now pipes the music that he taught, for that music which is of heaven, and described as being taught by Marsyas, enchants men through the power of the mouth. For if any musician, be he skilful or not, awakens this music it alone enables him to retain the minds of men, and from the divinity of its nature makes evident those who are in want of the gods and initiation. You differ only from Marsyas in this circumstance, that you effect without instruments, by mere words, all that he can do. For when we hear Pericles, or any other accomplished orator, deliver a discourse no one, as it were, cares anything about it. But when anyone hears you, or even your words related by another, though ever so rude and unskilful a speaker, be that person a woman, man or child, we are struck and retained, as it were, by the discourse clinging to our mind.

'If I was not afraid that I am a great deal too drunk I would confirm to you by an oath the strange effects which I assure you I have suffered from his words, and suffer still; for when I hear him speak, my heart leaps up far more than the hearts of those who celebrate the Corybantic mysteries; my tears are poured out as he talks, a thing I have seen happen to many others beside myself. I have heard Pericles and other excellent orators, and have been pleased with their discourses, but I suffered nothing of this kind; nor was my soul ever on those occasions disturbed and filled with self-reproach, as if it were slavishly laid prostrate. [216] But this Marsyas here has often affected me in the way I describe, until the life which I lead seemed hardly worth living. Do not deny it, Socrates, for I well know that if even now I chose to listen to you I could not resist, but should again suffer the same effects. For, my friends, he forces me to confess that while I myself am still in want of many things, I neglect my own necessities, and attend to those of the Athenians. I stop my ears, therefore, as from the Syrens, and flee away as fast as possible, that I may not sit down beside him and grow old in listening to his talk. For this man has reduced me to feel the sentiment of shame, which I imagine no one would readily believe was in me; he alone inspires me with remorse and awe. For I feel in his presence my incapacity of refuting what he says, or of refusing to do that which he directs; but when I depart from him, the glory which the multitude confers overwhelms me. I escape, therefore, and hide myself from him, and when I see him I am overwhelmed with humiliation, because I have neglected to do what I have confessed to him ought to be done; and often and often have I wished that he were no longer to be seen among men. But if that were to happen, I well know that I should suffer far greater pain; so that where I can turn, or what I can do with this man, I know not. All this have I and many others suffered from the pipings of this satyr.

'And observe, how like he is to what I said, and what a wonderful power he possesses. Know that there is not one of you who is aware of the real nature of Socrates; but since I have begun, I will make him plain to you. You observe how passionately Socrates affects the intimacy of those who are beautiful, and how ignorant he professes himself to be; appearances in themselves excessively Silenic. This, my friends, is the external form with which, like one of the sculptured Sileni, he has clothed himself; for if you open him you will find within admirable temperance and wisdom. For he cares not for mere beauty, but despises more than anyone can imagine all external possessions, whether it be beauty or wealth, or glory, or any other thing for which the multitude felicitates the possessor. He esteems these things and us who honour them, as nothing, and lives among men, making all the objects of their admiration the playthings of his irony. But I know not if anyone of you have ever seen the divine images which are within, when he has been opened and is serious. I have seen them, and they are so supremely beautiful, so golden, so divine, and wonderful, [217]

that everything which Socrates commands surely ought to be obeyed, even like the voice of a God.

[219] 'At one time we were fellow-soldiers, and had our mess together in the camp before Potidaea. Socrates there overcame not only me but everyone beside, in endurance of toils: when, as often happens in a campaign, we were reduced to few provisions, there were none who could sustain hunger like Socrates; [220] and when we had plenty he alone seemed to enjoy our military fare. He never drank much willingly, but when he was compelled he conquered all, even in that to which he was least accustomed; and what is most astonishing, no person ever saw Socrates drunk either then or at any other time. In the depth of winter (and the winters there are excessively rigid) he sustained calmly incredible hardships; and among other things, while the frost was intolerably severe, and no one went out of their tents, or if they went out, wrapt themselves up carefully, and put fleeces under their feet, and bound their legs with hairy skins, Socrates went out only with the same cloak on that he usually wore, and walked barefoot upon the ice; more easily, indeed, than those who had sandalled themselves so delicately: so that the soldiers thought that he did it to mock their want of fortitude. It would indeed be worth while to commemorate all that this brave man did and endured in that expedition. In one instance he was seen early in the morning, standing in one place wrapt in meditation; and as he seemed not to be able to unravel the subject of his thoughts, he still continued to stand as inquiring and discussing within himself, and when noon came, the soldiers observed him, and said to one another – "Socrates has been standing there thinking, ever since the morning." At last some Ionians came to the spot, and having supped, as it was summer, bringing their blankets, they lay down

to sleep in the cool; they observed that Socrates continued to stand there the whole night until morning, and that, when the sun rose, he saluted it with a prayer and departed.

'I ought not to omit what Socrates is in battle. For in that battle after which the generals decreed to me the prize of courage, Socrates alone of all men was the saviour of my life, standing by me when I had fallen and was wounded, and preserving both myself and my arms from the hands of the enemy. On that occasion I entreated the generals to decree the prize, as it was most due, to him. And this, O Socrates, you cannot deny, that the generals, wishing to conciliate a person of my rank, desired to give me the prize, you were far more earnestly desirous than the generals that this glory should be attributed not to your-self, but me.

'But to see Socrates when our army was defeated and scattered in flight at [Delium], was a spectacle worthy to behold. [221] On that occasion I was among the cavalry, and he on foot, heavily armed. After the total rout of our troops he and Laches retreated together; I came up by chance, and seeing them, bade them be of good cheer, for that I would not leave them. As I was on horseback, and therefore less occupied by a regard of my own situation, I could better observe than at Potidaea the beautiful spectacle ex-hibited by Socrates on this emergency. How superior was he to Laches in presence of mind and courage! Your representation of him on the stage, O Aristophanes, was not wholly unlike his real self on this occasion, for he walked and darted his regards around with a majestic composure, looking tranquilly both on his friends and enemies; so that it was evident to everyone, even from afar, that whoever should venture to attack him would encounter a desperate resistance. He and his companion thus

departed in safety; for those who are scattered in flight are pursued and killed, while men hesitate to touch those who exhibit such a countenance as that of Socrates even in defeat.

'Many other and most wonderful qualities might well be praised in Socrates; but such as these might singly be attributed to others. But that which is unparalleled in Socrates is that he is unlike, and above comparison with, all other men, whether those who have lived in ancient times, or those who exist now. For it may be conjectured that Brasidas and many others are such as was Achilles. Pericles deserves com-parison with Nestor and Antenor; and other excellent persons of various times may, with probability, be drawn into comparison with each other. But to such a singular man as this, both himself and his discourses are so uncommon, no one, should he seek, would find a parallel among the present or the past generations of mankind; unless they should say that he resembled those with whom I lately compared him, for, assuredly, he and his discourses are like nothing but the Sileni and the Satyrs. At first I forgot to make you observe how like his discourses are to those Satyrs when they are opened, for if anyone will listen to the talk of Socrates it will appear to him at first extremely ridiculous; the phrases and expressions which he employs fold around his exterior the skin, as it were, of a rude and wanton Satyr. He is always talking about great market-asses, and brass-founders, and leather-cutters, and skin-dressers; and this is his perpetual custom, so that any dull and unobservant person might easily laugh at his discourse. [222] But if anyone should see it opened, as it were, and get within the sense of his words, he would then find that they, alone of all that enters into the mind of man to utter, had a profound and persuasive meaning, and that they were most divine; and that they presented to the mind innumerable images of every excellence, and that they tended towards objects of the highest moment, or rather towards all that he who seeks the possession of what is supremely beautiful and good need regard as essential to the accomplishment of his ambition.

'These are the things, my friends, for which I praise Socrates.'

Alcibiades having said this, the whole party burst into a laugh at his frankness, and Socrates said, 'You seem to be sober enough, Alcibiades, else you would not have made such a circuit of words, only to hide the main design for which you made this long speech, and which, as it were carelessly, you just throw in at the last; now, as if you had not said all this for the mere purpose of dividing me and Agathon? You think that I ought to be your friend, and to care for no one else. I have found you out; it is evident enough for what design you invented all this Satyrical and Silenic drama. But, my dear Agathon, do not let his device succeed. I entreat you to permit no one to throw discord between us.' – 'No doubt,' said Agathon, 'he sat down between us only that he might divide us; but this shall not assist his scheme, for I will come and sit near you.' – 'Do so,' said Socrates, 'come, there is room for you by me.' – 'Oh, Jupiter!' exclaimed Alcibiades, 'what I endure from that man! He thinks to subdue every way; but, at least, I pray you, let Agathon remain between us.' – 'Impossible,' said Socrates, 'you have just praised me; I ought to praise him sitting at my right hand. If Agathon is placed beside you, will he not praise me before I praise him? Now, my dear friend, [223] allow the young man to receive what praise I can give him. I have a great desire to pronounce his encomium.' – 'Quick, quick, Alcibiades,' said Agathon, 'I cannot stay here, I must change

my place, or Socrates will not praise me.' – Agathon then arose to take his place near Socrates.

He had no sooner reclined than there came in a number of revellers – for someone who had gone out had left the door open – and took their places on the vacant couches, and everything became full of confusion; and no order being observed, everyone was obliged to drink a great quantity of wine. Eryximachus, and Phaedrus, and some others, said Aristodemus, went home to bed; that, for his part, he went to sleep on his couch, and slept long and soundly – the nights were then long – until the cock crew in the morning. When he awoke he found that some were still fast asleep, and others had gone home, and that Aristophanes, Agathon and Socrates had alone stood it out, and were still drinking out of a great goblet which they passed round and round. Socrates was disputing between them. The beginning of their discussion Aristodemus said that he did not recollect, because he was asleep; but it was terminated by Socrates forcing them to confess, that the same person is able to compose both tragedy and comedy, and that the foundations of the tragic and comic arts were essentially the same. They, rather convicted than convinced, went to sleep. Aristophanes first awoke, and then, it being broad daylight, Agathon. Socrates, having put them to sleep, went away, Aristodemus following him, and coming to the Lyceum he washed himself, as he would have done anywhere else, and after having spent the day there in his accustomed manner, went home in the evening. (212 C, omitting 217 A–219 E, tr. P. B. Shelley)

2.5.2.2 I thought that he was keen on my looks, and I thought this an incredible stroke of luck, a real gift of the gods. All that I had to do was to say Yes to him, and all his knowledge would be mine to listen to. I had pretty strong views about my looks. I worked it all out. Previously I'd never been in his presence on my own without a chaperon. Now I sent my attendant away. I was alone with Socrates. I'm telling you the absolute truth. Listen closely, and, Socrates, if what I say isn't true, just you pull me up. Friends, we were alone together. I thought that he'd immediately start the billing and cooing of lovers on their own together; it was a thrilling thought. Nothing of the kind. His conversation was the same as ever. We spent a whole day together, and at the end of it, off he went.

Next I proposed successfully that we might take some exercise together: I thought something was bound to happen there. He came to the gymnasium and wrestled with me several times without any spectators present. Would you believe it? I made no progress with him. I was getting nowhere. I decided on an all-out attack on the man; it would be irresistible. I had shown my hand; I had to find out how things stood. I invited him to dinner, a piece of direct seduction. He was in no hurry to accept, but eventually agreed to come. On the first occasion he had dinner and said he was going. I was too embarrassed to stop him. I tried again. After dinner I kept the conversation going far into the night. When he said that it was time to go, I protested the late hour, and insisted on his staying. He turned in on the couch next to mine – the one he'd been on for dinner. There was no one sleeping in the house except the two of us.

So far I've said nothing to bring a blush to my cheek. You'd never have heard the rest if there weren't something in the old saying 'Truth in wine': add children or not, as you like. Besides, I've come to give a testimonial to Socrates: it wouldn't be right to ignore his superior attitude to me. I'm like a man suffering from snake-bite. When this happens they said that you try to find people who've suffered in the same way: they're the only ones who will understand and sympathise if you lose control of your actions or your [218] tongue with the pain. I've been bitten by something worse than a snake. I've been bitten in the most sensitive part, the heart or soul or whatever you call it. I've been bitten by philosophical conversation. It's much fiercer than any snake; once it gets hold of a tender mind of reasonable ability, it does just what it likes. Look at Phaedrus and Agathon and Eryximachus and Pausanias and Aristodemus and Aristophanes and all. What about Socrates? What about all the rest of you? You've all experienced philosophic madness, philosophic inspiration. So you'll all listen. You'll all sympathise with what I did. You'll all sympathise with what I'm saying. The servants must shut their ears tight: so must any other uninitiated ignoramuses.

Friends, the servants had packed up, the lights were out. No need for embroidery, I said to myself; tell him straight what you want. So I shook him and said, 'Socrates are you asleep?' 'No,' he said. 'Do you know what I've decided?' 'No, what?' he said. 'I think you're the only lover I've ever had fit for me, but you're too shy to tell me. I'll tell you what I feel. You can have what you want. You can call on my resources or my friends too: it's all the same thing. If I've one ambition more than another it's to make the best of myself, and I can't think of a more competent collaborator. I should find it much harder to explain to the people who count why I refused to gratify a man of your quality than to explain to the people who don't count why I didn't refuse.'

He listened to what I said and replied with his characteristic mock-modesty: 'My dear Alcibiades, you must be a real genius if you're telling the truth, and I really have the power to effect an improvement in you. You must be able to see a beauty in me which leaves your good looks standing. So you've set your eyes on that; you're trying to get a share of it; you want to bargain beauty for beauty, and you intend to get the better of the bargain. You are plotting to get real beauty in exchange for sham; [219] that would be "Gold for bronze"! You'd better think twice. Suppose I were really worthless. You see the mind's eye begins to see clearly only when physical sight is over the top; yours isn't there yet.' I answered: 'I've said my say, and every word's true. You must decide what's best for both of us.' 'A good idea,' he said. 'We will indeed resolve for the future to do what's best for both of us – in this and in everything else.'

So we talked. I'd fired my shots, and suspected I'd scored a hit. So I got up. I didn't let him get another word in. I put my blanket over him – it was winter – climbed underneath his covering, threw both arms round him and lay there all through the night. What a man! He's out of this world. Socrates, you can't deny that I'm telling the truth. When I did this he had the effrontery to turn up his nose at my youth and good looks and jeer at the one thing I was really proud of, gentlemen of the jury – yes, you are a jury trying Socrates for arrogance. By all the gods – and goddesses – when I got up I'd no more *slept with* Socrates than if I'd been with my father or elder brother.

You can imagine what I felt like after that. I thought I'd been insulted, but I was still in love with his character, his courage, his control. I never thought to meet a man who combined intellectual brilliance and physical toughness as he did. I couldn't cut myself off from his company in a rage.

I couldn't find any way of winning him. I knew that money couldn't touch him any more than a sword could touch Ajax. The one means I thought was sure to catch him had already let me down. I was at my wits' end. Talk of slavery! You never saw anything like my slavery to him. (217 A–219 E)

This is the passage which Shelley was too prudish to include.

2.5.3 The Republic

2.5.3.1 While we were still in the middle of our discussion, Thrasymachus was, more than once, bent on interrupting the conversation with objections; but he was checked on each occasion by those who sat by, who wished to hear the argument out. However, when I had made this last remark and we had come to a pause he could restrain himself no longer, but, gathering himself up like a wild beast, he sprang upon us, as if he would tear us in pieces. I and Polemarchus were terrified and startled; while Thrasymachus, raising his voice to the company, said, What nonsense has possessed you and Polemarchus all this time, Socrates? And why do you play the fool together with your mutual complaisance? No; if you really wish to understand what justice is, do not confine yourself to asking questions, and making a display of refuting the answers that are returned (for you are aware that it is easier to ask questions than to answer them); but give us an answer also yourself, and tell us what you assert justice to be, and let me beg you to beware of defining it as the obligatory, or the advantageous, or the profitable, or the lucrative, or the expedient; but whatever your definition may be, let it be clear and precise: for I will not accept your answer, if you talk such trash as that.

When I heard this speech I was

astounded, and gazed at the speaker in terror; and I think if I had not set eyes on him before he eyed me I should have been struck dumb. But as it was, when he began to be exasperated by the conversation I had looked him in the face first: so that I was enabled to reply to him, and said with a slight tremble; Thrasymachus, do not be hard upon us. If I and Polemarchus are making mistakes in our examination of the subject, be assured that the error is involuntary. You do not suppose that if we were looking for a piece of gold we should ever willingly be so complaisant to one another in the search as to spoil the chance of finding it; and therefore, pray do not suppose that, in seeking for justice, which is a thing more precious than many pieces of gold, we should give way to one another so weakly as you describe, instead of doing our very best to bring it to light. You, my friend, may think so, if you choose; [337] but my belief is that the subject is beyond our powers. Surely, then, we might very reasonably expect to be pitied, not harshly treated, by such clever men as you.

When he had heard my reply he burst out laughing very scornfully, and said: O Hercules! here is an instance of that mock-humility which Socrates affects. I knew how it would be, and warned the company that you would refuse to answer, and would feign ignorance, and do anything rather than reply, if anyone asked you a question. (1, 336 B–337 A, tr. J. Ll. Davies and J. D. Vaughan)

2.5.3.2 Tell me, do you think there is such a thing as a horse's function?

I do.

Would you, then, describe the function of a horse, or of anything else whatever, as that work, for the accomplishment of which it is either the sole or the best instrument?

I do not understand.

Look at it this way. Can you see with anything besides eyes?

Certainly not.

Can you hear with anything besides ears?

No.

Then should we not justly say that seeing and hearing are the functions of these organs?

Yes, certainly.

[353] Again, you might cut off a vine-shoot with a carving knife, or chisel, or many other tools?

Undoubtedly.

But with no tool, I imagine, so well as with the pruning knife made for the purpose.

True.

Then shall we not define pruning to be the function of the pruning knife?

By all means.

Now then, I think, you will better understand what I wished to learn from you just now, when I asked whether the function of a thing is not that work for the accomplishment of which it is either the sole or the best instrument?

I do understand, and I believe that this is in every case the function of a thing.

Very well: do you not also think that everything which has an appointed function has also a proper *virtue*? Let us revert to the same instances; we say that the eyes have a function?

They have.

Then have the eyes a virtue also?

They have.

And the ears: did we assign them a function?

Yes.

Then have they a virtue also?

They have.

And is it the same with all other things?

The same.

Attend then: Do you suppose that the eyes could discharge their own function well if they had not their own proper virtue – that virtue being replaced by a vice?

How could they? You mean, probably, if sight is replaced by blindness.

I mean, whatever their virtue be; for I am not come to that question yet. At present I am asking whether it is through their own peculiar virtue that things perform their proper functions well, and through their own peculiar vice that they perform them ill?

You cannot be wrong in that.

Then, if the ears lose their own virtue, will they execute their functions ill?

Certainly.

May we include all other things under the same proposition?

I think we may.

Come, then, consider this point next. Has the soul any function which could not be executed by means of anything else whatsoever? For example, could we in justice assign superintendence and government, deliberation and the like, to anything but the soul, or should we pronounce them to be peculiar to it?

We could ascribe them to nothing else.

Again, shall we declare life to be a function of the soul?

Decidedly.

Do we not also maintain that the soul has a virtue?

We do.

Then can it ever so happen, Thrasymachus, that the soul will perform its functions well when destitute of its own peculiar virtue, or is that impossible?

Impossible.

Then a bad soul must needs exercise authority and superintendence ill, and a good soul must do all these things well.

Unquestionably.

Now did we not grant that justice was a virtue of the soul, and injustice a vice?

We did.

Consequently the just soul and the just man will live well, and the unjust man ill?

[354] Apparently, according to your argument.

And you will allow that he who lives well is blessed and happy, and that he who lives otherwise is the reverse.

Unquestionably.

Consequently the just man is happy, and the unjust man miserable.

Let us suppose them to be so.

But surely it is not misery, but happiness, that is advantageous.

Undoubtedly.

Never then, my excellent Thrasymachus, is injustice more advantageous than justice.

Well, Socrates, let this be your entertainment for the feast of Bendis.

I have to thank *you* for it, Thrasymachus, because you recovered your temper, and left off being angry with me. (1, 352 B–354 A, tr. J. Ll. Davies and J. D. Vaughan)

2.5.3.3 Unless it happen either that philosophers acquire the kingly power in states, or that those who are now called kings and potentates, be imbued with a sufficient measure of genuine philosophy, that is to say, unless political power and philosophy be united in the same person, most of those minds which at present pursue one to the exclusion of the other being peremptorily debarred from either, there will be no deliverance, my dear Glaucon, for cities, nor yet, I believe, for the human race; neither can the commonwealth, which we have now sketched in theory, ever till then grow into a possibility, and see the light of day. But a consciousness how entirely this would contradict the common opinion made me all along so reluctant to give expression to it: for it is difficult to see that there is no other way by which happiness can be attained, by the state or by the individual.

(5, 473 C–E, tr. J. Ll. Davies and J. D. Vaughan).

A key-passage, put in the mouth of Socrates but representing Plato's own development (cf. **2.7.2**).

2.5.4. Theaetetus

2.5.4.1 SOCRATES: Aha! you are in travail, my dear Theaetetus. It is pregnancy that is the matter with you.

THEAETETUS: I do not know, Socrates. I only tell you how I feel about it.

[149] SOCRATES: What! will you have the face to tell me you have never heard that I am the son of an excellent and lusty midwife, Phaenarete?

THEAETETUS: Yes, I have heard that.

SOCRATES: And have you heard, too, that I practise the same profession myself?

THEAETETUS: No indeed.

SOCRATES: Well, you must know that I certainly do. But do not tell it of me to others; for it has not been discovered that I have the art, my friend, and people, not knowing it, only say that I am a most curious person and go about puzzling men. You have heard that, perhaps?

THEAETETUS: Yes, I have.

SOCRATES: Shall I tell you the reason, then?

THEAETETUS: By all means.

SOCRATES: You must call to mind the whole principle of midwifery; and you will understand better what I mean. I suppose you know that no one practises as a midwife who can still conceive and bear children, but only those who are past child-bearing.

THEAETETUS: Certainly.

SOCRATES: Now they say that this goes back to Artemis, because she, a childless goddess, is the patroness of childbirth. Therefore she gave the art, not indeed to the barren, because

human nature is too week to deal aright with things of which it has no experience, but to those who can no longer bear through age, honouring in them the likeness to herself.

THEAETETUS: That seems likely.

SOCRATES: And is not this likely, too, or rather certain: that midwives can tell better than others whether women are pregnant or not?

THEAETETUS: Assuredly.

SOCRATES: Furthermore, they are able, by means of drugs and charms, to bring on the pains of labour and to deaden them at their will; yes, and to make those whose labour is hard bring forth; and if they think it best that the child should miscarry, they make it miscarry.

THEAETETUS: That is so.

SOCRATES: Well, then, have you noticed this, too, about them, that they are in addition the cleverest of matchmakers, being complete adepts at knowing what woman will bear the best children to what man?

THEAETETUS: I am not sure that I have heard that.

SOCRATES: Well, let me tell you that they pride themselves even more on this than on their actual midwifery. For consider a moment – is it the same art or two different arts, do you think, that deal with the culture and harvesting of crops, and with the selection of the best land for planting and sowing a particular sort?

THEAETETUS: One and the same, certainly.

SOCRATES: And do you think, my friend, that the corresponding arts in the case of a woman will be different?

[150] THEAETETUS: No, probably not.

SOCRATES: No indeed. But there is an immoral and unscientific method of bringing a man and a woman together which we know as procuring, and the existence of this makes the midwives, who are very self-respecting people, loth to act as matchmakers, for fear it may lead to the worse charge; though all the same it is, you will admit, only the true midwife that can be expected to make proper matches.

THEAETETUS: So it appears.

SOCRATES: These, then, are their functions; and very important ones they are, but not so important as mine. For in the case of women there is not the further difficulty that the offspring is sometimes genuine and sometimes spurious, and that it is hard to distinguish between them. Were it so, it would be their crowning achievement to decide which was true and which false – do you not think so?

THEAETETUS: I do.

SOCRATES: Now my method of midwifery is like theirs in most respects, but differs in that I apply it to men and not to women, and that it is their souls I treat and not their bodies. But my greatest feat is that I am able to test in every kind of way whether the offspring of a young man's intellect is an imposture and a lie, or something genuine and true. In one point I and the midwives are in the same position: I am sterile of wisdom, and the reproach that has often been made against me, that I ask questions of others, but never answer any by any chance myself, because I have nothing wise to say, is a true reproach. And the cause of it is this: it is divinely ordained that I should help others to bring forth, but bring forth nothing myself. I am, then, myself no such prodigy of wisdom nor can I point to any great invention, born of my soul; but those who pass their time with me, though at first they seem, some of them, quite unintelligent, nevertheless in my company all, as time goes on, all to whom heaven is kind, progress amazingly – or so it seems to them and to others. And all the while it is clear that they have never learnt anything from me, but have discovered for themselves in their own minds treasures manifold for their possession. Of this birth I under heaven am the cause. And this one can plainly see; for many ere now, who did not know it, thinking themselves the cause and holding me of slight account, have left me, either of their own motion or on the advice of friends, before their time; whereafter the rest of their ideas miscarried through evil associations, and those I had helped them to bring forth they reared badly and lost; for they cared less for truth than for lies and phantoms; and at the last they were seen by others and by themselves, too, to be unlearned fools. One of them was Aristides, the son of Lysimachus; and there are many others. [151] And when they come back to me, wanting my company, and begging me to take them, some of them the voice I hear within me forbids me to receive, but some it allows, and once again the good that is in them grows unbidden. Now those who spend their time with me are like women in travail in this way, too: they suffer pangs, and are plagued and perplexed day and night, and that far worse than women; and these pangs my art has power to excite and to allay. So much for them. But there are some whom I find not to be pregnant yet, and in no need of my skill; and for these, with the best will in the world, I seek out suitable matches, and, if I may say so, I divine fairly correctly whose intercourse will do them good. Many of them I have put out to Prodicus, and many to other giants of wisdom.

Now I have told you this long story, my friend, because I suspect that (as you think yourself) you are in travail with something that you have conceived in your mind. Approach me then, a midwife's son and myself skilled in midwifery, and try hard to answer my questions as you best can. But if, when I examine anything you say, I come to the conclusion that it is an imposture and false and therefore take it from you and cast it away, you must not rage like a mother over her first-born. My good friend, there have been many who are so angry with me when I rob them of some foolish notion of their own that they are positively ready to bite me; and they never think I do it in kindness, for they cannot understand that 'no god bears ill will to mortals', and nothing I do is done through ill will, but because it is not permitted to me to accept a lie or cover up the truth. Begin again, then, Theaetetus, and try to tell me what knowledge is. Never say that you cannot, for if heaven wills, and gives you heart, you can. (148 E–151 D, tr. H. F. Carlill)

2.5.4.2 To challenge Socrates to an argument is like challenging cavalry to fight in an open plain. If you start asking questions you'll get an earful in reply. (183 D)

2.6 Parmenides

Parmenides *purports to be a conversation between Parmenides in old age and Socrates in youth. Such a meeting was probably chronologically possible — though Plato's record of it has tended to affect scholars' dating of Parmenides. On the whole, it is unlikely to have taken place. Certainly the content of the dialogue cannot be authentic. It is impossible to think that Socrates received this radical critique of the Theory of Forms in his youth, and propounded the Theory with blind naïveté on his deathbed. See the Introduction.*

While Socrates was speaking, Pythodorus thought that Parmenides and Zeno were not altogether pleased at the successive steps of the argument; but still they gave the closest attention, and often looked at one another, and smiled as if in admiration of him. When he had finished, Parmenides expressed their feelings in the following words:

Socrates, he said, I admire the bent of your mind towards philosophy; tell me now, was this your own distinction between ideas in themselves and the things which partake of them? and do you think that there is an idea of likeness apart from the likeness which we possess, and of the one and many, and of the other things which Zeno mentioned?

I think that there are such ideas, said Socrates.

Parmenides proceeded: And would you also make absolute ideas of the just and the beautiful and the good, and of all that class?

Yes, he said, I should.

And would you make an idea of man apart from us and from all other human creatures, or of fire and water?

I am often undecided, Parmenides, as to whether I ought to include them or not.

And would you feel equally undecided, Socrates, about things of which the mention may provoke a smile? – I mean such things as hair, mud, dirt or anything else which is vile and paltry; would you suppose that each of these has an idea distinct from the actual objects with which we come into contact, or not?

Certainly not, said Socrates; visible things like these are such as they appear to us, and I am afraid that there would be an absurdity in assuming any idea of them, although I sometimes get disturbed, and begin to think that there is nothing without an idea; but then again, when I have taken up this position, I run away, because I am afraid that I may fall into a bottomless pit of nonsense, and perish; and so I return to the ideas of which I was just now speaking, and occupy myself with them.

Yes, Socrates, said Parmenides; that is because you are still young; the time will come, if I am not mistaken, when philosophy will have a firmer grasp of you, and then you will not despise even the meanest things; at your age you are too much disposed to regard the opinions of men. But I should like to know whether you mean that there are certain ideas of which all other things partake, and from which they derive their names; [131] that similars, for example, become similar, because they partake of similarity; and great things become great, because they partake of greatness; and that just and beautiful things become just and beautiful, because they partake of justice and beauty?

Yes, certainly, said Socrates, that is my meaning.

Then each individual partakes either of the whole of the idea or else of a part of the idea? Can there be any other mode of participation?

There cannot be, he said.

Then do you think that the whole idea is one, and yet, being one, is in each one of the many?

Why not, Parmenides? said Socrates.

Because one and the same thing will exist as a whole at the same time in many separate individuals, and will therefore be in a state of separation from itself.

Nay, but the idea may be like the day which is one and the same in many places at once, and yet continuous with itself; in this way each idea may be one and the same in all at the same time.

I like your way, Socrates, of making one in many places at once. You mean to say, that if I were to spread out a sail and cover a number of men there would be one whole including many — is not that your meaning?

I think so.

And would you say that the whole sail includes each man, or a part of it only, and different parts different men?

The latter.

Then, Socrates, the ideas themselves will be divisible, and things which participate in them will have a part of them only and not the whole idea existing in each of them?

That seems to follow.

Then would you like to say, Socrates, that the one idea is really divisible and yet remains one?

Certainly not, he said.

Suppose that you divide absolute greatness, and that of the many great things, each one is great in virtue of a portion of greatness less than absolute greatness — is that conceivable?

No.

Or will each equal thing, if possessing some small portion of equality less than absolute equality, be equal to some other thing by virtue of that portion only?

Impossible.

Or suppose one of us to have a portion of smallness; this is but a part of the small, and therefore the absolutely small is greater; if the absolutely small be greater, that to which the part of the small is added will be smaller and not greater than before.

How absurd!

Then in what way, Socrates, will all things participate in the ideas, if they are unable to participate in them either as parts or wholes?

Indeed, he said, you have asked a question which is not easily answered.

Well, said Parmenides, and what do you say of another question?

What question?

I imagine that the way in which you are led to assume one idea of each kind is as follows: [132] You see a number of great objects, and when you look at them there seems to you to be one and the same idea (or nature) in them all; hence you conceive of greatness as one.

Very true, said Socrates.

And if you go on and allow your mind in like manner to embrace in one view the idea of greatness and of great things which are not the idea, and to compare them, will not another greatness arise, which will appear to be the source of all these?

It would seem so.

Then another idea of greatness now comes into view over and above absolute greatness, and the individuals which partake of it; and then another, over and above all these, by virtue of which they will all be great, and so each idea instead of being one will be infinitely multiplied.

But may not the ideas, asked Socrates, be thoughts only, and have no proper existence except in our minds, Parmenides? For in that case each idea may still be one, and not experience this infinite multiplication.

And can there be individual thoughts which are thoughts of nothing?

Impossible, he said.

The thought must be of something?

Yes.

Of something which is or which is not?

Of something which is.

Must it not be of a single something, which the thought recognises as attaching to all, being a single form or nature?

Yes.

And will not the something which is apprehended as one and the same in all, be an idea?

From that, again, there is no escape.

Then, said Parmenides, if you say that everything else participates in the ideas, must you not say either that everything is made up of thoughts, and that all things think; or that they are thoughts but have no thought?

The latter view, Parmenides, is no more rational than the previous one. In my opinion, the ideas are, as it were, patterns fixed in nature, and other things are like them, and resemblances of them – what is meant by the participation of other things in the ideas, is really assimilation to them.

But if, said he, the individual is like the idea, must not the idea also be like the individual, in so far as the individual is a resemblance of the idea? That which is like, cannot be conceived of as other than the like of like.

Impossible.

And when two things are alike, must they not partake of the same idea?

They must.

And will not that of which the two partake, and which makes them alike, be the idea itself?

Certainly.

Then the idea cannot be like the individual, or the individual like the idea; for if they are alike, some further idea of likeness will always be coming to light, [133] and if that be like anything else, another; and new ideas will be always arising, if the idea resembles that which partakes of it?

Quite true.

The theory, then, that other things participate in the ideas by resemblance, has to be given up, and some other mode of participation devised?

It would seem so.

Do you see then, Socrates, how great is the difficulty of affirming the ideas to be absolute?

Yes, indeed.

And, further, let me say that as yet you only understand a small part of the difficulty which is involved if you make of each thing a single idea, parting it off from other things.

What difficulty? he said.

There are many, but the greatest of all is this: If an opponent argues that these ideas, being such as we say they ought to be, must remain unknown, no one can prove to him that he is wrong, unless he who denies their existence be a man of great ability and knowledge, and is willing to follow a long and laborious demonstration; he will remain unconvinced, and still insist that they cannot be known.

What do you mean, Parmenides? said Socrates.

In the first place, I think, Socrates, that you, or anyone who maintains the existence of absolute essences, will admit that they cannot exist in us.

No, said Socrates; for then they would be no longer absolute.

True, he said; and therefore when ideas are what they are in relation to one another their essence is determined by a relation among themselves, and has nothing to do with the resemblances, or whatever they are to be termed, which are in our sphere, and from which we receive this or that name when we partake of them. And the things which are within our sphere and have the same names with them are likewise only relative to one another, and not to the ideas which have the same names with them, but belong to themselves and not to them.

What do you mean? said Socrates.

I may illustrate my meaning in this way, said Parmenides: A master has a slave; now there is nothing absolute in the relation between them, which is simply a relation of one man to another. But there is also an idea of mastership in the abstract, which is relative to the idea of slavery in the abstract. [134] These natures have nothing to do with us, nor we with them; they are concerned with themselves only, and we with ourselves. Do you see my meaning?

Yes, said Socrates, I quite see your meaning.

And will not knowledge – I mean absolute knowledge – answer to absolute truth?

Certainly.

And each kind of absolute knowledge will answer to each kind of absolute being?

Yes.

But the knowledge which we have will answer to the truth which we have; and again, each kind of knowledge which we have will be a knowledge of each kind of being which we have?

Certainly.

But the ideas themselves, as you admit, we have not, and cannot have?

No, we cannot.

And the absolute natures or kinds are known severally by the absolute idea of knowledge?

Yes.

And we have not got the idea of knowledge?

No.

Then none of the ideas are known to us, because we have no share in absolute knowledge?

I suppose not.

Then the nature of the beautiful in itself, and of the good in itself, and all other ideas which we suppose to exist absolutely, are unknown to us?

It would seem so.

I think that there is a stranger consequence still.

What is it?

Would you, or would you not, say that absolute knowledge, if there is such a thing, must be a far more exact knowledge than our knowledge; and the same of beauty and of the rest?

Yes.

And if there be such a thing as participation in absolute knowledge no one is more likely than God to have this most exact knowledge?

Certainly.

But then, will God, having absolute knowledge, have a knowledge of human things?

Why not?

Because, Socrates, said Parmenides, we have admitted that the ideas are not valid in relation to human things; nor human things in relation to them; the relations of either are limited to their respective spheres.

Yes, that has been admitted.

And if God has this perfect authority,

and perfect knowledge, his authority cannot rule us, nor his knowledge know us, or any human thing; just as our authority does not extend to the gods, nor our knowledge know anything which is divine, so by parity of reason they, being gods, are not our masters, neither do they know the things of men.

Yet, surely, said Socrates, to deprive God of knowledge is monstrous.

[135] These, Socrates, said Parmenides, are a few, and only a few of the difficulties in which we are involved if ideas really are and we determine each one of them to be an absolute unity. He who hears what may be said against them will deny the very existence of them – and even if they do exist, he will say that they must of necessity be unknown to man; and he will seem to have reason on his side, and as we were remarking just now, will be very difficult to convince; a man must be gifted with very considerable ability before he can learn that everything has a class and an absolute essence; and still more remarkable will he be who discovers all these things for himself, and having thoroughly investigated them is able to teach them to others.

I agree with you, Parmenides, said Socrates; and what you say is very much to my mind.

And yet, Socrates, said Parmenides, if a man, fixing his attention on these and the like difficulties, does away with ideas of things and will not admit that every individual thing has its own determinate idea which is always one and the same, he will have nothing on which his mind can rest; and so he will utterly destroy the power of reasoning, as you seem to me to have particularly noted.

Very true, he said.

But, then, what is to become of philosophy? Whither shall we turn, if the ideas are unknown?

I certainly do not see my way at present. (130 A–135 C, tr. B. Jowett)

2.7 Epistles

There has been much discussion about the authenticity of the letters attributed to Plato. Some are clearly not by Plato, but many scholars today would accept the second and the seventh as genuine.

2.7.1 This is why I have never written anything on these subjects. There is not, and never will be, a work by Plato. What are now called Plato's works really belong to Socrates, a Socrates given youth and good looks. (314 C)

This passage has been used for diametrically opposed conclusions. Some scholars have taken it as an assertion that Plato is recording Socrates, not putting forward his own views. In fact, the last phrase is decisive. He acknowledges his debt to Socrates, but he is bringing him up to date.

2.7.2 When I was a young man I was affected as the many are. I thought, if I became quickly my own master, to betake myself immediately to the public affairs of the State. Now some such circumstances as these fell out relating to state affairs. Of the polity existing at that time, when it was abused by many, a change took place; and over the change one and fifty men presided as governors, eleven in the city, and ten in the Piraeus; and each of these had a jurisdiction about the Agora, and whatever else it was necessary to regulate in the cities, while thirty of them were invested with supreme authority. Some of these happened to be my relatives and acquaintances; and they forthwith invited me [to attend] to state-affairs, as being a suitable pursuit. And how I was affected is, on account of my youth, not at all wonderful. For I thought that they would, by leading the city from an unjust mode of living to a just one, administer it in the way it was meet; so that I diligently gave my mind to what they did. But when I saw these men proving in a short time that the previous form of government had been [as it were] gold, and that they committed other acts [unjustly], and sent my friend Socrates, advanced in years, whom I am not ashamed to say was nearly the most righteous man of those then living, together with certain others, against one of the citizens, and to bring him by force, in order that he might be executed, so that he [Socrates] might have a share in their deeds, whether he wished it or not, [325] and that he did not comply, but ran the risk of suffering everything, rather than take any part in their impious acts – all this when I saw, and other similar acts of no trifling kind, I felt indignant, and withdrew myself from the evil men of that period.

Not long after this, the power of the thirty fell by a revolution, together with the whole of the then existing form of government. Again, therefore, but somewhat more slowly, did a desire still drag me on to engage in public and political affairs. Now in these, as being in a troubled state, many things took place, at which anyone might be indignant; nor was it wonderful, that in revolutions the punishment of hostile factions should have been rather severe in the case of some; although they who returned acted with considerable clemency. But by some chance some of those in power brought before a court of justice our friend Socrates, laying upon him an accusation the most unholy, and belonging the least of all to Socrates. For some brought him to trial, and others gave their vote against him, and destroyed the man, who had been unwilling to share in the unholy act of a removal relating to one of his then exiled friends, when the exiles themselves were unfortunate. On re-flecting then upon these matters, and on the persons who managed political affairs, and on the laws and customs, the more I considered them, and I advanced in years, by so much the more difficult did it appear to me to administer correctly state affairs. For it is not possible to do so without friends and faithful associates; whom, existing at that time, it was not easy to find – for our city was then no longer administered according to the manners and institutions of our fathers – and it was impossible to acquire new with any facility; while the written laws and customs were corrupted, and [unholiness] was increasing to a degree how wonderful!

So that I, who had been at first full of ardour towards engaging in affairs of state, did, upon looking at these things and seeing them carried along in every way and on every side, become giddy; but not so as to withdraw from considering how at any time something better might take place respecting these very matters, [326] and likewise the whole form of government, but to be wisely waiting continually for opportunities of acting. At last I perceived that all states existing at present were badly governed. For what relates to their laws is nearly in an incurable state, without some wonderful arrangement in conjunction with fortune. I was therefore compelled to say, in praise of true philosophy, that through it we are enabled to perceive all that is just as regards the state and individuals; and hence that the human race will never cease from ills, until the race of those, who philosophise correctly and truthfully, shall come to political power, or persons of power in states shall, by a certain divine allotment, philosophise really.

Holding these sentiments, I arrived in Italy and Sicily, when I first came there. (324 B, tr. G. Burges)

Cf. **2.5.3.3.**

2.8 Probably Spurious Dialogues

2.8.1 1 Alcibiades. *Some scholars have argued hotly for the authenticity of this work. One problem is that its style resembles that of Plato's later period, its thought that of his earlier period. If it is not Plato's it is probably by an associate of his. It is of considerable interest in that of all the works of the Platonic Corpus it is the closest to portraying Socrates as we see him in Xenophon. It has indeed been described as a handbook of Socratic philosophy. The description begs a number of questions, but I have thought the work important enough to print in full. It is most unlikely to be a record of an actual conversation; but it shows a view of Socrates and his achievement which was preserved in the Academy.*

SOCRATES: I dare say that you may be surprised to find, O son of Cleinias, that I, who am your first lover, not having spoken to you for many years, when the rest of the world were wearying you with their attentions, am the last of your lovers who still speaks to you. The cause of my silence has been that I was hindered by a power more than human, of which I will some day explain to you the nature; this impediment has now been removed; I therefore here present myself before you, and I greatly hope that no similar hindrance will again occur. Meanwhile, I have observed that your pride has been too much for the pride of your admirers; they were numerous and high-spirited, but they have all run away, overpowered by your superior force of character; not one of them remains. [104] And I want you to understand the reason why you have been too much for them. You think that you have no need of them or of any other man, for you have great possessions and lack nothing, beginning with the body, and ending with the soul. In the first place, you say to yourself that you are

the fairest and tallest of the citizens, and this everyone who has eyes may see to be true; in the second place, that you are among the noblest of them, highly connected both on the father's and the mother's side, and sprung from one of the most distinguished families in your own state, which is the greatest in Hellas, and having many friends and kinsmen of the best sort, who can assist you when in need; and there is one potent relative, who is more to you than all the rest, Pericles the son of Xanthippus, whom your father left guardian of you, and of your brother, and who can do as he pleases not only in this city but in all Hellas, and among many and mighty barbarous nations. Moreover, you are rich; but I must say that you value yourself least of all upon your possessions. And all these things have lifted you up; you have overcome your lovers, and they have acknowledged that you were too much for them. Have you not remarked their absence? And now I know that you wonder why I, unlike the rest of them, have not gone away, and what can be my motive in remaining.

ALCIBIADES: Perhaps, Socrates, you are not aware that I was just going to ask you the very same question – What do you want? And what is your motive in annoying me, and always, wherever I am, making a point of coming? I do really wonder what you mean, and should greatly like to know.

SOCRATES: Then if, as you say, you desire to know, I suppose that you will be willing to hear, and I may consider myself to be speaking to an auditor who will remain, and will not run away?

ALCIBIADES: Certainly, let me hear.

SOCRATES: You had better be careful, for I may very likely be as unwilling to end as I have hitherto been to begin.

ALCIBIADES: Proceed, my good man, and I will listen.

SOCRATES: I will proceed; and, although no lover likes to speak with one who has no feeling of love in him I will make an effort, and tell you what I meant: [105] My love, Alcibiades, which I hardly like to confess, would long ago have passed away, as I flatter myself, if I saw you loving your good things, or thinking that you ought to pass life in the enjoyment of them. But I shall reveal other thoughts of yours, which you keep to yourself; whereby you will know that I have always had my eye on you. Suppose that at this moment some God came to you and said: Alcibiades, will you live as you are, or die in an instant if you are forbidden to make any further acquisition? – I verily believe that you would choose death. And I will tell you the hope in which you are at present living: Before many days have elapsed, you think that you will come before the Athenian assembly, and will prove to them that you are more worthy of honour than Pericles, or any other man that ever lived, and having proved this, you will have the greatest power in the State. When you have gained the greatest power among us you will go on to other Hellenic states, and not only to Hellenes but to all the barbarians who inhabit the same continent with us. And if the God were then to say to you again: Here in Europe is to be your seat of empire, and you must not cross over into Asia or meddle with Asiatic affairs, I do not believe that you would choose to live upon these terms; but the world, as I may say, must be filled with your power and name – no man less than Cyrus and Xerxes is of any account with you. Such I know to be your hopes – I am not guessing only – and very likely you, who know that I am speaking the truth, will reply, Well, Socrates, but what have my hopes to do with the explanation which you promised of your unwillingness to leave me? And that is what I am now going to tell you, sweet son of Cleinias and Dinomache. The explanation is, that all these designs of yours cannot be accomplished by you without my help; so great is the power which I believe myself to have over you and your concerns; and this I conceive to be the reason why the God has hitherto forbidden me to converse with you, and I have been long expecting his permission. For, as you hope to prove your own great value to the State, and having proved it, to attain at once to absolute power, so do I indulge a hope that I shall have the supreme power over you, if I am able to prove my own great value to you, and to show you that neither guardian, nor kinsman, nor anyone is able to deliver into your hands the power which you desire, but I only, God being my helper. When you were young and your hopes were not yet matured I should have wasted my time, and therefore, [106] as I conceive, the God forbade me to converse with you; but now, having his permission, I will speak, for now you will listen to me.

ALCIBIADES: Your silence, Socrates, was always a surprise to me. I never could understand why you followed me about, and now that you have begun to speak again I am still more amazed. Whether I think all this or not is a matter about which you seem to have already made up your mind, and therefore my denial will have no effect upon you. But granting, if I must, that you have perfectly divined my purposes, why is your assistance necessary to the attainment of them? Can you tell me why?

SOCRATES: You want to know whether I can make a long speech, such as you are in the habit of hearing; but that is not my way. I think, however, that I can prove to you the truth of what I am saying, if you will grant me one little favour.

ALCIBIADES: Yes, if the favour which you mean be not a troublesome one.

SOCRATES: Will you be troubled at having questions to answer?

ALCIBIADES: Not at all.

SOCRATES: Then please to answer.

ALCIBIADES: Ask me.

SOCRATES: Have you not the intention which I attribute to you?

ALCIBIADES: I will grant anything you like, in the hope of hearing what more you have to say.

SOCRATES: You do, then, mean, as I was saying, to come forward in a little while in the character of an adviser of the Athenians? And suppose that when you are ascending the bema, I pull you by the sleeve and say, Alcibiades, you are getting up to advise the Athenians – do you know the matter about which they are going to deliberate better than they? How would you answer?

ALCIBIADES: I should reply that I was going to advise them about a matter which I do know better than they.

SOCRATES: Then you are a good adviser about the things which you know?

ALCIBIADES: Certainly.

SOCRATES: And do you know anything but what you have learned of others, or found out yourself?

ALCIBIADES: That is all.

SOCRATES: And would you have ever learned or discovered anything, if you had not been willing either to learn of others or to examine yourself?

ALCIBIADES: I should not.

SOCRATES: And would you have been willing to learn or to examine what you supposed that you knew?

ALCIBIADES: Certainly not.

SOCRATES: Then there was a time when you thought that you did not know what you are now supposed to know?

ALCIBIADES: Certainly.

SOCRATES: I think that I know tolerably well the extent of your acquirements; and you must tell me if I forget any of them: according to my recollection, you learned the arts of writing, of playing on the lyre and of wrestling; the flute you never would learn; this is the sum of your accomplishments, unless there were some which you acquired in secret; and I think that secrecy was hardly possible, as you could not have come out of your door, either by day or night, without my seeing you.

ALCIBIADES: Yes, that was the whole of my schooling.

[107] SOCRATES: And are you going to get up in the Athenian assembly, and give them advice about writing?

ALCIBIADES: No, indeed.

SOCRATES: Or about the touch of the lyre?

ALCIBIADES: Certainly not.

SOCRATES: And they are not in the habit of deliberating about wrestling, in the assembly?

ALCIBIADES: Hardly.

SOCRATES: Then what are the deliberations in which you propose to advise them? Surely not about building?

ALCIBIADES: No.

SOCRATES: For the builder will advise better than you will about that?

ALCIBIADES: He will.

SOCRATES: Nor about divination?

ALCIBIADES: No.

SOCRATES: About that again the diviner will advise better than you will?

ALCIBIADES: True.

SOCRATES: Whether he be little or great, good or ill-looking, noble or ignoble – makes no difference.

ALCIBIADES: Certainly not.

SOCRATES: A man is a good adviser about anything, not because he has riches but because he has knowledge?

ALCIBIADES: Assuredly.

SOCRATES: Whether their counsellor is rich or poor is not a matter which will make any difference to the Athenians when they are deliberating about the health of the citizens; they only require that he should be a physician.

ALCIBIADES: Of course.

SOCRATES: Then what will be the subject of deliberation about which you will be justified in getting up and advising them?

ALCIBIADES: About their own concerns, Socrates.

SOCRATES: You mean about shipbuilding, for example, when the question is what sort of ships they ought to build?

ALCIBIADES: No, I should not advise them about that.

SOCRATES: I suppose, because you do not understand shipbuilding: is that the reason?

ALCIBIADES: It is.

SOCRATES: Then about what concerns of theirs will you advise them?

ALCIBIADES: About war, Socrates, or about peace, or about any other concerns of the State.

SOCRATES: You mean, when they deliberate with whom they ought to make peace, and with whom they ought to go to war, and in what manner?

ALCIBIADES: Yes.

SOCRATES: And they ought to go to war with those against whom it is better to go to war?

ALCIBIADES: Yes.

SOCRATES: And when it is better?

ALCIBIADES: Certainly.

SOCRATES: And for as long a time as is better?

ALCIBIADES: Yes.

SOCRATES: But suppose the Athenians to deliberate with whom they ought to close in wrestling, and whom they should grasp by the hand, would you, or the master of gymnastics, be a better adviser of them?

ALCIBIADES: Clearly, the master of gymnastics.

SOCRATES: And can you tell me on what grounds the master of gymnastics would decide, with whom they ought or ought not to close, and when and how? To take an instance: Would he not say that they should wrestle with those against whom it is best to wrestle?

ALCIBIADES: Yes.

[108] SOCRATES: And as much as is best?

ALCIBIADES: Certainly.

SOCRATES: And at such times as are best?

ALCIBIADES: Yes.

SOCRATES: Again; you sometimes accompany the lyre with the song and dance?

ALCIBIADES: Yes.

SOCRATES: When it is well to do so?

ALCIBIADES: Yes.

SOCRATES: And as much as is well?

ALCIBIADES: Just so.

SOCRATES: And as you speak of an excellence or art of the best in wrestling, and of an excellence in playing the lyre, I wish you would tell me what this latter is; the excellence of wrestling I call gymnastic, and I want to know what you call the other.

ALCIBIADES: I do not understand you.

SOCRATES: Then try to do as I do; for the answer which I gave is universally right, and when I say right, I mean according to rule.

ALCIBIADES: Yes.

SOCRATES: And was not the art of which I spoke gymnastic?

ALCIBIADES: Certainly.

SOCRATES: And I called the excellence in wrestling gymnastic?

ALCIBIADES: You did.

SOCRATES: And I was right?

ALCIBIADES: I think that you were.

SOCRATES: Well, now – for you should learn to argue prettily – let me ask you in return to tell me, first, what is that art of which playing and singing, and stepping properly in the dance, are parts – what is the name of the whole? I think that by this time you must be able to tell.

ALCIBIADES: Indeed I cannot.

SOCRATES: Then let me put the matter in another way: what do you call the Goddesses who are the patronesses of art?

ALCIBIADES: The Muses do you mean, Socrates?

SOCRATES: Yes, I do; and what is the name of the art which is called after them?

ALCIBIADES: I suppose that you mean music.

SOCRATES: Yes, that is my meaning; and what is the excellence of the art of music, as I told you truly that the excellence of wrestling was gymnastic – what is the excellence of music – to be what?

ALCIBIADES: To be musical, I suppose.

SOCRATES: Very good; and now please to tell me what is the excellence of war and peace; as the more musical was the more excellent, or the more gymnastical was the more excellent, tell me, what name do you give to the more excellent in war and peace?

ALCIBIADES: But I really cannot tell you.

SOCRATES: But if you were offering advice to another and said to him – This food is better than that, at this time and in this quantity, and he said to you – What do you mean, Alcibiades, by the word 'better'? you would have no difficulty in replying that you meant 'more wholesome', although you do not profess to be a physician: and when the subject is one of which you profess to have knowledge, and about which you are ready to get up and advise as if you knew, are you not ashamed, when you are asked, not to be able to answer the question? [109] Is it not disgraceful?

ALCIBIADES: Very.

SOCRATES: Well, then, consider and try to explain what is the meaning of 'better', in the matter of making peace and going to war with those against whom you ought to go to war? To what does the word refer?

ALCIBIADES: I am thinking, and I cannot tell.

SOCRATES: But you surely know what are the charges which we bring against one another, when we arrive at the point of making war, and what name we give them?

ALCIBIADES: Yes, certainly; we say that deceit or violence has been employed, or that we have been defrauded.

SOCRATES: And how does this happen? Will you tell me how? For there may be a difference in the manner.

ALCIBIADES: Do you mean by 'how', Socrates, whether we suffered these things justly or unjustly?

SOCRATES: Exactly.

ALCIBIADES: There can be no greater difference than between just and unjust.

SOCRATES: And would you advise the Athenians to go to war with the just or with the unjust?

ALCIBIADES: That is an awkward question; for certainly, even if a person did intend to go to war with the just, he would not admit that they were just.

SOCRATES: He would not go to war, because it would be unlawful?

ALCIBIADES: Neither lawful nor honourable.

SOCRATES: Then you, too, would address them on principles of justice?

ALCIBIADES: Certainly.

SOCRATES: What, then, is justice but that better, of which I spoke, in going to war or not going to war with those against whom we ought or ought not, and when we ought or ought not to go to war?

ALCIBIADES: Clearly.

SOCRATES: But how is this, friend Alcibiades? Have you forgotten that you do not know this, or have you been to the schoolmaster without my knowledge, and has he taught you to discern the just from the unjust? Who is he? I wish you would tell me, that I may go and learn of him – you shall introduce me.

ALCIBIADES: You are mocking, Socrates.

SOCRATES: No, indeed; I most solemnly declare to you by Zeus, who is the God of our common friendship, and whom I never will forswear, that I am not; tell me, then, who this instructor is, if he exists.

ALCIBIADES: But, perhaps, he does not exist; may I not have acquired the knowledge of just and unjust in some other way?

SOCRATES: Yes; if you have discovered them.

ALCIBIADES: But do you not think that I could discover them?

SOCRATES: I am sure that you might, if you inquired about them.

ALCIBIADES: And do you not think that I would inquire?

SOCRATES: Yes; if you thought that you did not know them.

ALCIBIADES: And was there not a time when I did so think?

SOCRATES: Very good; and can you tell me how long it is [110] since you thought that you did not know the nature of the just and the unjust? What do you say to a year ago? Were you, then, in a state of conscious ignorance and inquiry? or did you think that you knew? And please to answer truly, that our discussion may not be in vain.

ALCIBIADES: Well, I thought that I knew.

SOCRATES: And two years ago, and three years ago, and four years ago, you knew all the same?

ALCIBIADES: I did.

SOCRATES: And more than four years ago you were a child – were you not?

ALCIBIADES: Yes.

SOCRATES: And then I am quite sure that you thought you knew.

ALCIBIADES: Why are you so sure?

SOCRATES: Because I often heard you when a child, in your teacher's house, or elsewhere, playing at dice or some other game with the boys, not hesitating at all about the nature of the just and unjust; but very confident – crying and shouting that one of the boys was a rogue and a cheat, and had been cheating. Is it not true?

ALCIBIADES: But what was I to do, Socrates, when anybody cheated me?

SOCRATES: And how can you say, 'What was I to do'? if at the time you did not know whether you were wronged or not?

ALCIBIADES: To be sure I knew; I was quite aware that I was being cheated.

SOCRATES: Then you suppose yourself even when a child to have known the nature of just and unjust?

ALCIBIADES: Certainly; and I did know then.

SOCRATES: And when did you discover them – not, surely, at the time when you thought that you knew them?

ALCIBIADES: Certainly not.

SOCRATES: And when did you think that you were ignorant – if you consider, you will find that there never was such a time?

ALCIBIADES: Really, Socrates, I cannot say.

SOCRATES: Then you did not learn them by discovering them?

ALCIBIADES: Clearly not.

SOCRATES: But just before you said that you did not know them by learning; now, if you have neither discovered nor learned them, how and whence do you come to know them?

ALCIBIADES: I suppose that I was mistaken in saying that I knew them through my own discovery of them; whereas, in truth, I learned them in the same way that other people learn.

SOCRATES: So you said before, and I must again ask, of whom? Do tell me.

ALCIBIADES: Of the many.

SOCRATES: Do you take refuge in them? I cannot say much for your teachers.

ALCIBIADES: Why, are they not able to teach?

SOCRATES: They could not teach you how to play at draughts, which you would acknowledge (would you not) to be a much smaller matter than justice?

ALCIBIADES: Yes.

SOCRATES: And can they teach the better who are unable to teach the worse?

ALCIBIADES: I think that they can; at any rate, they can teach many far better things than to play at draughts.

[111] SOCRATES: What things?

ALCIBIADES: Why, for example, I learned to speak Greek of them, and I cannot say who was my teacher, or to whom I am to attribute my knowledge of Greek, if not to those good-for-nothing teachers, as you call them.

SOCRATES: Why, yes, my friend; and the many are good enough teachers of Greek, and some of their instructions in that line may be justly praised.

ALCIBIADES: Why is that?

SOCRATES: Why, because they have the qualities which good teachers ought to have.

ALCIBIADES: What qualities?

SOCRATES: Why, you know that knowledge is the first qualification of any teacher?

ALCIBIADES: Certainly.

SOCRATES: And if they know, they must agree together and not differ?

ALCIBIADES: Yes.

SOCRATES: And would you say that they knew the things about which they differ?

ALCIBIADES: No.

SOCRATES: Then how can they teach them?

ALCIBIADES: They cannot.

SOCRATES: Well, but do you imagine that the many would differ about the nature of wood and stone? are they not agreed if you ask them what they are? and do they not run to fetch the same thing, when they want a piece of wood or a stone? And so in similar cases, which I suspect to be pretty nearly all that you mean by speaking Greek.

ALCIBIADES: True.

SOCRATES: These, as we were saying, are matters about which they are agreed with one another and with themselves; both individuals and states use the same words about them; they do not use some one word and some another.

ALCIBIADES: They do not.

SOCRATES: Then they may be expected to be good teachers of these things?

ALCIBIADES: Yes.

SOCRATES: And if we want to instruct anyone in them we shall be right in sending him to be taught by our friends the many?

ALCIBIADES: Very true.

SOCRATES: But if we wanted further to know not only which are men and which are horses but which men or horses have powers of running, would the many still be able to inform us?

ALCIBIADES: Certainly not.

SOCRATES: And you have a sufficient proof that they do not know these things and are not the best teachers of them, inasmuch as they are never agreed about them?

ALCIBIADES: Yes.

SOCRATES: And suppose that we wanted to know not only what men are like but what healthy or diseased men are like – would the many be able to teach us?

ALCIBIADES: They would not.

SOCRATES: And you would have a proof that they were bad teachers of these matters, if you saw them at variance?

ALCIBIADES: I should.

SOCRATES: Well, but are the many agreed with themselves, or with one another, [112] about the justice or injustice of men and things?

ALCIBIADES: Assuredly not, Socrates.

SOCRATES: There is no subject about which they are more at variance?

ALCIBIADES: None.

SOCRATES: I do not suppose that you ever saw or heard of men quarrelling over the principles of health and disease to such an extent as to go to war and kill one another for the sake of them?

ALCIBIADES: No, indeed.

SOCRATES: But of the quarrels about justice and injustice, even if you have never seen them, you have certainly heard from many people, including Homer; for you have heard of the *Iliad* and *Odyssey*?

ALCIBIADES: To be sure, Socrates.

SOCRATES: A difference of just and unjust is the argument of these poems?

ALCIBIADES: True.

SOCRATES: Which difference caused all the wars and deaths of Trojans and Achaeans, and the deaths of the suitors of Penelope in their quarrel with Odysseus.

ALCIBIADES: Very true.

SOCRATES: And when the Athenians and Lacedaemonians and Boeotians fell at Tanagra, and afterwards in the battle of Coronea, at which your father Cleinias met his end, the question was one of justice – this was the sole cause of the battles, and of their deaths.

ALCIBIADES: Very true.

SOCRATES: But can they be said to understand that about which they are quarrelling to the death?

ALCIBIADES: Clearly not.

SOCRATES: And yet those whom you thus allow to be ignorant are the teachers to whom you are appealing.

ALCIBIADES: Very true.

SOCRATES: But how are you ever likely to know the nature of justice and injustice, about which you are so perplexed, if you have neither learned them of others nor discovered them yourself?

ALCIBIADES: From what you say, I suppose not.

SOCRATES: See, again, how inaccurately you speak, Alcibiades!

ALCIBIADES: In what respect?

SOCRATES: In saying that I say so.

ALCIBIADES: Why, did you not say that I know nothing of the just and unjust?

SOCRATES: No; I did not.

ALCIBIADES: Did I, then?

SOCRATES: Yes.

ALCIBIADES: How was that?

SOCRATES: Let me explain. Suppose I were to ask you which is the greater number, two or one; you would reply 'two'?

ALCIBIADES: I should.

SOCRATES: And by how much greater?

ALCIBIADES: By one.

SOCRATES: Which of us now says that two is more than one?

ALCIBIADES: I do.

SOCRATES: Did not I ask, and you answer the question?

ALCIBIADES: Yes.

[113] SOCRATES: Then who is speaking? I who put the question, or you who answer me?

ALCIBIADES: I am.

SOCRATES: Or suppose that I ask and you tell me the letters which make up the name Socrates, which of us is the speaker?

ALCIBIADES: I am.

SOCRATES: Now let us put the case generally: whenever there is a question and answer, who is the speaker – the questioner or the answerer?

ALCIBIADES: I should say, Socrates, that the answerer was the speaker.

SOCRATES: And have I not been the questioner all through?

ALCIBIADES: Yes.

SOCRATES: And you the answerer?

ALCIBIADES: Just so.

SOCRATES: Which of us, then, was the speaker?

ALCIBIADES: The inference is, Socrates, that I was the speaker.

SOCRATES: Did not someone say that Alcibiades, the fair son of Cleinias, not understanding about just and unjust, but thinking that he did understand, was going to the assembly to advise the Athenians about what he did not know? Was not that said?

ALCIBIADES: Very true.

SOCRATES: Then, Alcibiades, the result may be expressed in the language of Euripides. I think that you have heard all this 'from yourself, and not from me'; nor did I say this, which you erroneously attribute to me, but you yourself, and what you said was very true. For indeed, my dear fellow, the design which you meditate of teaching what you do not know, and have not taken any pains to learn, is downright insanity.

ALCIBIADES: But, Socrates, I think that the Athenians and the rest of the Hellenes do not often advise as to the more just or unjust; for they see no difficulty in them, and therefore they leave them, and consider which course of action will be most expedient; for there is a difference between justice and expediency. Many persons have done great wrong and profited by their injustice; others have done rightly and come to no good.

SOCRATES: Well, but granting that the just and the expedient are ever so much opposed, you surely do not imagine that you know what is expedient for mankind, or why a thing is expedient?

ALCIBIADES: Why not, Socrates? – But I am not going to be asked again from whom I learned, or when I made the discovery.

SOCRATES: What a way you have! When you make a mistake which might be refuted by a previous argument you insist on having a new and different refutation; the old argument is a worn-out garment which you will no longer put on, but someone must produce another which is clean and new. [114] Now I shall disregard this move of yours, and shall ask over again, Where did you learn and how do you know the nature of the expedient, and who is your teacher? All this I comprehend in a single question, and now you will manifestly be in the old difficulty, and will not be able to show that you know the expedient, either because you learned or because you discovered it yourself. But, as I perceive that you are dainty, and dislike the taste of a stale argument, I will inquire no further into your knowledge of what is expedient or what is not expedient for the Athenian people, and simply request you to say why you do not explain whether justice and expediency are the same or different? And if you like you may examine me as I have examined you, or, if you would rather, you may carry on the discussion by yourself.

ALCIBIADES: But I am not certain, Socrates, whether I shall be able to discuss the matter with you.

SOCRATES: Then imagine, my dear fellow, that I am the demus and the ecclesia; for in the ecclesia, too, you will have to persuade men individually.

ALCIBIADES: Yes.

SOCRATES: And is not the same person able to persuade one individual singly and many individuals of the things which he knows? The grammarian, for example, can persuade one and he can persuade many about letters.

ALCIBIADES: True.

SOCRATES: And about number, will not the same person persuade one and persuade many?

ALCIBIADES: Yes.

SOCRATES: And this will be he who knows number, or the arithmetician?

ALCIBIADES: Quite true.

SOCRATES: And cannot you persuade one man about that of which you can persuade many?

ALCIBIADES: I suppose so.

SOCRATES: And that of which you can persuade either is clearly what you know?

ALCIBIADES: Yes.

SOCRATES: And the only difference between one who argues as we are doing and the orator who is addressing an assembly is that the one seeks to persuade a number, and the other an individual, of the same things.

ALCIBIADES: I suppose so.

SOCRATES: Well, then, since the same person who can persuade a multitude can persuade individuals, try conclusions upon me, and prove to me that the just is not always expedient.

ALCIBIADES: You take liberties, Socrates.

SOCRATES: I shall take the liberty of proving to you the opposite of that which you will not prove to me.

ALCIBIADES: Proceed.

SOCRATES: Answer my questions – that is all.

ALCIBIADES: Nay, I should like you to be the speaker.

SOCRATES: What, do you not wish to be persuaded?

ALCIBIADES: Certainly I do.

SOCRATES: And can you be persuaded better than out of your own mouth?

ALCIBIADES: I think not.

SOCRATES: Then you shall answer: and if you do not hear the words, that the just is the expedient, coming from your own lips, never believe another man again.

ALCIBIADES: I won't; but answer I will, for I do not see how I can come to any harm.

[115] SOCRATES: A true prophecy! Let me begin then by inquiring of you whether you allow that the just is sometimes expedient and sometimes not?

ALCIBIADES: Yes.

SOCRATES: And sometimes honourable and sometimes not?

ALCIBIADES: What do you mean?

SOCRATES: I am asking if you ever knew anyone who did what was dishonourable and yet just?

ALCIBIADES: Never.

SOCRATES: All just things are honourable?

ALCIBIADES: Yes.

SOCRATES: And are honourable things sometimes good and sometimes not good, or are they always good?

ALCIBIADES: I rather think, Socrates, that some honourable things are evil.

SOCRATES: And are some dishonourable things good?

ALCIBIADES: Yes.

SOCRATES: You mean in such a case as the following: In time of war, men have been wounded or have died in rescuing a companion or kinsman, when others who have neglected the duty of rescuing them have escaped in safety?

ALCIBIADES: True.

SOCRATES: And to rescue another in such circumstances is honourable, in respect of the attempt to save those whom we ought to save; and this is courage?

ALCIBIADES: True.

SOCRATES: But evil in respect of death and wounds?

ALCIBIADES: Yes.

SOCRATES: And the courage which is shown in the rescue is one thing, and the death another?

ALCIBIADES: Certainly.

SOCRATES: Then the rescue of one's friends is honourable in one point of view, but evil in another?

ALCIBIADES: True.

SOCRATES: And if honourable, then also good: Will you consider now whether I may not be right, for you were acknowledging that the courage which is shown in the rescue is honourable? Now is this courage good or evil? Look at the matter thus: which would you rather choose, good or evil?

ALCIBIADES: Good.

SOCRATES: And the greatest goods you would be most ready to choose, and would least like to be deprived of them?

ALCIBIADES: Certainly.

SOCRATES: What would you say of courage? At what price would you be willing to be deprived of courage?

ALCIBIADES: I would rather die than be a coward.

SOCRATES: Then you think that cowardice is the worst of evils?

ALCIBIADES: I do.

SOCRATES: As bad as death, I suppose?

ALCIBIADES: Yes.

SOCRATES: And life and courage are the extreme opposites of death and cowardice?

ALCIBIADES: Yes.

SOCRATES: And they are what you would most desire to have, and their opposites you would least desire?

ALCIBIADES: Yes.

SOCRATES: Is this because you think life and courage the best, and death and cowardice the worst?

ALCIBIADES: Yes.

SOCRATES: And you would term the rescue of a friend in battle honourable, in as much as courage does a good work?

ALCIBIADES: I should.

SOCRATES: But evil because of the death which ensues?

ALCIBIADES: Yes.

SOCRATES: Might we not describe their different effects as follows: You may call either of them evil in respect of the evil which is the result, and good in respect of the good which is the result of either of them?[116]

ALCIBIADES: Yes.

SOCRATES: And they are honourable in so far as they are good, and dishonourable in so far as they are evil?

ALCIBIADES: True.

SOCRATES: Then when you say that the rescue of a friend in battle is honourable and yet evil, that is equivalent to saying that the rescue is good and yet evil?

ALCIBIADES: I believe that you are right, Socrates.

SOCRATES: Nothing honourable, regarded as honourable, is evil; nor anything base, regarded as base, good.

ALCIBIADES: Clearly not.

SOCRATES: Look at the matter yet once more in a further light: he who acts honourably acts well?

ALCIBIADES: Yes.

SOCRATES: And he who acts well is happy?

ALCIBIADES: Of course.

SOCRATES: And the happy are those who obtain good?

ALCIBIADES: True.

SOCRATES: And they obtain good by acting well and honourably?

ALCIBIADES: Yes.

SOCRATES: Then acting well is a good?

ALCIBIADES: Certainly.

SOCRATES: And happiness is a good?

ALCIBIADES: Yes.

SOCRATES: Then the good and the honourable are again identified.

ALCIBIADES: Manifestly.

SOCRATES: Then, if the argument holds, what we find to be honourable we shall also find to be good?

ALCIBIADES: Certainly.

SOCRATES: And is the good expedient or not?

ALCIBIADES: Expedient.

SOCRATES: Do you remember our admissions about the just?

ALCIBIADES: Yes; if I am not mistaken, we said that those who acted justly must also act honourably.

SOCRATES: And the honourable is the good?

ALCIBIADES: Yes.

SOCRATES: And the good is expedient?

ALCIBIADES: Yes.

SOCRATES: Then, Alcibiades, the just is expedient?

ALCIBIADES: I should infer so.

SOCRATES: And all this I prove out of your own mouth, for I ask and you answer?

ALCIBIADES: I must acknowledge it to be true.

SOCRATES: And having acknowledged that the just is the same as the expedient, are you not (let me ask) prepared to ridicule anyone who, pretending to understand the principles of justice and injustice, gets up to advise the noble Athenians or the ignoble Peparethians, that the just may be the evil?

ALCIBIADES: I solemnly declare, Socrates, that I do not know what I am saying. Verily, I am in a strange state, for when you put questions to me I am of different minds in successive instants.

SOCRATES: And are you not aware of the nature of this perplexity, my friend?

ALCIBIADES: Indeed I am not.

SOCRATES: Do you suppose that if someone were to ask you whether you have two eyes or three, or two hands or four, or anything of that sort, you would then be of different minds in successive instants?

[117] ALCIBIADES: I begin to distrust myself, but still I do not suppose that I should.

SOCRATES: You would feel no doubt; and for this reason – because you would know?

ALCIBIADES: I suppose so.

SOCRATES: And the reason why you involuntarily contradict yourself is clearly that you are ignorant?

ALCIBIADES: Very likely.

SOCRATES: And if you are perplexed in answering about just and unjust, honourable and dishonourable, good and evil, expedient and inexpedient, the reason is that you are ignorant of

them, and therefore in perplexity. Is not that clear?

ALCIBIADES: I agree.

SOCRATES: But is this always the case, and is a man necessarily perplexed about that of which he has no knowledge?

ALCIBIADES: Certainly he is.

SOCRATES: And do you know how to ascend into heaven?

ALCIBIADES: Certainly not.

SOCRATES: And in this case, too, is your judgement perplexed?

ALCIBIADES: No.

SOCRATES: Do you see the reason why, or shall I tell you?

ALCIBIADES: Tell me.

SOCRATES: The reason is, that you not only do not know, my friend, but you do not think that you know.

ALCIBIADES: There again; what do you mean?

SOCRATES: Ask yourself; are you in any perplexity about things of which you are ignorant? You know, for example, that you know nothing about the preparation of food.

ALCIBIADES: Very true.

SOCRATES: And do you think and perplex yourself about the preparation of food: or do you leave that to someone who understands the art?

ALCIBIADES: The latter.

SOCRATES: Or if you were on a voyage, would you bewilder yourself by considering whether the rudder is to be drawn inwards or outwards, or do you leave that to the pilot, and do nothing?

ALCIBIADES: It would be the concern of the pilot.

SOCRATES: Then you are not perplexed about what you do not know, if you know that you do not know it?

ALCIBIADES: I imagine not.

SOCRATES: Do you not see, then, that mistakes in life and practice are likewise to be attributed to the ignorance which has conceit of knowledge?

ALCIBIADES: Once more, what do you mean?

SOCRATES: I suppose that we begin to act when we think that we know what we are doing?

ALCIBIADES: Yes.

SOCRATES: But when people think that they do not know they entrust their business to others?

ALCIBIADES: Yes.

SOCRATES: And so there is a class of ignorant persons who do not make mistakes in life because they trust others about things of which they are ignorant?

ALCIBIADES: True.

SOCRATES: Who, then, are the persons who make mistakes? They cannot, of course, be those who know?

ALCIBIADES: Certainly not.

SOCRATES: But if neither those who know nor those who know that they do not know make mistakes, [118] there remain those only who do not know and think that they know.

ALCIBIADES: Yes, only those.

SOCRATES: Then this is ignorance of the disgraceful sort which is mischievous?

ALCIBIADES: Yes.

SOCRATES: And most mischievous and most disgraceful when having to do with the greatest matters?

ALCIBIADES: By far.

SOCRATES: And can there be any matters greater than the just, the honourable, the good and the expedient?

ALCIBIADES: There cannot be.

SOCRATES: And these, as you were saying, are what perplex you?

ALCIBIADES: Yes.

SOCRATES: But if you are perplexed, then, as the previous argument has shown, you are not only ignorant of the greatest matters but being ignorant you fancy that you know them?

ALCIBIADES: I fear that you are right.

SOCRATES: And now see what has happened to you, Alcibiades! I hardly like to speak of your evil case, but as we are alone I will: My good friend, you are wedded to ignorance of the most disgraceful kind, and of this you are convicted, not by me but out of your own mouth and by your own argument; wherefore also you rush into politics before you are educated. Neither is your case to be deemed singular. For I might say the same of almost all our statesmen, with the exception, perhaps, of your guardian, Pericles.

ALCIBIADES: Yes, Socrates; and Pericles is said not to have got his wisdom by the light of nature, but to have associated with several of the philosophers; with Pythocleides, for example, and with Anaxagoras, and now in advanced life with Damon, in the hope of gaining wisdom.

SOCRATES: Very good; but did you ever know a man wise in anything who was unable to impart his particular wisdom? For example, he who taught you letters was not only wise but he made you and any others whom he liked wise.

ALCIBIADES: Yes.

SOCRATES: And you, whom he taught, can do the same?

ALCIBIADES: True.

SOCRATES: And in like manner the harper and gymnastic-master?

ALCIBIADES: Certainly.

SOCRATES: When a person is enabled to impart knowledge to another he thereby gives an excellent proof of his own understanding of any matter.

ALCIBIADES: I agree.

SOCRATES: Well, and did Pericles make anyone wise; did he begin by making his sons wise?

ALCIBIADES: But, Socrates, if the two sons of Pericles were simpletons, what has that to do with the matter?

SOCRATES: Well, but did he make your brother, Cleinias, wise?

ALCIBIADES: Cleinias is a madman; there is no use in talking of him.

SOCRATES: But if Cleinias is a madman and the two sons of Pericles were simpletons, what reason can be given why he neglects you, and lets you be as you are?

ALCIBIADES: I believe that I am to blame for not listening to him.

SOCRATES: But did you ever hear of any other Athenian or foreigner, bond or free, who was deemed to have grown wiser in the society of Pericles [119] – as I might cite Pythodorus, the son of Isolochus, and Callias, the son of Calliades, who have grown wiser in the society of Zeno, for which privilege they have each of them paid him the sum of a hundred minae to the increase of their wisdom and fame.

ALCIBIADES: I certainly never did hear of anyone.

SOCRATES: Well, and in reference to your own case, do you mean to remain as you are, or will you take some pains about yourself?

ALCIBIADES: With your aid, Socrates, I will. And indeed, when I hear you speak, the truth of what you are saying strikes home to me and I agree with you, for our statesmen, all but a few, do appear to be quite uneducated.

SOCRATES: What is the inference?

ALCIBIADES: Why, that if they were educated they would be trained athletes, and he who means to rival them ought to have knowledge and experience when he attacks them; but now, as they have become politicians without any special training, why should I have the trouble of learning and practising? For I know well that by the light of nature I shall get the better of them.

SOCRATES: My dear friend, what a sentiment! And how unworthy of your noble form and your high estate!

ALCIBIADES: What do you mean, Socrates; why do you say so?

SOCRATES: I am grieved when I think of our mutual love.

ALCIBIADES: At what?

SOCRATES: At your fancying that the contest on which you are entering is with people here.

ALCIBIADES: Why, what others are there?

SOCRATES: Is that a question which a magnanimous soul should ask?

ALCIBIADES: Do you mean to say that the contest is not with these?

SOCRATES: And suppose that you were going to steer a ship into action, would you only aim at being the best pilot on board? Would you not, while acknowledging that you must possess this degree of excellence, rather look to your antagonists, and not, as you are now doing, to your fellow combatants? You ought to be so far above these latter, that they will not even dare to be your rivals; and, being regarded by you as inferiors, will do battle for you against the enemy; this is the kind of superiority which you must establish over them, if you mean to accomplish any noble action really worthy of yourself and of the State.

ALCIBIADES: That would certainly be my aim.

SOCRATES: Verily, then, you have good reason to be satisfied, if you are better than the soldiers; and you need not, when you are their superior and have your thoughts and actions fixed upon them, look away to the generals of the enemy.

ALCIBIADES: Of whom are you speaking, Socrates?

[120] SOCRATES: Why, you surely know that our city goes to war now and then with the Lacedaemonians and with the great king?

ALCIBIADES: True enough.

SOCRATES: And if you meant to be the ruler of this city, would you not be right in considering that the Lacedaemonian and Persian king were your true rivals?

ALCIBIADES: I believe that you are right.

SOCRATES: Oh, no, my friend, I am

quite wrong, and I think that you ought rather to turn your attention to Midias the quail-breeder and others like him, who manage our politics; in whom, as the women would remark, you may still see the slaves' cut of hair, cropping out in their minds as well as on their pates; and they come with their barbarous lingo to flatter us and not to rule us. To these, I say, you should look, and then you need not trouble yourself about your own fitness to contend in such a noble arena; there is no reason why you should either learn what has to be learned or practise what has to be practised, and only when thoroughly prepared enter on a political career.

ALCIBIADES: There, I think, Socrates, that you are right; I do not suppose, however, that the Spartan generals or the great king are really different from anybody else.

SOCRATES: But, my dear friend, do consider what you are saying.

ALCIBIADES: What am I to consider?

SOCRATES: In the first place, will you be more likely to take care of yourself, if you are in a wholesome fear and dread of them, or if you are not?

ALCIBIADES: Clearly, if I have such a fear of them.

SOCRATES: And do you think that you will sustain any injury if you take care of yourself?

ALCIBIADES: No, I shall be greatly benefited.

SOCRATES: And this is one very important respect in which that notion of yours is bad.

ALCIBIADES: True.

SOCRATES: In the next place, consider that what you say is probably false.

ALCIBIADES: How so?

SOCRATES: Let me ask you whether better natures are likely to be found in noble races or not in noble races?

ALCIBIADES: Clearly in noble races.

SOCRATES: Are not those who are well born and well bred most likely to be perfect in virtue?

ALCIBIADES: Certainly.

SOCRATES: Then let us compare our antecedents with those of the Lacedaemonian and Persian kings; are they inferior to us in descent? Have we not heard that the former are sprung from Heracles, and the latter from Achaemenes, and that the race of Heracles and the race of Achaemenes go back to Perseus, son of Zeus?

[121] ALCIBIADES: Why, so does mine go back to Eurysaces, and he to Zeus!

SOCRATES: And mine, noble Alcibiades, to Daedalus, and he to Hephaestus, son of Zeus. But, for all that, we are far inferior to them. For they are descended 'from Zeus', through a line of kings – either kings of Argos and Lacedaemon or kings of Persia, a country which the descendants of Achaemenes have always possessed, besides being at various times sovereigns of Asia, as they now are; whereas, we and our fathers were but private persons. How ridiculous would you be thought if you were to make a display of your ancestors and of Salamis, the island of Eurysaces, or of Aegina, the habitation of the still more ancient Aeacus, before Artaxerxes, son of Xerxes. You should consider how inferior we are to them both in the derivation of our birth and in other particulars. Did you never observe how great is the property of the Spartan kings? And their wives are under the guardianship of the Ephori, who are public officers and watch over them, in order to preserve as far as possible the purity of the Heracleid blood. Still greater is the difference among the Persians; for no one entertains a suspicion that the father of a prince of Persia can be anyone but the king. Such is the awe which invests the person of the queen that any other guard is needless. And when the heir of the kingdom is born, all the subjects of the king feast;

and the day of his birth is for ever afterwards kept as a holiday and time of sacrifice by all Asia; whereas, when you and I were born, Alcibiades, as the comic poet says, the neighbours hardly knew of the important event. After the birth of the royal child he is tended not by a good-for-nothing woman nurse but by the best of the royal eunuchs, who are charged with the care of him, and especially with the fashioning and right formation of his limbs, in order that he may be as shapely as possible; which being their calling, they are held in great honour. And when the young prince is seven years old he is put upon a horse and taken to the riding-masters, and begins to go out hunting. And at fourteen years of age he is handed over to the royal schoolmasters, as they are termed: these are four chosen men, reputed to be the best among the Persians of a certain age; and one of them is the wisest, another the justest, a third the most temperate and a fourth the most valiant. The first instructs him in the magianism of Zoroaster, the son of Oromasus, [122] which is the worship of the Gods, and teaches him also the duties of his royal office; the second, who is the justest, teaches him always to speak the truth; the third, or most temperate, forbids him to allow any pleasure to be lord over him, that he may be accustomed to be a freeman and king indeed – lord of himself first, and not a slave; the most valiant trains him to be bold and fearless, telling him that if he fears he is to deem himself a slave; whereas Pericles gave you, Alcibiades, for a tutor Zopyrus the Thracian, a slave of his who was past all other work. I might enlarge on the nurture and education of your rivals, but that would be tedious; and what I have said is a sufficient sample of what remains to be said. I have only to remark, by way of contrast, that no one cares about your birth or nurture or education, or, I may say, about that of any other Athenian,

unless he has a lover who looks after him. And if you cast an eye on the wealth, the luxury, the garments with their flowing trains, the anointings with myrrh, the multitudes of attendants and all the other bravery of the Persians you will be ashamed when you discern your own inferiority; or if you look at the temperance and orderliness and ease and grace and magnanimity and courage and endurance and love of toil and desire of glory and ambition of the Lacedaemonians – in all these respects you will see that you are but a child in comparison of them. Even in the matter of wealth, if you value yourself upon that, I must reveal to you how you stand; for if you form an estimate of the wealth of the Lacedaemonians you will see that our possessions fall far short of theirs. For no one here can compete with them either in the extent and fertility of their own and the Messenian territory or in the number of their slaves, and especially of the Helots, or of their horses, or of the animals which feed on the Messenian pastures. But I have said enough of this: and as to gold and silver, there is more of them in Lacedaemon than in all the rest of Hellas, for during many generations gold has been always flowing in to them from the whole Hellenic world, and often from the barbarian also, and never going out, [123] as in the fable of Aesop the fox said to the lion, 'The prints of the feet of those going in are distinct enough'; but who ever saw the trace of money going out of Lacedaemon? and therefore you may safely infer that the inhabitants are the richest of the Hellenes in gold and silver, and that their kings are the richest of them, for they have a larger share of these things, and they have also a tribute paid to them which is very considerable. Yet the Spartan wealth, though great in comparison of the wealth of the other Hellenes, is as nothing in comparison of that of the

Persians and their kings. Why, I have been informed by a credible person who went up to the king [at Susa] that he passed through a large tract of excellent land, extending for nearly a day's journey, which the people of the country called the queen's girdle, and another, which they called her veil; and several other fair and fertile districts, which were reserved for the adornment of the queen, and are named after her several habiliments. Now, I cannot help thinking to myself, What if someone were to go to Amestris, the wife of Xerxes and mother of Artaxerxes, and say to her, There is a certain Dinomache, whose whole wardrobe is not worth fifty minae – and that will be more than the value – and she has a son who is possessed of a three-hundred acre patch at Erchiae, and he has a mind to go to war with your son – would she not wonder to what this Alcibiades trusts for success in the conflict? 'He must rely,' she would say to herself, 'upon his training and wisdom – these are the things which Hellenes value.' And if she heard that this Alcibiades who is making the attempt is not as yet twenty years old, and is wholly uneducated, and when his lover tells him that he ought to get education and training first, and then go and fight the king he refuses, and says that he is well enough as he is, would she not be amazed, and ask, 'On what, then, does the youth rely?' And if we replied: He relies on his beauty, and stature, and birth, and mental endowments, she would think that we were mad, Alcibiades, when she compared the advantages which you possess with those of her own people. [124] And I believe that even Lampido, the daughter of Leotychides, the wife of Archidamus and mother of Agis, all of whom were kings, would have the same feeling; if, in your present uneducated state, you were to turn your thoughts against her son she, too, would be equally astonished. But how disgraceful that we should not have as high a notion of what is required in us as our enemies' wives and mothers have of the qualities which are required in their assailants? O my friend, be persuaded by me, and hear the Delphic inscription, 'Know thyself' – not the men whom you think, but these kings are our rivals, and we can only overcome them by pains and skill. And if you fail in the required qualities you will fail also in becoming renowned among Hellenes and Barbarians, which you seem to desire more than any other man ever desired anything.

ALCIBIADES: I entirely believe you; but what are the sort of pains which are required, Socrates – can you tell me?

SOCRATES: Yes, I can; but we must take counsel together concerning the manner in which both of us may be most improved. For what I am telling you of the necessity of education applies to myself as well as to you; and there is only one point in which I have an advantage over you.

ALCIBIADES: What is that?

SOCRATES: I have a guardian who is better and wiser than your guardian, Pericles.

ALCIBIADES: Who is he, Socrates?

SOCRATES: God, Alcibiades, who up to this day has not allowed me to converse with you; and he inspires in me the faith that I am especially designed to bring you to honour.

ALCIBIADES: You are jesting, Socrates.

SOCRATES: Perhaps; at any rate, I am right in saying that all men greatly need pains and care, and you and I above all men.

ALCIBIADES: You are not far wrong about me.

SOCRATES: And certainly not about myself.

ALCIBIADES: But what can we do?

SOCRATES: There must be no hesitation or cowardice, my friend.

ALCIBIADES: That would not become us, Socrates.

SOCRATES: No, indeed, and we ought to take counsel together: for do we not wish to be as good as possible?

ALCIBIADES: We do.

SOCRATES: In what sort of virtue?

ALCIBIADES: Plainly, in the virtue of good men.

SOCRATES: Who are good in what?

ALCIBIADES: Those, clearly, who are good in the management of affairs.

SOCRATES: What sort of affairs? Equestrian affairs?

ALCIBIADES: Certainly not.

SOCRATES: You mean that about them we should have recourse to horsemen?

ALCIBIADES: Yes.

SOCRATES: Well; naval affairs?

ALCIBIADES: No.

SOCRATES: You mean that we should have recourse to sailors about them?

ALCIBIADES: Yes.

SOCRATES: Then what affairs? And who do them?

[125] ALCIBIADES: The affairs which occupy Athenian gentlemen.

SOCRATES: And when you speak of gentlemen, do you mean the wise or the unwise?

ALCIBIADES: The wise.

SOCRATES: And a man is good in respect of that in which he is wise?

ALCIBIADES: Yes.

SOCRATES: And evil in respect of that in which he is unwise?

ALCIBIADES: Certainly.

SOCRATES: The shoemaker, for example, is wise in respect of the making of shoes?

ALCIBIADES: Yes.

SOCRATES: Then he is good in that?

ALCIBIADES: He is.

SOCRATES: But in respect of the making of garments he is unwise?

ALCIBIADES: Yes.

SOCRATES: Then in that he is bad?

ALCIBIADES: Yes.

SOCRATES: Then upon this view of the matter the same man is good and also bad?

ALCIBIADES: True.

SOCRATES: But would you say that the good are the same as the bad?

ALCIBIADES: Certainly not.

SOCRATES: Then whom do you call the good?

ALCIBIADES: I mean by the good those who are able to rule in the city.

SOCRATES: Not, surely, over horses?

ALCIBIADES: Certainly not.

SOCRATES: But over men?

ALCIBIADES: Yes.

SOCRATES: When they are sick?

ALCIBIADES: No.

SOCRATES: Or on a voyage?

ALCIBIADES: No.

SOCRATES: Or reaping the harvest?

ALCIBIADES: No.

SOCRATES: When they are doing something or nothing?

ALCIBIADES: When they are doing something, I should say.

SOCRATES: I wish that you would explain to me what this something is.

ALCIBIADES: When they are having dealings with one another, and using one another's services, as we citizens do in our daily life.

SOCRATES: Those of whom you speak are ruling over men who are using the services of other men?

ALCIBIADES: Yes.

SOCRATES: Are they ruling over the signal-men who give the time to the rowers?

ALCIBIADES: No; they are not.

SOCRATES: That would be the office of the pilot?

ALCIBIADES: Yes.

SOCRATES: But, perhaps you mean that they rule over flute-players, who lead the singers and use the services of the dancers?

ALCIBIADES: Certainly not.

SOCRATES: That would be the business of the teacher of the chorus?

ALCIBIADES: Yes.

SOCRATES: Then what is the meaning of being able to rule over men who use other men?

ALCIBIADES: I mean that they rule over men who have common rights of citizenship, and dealings with one another.

SOCRATES: And what sort of an art is this? Suppose that I ask you again, as I did just now, What art makes men know how to rule over their fellow-sailors – how would you answer?

ALCIBIADES: The art of the pilot.

SOCRATES: And if I may recur to another old instance, what art enables them to rule over their fellow-singers?

ALCIBIADES: The art of the teacher of the chorus, which you were just now mentioning.

SOCRATES: And what do you call the art of fellow-citizens?

ALCIBIADES: I should say, good counsel, Socrates.

SOCRATES: And is the art of the pilot evil counsel?

ALCIBIADES: No.

SOCRATES: But good counsel?

[126] ALCIBIADES: Yes, that is what I should say – good counsel, of which the aim is the preservation of the voyagers.

SOCRATES: True. And what is the aim of that other good counsel of which you speak?

ALCIBIADES: The aim is the better order and preservation of the city.

SOCRATES: And what is that of which the absence or presence improves and preserves the order of the city? Suppose you were to ask me, what is that of which the presence or absence improves or preserves the order of the body? I should reply, the presence of health and the absence of disease. You would say the same?

ALCIBIADES: Yes.

SOCRATES: And if you were to ask me the same question about the eyes I should reply in the same way, 'the presence of sight and the absence of blindness'; or about the ears, I should reply that they were improved and were in better case when deafness was absent and hearing was present in them.

ALCIBIADES: True.

SOCRATES: And what would you say of a state? What is that by the presence or absence of which the State is improved and better managed and ordered?

ALCIBIADES: I should say, Socrates: the presence of friendship and the absence of hatred and division.

SOCRATES: And do you mean by friendship agreement or disagreement?

ALCIBIADES: Agreement.

SOCRATES: What art makes cities agree about numbers?

ALCIBIADES: Arithmetic.

SOCRATES: And private individuals?

ALCIBIADES: The same.

SOCRATES: And what art makes each individual agree with himself?

ALCIBIADES: The same.

SOCRATES: And what art makes each of us agree with himself about the comparative length of the span and of the cubit? Does not the art of measure?

ALCIBIADES: Yes.

SOCRATES: Individuals are agreed with one another about this; and states, equally?

ALCIBIADES: Yes.

SOCRATES: And the same holds of the balance?

ALCIBIADES: True.

SOCRATES: But what is the other agreement of which you speak, and about what? what art can give that agreement? And does that which gives it to the State give it also to the individual, so as to make him consistent with himself and with another?

ALCIBIADES: I should suppose so.

SOCRATES: But what is the nature of the agreement? – answer, and faint not.

ALCIBIADES: I mean to say that there should be such friendship and agreement as exists between an affectionate father and mother and their son, or between brothers, or between husband and wife.

SOCRATES: But can a man, Alcibiades, agree with a woman about the spinning of wool, which she understands and he does not?

ALCIBIADES: No, truly.

SOCRATES: Nor has he any need, for spinning is a female accomplishment.

ALCIBIADES: Yes.

[127] SOCRATES: And would a woman agree with a man about the science of arms, which she has never learned?

ALCIBIADES: Certainly not.

SOCRATES: I suppose that the use of arms would be regarded by you as a male accomplishment?

ALCIBIADES: It would.

SOCRATES: Then, upon your view, women and men have two sorts of knowledge?

ALCIBIADES: Certainly.

SOCRATES: Then in their knowledge there is no agreement of women and men?

ALCIBIADES: There is not.

SOCRATES: Nor can there be friendship, if friendship is agreement?

ALCIBIADES: Plainly not.

SOCRATES: Then women are not loved by men when they do their own work?

ALCIBIADES: I suppose not.

SOCRATES: Nor men by women when they do their own work?

ALCIBIADES: No.

SOCRATES: Nor are states well administered when individuals do their own work?

ALCIBIADES: I should rather think, Socrates, that the reverse is the truth.

SOCRATES: What! do you mean to say that states are well administered when friendship is absent, the presence of which, as we were saying, alone secures their good order?

ALCIBIADES: But I should say that there is friendship among them, for this very reason, that the two parties respectively do their own work.

SOCRATES: That was not what you were saying before; and what do you mean now by affirming that friendship exists when there is no agreement? How can there be agreement about matters which the one party knows and of which the other is in ignorance?

ALCIBIADES: Impossible.

SOCRATES: And when individuals are doing their own work, are they doing what is just or unjust?

ALCIBIADES: What is just, certainly.

SOCRATES: And when individuals do what is just in the State, is there no friendship among them?

ALCIBIADES: I suppose that there must be, Socrates.

SOCRATES: Then what do you mean by this friendship or agreement about which we must be wise and discreet in order that we may be good men? I cannot make out where it exists or among whom; according to you, the same persons may sometimes have it, and sometimes not.

ALCIBIADES: But, indeed, Socrates, I do not know what I am saying; and I have long been, unconsciously to myself, in a most disgraceful state.

SOCRATES: Nevertheless, cheer up; at fifty, if you had discovered your deficiency you would have been too old, and the time for taking care of yourself would have passed away, but yours is just the age at which the discovery should be made.

ALCIBIADES: And what should he do, Socrates, who would make the discovery?

SOCRATES: Answer questions, Alcibiades; and that is a process which, by the grace of God, if I may put any faith in my oracle, will be very improving to both of us.

ALCIBIADES: If I can be improved by answering, I will answer.

[128] SOCRATES: And first of all, that we may not peradventure be de-

ceived by appearances, fancying, perhaps, that we are taking care of ourselves when we are not, what is the meaning of a man taking care of himself? and when does he take care? Does he take care of himself when he takes care of what belongs to him?

ALCIBIADES: I should think so.

SOCRATES: When does a man take care of his feet? Does he not take care of them when he takes care of that which belongs to his feet?

ALCIBIADES: I do not understand.

SOCRATES: Let me take the hand as an illustration; does not a ring belong to the finger, and to the finger only?

ALCIBIADES: Yes.

SOCRATES: And the shoe in like manner to the foot?

ALCIBIADES: Yes.

SOCRATES: And when we take care of our shoes, do we not take care of our feet?

ALCIBIADES: I do not comprehend, Socrates.

SOCRATES: But you would admit, Alcibiades, that to take proper care of a thing is a correct expression?

ALCIBIADES: Yes.

SOCRATES: And taking proper care means improving?

ALCIBIADES: Yes.

SOCRATES: And what is the art which improves our shoes?

ALCIBIADES: Shoemaking.

SOCRATES: Then by shoemaking we take care of our shoes?

ALCIBIADES: Yes.

SOCRATES: And do we by shoemaking take care of our feet, or by some other art which improves the feet?

ALCIBIADES: By some other art.

SOCRATES: And the same art improves the feet which improves the rest of the body?

ALCIBIADES: Very true.

SOCRATES: Which is gymnastic?

ALCIBIADES: Certainly.

SOCRATES: Then by gymnastic we take care of our feet, and by shoemaking of that which belongs to our feet?

ALCIBIADES: Very true.

SOCRATES: And by gymnastic we take care of our hands, and by the art of graving rings of that which belongs to our hands?

ALCIBIADES: Yes.

SOCRATES: And by gymnastic we take care of the body, and by the art of weaving and the other arts we take care of the things of the body?

ALCIBIADES: Clearly.

SOCRATES: Then the art which takes care of each thing is different from that which takes care of the belongings of each thing?

ALCIBIADES: True.

SOCRATES: Then in taking care of what belongs to you, you do not take care of yourself?

ALCIBIADES: Certainly not.

SOCRATES: For the art which takes care of our belongings appears not to be the same as that which takes care of ourselves?

ALCIBIADES: Clearly not.

SOCRATES: And now let me ask you what is the art with which we take care of ourselves?

ALCIBIADES: I cannot say.

SOCRATES: At any rate, thus much has been admitted, that the art is not one which makes any of our possessions, but which makes ourselves better?

ALCIBIADES: True.

SOCRATES: But should we ever have known what art makes a shoe better, if we did not know a shoe?

ALCIBIADES: Impossible.

SOCRATES: Nor should we know what art makes a ring better if we did not know a ring?

ALCIBIADES: That is true.

[129] SOCRATES: And can we ever know what art makes a man better if we do not know what we are ourselves?

ALCIBIADES: Impossible.

SOCRATES: And is self-knowledge

such an easy thing, and was he to be lightly esteemed who inscribed the text on the temple at Delphi? Or is self-knowledge a difficult thing, which few are able to attain?

ALCIBIADES: At times I fancy, Socrates, that anybody can know himself; at other times the task appears to be very difficult.

SOCRATES: But whether easy or difficult, Alcibiades, still there is no other way; knowing what we are, we shall know how to take care of ourselves, and if we are ignorant we shall not know.

ALCIBIADES: That is true.

SOCRATES: Well, then, let us see in what way the self-existent can be discovered by us; that will give us a chance of discovering our own existence, which otherwise we can never know.

ALCIBIADES: You say truly.

SOCRATES: Come, now, I beseech you, tell me with whom you are conversing? – with whom but with me?

ALCIBIADES: Yes.

SOCRATES: As I am, with you?

ALCIBIADES: Yes.

SOCRATES: That is to say, I, Socrates, am talking?

ALCIBIADES: Yes.

SOCRATES: And Alcibiades is my hearer?

ALCIBIADES: Yes.

SOCRATES: And I in talking use words?

ALCIBIADES: Certainly.

SOCRATES: And talking and using words have, I suppose, the same meaning?

ALCIBIADES: To be sure.

SOCRATES: And the user is not the same as the thing which he uses?

ALCIBIADES: What do you mean?

SOCRATES: I will explain; the shoemaker, for example, uses a square tool, and a circular tool, and other tools for cutting?

ALCIBIADES: Yes.

SOCRATES: But the tool is not the same as the cutter and user of the tool?

ALCIBIADES: Of course not.

SOCRATES: And in the same way the instrument of the harper is to be distinguished from the harper himself?

ALCIBIADES: It is.

SOCRATES: Now the question which I asked was whether you conceive the user to be always different from that which he uses?

ALCIBIADES: I do.

SOCRATES: Then what shall we say of the shoemaker? Does he cut with his tools only or with his hands?

ALCIBIADES: With his hands as well.

SOCRATES: He uses his hands too?

ALCIBIADES: Yes.

SOCRATES: And does he use his eyes in cutting leather?

ALCIBIADES: He does.

SOCRATES: And we admit that the user is not the same with the things which he uses?

ALCIBIADES: Yes.

SOCRATES: Then the shoemaker and the harper are to be distinguished from the hands and feet which they use?

ALCIBIADES: Clearly.

SOCRATES: And does not a man use the whole body?

ALCIBIADES: Certainly.

SOCRATES: And that which uses is different from that which is used?

ALCIBIADES: True.

SOCRATES: Then a man is not the same as his own body?

ALCIBIADES: That is the inference.

SOCRATES: What is he, then?

ALCIBIADES: I cannot say.

SOCRATES: Nay, you can say that he is the user of the body.

ALCIBIADES: Yes.

[130] SOCRATES: And the user of the body is the soul?

ALCIBIADES: Yes, the soul.

SOCRATES: And the soul rules?

ALCIBIADES: Yes.

SOCRATES: Let me make an assertion which will, I think, be universally admitted.

ALCIBIADES: What is it?

SOCRATES: That man is one of three things.

ALCIBIADES: What are they?

SOCRATES: Soul, body, or both together forming a whole.

ALCIBIADES: Certainly.

SOCRATES: But did we not say that the actual ruling principle of the body is man?

ALCIBIADES: Yes, we did.

SOCRATES: And does the body rule over itself?

ALCIBIADES: Certainly not.

SOCRATES: It is subject, as we were saying?

ALCIBIADES: Yes.

SOCRATES: Then that is not the principle which we are seeking?

ALCIBIADES: It would seem not.

SOCRATES: But may we say that the union of the two rules over the body, and consequently that this is man?

ALCIBIADES: Very likely.

SOCRATES: The most unlikely of all things; for if one of the members is subject the two united cannot possibly rule.

ALCIBIADES: True.

SOCRATES: But since neither the body nor the union of the two is man, either man has no real existence or the soul is man?

ALCIBIADES: Just so

SOCRATES: Is anything more required to prove that the soul is man?

ALCIBIADES: Certainly not; the proof is, I think, quite sufficient.

SOCRATES: And if the proof, although not perfect, be sufficient, we shall be satisfied; more precise proof will be supplied when we have discovered that which we were led to omit, from a fear that the inquiry would be too much protracted.

ALCIBIADES: What was that?

SOCRATES: What I meant, when I said that absolute existence must be first considered; but now, instead of absolute existence, we have been considering the nature of individual existence, and this may, perhaps, be sufficient; for surely there is nothing which may be called more properly ourselves than the soul?

ALCIBIADES: There is nothing.

SOCRATES: Then we may truly conceive that you and I are conversing with one another, soul to soul?

ALCIBIADES: Very true.

SOCRATES: And that is just what I was saying before – that I, Socrates, am not arguing or talking with the face of Alcibiades, but with the real Alcibiades; or in other words, with his soul.

ALCIBIADES: True.

SOCRATES: Then he who bids a man know himself would have him know his soul?

ALCIBIADES: That appears to be true.

[131] SOCRATES: He whose knowledge only extends to the body, knows the things of a man, and not the man himself?

ALCIBIADES: That is true.

SOCRATES: Then neither the physician regarded as a physician, nor the trainer regarded as a trainer, knows himself?

ALCIBIADES: He does not.

SOCRATES: The husbandmen and the other craftsmen are very far from knowing themselves, for they would seem not even to know their own belongings? When regarded in relation to the arts which they practise they are even further removed from self-knowledge, for they only know the belongings of the body, which minister to the body.

ALCIBIADES: That is true.

SOCRATES: Then if temperance is the knowledge of self, in respect of his art none of them is temperate?

ALCIBIADES: I agree.

SOCRATES: And this is the reason

why their arts are accounted vulgar, and are not such as a good man would practise?

ALCIBIADES: Quite true.

SOCRATES: Again, he who cherishes his body cherishes not himself, but what belongs to him?

ALCIBIADES: That is true.

SOCRATES: But he who cherishes his money, cherishes neither himself nor his belongings, but is in a stage yet further removed from himself?

ALCIBIADES: I agree.

SOCRATES: Then the money-maker has really ceased to be occupied with his own concerns?

ALCIBIADES: True.

SOCRATES: And if anyone has fallen in love with the person of Alcibiades, he loves not Alcibiades, but the belongings of Alcibiades?

ALCIBIADES: True.

SOCRATES: But he who loves your soul is the true lover?

ALCIBIADES: That is the necessary inference.

SOCRATES: The lover of the body goes away when the flower of youth fades?

ALCIBIADES: True.

SOCRATES: But he who loves the soul goes not away, as long as the soul follows after virtue?

ALCIBIADES: Yes.

SOCRATES: And I am the lover who goes not away, but remains with you, when you are no longer young and the rest are gone?

ALCIBIADES: Yes, Socrates; and therein you do well, and I hope that you will remain.

SOCRATES: Then you must try to look your best.

ALCIBIADES: I will.

SOCRATES: The fact is, that there is only one lover of Alcibiades the son of Cleinias; there neither is nor ever has been seemingly any other; and he is his darling – Socrates, the son of Sophroniscus and Phaenarete.

ALCIBIADES: True.

SOCRATES: And did you not say, that if I had not spoken first, you were on the point of coming to me, and inquiring why I only remained?

ALCIBIADES: That is true.

SOCRATES: The reason was that I loved you for your own sake, whereas other men love what belongs to you; and your beauty, [132] which is not you, is fading away, just as your true self is beginning to bloom. And I will never desert you, if you are not spoiled and deformed by the Athenian people; for the danger which I most fear is that you will become a lover of the people and will be spoiled by them. Many a noble Athenian has been ruined in this way. For the demus of the great-hearted Erechtheus is of a fair countenance, but you should see him naked; wherefore observe the caution which I give you.

ALCIBIADES: What caution?

SOCRATES: Practise yourself, sweet friend, in learning what you ought to know, before you enter on politics; and then you will have an antidote which will keep you out of harm's way.

ALCIBIADES: Good advice, Socrates, but I wish that you would explain to me in what way I am to take care of myself.

SOCRATES: Have we not made an advance? for we are at any rate tolerably well agreed as to what we are, and there is no longer any danger, as we once feared, that we might be taking care not of ourselves but of something which is not ourselves.

ALCIBIADES: That is true.

SOCRATES: And the next step will be to take care of the soul, and look to that?

ALCIBIADES: Certainly.

SOCRATES: Leaving the care of our bodies and of our properties to others?

ALCIBIADES: Very good.

SOCRATES: But how can we have a perfect knowledge of the things of the soul? – For if we know them, then I suppose we shall know ourselves. Can we really be ignorant of the excellent meaning of the Delphian inscription, of which we were just now speaking?

ALCIBIADES: What have you in your thoughts, Socrates?

SOCRATES: I will tell you what I suspect to be the meaning and lesson of that inscription. Let me take an illustration from sight, which I imagine to be the only one suitable to my purpose.

ALCIBIADES: What do you mean?

SOCRATES: Consider; if someone were to say to the eye, 'See thyself,' as you might say to a man, 'Know thyself,' what is the nature and meaning of this precept? Would not his meaning be: That the eye should look at that in which it would see itself?

ALCIBIADES: Clearly.

SOCRATES: And what are the objects in looking at which we see ourselves?

ALCIBIADES: Clearly, Socrates, in looking at mirrors and the like.

SOCRATES: Very true; and is there not something of the nature of a mirror in our own eyes?

ALCIBIADES: Certainly.

SOCRATES: Did you ever observe that the face of the person looking into the eye of another is reflected as in a mirror; and in the visual organ which is over against him [133] and which is called the pupil, there is a sort of image of the person looking?

ALCIBIADES: That is quite true.

SOCRATES: Then the eye, looking at another eye, and at that in the eye which is most perfect, and which is the instrument of vision, will there see itself?

ALCIBIADES: That is evident.

SOCRATES: But looking at anything else either in man or in the world, and not to what resembles this, it will not see itself?

ALCIBIADES: Very true.

SOCRATES: Then if the eye is to see itself, it must look at the eye, and at that part of the eye where sight which is the virtue of the eye resides?

ALCIBIADES: True.

SOCRATES: And if the soul, my dear Alcibiades, is ever to know herself, must she not look at the soul; and especially at that part of the soul in which her virtue resides, and to any other which is like this?

ALCIBIADES: I agree, Socrates.

SOCRATES: And do we know of any part of our souls more divine than that which has to do with wisdom and knowledge?

ALCIBIADES: There is none.

SOCRATES: Then this is that part of the soul which resembles the divine; and he who looks at this and at the whole class of things divine, will be most likely to know himself?

ALCIBIADES: Clearly.

SOCRATES: And self-knowledge we agree to be wisdom?

ALCIBIADES: True.

SOCRATES: But if we have no self-knowledge and no wisdom, can we ever know our own good and evil?

ALCIBIADES: How can we, Socrates?

SOCRATES: You mean, that if you did not know Alcibiades, there would be no possibility of your knowing that what belonged to Alcibiades was really his?

ALCIBIADES: It would be quite impossible.

SOCRATES: Nor should we know that we were the persons to whom anything belonged, if we did not know ourselves?

ALCIBIADES: How could we?

SOCRATES: And if we did not know our own belongings, neither should we know the belongings of our belongings?

ALCIBIADES: Clearly not.

SOCRATES: Then we were not altogether right in acknowledging just now that a man may know what belongs to him and yet not know himself; nay, rather he cannot even know the belongings of his belongings; for the discernment of the things of self, and of the things which belong to the things of self, appear all to be the business of the same man, and of the same art.

ALCIBIADES: So much may be supposed.

SOCRATES: And he who knows not the things which belong to himself, will in like manner be ignorant of the things which belong to others?

ALCIBIADES: Very true.

SOCRATES: And if he knows not the affairs of others, he will not know the affairs of states?

ALCIBIADES: Certainly not.

SOCRATES: Then such a man can never be a statesman?

ALCIBIADES: He cannot.

SOCRATES: Nor an economist?

ALCIBIADES: He cannot.

[134] SOCRATES: He will not know what he is doing?

ALCIBIADES: He will not.

SOCRATES: And will not he who is ignorant fall into error?

ALCIBIADES: Assuredly.

SOCRATES: And if he falls into error will he not fail both in his public and private capacity?

ALCIBIADES: Yes, indeed.

SOCRATES: And failing, will he not be miserable?

ALCIBIADES: Very.

SOCRATES: And what will become of those for whom he is acting?

ALCIBIADES: They will be miserable also.

SOCRATES: Then he who is not wise and good cannot be happy?

ALCIBIADES: He cannot.

SOCRATES: The bad, then, are miserable?

ALCIBIADES: Yes, very.

SOCRATES: And if so, not he who has riches, but he who has wisdom, is delivered from his misery?

ALCIBIADES: Clearly.

SOCRATES: Cities, then, if they are to be happy, do not want walls, or triremes, or docks, or numbers, or size, Alcibiades, without virtue?

ALCIBIADES: Indeed they do not.

SOCRATES: And you must give the citizens virtue, if you mean to administer their affairs rightly or nobly?

ALCIBIADES: Certainly.

SOCRATES: But can a man give that which he has not?

ALCIBIADES: Impossible.

SOCRATES: Then you or anyone who means to govern and superintend not only himself and the things of himself but the State and the things of the State must in the first place acquire virtue.

ALCIBIADES: That is true.

SOCRATES: You have not therefore to obtain power or authority in order to enable you to do what you wish for yourself and the State, but justice and wisdom.

ALCIBIADES: Clearly.

SOCRATES: You and the State, if you act wisely and justly, will act according to the will of God?

ALCIBIADES: Certainly.

SOCRATES: As I was saying before, you will look only at what is bright and divine, and act with a view to them?

ALCIBIADES: Yes.

SOCRATES: In that mirror you will see and know yourselves and your own good?

ALCIBIADES: Yes.

SOCRATES: And so you will act rightly and well?

ALCIBIADES: Yes.

SOCRATES: In which case I will be security for your happiness.

ALCIBIADES: I accept the security.

SOCRATES: But if you act unrighteously your eye will turn to the dark and godless, and being in darkness and ignorance of yourselves, you will probably do deeds of darkness.

ALCIBIADES: Very possibly.

SOCRATES: For if a man, my dear

Alcibiades, has the power to do what he likes, but has no understanding, what is likely to be the result, [135] either to him as an individual or to the State – for example, if he be sick and is able to do what he likes, not having the mind of a physician – having, moreover, tyrannical power, and no one daring to reprove him, what will happen to him? Will he not be likely to have his constitution ruined?

ALCIBIADES: That is true.

SOCRATES: Or again, in a ship, if a man having the power to do what he likes has no intelligence or skill in navigation, do you see what will happen to him and to his fellow-sailors?

ALCIBIADES: Yes; I see that they will all perish.

SOCRATES: And in like manner, in a state, and where there is any power and authority which is wanting in virtue, will not misfortune, in like manner, ensue?

ALCIBIADES: Certainly.

SOCRATES: Not tyrannical power, then, my good Alcibiades, should be the aim either of individuals or states, if they would be happy, but virtue.

ALCIBIADES: That is true.

SOCRATES: And before they have virtue, to be commanded by a superior is better for men as well as for children?

ALCIBIADES: That is evident.

SOCRATES: And that which is better is also nobler?

ALCIBIADES: True.

SOCRATES: And what is nobler is more becoming?

ALCIBIADES: Certainly.

SOCRATES: Then to the bad man slavery is more becoming, because better?

ALCIBIADES: True.

SOCRATES: Then vice is only suited to a slave?

ALCIBIADES: Yes.

SOCRATES: And virtue to a freeman?

ALCIBIADES: Yes.

SOCRATES: And, O my friend, is not the condition of a slave to be avoided?

ALCIBIADES: Certainly, Socrates.

SOCRATES: And are you now conscious of your own state? And do you know whether you are a freeman or not?

ALCIBIADES: I think that I am very conscious indeed of my own state.

SOCRATES: And do you know how to escape out of a state which I do not even like to name to my beauty?

ALCIBIADES: Yes, I do.

SOCRATES: How?

ALCIBIADES: By your help, Socrates.

SOCRATES: That is not well said, Alcibiades.

ALCIBIADES: What ought I to have said?

SOCRATES: By the help of God.

ALCIBIADES: I agree; and I further say, that our relations are likely to be reversed. From this day forward, I must and will follow you as you have followed me; I will be the disciple, and you shall be my master.

SOCRATES: O that is rare! My love breeds another love: and so like the stork I shall be cherished by the bird whom I have hatched.

ALCIBIADES: Strange, but true; and henceforward I shall begin to think about justice.

SOCRATES: And I hope that you will persist; although I have fears, not because I doubt you; but I see the power of the State, which may be too much for both of us. (tr. B. Jowett)

2.8.2 Theages. *This can hardly be by Plato: it draws extensively on his work, and Stallbaum thought (wrongly) that it was written in the second century B.C. or later. It is a justification of Socrates as an educator. Its chief interest lies in the account of Socrates' divine sign: the description of it comes from Plato's Apology 31 D, but there are stories which are not otherwise recorded, notably in Socrates being led to check* *the acts of others* (cf. **9.7.14**). *As in Plato the sign acts negatively, but there is a curious suggestion that it also helps in the process of education through association with Socrates. There is a notable tribute to Socrates' personality towards the end of the dialogue.*

SOCRATES: There is, by a divine allotment, a certain daemon that has followed me, beginning from childhood. This is a voice, which, when it exists, always signifies to me the abandonment of what I am about to do; but it never at any time incites me. And, if anyone of my friends communicates anything to me and there is the voice, it dissuades me from that very thing, and it does not suffer me to do it. Of this I will produce you witnesses. You know the beautiful Charmides, the son of Glauco. He once happened to communicate to me that he was about to contend for the stadium at Nemea; and immediately, on his beginning to say, that he meant to contend, there was the voice. And I forbade him, and said, While you were speaking to me, there was the voice of the daemon; do not, therefore, contend. Perhaps, said he, the voice signified to you that I should not conquer; but though I should not be victorious, yet, by exercising myself at this time, I shall be benefited. Having thus spoken, he engaged in the contest. It is worth while, therefore, to inquire of him what happened to him after this very act of contending. [129] And if you are willing to inquire of Clitomachus, the brother of Timarchus, what Timarchus said to him, when, being about to die, he went right against the daemon, both he and Euathlus, the runner in the stadium, who received Timarchus when he was an exile, will tell you what he then said.

THEAGES: What did he say?

SOCRATES: O Clitomachus, said he, I indeed am now going to die, because I was unwilling to be persuaded by Socrates. But why Timarchus said this, I will tell you. When Timarchus rose from the banquet, together with Philemon the son of Philemonides, with the view of murdering Nicias the son of Heroscomander, they two alone were cognisant of the plot; and Timarchus, as he rose, said to me, What do you say, Socrates? Do you continue drinking; but I must rise up [and go] somewhere. I will, however, return shortly, if I am successful. And there was the voice. And I said to him, By no means, said I, rise up; for there has been to me the usual daemon signal. Upon this he stayed. And after a slight interval he was again going away, and said – Socrates, I am going. And there was again the voice. Again, therefore, I compelled him to stay. The third time, wishing to escape me unnoticed, he rose up without saying anything to me, and escaped unnoticed, having watched me, while I had my attention otherwise engaged; and thus departing he perpetrated the acts, through which he went away about to die. Hence he told his brother, what I have now told you, that he was going to die, through his not believing in me. Further still, you will hear from many respecting the events in Sicily what I said concerning the destruction of the army. And the things that are past you may hear from those that know them; but you may now make trial of the daemon signal, if it says anything to the purpose. For on the departure of Sannio the beautiful for the army there came to me the signal; and he is now gone with Thrasyllus, to carry on the campaign right through Ephesus and Ionia. And I think that he will either die or that he will meet with an end something near to it. And I very much fear for the rest of the enterprise. All these things have I said to you, because this power of this daemon is able to effect everything with respect to the intercourse of those who pass their time with me. For it is opposed to many; and it is not possible for those to be benefited by passing their time with me, so that it is not possible for me to live with them. With many, however, it does not prevent me from conversing; and yet they are not at all benefited by being with me. But they, whom the power of the daemon assists to the intercourse, are those whom you have noticed; for in a short time they make progress. [130] And of those who make progress some have the benefit firm and lasting; but many, as long as they are with me, advance in a wonderful manner; but when they separate themselves from me they again differ in no respect from any person whatever. This did Aristides, the son of Lysimachus and grandson of Aristides, suffer; for while passing his time with me he made very great progress in a short period; but afterwards an expedition took place, and he went away, sailing with it. On his return he found Thucydides, the son of Melesias and grandson of Thucydides, passing his time with me. Now this Thucydides, the day before, had felt some ill against me during a conversation. Aristides, therefore, after he had seen and saluted me, and other matters had been talked of, observed – I hear, Socrates, that Thucydides thinks highly of himself, on some points, and is angry with you, as if he were really something. It is so, said I. What, then, said he, does he not know what a slave he was before he associated with you? By the gods, said I, it does not seem that he does. But I too, said he, am in a ridiculous situation, Socrates. What is it? said I. It is, said he, that before I sailed away I was able to converse with any man whatever, and not to appear inferior to anyone in argument, so that I sought the society of men the most elegant; but now, on the contrary, I shun anyone whom I perceive to be instructed, so ashamed am I of my own littleness. But, said I, whether did this power leave you suddenly or by degrees? By degrees, he

replied. When was it present with you, said I? Was it present while you were learning something from me, or was it in some other way? I will tell you, said he, Socrates, a thing incredible indeed, by the gods, but true. I never at any time learnt anything from you, as you know. I made progress, however, when I associated with you, even if I was only in the same house, though not in the same room; but more so when I was in the same room with you; and I seemed to myself to improve much more when, being in the same room, I looked at you when you were speaking than when I looked another way. But I made by far the greatest progress when I sat near you and touched you. Now, however, said he, all that habit has entirely oozed away. Of such kind then is, Theages, the intercourse with myself; for if it is pleasing to the god you will make very great and rapid progress; but if not, not. See, then, whether it is not safer for you to be instructed by someone of those, who have a power over the benefit, with which they benefit men, than by me, who [have the power] to do only whatever may happen.

[131] THEAGES: It appears to me, Socrates, that we should act in this manner, namely, to make a trial of this daemon by associating together. And if he is favourable to us this will be the best; but if not, then let us immediately consult what we shall do, whether we shall associate with some other person or endeavour to appease the divine power that is present with you, by prayers and sacrifices, or any other method that the diviners may explain.

DEMODOCUS: Do not, Socrates, oppose the lad any longer on these points; for Theages speaks well.

SOCRATES: If it appears proper so to act, let us act so. (128 D–131 A, tr. G. Burges altd.)

PART THREE

XENOPHON (c. 430–354 B.C.)

An Athenian soldier and man of letters, who knew Socrates and was influenced by him. His evidence is thus of considerable importance, but that importance is qualified by the facts that

(*a*) He was away from Athens from 401; he can have known Socrates only for a limited period before that.

(*b*) He himself was young at the time and his judgement immature.

(*c*) He does not claim to have known Socrates closely.

(*d*) His response to Socrates is largely in terms of his own conventional piety and morality.

But he had access to other writings about Socrates, lost to us, and he is at least evidence of how Socrates struck one young man.

In 401, despite a warning from Socrates, he joined Cyrus's expedition 'up-country' and embarked on the adventures he later narrated in his *Anabasis*. His friendship for Cyrus and sympathies with Sparta led to a sentence of banishment, though this was later rescinded. For most of his settled life he lived as a country gentleman in the Peloponnese.

His romantic work *The Education of Cyrus* (Cyrus the Elder) contains parallels with the books about Socrates, and makes us wonder how far Socrates moulded Xenophon's whole outlook and how far Xenophon put his own ideas into Socrates' mouth.

I have not here included anything from the undoubtedly spurious letters: one extract will be found under Stobaeus, **11.1.3** and others in **15.5**.

3.1 Apology

Xenophon was not in Athens at the time of Socrates' trial, and his account of Socrates' defence has little claim to authenticity, though he names as his informant Hermogenes, whom Plato records as visiting Socrates' death-bed (Phaedo 59 B). *The importance of the work (which we cannot date, even in relation to Plato's* Apology) *is that it shows that either there were very different memories of Socrates' defence or that it was regarded as nothing abnormal to invent a defence for him.*

I have always considered the manner in which Socrates behaved after he had been summoned to his trial as most worthy of our remembrance; and that not only with respect to the defence he made for himself when standing before his judges, but the sentiments he expressed concerning his dissolution. For although there be many who have written on this subject, and all concur in setting forth the wonderful courage and intrepidity wherewith he spake to the assembly – so that it remaineth incontestable that Socrates did thus speak – yet that it was his full persuasion, that death was more eligible for him than life at such a season, they have by no means so clearly manifested; whereby the loftiness of his style, and the boldness of his speech, may wear at least the appearance of being imprudent and unbecoming.

But Hermogenes, the son of Hipponicus, was his intimate friend; and from him it is we have heard those things of Socrates, as sufficiently prove the sublimity of his language was only conformable to the sentiments of his mind. For, having observed him, as he tells us, choosing rather to discourse on any other subject than the business of his trial; he asked him, 'If it was not necessary to be preparing for his defence?' And 'What!' said he, 'my

Hermogenes, suppose you I have not spent my whole life in preparing for this very thing?' Hermogenes desiring he would explain himself: 'I have,' said he, 'steadily persisted, throughout life, in a diligent endeavour to do nothing which is unjust; and this I take to be the best and most honourable preparation.'

'But see you not,' said Hermogenes, 'that oft times here in Athens the judges, influenced by the force of oratory, condemn those to death who no way deserve it; and not less frequently acquit the guilty, when softened into compassion by the moving complaints, or the insinuating eloquence of those who plead their cause before them?'

'I know it,' replied Socrates; 'and therefore twice have I attempted to take the matter of my defence under consideration: but the Genius always opposed me.'

Hermogenes having expressed some astonishment at these words, Socrates proceeded:

'Doth it then appear marvellous to you, my Hermogenes, that God should think this the very best time for me to die? Know you not that hitherto I have yielded to no man that he hath lived more uprightly or even more pleasurably than myself; possessed, as I was, of that well-grounded self-approbation, arising from the consciousness of having done my duty both to the gods and men: my friends also bearing their testimony to the integrity of my conversation! But now – if my life is prolonged, and I am spared even to old age – what can hinder, my Hermogenes, the infirmities of old age from falling upon me? My sight will grow dim; my hearing, heavy; less capable of learning, as more liable to forget what I have already learned; and if, to all this, I become sensible of my decay and bemoan myself on the account of it; how can I say that I still lived pleasantly? It may be too,' continued Socrates, 'that God, through his goodness, hath appointed for me, not only that my life should terminate at a time which seems the most seasonable, but the manner in which it will be terminated shall also be the most eligible: for, if my death is now resolved upon it must needs be that they who take charge of this matter will permit me to choose the means supposed the most easy; free too from those lingering circumstances which keep our friends in anxious suspense for us, and fill the mind of the dying man with much pain and perturbation. And when nothing offensive, nothing unbecoming, is left on the memory of those who are present, but the man is dissolved while the body is yet sound, and the mind still capable of exerting itself benevolently, who can say, my Hermogenes, that so to die is not most desirable? And with good reason,' continued Socrates, 'did the gods oppose themselves at what time we took the affair of my escape under deliberation, and determined that every means should be diligently sought after to effect it; since if our designs had been carried into execution, instead of terminating my life in the manner I am now doing, I had only gained the unhappy privilege of finding it put an end to by the torments of some disease, or the lingering decays incident to old age, when all things painful flow in upon us together, destitute of every joy which might serve to soften and allay them.

'Yet think not, my Hermogenes, the desire of death shall influence me beyond what is reasonable: I will not set out with asking it at their hands; but if, when I speak my opinion of myself and declare what I think I have deserved both of gods and men, my judges are displeased I will much sooner submit to it than meanly entreat the continuance of my life, whereby I should only bring upon myself many and far greater evils than any I had taken such unbecoming pains to deprecate.'

In this manner Socrates replied to Hermogenes and others: and his enemies having accused him of 'not believing in the gods whom the city held sacred; but as designing to introduce other and new deities; and, likewise, of his having corrupted the youth': Hermogenes further told me that Socrates, advancing towards the tribunal, thus spake:

'What I chiefly marvel at, O ye judges! is this; whence Meletus inferreth that I esteem not those as gods whom the city hold sacred. For that I sacrifice at the appointed festivals, on our common altars, was evident to all others; and might have been to Meletus, had Meletus been so minded. Neither yet doth it seem to be asserted with greater reason that my design was to introduce new deities among us, because I have often said, 'That it is the voice of God which giveth me significations of what is most expedient'; since they themselves, who observe the chirping of birds, or those ominous words spoken by men, ground their conclusions on no other than voices. For who among you doubteth whether thunder sendeth forth a voice? or whether it be not the very greatest of all auguries? The Pythian priestess herself; doth not she likewise from the tripod declare, by a voice, the divine oracles? And, truly, that God foreknoweth the future, and also showeth it to whomsoever he pleaseth, I am no way singular either in believing or asserting; since all mankind agree with me herein, this difference only excepted, that whereas they say it is from auguries, omens, symbols and diviners whence they have their notices of the future; I, on the contrary, impute all those premonitions wherewith I am favoured to a genius; and I think that, in so doing, I have spoken not only more truly but more piously than they who attribute to birds the divine privilege of declaring things to come: and that I lied not against God, I have this indisputable proof, that whereas I have often communicated to many of my friends the divine counsels, yet hath no man ever detected me of speaking falsely.'

No sooner was this heard but a murmuring arose among his judges; some disbelieving the truth of what he had said, while others envied him for being, as they thought, more highly favoured of the gods than they. But Socrates, still going on; 'Mark!' said he, 'I pray; and attend to what is yet more extraordinary, that such of you as are willing may still the more disbelieve that I have been thus favoured of the deity: Chaerephon, inquiring of the oracle at Delphi concerning me, was answered by Apollo himself, in the presence of many people, 'That he knew no man more free, more just or more wise than *I*.'

On hearing this, the tumult among them visibly increased; but Socrates, still going on, – 'And yet Lycurgus, the Lacedaemonian lawgiver, had still greater things declared of him: for, on his entering into the temple, the deity thus accosted him: "I am considering," said he, "whether I shall call thee a god, or a man!" Now Apollo compared me not to a god. This, indeed he said, 'That I by far excelled man." Howbeit, credit not too hastily what ye have heard, though coming from an oracle; but let us thoroughly examine those things which the deity spake concerning me.

'Say, then, where have you ever known anyone less enslaved to sensual appetite; whom more free than the man who submits not to receive gift or reward from the hands of any other? Whom can you deservedly esteem more just than he who can so well accommodate himself to what he hath already in his own possession as not even to desire what belongeth to another? Or how can he fail of being accounted wise who, from the time he first began to comprehend what was spoken, never ceased to seek, and search out, to the very best of his power, whatever was virtuous and good for man? And, as a proof that in so doing I have not laboured in vain, ye yourselves know, that many of our citizens, yea, and many foreigners also, who made virtue their pursuit, always preferred, as their chief pleasure, the conversing with me. Whence was it, I pray you, that when everyone knew my want of power to return any kind of pecuniary favour so many should be ambitious to bestow them on me? Why doth no man call me his debtor, yet many acknowledge they owe me much? When the city is besieged, and every other person bemoaning his loss, why do *I* appear as in no respect the poorer than while it remained in its most prosperous state? And what is the cause that when others are under a necessity to procure their delicacies from abroad, at an exorbitant rate, *I* can indulge in pleasures far more exquisite, by recurring to the reflections in my own mind? And now, O ye judges! if, in whatsoever I have declared of myself, no one is able to confute me as a false speaker, who will say I merit not approbation, and that not only from the gods but men?

'Nevertheless, you, O Meletus, have asserted, that I – diligently applying myself to the contemplation and practice of whatever is virtuous – "*corrupt the youth:*" – and, indeed, we well know what it is to corrupt them. But show us, if in your power, whom, of pious, I have made impious; of modest, shameless; of frugal, profuse? Who, from temperate is become drunken; from laborious, idle or effeminate, by associating with me? Or, where is the man who hath been enslaved, by my means, to any vicious pleasure whatsoever?'

'Nay, verily!' said Meletus; 'but I know of many whom thou has persuaded to obey thee rather than their parents.'

'And with good reason,' replied Socrates, 'when the point in question concerned education; since no man but knows that I made this my chief study: and which of you, if sick, prefers not the advice of the physician to his parents? Even the whole body of the Athenian people – when collected in the public assembly – do not they follow the opinion of him whom they think the most able, though he be not of their kindred? And in the choice of a general, do you not to your fathers, brothers, nay, even to yourselves, prefer the man whom ye think the best skilled in military discipline?'

'Certainly,' returned Meletus; 'neither can anyone doubt of its being most expedient.'

'How, then, could it escape being regarded even by you, Meletus, as a thing deserving the highest admiration, that while in every other instance the man who excels in any employment is supposed not only entitled to a common regard but receives many, and those very distinguishing, marks of honour; I, on the contrary, am persecuted even to death, because I am thought by many to have excelled in that employment which is the most noble, and which hath for its aim the greatest good to mankind; by instructing our youth in the knowledge of their duty, and planting in the mind each virtuous principle!'

Now, doubtless, there were many other things spoken at the trial, not only by Socrates but his friends, who were most zealous to support him; but I have not been careful to collect all that was spoken, yet think I have done enough to show, and that most plainly, that the design of Socrates in speaking at this time was no other than to exculpate himself from anything that might have the least appearance of impiety towards the gods or of injustice towards men. For, with regard to death, he was no way solicitous to importune his judges, as the custom was with others: on the contrary, he thought it the best time for him to die. And, that he had thus determined with himself, was still the more evident after his condemnation: for when he was ordered to fix his own penalty he refused to do it, neither would he suffer any other to do it for him; saying that to fix a penalty implied a confession of guilt. And afterwards, when his friends would have withdrawn him privately he would not consent; but asked them with a smile, 'If they knew of any place beyond the borders of Attica where death could not approach him?'

The trial being ended, Socrates, as it is related, spake to his judges in the following manner:

'It is necessary, O ye judges! that all they who instructed the witnesses to bear, by perjury, false testimony against me, as well as all those who too readily obeyed their instructions, should be conscious to themselves of much impiety and injustice: but that I, in any wise, should be more troubled and cast down than before my condemnation, I see not, since I stand here unconvicted of any of the crimes whereof I was accused: for no one hath proved against me that I sacrificed to any new deity; or by oath appealed to, or even made mention of the names of, any other than Jupiter, Juno and the rest of the deities, which, together with these, our city holds sacred: neither have they once shown what were the means I made use of to corrupt the youth at the very time that I was inuring them to a life of patience and frugality. As for those crimes to which our laws have annexed death as the only proper punishment – sacrilege, man-stealing, undermining of walls or betraying of the city – my enemies do not even say that any of these things were even once practised by me. Wherefore I the rather marvel that ye have now judged me worthy to die.

'But it is not for *me* to be troubled on that account: for, if I die unjustly, the shame must be theirs who put me unjustly to death; since if injustice is shameful, so likewise every act of it; but no disgrace can it bring on me that others have not seen that I was innocent. Palamedes likewise affords me this further consolation: for being, like me, condemned undeservedly, he furnishes, to this very day, more noble subjects for praise than the man who had iniquitously caused his destruction. And I am persuaded that I also shall have the attestation of the time to come, as well as of that which is past already, that I never wronged any man, or made him more depraved; but, contrariwise, have steadily endeavoured, throughout life, to benefit those who conversed with me; teaching them, to the very utmost of my power, and that without reward, whatever could make them wise and happy.'

Saying this, he departed; the cheerfulness of his countenance, his gesture and whole deportment bearing testimony to the truth of what he had just declared. And seeing some of those who accompanied him weeping, he asked what it meant. And why they were now afflicted. 'For, knew ye not,' said he, 'long ago, even by that whereof I was produced, that I was born mortal? If, indeed, I had been taken away when the things which are most desirable flowed in upon me abundantly, with good reason it might have been lamented, and by myself as well as others; but if I am only to be removed when difficulties of every kind are ready to break in upon me we ought rather to rejoice, as though my affairs went on the most prosperously.'

Apollodorus being present – one who loved Socrates extremely, though otherwise a weak man – he said to him, 'But it grieveth me, my Socrates! to have you die so unjustly!' Socrates, with much tenderness, laying his hand upon his head, answered, smiling, 'And what, my much-loved Apollodorus! wouldst thou rather they had condemned me justly?'

It is likewise related that on seeing Anytus pass by, 'There goes a man,' said he, 'not a little vain-glorious, on supposing he shall have achieved something great and noble, in putting me to death, because I once said, "that since he himself had been dignified with some of the chief offices in the city, it was wrong in him to breed up his son to the trade of a tanner." But he must be a fool,' continued Socrates, 'who seeth not that he who at all times performs things useful and excellent is alone the hero. And, truly,' added Socrates, 'as Homer makes some, who were near the time of their dissolution, look forward into futurity; I, likewise, have a mind to speak somewhat oraculously. Now it happened I was once, for a short time, with this same son of Anytus; and plainly perceiving he neither wanted talents nor activity, therefore I said, it was not fitting that the young man should continue in such a station; but continuing, as he still doth, destitute at the same time of any virtuous instructor, to guide and restrain him within the bounds of duty, he must soon fall a prey to some evil inclination that will hurry him headlong into vice and ruin.'

And, in thus speaking, Socrates prophesied not untruly; for the young man delighted so much in wine that he ceased not drinking, whether night or day; whereby he became perfectly useless to his country, to his friends and even to himself. The memory of Anytus was likewise held in the highest detestation; and that not only on the account of his other crimes but for the scandalous manner in which he had educated his son.

Now it cannot be doubted but Socrates, by speaking thus highly of himself, incurred the more envy, and made his judges still the more eager to condemn him; yet I think, indeed, he obtained only that fate which the gods decree to those they most love: a discharge from life, when life is become a burthen; and that by a means, of all others, the most easy. Yet here, as well as on every other occasion, Socrates demonstrated the firmness of his soul. For although he was fully persuaded that to die would be the best for him, yet did he not discover any anxious solicitude, any womanish longings for the hour of his dissolution; but waited its approach with the same steady tranquillity, and unaffected complacency, with which he afterwards went out of life. And, truly, when I consider the wisdom and greatness of soul, so essential to this man, I find it not more out of my power to forget him than to remember and not praise him. And if among those who are most studious to excel in virtue there be any who hath found a person to converse with more proper than Socrates for promoting his design – verily, we may well pronounce him the most fortunate of all mankind. (tr. S. Fielding)

3.2 Memoirs of Socrates

These Memoirs *were doubtless written over a number of years, and there is little that we can say about them with complete certainty. The following points would be widely agreed:*

(a) *The opening is a defence of Socrates against a pamphlet attack by a*
sophist named Polycrates (*whom Xenophon calls 'his accuser':* 1, 2, 12, *and, despite the translation here printed,* 1, 2, 9).

(b) *The work as a whole consists of independent anecdotes, some of which are brought together because of similarity of subject.*

(c) *Xenophon draws on some of the writings of Plato and other followers of Socrates, but turns what he borrows to his own purposes.*

(d) *No credence can be placed on the fact that Xenophon suggests that he was present on several of the occasions: this is a simple literary device.*

In all we have a Socrates who is worthy, moral, pious, sententious and somewhat dull.

These passages are all from Sarah Fielding's version.

3.2.1 [1] I have often wondered by what arguments the accusers of Socrates could persuade the Athenians that he had behaved in such a manner towards the republic as to deserve death; for the accusation preferred against him was to this effect:

'Socrates is criminal; inasmuch as he acknowledgeth not the gods whom the republic holds sacred, but introduceth other and new deities. – He is likewise criminal, because he corrupteth the youth.'

[2] Now, as to the first of these, that he acknowledged not the gods whom the republic held sacred – what proof could they bring of this, since it was manifest that he often sacrificed both at home and on the common altars? Neither was it in secret that he made use of divination; it being a thing well known among the people, that Socrates should declare his genius gave him frequent intimations of the future; whence, principally, as it seems to me, his accusers imputed to him the crime of introducing new deities. [3] But, surely, herein Socrates introduces nothing

newer, or more strange, than any other, who, placing confidence in divination, makes use of auguries, and omens, and symbols, and sacrifices. For these men suppose not that the birds or persons they meet unexpectedly, know what is good for them but that the gods by their means give certain intimations of the future, to those who apply themselves to divination. [4] And the same also was his opinion, only with this difference, that while the greatest part say they are persuaded by the flights of birds or some accidental occurrence, Socrates, on the contrary, so asserted concerning these matters as he knew them from an internal consciousness; declaring it was his genius from whom he received his information. And, in consequence of these significations, (communicated, as he said, by his genius,) Socrates would frequently forewarn his friends what might be well for them to do, and what to forbear; and such as were guided by his advice found their advantage in so doing, while those who neglected it had no small cause for repentance.

[5] Now, who is there that will not readily acknowledge, that Socrates could have no desire to appear to his friends either as an enthusiast or arrogant boaster? which, however, would have been unavoidable, had he openly asserted that notices of the future had been given him by the Deity; while a failure in the event made the falsehood of the assertion notorious to all. Wherefore, it is manifest Socrates foretold nothing but what he firmly believed would, hereafter, be fulfilled: – But where could he place this full confidence, exclusive of a deity; and how could one, who thus confided, be said to acknowledge no gods?

[6] Further: – although Socrates always advised his followers to perform the necessary affairs of life in the best manner they were able; yet, with regard to every thing, the event whereof was doubtful, he constantly sent them to consult the oracle, whether it ought or ought not to be undertaken. [7] He likewise asserted, that the science of divination was necessary for all such as would govern successfully either cities or private families: for, although he thought every one might choose his own way of life, and afterwards, by his industry, excel therein; whether architecture, mechanics, agriculture, superintending the labourer, managing the finances, or practising the art of war; [8] yet even here, the gods, he would say, thought proper to reserve to themselves, in all these things, the knowledge of that part of them which was of the most importance; since he, who was the most careful to cultivate his field, could not know, of a certainty, who should reap the fruit of it. He who built his house the most elegantly was not sure who should inhabit it. He who was the best skilled in the art of war could not say whether it would be for his interest to command the army: neither he who was the most able to direct in the administration, whether for his to preside over the city. The man who married a fair wife in hopes of happiness might procure for himself a source of much sorrow; and he who formed the most powerful alliances might come in time, by their means, to be expelled his country. [9] Socrates, therefore, esteemed all those as no other than madmen who, excluding the Deity, referred the success of their designs to nothing higher than human prudence. He likewise thought those not much better who had recourse to divination on every occasion, as if a man was to consult the oracle whether he should give the reins of his chariot into the hands of one ignorant or well versed in the art of driving; or place at the helm of his ship a skilful or unskilful pilot. He also thought it a kind of impiety to importune the gods with our inquiries concerning things of which we

may gain the knowledge by number, weight or measure; it being, as it seemed to him, incumbent on man to make himself acquainted with whatever the gods had placed within his power: as for such things as were beyond his comprehension, for these he ought always to apply to the oracle; the gods being ever ready to communicate knowledge to those whose care had been to render them propitious.

[10] Socrates was almost continually in men's sight. The first hours of the morning were usually spent in the places set apart for walking or the public exercises; and from thence he went to the forum, at the time when the people were accustomed to assemble. The remainder of the day was passed where might be seen the greatest concourse of the Athenians; and for the most part he so discoursed that all who were willing might hear whatsoever he said: yet no one ever observed Socrates either speaking or practising anything impious or profane; [11] neither did he amuse himself, like others, with making curious researches into the works of Nature; and finding out how this, which sophists call the world, had its beginning, or what those powerful springs which influence celestial bodies. On the contrary, he demonstrated the folly of those who busied themselves much in such fruitless disquisitions; asking, [12] whether they thought they were already sufficiently instructed in human affairs that they undertook only to meditate on divine? Or if passing over the first and confining their inquiries altogether to the latter they appeared, even to themselves, to act wisely and as became men. [13] He marvelled they should not perceive it was not for man to investigate such matters; for those among them who arrogated the most to themselves, because they could with the greatest facility talk on these subjects, never agreed in the same opinion; [14]

but like madmen, some of whom tremble when no danger is near, while others fear no harm at the approach of things hurtful: so these philosophers; some of them asserting there was no shame in saying or doing anything before the people; others sending their disciples into solitude, as if nothing innocent could be performed by us in public: some regarding neither temples nor altars, nor reverencing anything whatsoever as divine; while others thought nothing could be found too vile for an object of their adoration. Even among those who laboriously employed themselves in studying the universe, and the nature of all things, some imagined the whole of being to be simply one only; others that beings are in number infinite: some that all things are eternally moving; others that nothing can be moved at all; some that all things are generated and destroyed; others that there can never be any generation or destruction of anything.

[15] He would ask, concerning these busy inquirers into the nature of such things as are only to be produced by a divine power, whether as those artists who have been instructed in some art believe they are able to practise it at pleasure, so they, having found out the immediate cause, believe they shall be able, for their own benefit or that of others, to produce winds and rain, the vicissitudes of time or the change of seasons? Or if indeed altogether destitute of this hope they could content themselves with such fruitless knowledge?

[16] In this manner would he reason concerning those people who gave themselves up to such useless speculations. As for himself, man and what related to man were the only subjects on which he chose to employ himself. To this purpose, all his inquiries and conversation turned upon what was pious, what impious; what honourable, what base; what just, what unjust; what

wisdom, what folly; what courage, what cowardice; what a state or political community, what the character of a statesman or politician; what a government of men, what the character of one equal to such government. It was on these, and other matters of the same kind, that he used to dissert; in which subjects those who were knowing he used to esteem men of honour and goodness; and those who were ignorant to be no better than the basest of slaves.

[17] That the judges of Socrates should err concerning him, in points wherein his opinion might not be apparently manifest, I marvel not; but that such things as had been spoken plainly and acted openly, should have no weight with them, is indeed wonderful; [18] for, being of the senate and having taken, as was customary, the senatorial oath, by which he bound himself to act in all things conformable to the laws, and arriving in his turn to be president of the assembly of the people, he boldly refused to give his suffrage to the iniquitous sentence which condemned the nine captains, two of whom were Erasmides and Thrasellus, to an unjust death; being neither intimidated with the menaces of the great nor the fury of the people, but steadily preferring the sanctity of an oath to the safety of his person; [19] for he was persuaded the gods watched over the actions and the affairs of men in a way altogether different to what the vulgar imagined; for while these limited their knowledge to some particulars only, Socrates, on the contrary, extended it to all; firmly persuaded that every word, every action, nay, even our most retired deliberations, were open to their view; that they were everywhere present and communicated to mankind all such knowledge as related to the conduct of human life: [20] wherefore, I greatly wonder the Athenians could ever suffer themselves to be persuaded that Socrates retained

sentiments injurious to the Deity! He in whom nothing was ever observed unbecoming that reverence so justly due to the gods; but, on the contrary, so behaved towards them both in regard to his words and his actions that whoever shall hereafter demean himself in such a manner must be in fact, and ought also to be esteemed, a man of the truest and most exemplary piety. (1, 1–20, tr. S. Fielding)

3.2.2 [1] But it is still matter of more wonder to me that anyone could be prevailed on to believe that Socrates was a corrupter of youth! Socrates, the most sober and the most chaste of all mankind! supporting with equal cheerfulness the extreme, whether of heat or cold! who shrunk at no hardships, declined no labour and knew so perfectly how to moderate his desires as to make the little he possessed altogether sufficient for him! [2] Could such a one be an encourager of impiety, injustice, luxury, intemperance, effeminacy? But so far from any such thing, that on the contrary he reclaimed many from these vices, by kindling in their minds a love of virtue; encouraging them to think that by a steadfast perseverance they might make themselves esteemed by becoming virtuous men; [3] and although he never undertook to be a teacher of others, yet, as he practised the virtues he sought to recommend, those who conversed with him were animated with the hopes of becoming one day wise from the influence of his example. (2, 1–3, tr. S. Fielding)

3.2.3 [9] But, say his accusers, 'Socrates makes those who converse with him contemners of the laws; calling it madness to leave to chance the election of our magistrates; while no one would be willing to take a pilot, an architect or even a teacher of music on the same terms; though mistakes in such things would be far less fatal than errors in the administration.' With these, and the like discourses, he brought (as was said) the youth by degrees to ridicule and contemn the established form of government; and made them thereby the more headstrong and audacious. (1, 2, 9, tr. S. Fielding)

3.2.4 [12] 'But,' adds his accuser, 'Critias and Alcibiades were two of his intimate friends; and these were not only the most profligate of mankind but involved their country in the greatest misfortunes; for, as among the thirty none was ever found so cruel and rapacious as Critias; so during the democracy none was so audacious, so dissolute or so insolent as Alcibiades.' [13] Now I shall not take upon me to exculpate either of these men; but shall only relate at what time, and, as I think, to what end, they became the followers of Socrates. [14] Critias and Alcibiades were, of all the Athenians, by nature the most ambitious; aiming, at what price soever, to set themselves at the head of the commonwealth, and thereby exalt their names beyond that of any other: they saw that Socrates lived well satisfied with his own scanty possessions; that he could restrain every passion within its proper bounds, and lead the minds of his hearers, by the power of his reasoning, to what purpose he most desired. [15] Understanding this, and being such men as we have already described them, will any one say it was the temperance of Socrates, or his way of life, they were in love with; and not rather, that by hearing his discourses, and observing his actions, they might the better know how to manage their affairs, and harangue the people? [16] And, truly, I am thoroughly persuaded that if the gods had given to these men the choice of passing their whole lives after the manner of Socrates, or dying the next moment, the last

would have been preferred, as by much the most eligible. And their own behaviour bears sufficient testimony to the truth of this assertion; for, no sooner did they imagine they surpassed in knowledge the rest of their contemporaries, who, together with themselves, had attended on Socrates but they left him to plunge into business and the affairs of the administration; the only end they could propose in desiring to associate with him. [17] But, perhaps, it may be objected that Socrates ought not to have discoursed with his followers on the affairs of government till he had first instructed them how to behave with temperance and discretion. Far am I from saying otherwise, and shall only observe that it is commonly the practice with those who are teachers of others to perform in the presence of their pupils the things they would recommend; to the end that while they enforced them on their minds, by the strength of their reasonings, they might set forth, by their example, the manner in which they are done.

Now, with respect to either of these methods of instruction, I know not of any who went beyond Socrates; his whole life serving as an example of the most unblemished integrity; at the same time that he ever reasoned with a peculiar force and energy, on virtue and those several duties which are becoming us as men. [18] And it is certain, that even Critias and Alcibiades themselves behaved soberly and wisely all the time they conversed with him; not that they feared punishment; but as supposing a regular conduct would best serve the end they had in view. (1, 2, 12–18, tr. S. Fielding)

3.2.5 [29] But far from Socrates were all such compliances! On the contrary, when Critias was ensnared with the love of Euthydemus he earnestly endeavoured to cure him of so base a passion; showing how illiberal, how indecent, how unbecoming the man of honour, to fawn, and cringe, and meanly act the beggar; before him, too, whom of all others he the most earnestly strove to gain the esteem of and, after all, for a favour which carried along with it the greatest infamy. [30] And when he succeeded not in his private remonstrances, Critias still persisting in his unwarrantable designs, Socrates, it is said, reproached him in the presence of many, and even before the beloved Euthydemus; resembling him to a swine, the most filthy and disgusting of all animals. [31] For this cause Critias hated him ever after; and when one of the Thirty, being advanced, together with Charicles, to preside in the city, he forgot not the affront; but, in order to revenge it, made a law, wherein it was forbidden that any should teach philosophy in Athens: by which he meant, having nothing in particular against Socrates, to involve him in the reproach cast by this step on all the philosophers, and thereby render him, in common with the rest, odious to the people; for I never heard Socrates say that he taught philosophy; neither did I know any who ever did hear him; but Critias was stung, and he determined to show it. – [32] Now, after the Thirty had put to death many of the citizens, and some of them of the best rank, and had given up the reins to all manner of violence and rapine, Socrates had said somewhere 'that it would astonish him much if he who lost part of the herd every day, while the rest grew poorer and weaker under his management, should deny his being a bad herdsman; but it would astonish him still more if he who had the charge of the city, and saw the number of his citizens decrease hourly, while the rest became more dissolute and depraved under his administration, should be shameless enough not to acknow-

ledge himself an evil ruler.' (1, 2, 29–32, tr. S. Fielding)

3.2.6 [37] 'It is hardly intended to prohibit such things,' returned Charicles: when Critias interrupting them; 'And I, Socrates, I can inform thee of something more thou hast to refrain from: keep henceforth at a proper distance from the carpenters, smiths and shoemakers; and let us have no more of your examples from among them. And, besides, I fancy they are sufficiently tired with your bringing them in so often in your long discourses.'

'Must I likewise give up the consequences,' said Socrates, 'deducible from these examples, and concern myself no longer with justice and piety, and the rules of right and wrong?'

'Thou must, by Jupiter!' replied Charicles. 'And, Socrates,' said he, 'to make all sure, trouble not thyself any more with the herdsmen, for fear thou shouldst occasion the loss of more cattle.'

[38] Now from this it is evident that what Socrates once said concerning the cattle, being told these men, had greatly inflamed their rage against him. Hence also may be seen how long Critias continued to associate with Socrates, and what the affection they had for each other. (1, 2, 37–8, tr. S. Fielding)

3.2.7 [53] And I remember him saying, 'that when the soul, in which thought and reason alone reside, retires from the body, although it may be the body of a father, or a friend, we remove it from our sight as speedily as well may be.' (1, 2, 53, tr. S. Fielding)

3.2.8 [1] Now, as I am persuaded, the benefit arising to all those who accompanied with Socrates was not less owing to the irresistible force of his example than to the excellency of his discourses, I will set down whatever occurs to my memory, whether it relates to his words or his actions.

And first, with respect to sacred rites and institutions. In these things it was ever his practice to approve himself a strict observer of the answer the Pythian priestess gives to all who inquire the proper manner of sacrificing to the gods, or paying honours to their deceased ancestors: 'Follow,' saith the god, 'the custom of your country': and therefore Socrates, in all those exercises of his devotion and piety, confined himself altogether to what he saw practised by the republic; and to his friends he constantly advised the same thing, saying it only savoured of vanity and supersition in all those who did otherwise.

[2] When he prayed, his petition was only this – 'That the gods would give to him those things that were good.' And this he did, forasmuch as they alone knew what was good for man. But he who should ask for gold or silver, or increase of dominion, acted not, in his opinion, more wisely than one who should pray for the opportunity to fight, or game, or anything of the like nature, the consequence whereof, being altogether doubtful, might turn, for aught he knew, not a little to his disadvantage. (1, 3, 1–2, tr. S. Fielding)

3.2.9 [5] As to his manner of living, it may be said that whoever is willing to regulate and discipline his body and his mind after the example of Socrates can hardly fail, no deity opposing, to procure for himself that degree of health and strength as cannot easily be shaken. Neither shall he want large sums for such a purpose. On the contrary, such was his moderation that I question whether there ever was any man, if able to work at all, but might have earned sufficient to have supported Socrates. His custom was to eat as long as it gave him any pleasure; and a good appetite was to him what delicious fare is to another: and as he drank only when thirst compelled him,

whatever served to allay it could not fail of being grateful. (1, 3, 5, tr. S. Fielding)

3.2.10 [1] Now, should there be any inclined to believe what some on conjecture have undertaken to advance, both in their conversations and writings, 'that Socrates could indeed inflame his hearers with the love of virtue, but could never influence them so far as to bring them to make any great proficiency therein': let these, I say, consider what his arguments were not only when his design was to refute such men as pretended to know everything but even in his retired and familiar conversation, and then let them judge whether Socrates was not fully qualified for the bringing his followers and his friends to make proficiency in the paths of virtue. (1, 4, 1, tr. S. Fielding)

3.2.11 [5] 'But it is evidently apparent that He, who at the beginning made man, endued him with senses because they were good for him; eyes, wherewith to behold whatever was visible; and ears, to hear whatever was to be heard. For say, Aristodemus, to what purpose should odours be prepared if the sense of smelling had been denied? Or why the distinctions of bitter and sweet, of savoury and unsavoury, unless a palate had been likewise given, conveniently placed, to arbitrate between them, and declare the difference? (1, 4, 5, tr. S. Fielding)

3.2.12 [17] Consider, my Aristodemus, that the soul which resides in thy body can govern it at pleasure; why, then, may not the soul of the universe, which pervades and animates every part of it, govern it in like manner? If thine eye hath the power to take in many objects, and these placed at no small distance from it, marvel not if the eye of the Deity can, at one glance, comprehend the whole! And as thou perceivest it not beyond thy ability to extend thy care, at the same time, to the concerns of Athens, Egypt, Sicily; why thinkest thou, my Aristodemus, that the providence of God may not easily extend itself throughout the whole universe? [18] As, therefore, among men we make best trial of the affection and gratitude of our neighbour, by showing him kindness; and discover his wisdom, by consulting him in our distress; do thou, in like manner, behave towards the gods: and if thou wouldst experience what their wisdom, and what their love, render thyself deserving the communication of some of those divine secrets which may not be penetrated by man; and are imparted to those alone who consult, who adore, who obey the Deity. Then shalt thou, my Aristodemus, understand there is a being whose eye pierceth throughout all nature, and whose ear is open to every sound; extended to all places; extending through all time; and whose bounty and care can know no other bounds than those fixed by his own creation!'

[19] By this discourse, and others of the like nature, Socrates taught his friends that they were not only to forbear whatever was impious, unjust or unbecoming before men; but even, when alone, they ought to have a regard to all their actions; since the gods have their eyes continually upon us; and none of our designs can be concealed from them.

(1, 4, 17–19, tr. S. Fielding)

3.2.13 [10] It should seem your opinion, Antipho, that happiness consisted in luxury and profusion; whereas, in truth, I consider it as a perfection in the gods that they want nothing; and consequently, he cometh the nearest to the divine nature who standeth in want of the fewest things: and seeing there is nothing which can transcend the divine nature, whoever approacheth the nearest thereto approaches the nearest to sovereign excellence.' (1, 6, 10, tr. S. Fielding)

3.2.14 [1] I remember Socrates once saying to Diodorus, 'Suppose, Diodorus, one of your slaves ran away from you, would you be at any pains to recover him?'

[2] 'Yes, certainly,' said the other; 'and I would even go so far as to publish a reward for whoever would bring him to me.'

'And if any of them were sick you would take care of them, I imagine, and send for a physician to try to save them?'

'Undoubtedly.'

'But what if a friend, something of more worth to you than a thousand slaves, were reduced to want, would it not become you, Diodorus, to relieve him? [3] You know him for a man incapable of ingratitude; nay, one who would even blush to lie under an obligation without endeavouring to return it. You know, too, that the service of him who serves from inclination – who not only can execute what you command but of himself find out many things that may be of use to you – who can deliberate, foresee and assist you with good counsel – is infinitely of more value than many slaves? [4] Now good economists tell us, it is right to purchase when things are most cheap; and we can scarcely recollect the time, at Athens, when a good friend might be had for such a pennyworth.'

[5] 'You are in the right,' said Diodorus; 'therefore you may bid Hermogenes come to me.'

'Not so neither,' returned Socrates; 'for, since the benefit will be reciprocal, it seems just as reasonable that you go to him, as he come to you.'

[6] In consequence of this discourse, Diodorus went himself to Hermogenes, and, for a small consideration, secured a valuable friend, whose principal

care was to approve his gratitude, and return the kindness shown him with many real services. (2, 10, 1–6, tr. S. Fielding)

One of many anecdotes showing Socrates giving practical advice.

3.2.15 [5] Agreeable to this, Socrates would often say, 'That justice, together with every other virtue, was wisdom; for that all their actions being fair and good, must be preferred as such by all who were possessed of a right discernment; but ignorance and folly could perform nothing fair and good; because, if attempted, it would miscarry in their hands. Whence it follows that as whatever is just and fair must be the result of sound wisdom; and as nothing can be fair and just where virtue is wanting; therefore justice and every other virtue is wisdom.' (3, 8, 5, tr. S. Fielding)

3.2.16 [4] Socrates seeing one beat his servant immoderately, asked him, 'What offence the man had committed?'

'I beat him,' replied the other, 'because he is not only a drunkard and a glutton, but avaricious and idle.'

'You do well,' said Socrates; 'but judge for yourself which deserves the most stripes, your servant, or you?' (3, 13, 4, tr. S. Fielding)

3.2.17 [2] He would frequently assume the character and the language of a lover; but it was easy to perceive it was the charms of the mind not those of the body with which he was enamoured, as the objects he sought after were always such as he saw naturally inclining towards virtue. Now he thought an aptness to learn, together with a strength of memory to retain what was already learned, accompanied with a busy inquisitiveness into such things as might be of use for the right

conduct of life, whether as head only of a single family or governor of the whole state, indicated a mind well fitted for instruction, which, if duly cultivated, would render the youths in whom they were found not only happy in themselves, and their own families, but give them the power of making many others the same; since the benefits arising from thence would be diffused throughout the whole community. (4, 1, 2, tr. S. Fielding)

3.2.18 [3] Socrates went no farther at that time; but plainly perceiving that Euthydemus cautiously avoided his company, that he might not be taken for one of his followers, he determined to attack him something more openly. To this purpose, when he was next along with him, Socrates, turning to some who were present, 'May we not expect,' said he, 'from the manner in which this young man pursues his studies, that he will not fail to speak his opinion even the very first time he appears in the assembly, should there be any business of importance then in debate? I should suppose, too, that the proem to his speech, if he begins with letting them know that he hath never received any instruction, must have something in it not unpleasant. [4] "Be it known to you," will he say, "O ye men of Athens! I never learnt anything of any man: I never associated with persons of parts or experience; never sought out for people who could instruct me; but, on the contrary, have steadily persisted in avoiding all such; as not only holding in abhorrence the being taught by others but careful to keep clear of even the least suspicion of it; but I am ready, notwithstanding, to give you such advice as chance shall suggest to me." [5] –Not unlike the man,' continued Socrates, 'who should tell the people, while soliciting their voices; "It is true, gentlemen, I never once thought of making physic my study; I never once applied to anyone for instruction; and so far was I from desiring to be well versed in this science, I even wished not to have the reputation of it; but, gentlemen, be so kind as to choose me your physician; and I will gain knowledge by making experiments upon you."'

Every one present laughed at the absurdity of such a preface. (4, 2, 3–5, tr. S. Fielding)

3.2.19 'Most assuredly,' said Socrates; 'for it is far better to change our opinion, than to persist in a wrong one. [19] However,' continued he, 'that we may pass over nothing without duly examining it: which of the two, Euthydemus, appears to you the most unjust; he who deceives his friend wittingly, or he who does it without having any such design?'

'Truly,' said Euthydemus, 'I am not certain what I should answer, or what I should think; for you have given such a turn to all I have hitherto advanced as to make it appear very different to what I before thought it: however, I will venture so far as to declare that man the most unjust who deceiveth his friend designedly.'

[20] 'Is it your opinion, Euthydemus, that a man must learn to be just and good, in like manner as he learneth to write and read?'

'I believe so.'

'And which,' said Socrates, 'do you think the most ignorant, he who writes or reads ill designedly or he who doth it for want of knowing better?'

'The last, certainly,' replied Euthydemus; 'since the other can do right whenever he pleases.'

'It then follows that he who reads ill, from design, knows how to read well; but the other doth not?'

'It is true.'

'Pray tell me,' continued Socrates, 'which of the two knoweth best what justice is, and what he ought to do; he who offends against the truth and deceives designedly, or he who does it without having any such design?'

'He, no doubt, who deceives designedly,' replied Euthydemus.

'But you said, Euthydemus, that he who understands how to read is more learned than one who does not?'

'I did so, Socrates; and it is certainly true.'

'Then he who knows wherein justice consists, is more just than he who knows nothing of the matter?'

'So it seems,' said Euthydemus; 'and I know not how I came to say otherwise.'

[21] 'But what would you think of the man, Euthydemus, who, however willing he might be to tell the truth, never tells you twice together the same thing, but if you ask him about the road, will show you today to the east, and tomorrow to the west; and make the very same sum amount sometimes to fifty, and sometimes to a hundred; what would you say to this man, Euthydemus?'

'That it was plain he knew nothing of what he pretended to know.'

[22] Socrates still went on, and said, 'Have you never heard people called base and servile?'

'Frequently.'

'And why were they so called? for their ignorance, or knowledge?'

'Not for their knowledge, certainly.'

'What then? for their ignorance in the business of a brazier? building a house? or sweeping a chimney?'

'Nor this, nor that,' replied Euthydemus; 'for the men who are the most expert in employments of this nature are generally the most abject and servile in their minds.'

'It should seem then, Euthydemus, these appellatives only belong to those who are ignorant of what is just and good?'

'So I imagine.'

[23] 'Doth it not then follow that we ought to exert our powers to the utmost, to avoid this ignorance, which debases men so low?' (4, 2, 18–23, tr. S. Fielding)

3.2.20 [24] 'Have you ever been at Delphi?'

'I have been there twice.'

'Did you observe this inscription somewhere on the front of the temple – *Know thyself*?'

'Yes, I read it.'

'But it seems scarcely sufficient to have read it, Euthydemus: did you consider it? and, in consequence of the admonition, set yourself diligently to find out what you are?'

'I certainly did not,' said Euthydemus; 'for I imagined I must know this sufficiently already: and, indeed, it will be difficult for us to know any thing, if we can be supposed at a loss here.'

[25] 'But for a man to know himself properly,' said Socrates, 'it is scarcely enough that he knows his own name. He who desires to purchase a horse doth not imagine he hath made the proper trial of his merit, till by mounting him he hath found out whether he is tractable or unruly, strong or weak, fleet or heavy, with everything else, either good or bad, in him: so likewise we should not say he knows himself as he ought who is ignorant of his own powers; or those duties which, as man, it is incumbent upon him to perform.'

'It must be confessed,' replied Euthydemus, 'that he who knoweth not his own powers cannot be said to know himself.' (4, 2, 24–5, tr. S. Fielding)

3.2.21 [9] 'But it is certain,' said Hippias, 'you will not know it without first telling us your sentiments concerning justice, or this rule of right: for you content yourself, Socrates, with asking questions, and afterwards confuting the answers that are made you, in order to turn those who make them into ridicule; but never advance anything of your own, that you may not be called upon to support your opinion.' (4, 4, 9, tr. S. Fielding)

3.2.22 [12] Socrates likewise added, that by a constant exercise of this discriminating power, men were taught to reason well: and that the term conference, given to their assemblies, implied that the very end of their meeting was in order to examine into the nature of things and class them properly and he advised his followers to the frequent holding of these conferences; saying, 'It would be the best means to mature their judgement; making them thereby truly great and capable of governing both themselves and others.' (4, 5, 12, tr. S. Fielding)

3.2.23 [1] Neither must I omit to mention how solicitous Socrates always showed himself to have his friends become capable of performing their own business that they might not stand in need of others to perform it for them. For this reason he made it his study more than any man I ever knew to find out wherein any of his followers were likely to excel in things not unbecoming a wise and good man; and in such points as he himself could give them any instruction he did it with the utmost readiness; and where he could not was always forward to carry them to some more skilful master. [2] Yet was he very careful to fix the bounds in every science; beyond which, he would say, no person properly instructed ought to pass. And, therefore – in geometry, for example – he thought it sufficient if so much of it was known as would secure a man from being imposed upon in the buying and selling of land; direct him in the proper distributions of the several portions of an inheritance, and in measuring out the labourer's work: all which, he said, was so easy to be done, that he who applied himself to this science, though almost ever so slightly, might soon find out in what manner to measure the whole earth and describe its circumference. [3] But to dive deep into such things, and perplex the mind with various uncouth figures, and hard to be understood, although he himself had much knowledge therein, he approved not of it, as seeing no use in these nice inquiries; which consume all his time and engross the whole man, taking off his thoughts from more profitable studies. [4] He also advised his friends to gain such a knowledge of astronomy as to be able to tell by the stars the hours of the night, the day of the month and the seasons of the year that they should not be at a loss when to relieve the sentinel, begin a journey or a voyage, or do any other thing which depends on this science: all which, he said, was easily to be learnt by conversing with seafaring men, or those whose custom it was to hunt in the night. [5] But to go further, in order to find out what planets were in the same declension, explain their different motions, tell their distances from the earth, their influences, together with the time necessary for the performance of their respective revolutions; these, and things like these, he strongly dissuaded his followers from attempting: not as being ignorant of them himself; but he judged of this science as he did of the former, that to examine deeply into the nature of such things would rob us of all our time, divert our thoughts from useful studies and, after all, produce nothing that could turn to our advantage. [6] In short, he would not that men should too curiously search into that marvellous art, wherewith the Maker of the universe had disposed the several parts of it, seeing it was a subject incomprehensible to the mind of man; neither

yet pleasing to the gods to attempt to discover the things which they in their wisdom had thought fit to conceal. He also said 'that the understanding, unable to bear these towering speculations, ofttimes lost itself in the inquiry; as was the case with Anaxagoras, who gloried not a little in the extent of his knowledge: [7] yet this very man asserted, "that the sun was the same as fire; forgetful that the eye can bear the light of the fire, whereas the lustre of the sun is too dazzling for it to behold. Neither did he consider that the rays of the sun change the skin black, which the fire doth not: as also, that its warmth produces and brings to perfection trees and flowers, and fruits of the earth, while it is the property of the fire to wither and consume them. He said, moreover, "that the sun was no other than a stone thoroughly inflamed"; not perceiving,' added Socrates, 'that the stone shineth not in the fire; neither can remain there any long time without wasting; whereas the sun abideth still the same – an inexhaustible source of light and warmth to us.'

[8] Socrates also recommended the study of arithmetic to his friends; and assisted them, as was his custom, in tracing out the several parts of it as far as might be useful: but here, as elsewhere, fixed bounds to their inquiries; never suffering them to run out into vain and trifling disquisitions, which could be of no advantage either to themselves or others.

[9] He always earnestly exhorted his friends to be careful of their health: and, to this end, not only advised them to consult those who were skilful therein but of themselves to be continually attentive to their diet and exercise; always preferring what would keep them in the best health; since they who did this would seldom, he said, want |a better physician. [10] And when he found any who could not satisfy themselves with the knowledge that lay

within the reach of human wisdom Socrates advised that they should diligently apply to the study of divination: asserting that whoever was acquainted with those mediums which the gods made use of when they communicated anything to man should never be left destitute of divine counsel. (4, 7, 1–10, tr. S. Fielding)

3.2.24 [11] In this manner did Socrates continue to discourse with Hermogenes and others: nor are there any among those who knew him, if lovers of virtue, who do not daily regret the loss of his conversation; convinced how much they might have been advantaged thereby.

As to myself, knowing him of a truth to be such a man as I have described; so pious towards the gods as never to undertake anything without having first consulted them: so just towards men as never to do an injury, even the very slightest, to anyone; while many and great were the benefits he conferred on all with whom he had any dealings; so temperate and chaste as not to indulge any appetite or inclination at the expense of whatever was modest or becoming; so prudent as never to err in judging of good and evil, nor wanting the assistance of others to discriminate rightly concerning them; so able to discourse upon, and define with the greatest accuracy not only those points of which we have been speaking but likewise of every other, and looking as it were into the minds of men, discover the very moment for reprehending vice or stimulating to the love of virtue. Experiencing, as I have done, all these excellencies in Socrates, I can never cease considering him as the most virtuous and the most happy of all mankind. But if there is anyone who is disposed to think otherwise, let him go and compare Socrates with any other, and afterwards let him determine. (4, 8, 11, tr. S. Fielding)

3.3 Oeconomicus

Oeconomicus or 'How to Run a Farm and House' is in large measure a discussion between Socrates and one Ischomachus, a thin disguise for Xenophon himself.

3.3.1 'But how could I of all people presume to reform a finished gentleman, when I'm well known for the nonsense I talk, for trying to measure air, and – of all the stupid criticisms to bring – for my poverty.' (11, 3)

Socrates is speaking: a good example of his 'irony'. The criticisms are those of Aristophanes, The Clouds 225; 1480: adoleschein, 'talking nonsense', was evidently a familiar gibe.

3.3.2 'Ischomachus, I can't help thinking about the value of a good simile. You really got me worked up against the weeds when you compared them to drones, much more than when you were just talking about weeds.' (17, 15)

A Socratic method.

3.3.3 'Ischomachus, is a question really a form of education? I've just realised the point of all your questions. You lead me along familiar paths of knowledge, you point out to me objects similar to those I know, and persuade me that I really know things which I didn't realise I knew.' (19, 15)

'Irony' again: it is an excellent description of Socrates' own method. The first sentence is magnificent.

3.4 The Banquet

The Banquet was probably written about 380 B.C. The scene depicted can be dated to 422 B.C. Xenophon says that he was *present, but he was not old enough. The work was evidently written in emulation of Plato's work of the same name. Xenophon's is less exalted in tone but vivid and realistic.*

3.4.1 Then Socrates said, 'You're always turning your nose up at us, because you've paid heavy fees to Protagoras, Gorgias, Prodicus and lots of others for a course in wisdom, and you see that we have to improvise our philosophy.' (1, 5)

3.4.2 'But we want perfumes to make up the treat,' answered Callias: 'What say you to that?' – 'Not at all,' replied Socrates; 'perfumes, like habits, are to be used according to decency; some become men, and others women; but I would not that one man should perfume himself for the sake of another: and for the women, especially such as the wife of Critobulus or Nicerates, they have no occasion for perfumes, their natural sweetness supplying the want of them. But it is otherwise if we talk of the smell of that oil that is used in the Olympic games, or other places of public exercise. This, indeed, is sweeter to the men than perfumes to the women; and when they have been for some time disused to it, they only think on it with a greater desire. [4] If you perfume a slave and a freeman, the difference of their birth produces none in the smell; and the scent is perceived as soon in the one as the other: but the odour of honourable toil, as it is acquired with great pains and application, so it is ever sweet, and worthy of a brave man.' – 'This is agreeable to young men,' said Lycon; 'but as for you and me, who are past the age of these public exercises, what perfumes ought we to have?' – 'That of virtue and honour,' said Socrates.

LYCON: And where is this sort of perfume to be had?

SOCRATES: Not in the shops, I assure you.

LYCON: Where then?

SOCRATES: Theognis sufficiently discovers where, when he tells us in his poem:

When virtuous thoughts warm the celestial
    mind
With generous heat, each sentiment's
    refin'd:
Th'immortal perfumes breathing from
    the heart,
With grateful odours sweeten every part.

But when our vicious passions fire the
    soul,
The clearest fountains grow corrupt and
    foul;
The virgin springs, which should untainted flow,
Run thick, and blacken all the stream
    below.   (2, 3–4, tr. J. Welwood)

A famous passage much alluded to by later writers.

3.4.3 [8] At the same time the other girl took her flute; the one played and the other danced to admiration; the dancing girl throwing up and catching again her cymbals so as to answer exactly the cadency of the music, and that with a surprising dexterity. [9] Socrates, who observed her with pleasure, thought it deserved some reflection: and therefore, said he, 'This young girl has confirmed me in the opinion I have had of a long time, that the female sex are nothing inferior to ours, excepting only in strength of body, or perhaps steadiness of judgement. Now you, gentlemen, that have wives among us, may take my word for it they are capable of learning anything you are willing they should know to make them more useful to you.' [10] 'If so, sir,' said Antisthenes; 'if this be the real sentiment of your heart how comes it you do not instruct Xanthippe, who is, beyond dispute, the most insupportable woman that is, has been or ever will be?' – 'I do with her,' said Socrates, 'like those who would learn horsemanship: they do not choose easy tame horses, or such as are manageable at pleasure, but the highest metalled and hardest mouthed; believing if they can tame the natural heat and impetuosity of these there can be none too hard for them to manage. I propose to myself very near the same thing; for having designed to converse with all sorts of people, I believed I should find nothing to disturb me in their conversation or manners, being once accustomed to bear the unhappy temper of Xanthippe.'

The company relished what Socrates said, and the thought appeared very reasonable. (2, 8–10, tr. J. Welwood)

It is interesting to compare this view of ' the equality of the sexes' with that in Plato's Republic.

3.4.4 [19] 'Why, Critobulus, do you give yourself this air of vanity,' said Socrates, 'as if you were handsomer than me?' – 'Doubtless,' replied Critobulus, 'if I have not the advantage of you in beauty, I must be uglier than the Sileni, as they are painted by the poets.' Now Socrates had some resemblance to those figures. (4, 19, tr. J. Welwood)

3.4.5 [1] Now you have heard in what manner every one spoke, when Callias began again, and said to Critobulus, 'Will you not then venture into the lists with Socrates, and dispute beauty with him?'

SOCRATES: I believe not; for he knows my art gives me some interest with the judges.

[2] CRITOBULUS: Come, I will not refuse to enter the lists for once with you; pray, then, use all your eloquence, and let us know how you prove yourself to be handsomer than I.

SOCRATES: That shall be done presently; bring but a light, and the thing is done.

CRITOBULUS: But in order to state the question well you will give me leave to ask a few questions?

SOCRATES: I will.

CRITOBULUS: But on second thoughts I will give you leave to ask what questions you please first.

[3] SOCRATES: Agreed. Do you believe beauty is nowhere to be found but in man?

CRITOBULUS: Yes, certainly, in other creatures too, whether animate, as a horse or bull, or inanimate things, as we say that is a handsome sword, or a fine shield, etc.

[4] SOCRATES: But how comes it, then, that things so very different as these should yet all of them be handsome?

CRITOBULUS: Because they are well made, either by art or nature, for the purposes they are employed in.

[5] SOCRATES: Do you know the use of eyes?

CRITOBULUS: To see.

SOCRATES: Well! it is for that very reason mine are handsomer than yours.

CRITOBULUS: Your reason?

SOCRATES: Yours see only in a direct line; but, as for mine, I can look not only directly forward, as you, but sideways too, they being seated on a kind of ridge on my face, and staring out.

CRITOBULUS: At that rate a crab has the advantage of all other animals in matter of eyes?

SOCRATES: Certainly: for theirs are incomparably more solid and better situated than any other creature's.

[6] CRITOBULUS: Be it so as to eyes; but as to your nose, would you make me believe that yours is better shaped than mine?

SOCRATES: There is no room for doubt, if it be granted that God made the nose for the sense of smelling; for your nostrils are turned downward, but mine are wide and turned up towards heaven, to receive smells that come from every part, whether from above or below.

CRITOBULUS: What! is a short flat

nose, then, more beautiful than another?

SOCRATES: Certainly; because being such, it never hinders the sight of both eyes at once; whereas a high nose parts the eyes so much by its rising that it hinders their seeing both of them in a direct line.

[7] CRITOBULUS: As to your mouth, I grant it you; for if God has given us a mouth to eat with it is certain yours will receive and chew as much at once as mine at thrice.

SOCRATES: Don't you believe too that my kisses are more luscious and sweet than yours, having my lips so thick and large?

CRITOBULUS: According to your reckoning, then, an ass's lips are more beautiful than mine.

SOCRATES: And lastly, I must excel you in beauty, for this reason: the Naiades, notwithstanding they are sea-goddesses, are said to have brought forth the Sileni; and sure I am much more like them than you can pretend to be. What say you to that?

[8] CRITOBULUS: I say it is impossible to hold a dispute with you, Socrates; and therefore let us determine this point by balloting; and so we shall know presently who has the best of it, you or I: but pray let it be done in the dark, lest Antisthenes' riches and your eloquence should corrupt the judges. (5, 1–8, tr. J. Welwood)

3.4.6 [6] As they were talking thus, the Syracusan observing they took no great notice of anything he could show them, but that they entertained one another on subjects out of his road, was out of all temper with Socrates, who he saw gave occasion at every turn for some new discourse. 'Are you,' said he to him, 'that Socrates who is surnamed the Contemplative'?

SOCRATES: Yes; and is it not much more preferable to be called so than by another name for some opposite quality?

SYRACUSAN: Let that pass. But they do not only say in general that Socrates is contemplative, but that he contemplates things that are sublime.

[7] SOCRATES: Know you anything in the world so sublime and elevated as the gods?

SYRACUSAN: No. But I am told your contemplations run not that way. They say they are but trifling; and that, in searching after things above your reach, your inquiries are good for nothing.

SOCRATES: It is by this, if I deceive not myself, that I attain to the knowledge of the gods: for it is from above that the gods make us sensible of their assistance; it is from above they inspire us with knowledge. But if what I have said appears dry and insipid you are the cause, for forcing me to answer you.

[8] SYRACUSAN: Let us then talk of something else. Tell me, then, the just measure of the skip of a flea; for I hear you are a subtle geometrician, and understand the mathematics perfectly well. (6, 6–8, tr. J. Welwood)

The last jibe reminds us of Aristophanes.

3.4.7 Then Antisthenes said: 'Anyone can see through you, you're always the same, always the pander with yourself as the goods. You're always refusing to talk with me: sometimes your divine sign's the excuse, sometimes something else.' (8, 5)

3.5 Anabasis

Xenophon read the letter and communicated with Socrates the Athenian about the expedition. Socrates suspected that friendship with Cyrus might be politically dangerous, in that Cyrus was reputed to have been an enthusiastic ally of Sparta against Athens. He advised Xenophon to go to Delphi and consult the god about the expedition. Xenophon went and asked Apollo to which of the gods he should pray and sacrifice so as to ensure that his journey was as successful as possible and that he returned successfully and safely. Apollo responded with the gods to whom he had to sacrifice. On his arrival back, Xenophon told Socrates about the oracle. Socrates listened to him and criticised him because he did not begin by asking whether it was better for him to go at all or to stay behind; he had taken the decision to go and then asked how to make a success of the journey. 'However,' he added, 'since you put the question in that form, you must fulfil the god's instructions.' (3, 1, 5)

PART FOUR

CONTEMPORARY COMIC DRAMATISTS

The Old Comedy of the fifth century B.C. drew much of its material from the contemporary scene, and Socrates was too prominent a figure to escape the caricatures of the stage. In evaluating the picture given we must remember three things. First, this is the earliest evidence we have; when Aristophanes put on *The Clouds* Xenophon and Plato were not long out of their cradles. Second, a caricature is not a portrait. Third, unless a caricature has some basis in fact it is pointless.

4.1 Aristophanes

Aristophanes (c. 430–385 B.C.): the greatest of Greek comic dramatists, and one of the greatest of all comic dramatists. We have eleven of his plays, and no complete comedy from anyone else before Menander. Several of them form a vigorous political commentary upon current events, especially on the war between Athens and Sparta. In 423 B.C. he put on The Clouds, *an attack on the New Learning with Socrates as its representative. The play was a failure, and he rewrote it: the version we have owes something to the revision. There is an excellent discussion of all the problems in K. J. Dover's edition. References to Socrates in other plays are secondary and incidental.*

4.1.1 The Clouds

4.1.1.1 (*There is a two-storey stage-building with large central double-doors. Standing by the doors is a large round jar. All the characters are grotesquely masked.*)

STREPSIADES (*an old man, ruddy-faced, seeking the New Learning*):
I'm down but not out.
I'll offer a prayer to the gods and then go
to enrol in person in the Think-Tank.
Hey! I'm old, absent-minded, slow.
[130] How can I master their logic, their hair-splitting?
On, Strepsiades. Stop trailing your heels.
Knock on their door. ₍(*He does so.*)
Porter! PORTER!!

STUDENT (*putting a very pale, cadaverous face round the door*):
Go to hell! Who's that banging on our door?

STREPSIADES:
Strepsiades, Phaedon's son, from Cicynna.

STUDENT:
Clearly illiterate. D'you realise that by banging

at our door when we weren't expecting it you've
caused the miscarriage of a scientific discovery?

STREPSIADES:
I'm sorry. I'm country born and bred.
What was that about a miscarriage?

STUDENT:
[140] Sacred. Hush-hush. Only for registered students.

STREPSIADES:
C'm on. Tell me. I've come
to register as a student in the Think-Tank.

STUDENT (*Conspiratorially*):
All right. But not to be revealed to the uninitiated.
Sh! Socrates was examining Chaerephon.
How many of its own feet can a flea jump?
One bit Chaerephon's eyebrow
and jumped on to Socrates' bald patch!

STREPSIADES:
How on earth did he measure that?

STUDENT: Brilliantly,
He melted some wax. Next he caught the flea,
[150] dipped its two feet in the wax;
when it cooled, there were Persian slippers;
slipped them off and measured the distance.

STREPSIADES:
God in heaven! What a brain!

STUDENT:
What about this other brainwave of Socrates?

STREPSIADES:
        What? *Do* tell me!

STUDENT:
Our friend Chaerephon asked him
his view. Which is right? Do gnats
buzz through their mouth or through their rear?

STREPSIADES:
What did he answer about the gnat?

STUDENT:

[160] He explained that the gnat's
    intestinal tract
is narrow, the gastric gas is forced
to flow through this slender channel
    into the rear.
The force of the explosion makes the
    gnat fart.

STREPSIADES:

So the gnat has a trumpet in its
    arse.
What fascinating inside-informa-
    tion!
Anyone who's mastered a gnat's
    innards
could easily get off any lawsuit.

STUDENT:

Ah, but yesterday he was done out
    of a brilliant idea,
and all by a gecko.

STREPSIADES:

                [170] What d'you
    mean 'done out'?
    Do tell me!

STUDENT:

He was investigating the moon's
    course,
its orbit. He was looking up, with his
    mouth open.
It was dark, and gecko on the roof –
um – evacuated over him.

STREPSIADES (*laughing*):

I like that! A gecko crapping on
    Socrates.

STUDENT:

Yesterday night there was nothing
    for dinner.

STREPSIADES:

O.K. How did he – um – excogitate
    some grub?

STUDENT:

First he sprinkled the table with
    some fine – ash –
took a skewer, bent it to make a pair
    of compasses –
and hooked someone's cloak from
    the changing-rooms.

STREPSIADES:

[180] That's real mathematics. Who
    was Thales anyway?

(*Knocking with increasing vigour*)

Open up! Get a move on! Open up!
    I want to get inside
the Think-Tank and see Socrates –
    this very minute.
I *must* have education. Open the
    bloody door.

(*The double-doors open and a wheeled plat-
form is pushed out. On it is a tableau of
fantastic scientific apparatus, including a
large map crudely showing the Mediterranean
world, and an old bed and a group of
students. Their clothes are filthy and ragged,
their masks lean and pale. They are staring
downwards, some standing rapt and upright,
others like ostriches, peering closely at the
ground, with their rumps sticking in-
decorously upwards.*)

Good God! What curious creatures!

STUDENT:

What's up? Do they remind you of
    anyone?

STREPSIADES:

Spartan troops captured at Pylos.
What on earth are they staring at
    the ground for?

STUDENT:

They're studying geology.

STREPSIADES:

                They're looking for
mushrooms. (*Going up to them*) Here –
    this isn't work for the Think-
    Tank.
[190] I'll tell you where to get lovely
    big ones.
What are those blokes up to with
    their noses in the ground?

STUDENT:

An advanced course on the Under-
    world.

STREPSIADES:

What the hell are their arses staring
    at the sky for?

STUDENT:

It's registered for a special course in
    astronomy.

(*He hears a creaking as over the top of the
stage building a crane hoists a basket. In it
is Socrates, caricatured but clearly recog-
nisable with pop-eyes, snub nose, bald head*)

and beard. The basket can be seen by the audience, not yet by actors).

Cave *or the Beak'll catch you.*

(*The tableau jerks into sudden movement*).

STREPSIADES:

Hold on, hold on. (*The tableau freezes.*)
Don't let them go.
I've some business to discuss with them.

STUDENT:

Es ist strengstens verboten. It's against the rules
to spend too long in the fresh air.

(*The tableau unfreezes, and the students scamper inside. Strepsiades starts examining the apparatus. He looks at a large globe and some tablets with geometrical diagrams.*)

STREPSIADES:

[200] Good God! What's all this?

STUDENT:

That's astronomy.

STREPSIADES (*with surveying instruments*):

What about this?

STUDENT:

Geometry.

STREPSIADES:

What can you do with it?

STUDENT:

Measure land.

STREPSIADES:

You mean my allotment?

STUDENT:

No, the whole world.

STREPSIADES:

You're joking!
That would be pretty useful in politics.

STUDENT (*with bronze map*):

This is the whole circuit of the earth.
D'you see?
Here's Athens (*pointing*).

STREPSIADES (*peering*):

What? I don't believe you.
I can't see a single law-court in session.

STUDENT:

It really is the land of Attica.

STREPSIADES:

[210] Then where's Cicynna? Where are my neighbours?

STUDENT:

Inside. (*Strepsiades is puzzled, shakes the map, looks underneath it.*) Here's Euboea. Look.
Here. Stretching out for ever such a long way.

STREPSIADES:

Oh, yes. It was Pericles helped us put them on the rack.
Well, where the devil's Sparta?

STUDENT:

Where's Sparta? Here.

STREPSIADES:

Much too near. The Think-Tank had better
think again, and move them a lot farther away from us.

STUDENT:

It can't be done.

STREPSIADES:

Then you'll be sorry for it.

(*The basket with Socrates has by now swung into view: he is sitting on a cross-bar holding on to a rope.*)

Here. Who's that guy at the end of the guy-rope?

STUDENT:

Himself.

STREPSIADES:

What self?

STUDENT:

Socrates.

STREPSIADES (*overcome with excitement, calling in a spluttering whisper*):

Socrates!
[220] Here, you call him. Give him a good big shout.

STUDENT:

Call him yourself. I've work to do.

(*Exit.*)

STREPSIADES:

Socrates! Socrates dear!

SOCRATES:

Yes, mortal?

STREPSIADES:

Please, what *are* you doing? Do tell me.

SOCRATES:

Treading the air, and letting my
thought move round the sun.

STREPSIADES:

Well it's a good perch for looking
down on the gods,
better than earth, if that's what
you're up to.

SOCRATES:

True.

I could never have made my revolutionary discoveries in meteoro-
logy
without suspending my intellect, my
thought,
[230] blending its rarity with the
rarefied atmosphere.
To pursue elevated inquiries from
down on earth
would negate my theories. Earth is
gross.
It draws to itself the liquidity of
thought.
The same thing happens with water-
cress.

STREPSIADES

Really?
Thought draws liquidity into water-
cress?
Socrates dear, please drop down to
my level
and teach me what I've come here
for.

SOCRATES:

Your object being . . . ?

STREPSIADES:

I want to
learn Public Speaking.
[240] It's debts. My creditors are
real brutes,
straining and distraining. My property's in danger.

SOCRATES:

But didn't you realise you were falling
into debt?

STREPSIADES:

Oh, doctor, I'm worn out by the
horse-pox; it's fair eating me up.
Just teach me your Second Logical
Principle,

the Get-off-scot-free one. I'll pay
your fees. I swear it. By the gods.

SOCRATES:

Gods? What gods. The first lesson.
Gods
are not legal tender here.

STREPSIADES:

Then what
d'you swear by?
Are iron bars current, like in Byzantium?

SOCRATES:

[250] Divinity – d'you really want
to know the truth, the whole
truth
and nothing but the truth about it?

STREPSIADES:

Ooh yes, if it's on.

SOCRATES:

D'you earnestly and truly desire
intercourse
with our goddesses, the Clouds?

STREPSIADES:

Intercourse? Ooh yes!

SOCRATES:

Take your seat on the sacred throne.
(*It is an old truckle-bed. He does so, and
Socrates dances round him in parody of an
initiation ritual.*)

STREPSIADES:

O.K. I'm waiting.

SOCRATES:

Take this garland.
Put it on.
(*It is a garland of weeds.*)

STREPSIADES (*jumping to his feet*):

Garland! Oh, Socrates,
please don't sacrifice me – like
Athamas in the play.

SOCRATES:

Don't be silly. We do this to all
initiates. (*Strepsiades sits down again.*)

STREPSIADES:

What do I get out of it?

SOCRATES (*sprinkling flour over him till
he's as ghastly as the others*):

[260] You'll be reborn the fine flour
of a public speaker, a rattling good
one.
Stop fidgeting.

STREPSIADES:

By God, you're right
in one thing

I shall be a fine flour by the time
you've done baptising me.

SOCRATES:

Stop talking, you old fool, and
listen to my prayer. This is sacred.

(*He looks up with arms spread and palms
upwards and intones*)

Almighty Lord, infinite Air, who dost
hold the earth in equilibrium,

and thou, Translucent Ether, and ye
Clouds, holy thunder-and-lightning
goddesses,

arise, be known on high to your
Thinker, mighty powers. (131–266)

*At 137 the 'miscarriage' looks much like
a joke at the expense of Socrates' claim to be
an intellectual midwife.*

4.1.1.2

(*The Chorus of Clouds have arrived, some
lowered by the crane in parody of a similarly
spectacular entrance in Aeschylus' Pro-
theus.*)

CHORUS (*to Strepsiades*):

Hail, you superannuated antique,
hunter of the Muses' learning.

(*to Socrates*):

Hail, high-priest of subtle bilge,
tell us what you're now requesting.

[360] Of all the present-day professors you're the only one we've
time for –

apart from Prodicus. We value his
wisdom and his judgement; you,

swaggering along the streets as your
eyes dart shifty glances,

barefoot, putting up with trouble,
looking disdainfully – all for us.

STREPSIADES:

Name of Earth, what a voice, solemn,
spectacular, out of this world!

SOCRATES:

Of course. These are the only gods.
All other religion is just nonsense.

STREPSIADES:

But Zeus – name of Earth! – Olym-
pian Zeus – isn't he a god?

SOCRATES:

Zeus! What Zeus? Don't talk rubbish.
There isn't any Zeus.

STREPSIADES:

What d'you mean?
Who makes the rain? Answer me
that before you go any farther.

SOCRATES:

[370] *They* do of course. And I'll
prove it you by irrefutable evidence –

come along now. When did you ever
see it raining, and no cloud in the
sky?

Zeus ought to be able to give the
clouds a holiday and rain out of a
clear sky.

STREPSIADES:

Apollo, that's right. What a splendid
piece of graft!

And I always used to think the rain
was Zeus pissing into a sieve.

Ah, but who causes the thunder? It
makes me go hot and cold to talk
about it.

SOCRATES:

They do. The thunder is the sound
of their rolling.

STREPSIADES:

You've an answer
for everything. How?

SOCRATES:

They are hydroelectric spheres. A
disequilibrium of forces

operates the laws of motion. Hydro-
statics in suspension

become hydrodynamics. Result: collision of mass, explosion, resonance.

STREPSIADES:

But the disequitable force that operates the laws of motion – that's
Zeus.

SOCRATES:

Oh, no. It's an atmospheric vortex.

STREPSIADES:

[380] Vortex? Well, I never did.
Poor old Zeus is non-existent. Vortex
is on the throne instead.

Here! you've not explained to me
about the resonance, the thunder.

SOCRATES:

Don't you take anything in? I *told*
you that the clouds are hydroelectric.

Mutual collision and the density
produces resonance.

STREPSIADES:

What's the evidence for that?

SOCRATES:

You are, as I'll show you.

Remember the Panathenaea? How
you stuffed yourself with stew?

Result: stomach-ache, and a sudden
tendency to rumble.

STREPSIADES:

Apollo, yes. I felt awful. I had a
dreadful time.

That stew made a noise just like
thunder. God, it was a fearful
racket.

[390] Quite quiet at first – pappax!
pappax! – then, louder, papappax.

Then when I was crapping, proper
thunder, papapappax, just like the
Clouds.

SOCRATES:

Right. Your inside's very small and
it produces a tiny little fart.

The atmosphere is infinite; you
expect the thunder to be loud.

After all, both you and the Clouds
break wind; it's the same thing.

STREPSIADES:

Well, then – what about the lightning flashing on its fiery course?

When it strikes it's incineration for
some, and a mild roasting for
others.

It's clear. It *must* be Zeus's punishment on perjurers.

SOCRATES:

Go to the bottom of the class, you
square, you generation-gap.

If Zeus strikes perjurers, how on
earth has he failed to burn up

[400] Simon, Cleonymus, Theorus?
They are perjurers all right!

Instead he strikes his own temple,
or the Athenians' high spot,
Sunium,

or tall oak trees. What's the point of
that? Oak trees don't commit
perjury!

STREPSIADES:

I don't understand. It sounds all
right to me. Then what is the
lightning?

SOCRATES:

The Clouds again. An arid airstream
moves upwards into a confined
space,

and inflates them like a bladder. The
laws of nature operate.

There is an explosion. Density drives
the air out with accelerated

velocity. Result: impetus, effer-
vescence, ignition. (358–407)

4.1.1.3

CHORUS:

Take this mature student and
give him a preliminary examination.

Get his mind working and test his
I.Q.

SOCRATES:

Now, sir, first, some information
about yourself.

The knowledge is needed to decide
what new

[480] maxims I should bring to bear
on you.

STREPSIADES:

Maxims? Good God! Are you declaring war?

SOCRATES:

No. I want to ask you a few questions.
Have you a good memory?

STREPSIADES:

Yes and no.

If anyone owes me money, very
good.

If I owe anyone money, very
bad.

SOCRATES:

Have you any talent for public
speaking?

STREPSIADES:

Less for public speaking than for
private sneaking.

SOCRATES:
How on earth are you going to learn anything?

STREPSIADES:
        Oh, I'll manage all right.

SOCRATES:
[490] Well then, if I toss you off a piece of scholarship
about cosmology, will you catch the point?

STREPSIADES: Am I a performing dog, snapping scholarship as it's tossed up?

SOCRATES:
The man's completely illiterate!
(476–92)

4.1.1.4 (*Enter Socrates from the Think-Tank.*)

SOCRATES:
Great Respiration! For Chaos' sake! What the Atmosphere!
I never saw such a country bumpkin, such an idiot, dope, moron.
[630] I teach him a few hoary chestnuts of science,
(*there is a pun here with an obscene gesture*)
he's forgotten them before he's started. Still
I'll call him out here. He needs light. Strepsiades! Get your mattress and come outside.
(*Strepsiades half-enters pulling a palliasse which sticks in the door.*)

STREPSIADES:
The bed-bugs are barring me from bringing it.

SOCRATES:
Come along, put it down and pay attention.

STREPSIADES:
        O.K.

SOCRATES:
Right. Now which part of our curriculum which you've not
yet covered would you like to begin with. Out with it!
Measure-analysis? Grammatical linguistics? Rhythm-analysis?

STREPSIADES:
Measure-analysis for me! Only the other day
[640] the grocer did me out of several ounces.

SOCRATES:
You've got it all wrong. I'm asking which you think
the finest measure – heroic or alexandrine?

STREPSIADES:
I'll settle for a yard any day.

SOCRATES:
You don't know what you're talking about.

STREPSIADES:
        But
isn't a yard the same as three feet?

SOCRATES:
To hell with it. You're an illiterate country-bumpkin.
Perhaps you'll be able to make something of rhythm-analysis.

STREPSIADES:
What's rhythm-analysis got to do with my next meal?

SOCRATES:
It makes an impression in high society
[650] if a man understands rhythm-analysis,
what suits victory-odes and what suits epic.

STREPSIADES:
Victory? Good God, I know all about that.

SOCRATES:
        Carry on then.

STREPSIADES:
Well of course it means this.
(*He gives the V-sign.*)
But when I was a kid we did it like this.
(*He turns it into an obscene gesture.*)

SOCRATES:
Vulgar oaf!

STREPSIADES
        Poor Socrates! This isn't the sort of stuff I want to know.

SOCRATES:
What *do* you want to know?

STREPSIADES:
I keep telling you – logic: the logic
of injustice.

SOCRATES:
Well there are a few preliminary
lessons.
First, gender. What quadrupeds are
properly male?

STREPSIADES:
[660] I *would* be a loony if I couldn't
answer that –
rams, bulls, dogs, fowls.

SOCRATES:
Stop. D'you see what's happening?
You're using
for the male a word which also
applies to the female.

STREPSIADES:
What's that? I don't get it.

SOCRATES:
Fowl-male. Fowl-female.

STREPSIADES:
Poseidon! What ought I to call them?

SOCRATES:
The female a fow*less*, and the male a
fow*ler*.

STREPSIADES:
Fowless? That's good, by Atmo-
sphere.
For that lesson, apart from anything
else
I'll fill your basket to the brim.

SOCRATES:
[670] Stop. You've done it again.
You're making
basket masculine. It's feminine.

STREPSIADES:
What d'you mean?
I'm making basket masculine?

SOCRATES:
Yes,
just like Cleonymus.

STREPSIADES: I don't get that.

SOCRATES:
Cleonymus is nothing but a basket.

STREPSIADES:
My dear good man, Cleonymus
doesn't own a basket;

*(cupping his hands and miming mastur-
bation)*
he kneads his dough in a round
basin.
What word should I use in the future?

SOCRATES:
Why,
baskette, just like suffragette.

STREPSIADES:
A female baskette.

SOCRATES:
That's right.

STREPSIADES:
[680] That's what it should have
been all along – baskette, Cleo-
nyme.

SOCRATES:
The next part of the curriculum deals
with proper names. (627–81)

*In this scene Socrates appears as a lin-
guistic philosopher, concerned with the
minutiae of grammar and metrical analysis.
Greek being an inflected language, the jokes
do not always work in English. At 645
'yard' is borrowed from William Arrow-
smith's version. At 651 the joke is adapted.
The Greek rhythm 'dactyl' means literally
'finger'; but the use of the obscene gesture
is in the original. 661 is curious (the original
has 'goat' in as well) since the Greek word
for 'dog' is also used of bitches, and a
fowl is not a quadruped. Cleonymus was a
well-known queer. I have introduced an
additional point at 674, but Aristophanes
would have approved. At 634 there is a hit
at Socrates' spiritual voice which always
said No.*

4.1.1.5 *(Socrates has left Strepsiades to a
period of meditation, on the palliasse, completely covered with a pile of sheepskins.
He picks up a corner and looks in.)*

SOCRATES:
Now how are you getting on?
Thinking?

STREPSIADES:
Who, me?
God, yes.

SOCRATES:
What Thoughts have come?

STREPSIADES:
Whether these blasted bugs are going to leave anything of me.

SOCRATES:
Damn and blast you.

STREPSIADES:
I am damned and blasted. (*Exit Socrates.*)

CHORUS:
Don't be such a coward. Cover up your head.
Excogitate a scheme. Evasive.
Casuistical.

STREPSIADES:
Ow! Oh! I wish someone'd propose
[730] a scheme for evading these skins.

(*A pause. The sheepskins are in a turmoil of tossing. Then they subside. Re-enter Socrates.*)

SOCRATES:
Well now, let's see how he's getting on.

(*A snore is heard. Socrates picks up the skins.*)
Here, you. Have you gone to sleep?

STREPSIADES:
Sleep? Good God, no.

SOCRATES:
Got anything yet?

STREPSIADES:
Not a thing.

SOCRATES:
Nothing at all?

STREPSIADES:
Only my cock in my hand.

SOCRATES:
Get under the covers double quick and THINK!

STREPSIADES:
What about? Socrates, you'd better tell me.

SOCRATES:
You tell *me* when you know what you want.

STREPSIADES:
I've told you a million times what I want –
to avoid paying my debts.

SOCRATES:
All right. Get under the covers. (*He does so, reluctantly.*)
[740] Now try and refine your mind. Meditate minutely on the matter in hand.
Get your distinctions straight. Examine them carefully.

STREPSIADES (*with a great heave of the skins*):
Ow!

SOCRATES:
And stop fidgeting. Should your investigations reach an impasse,
drop them for a time, then with a fresh mind
stir them up and weigh the result.

(*The skins subside. There is a pause. Socrates makes to return to the Think-Tank. Suddenly there is a whirl of skins and Strepsiades emerges panting and triumphant. Two students unobtrusively cart away the palliasse.*)

STREPSIADES:
Socrates, Socrates darling.

SOCRATES:
Well?

STREPSIADES:
I've got a scheme for evading my debts.

SOCRATES:
Expound.

STREPSIADES:
Just suppose—

SOCRATES:
Suppose what?

STREPSIADES:
Suppose I hired a witch from Thessaly,
[750] caught the moon down from the sky one night, then
shut her up firmly in a mirror-case,
just like a mirror, and kept her all for mine.

SOCRATES:
What good would that do you?

STREPSIADES:
Easy?
If the moon never again appeared in the sky
I shouldn't have to pay my debts.

SOCRATES:
Why not?
STREPSIADES:
Because debts are collected on a monthly basis. (723–56)
Socrates may well have encouraged his friends to periods of meditation, like, for example, M.R.A. This scene leads towards the argument between the logic of justice and the logic of injustice.

4.1.1.6
STREPSIADES:
You swore by Zeus.
PHEIDIPPIDES:
I did.
STREPSIADES:
What a splendid thing learning is! Pheidippides, there's no such person as Zeus.
PHEIDIPPIDES:
Who is there then?
STREPSIADES:
Vortex has kicked Zeus out and holds the throne.
PHEIDIPPIDES:
You're crazy!
STREPSIADES:
It's true.
PHEIDIPPIDES:
Who says so?
STREPSIADES:
Socrates of Melos
And Chaerephon who understands how fleas jump. (825–31)
Diagoras of Melos was a well-known atheist.

4.1.2 The Wasps (*422* B.C.)
CHORUS:
So much for him [Cleon]. Last season
your poet moved his hand against those fever-ridden nightmares
who tried to strangle your fathers in the dark and choke out the life of their fathers,
who took to their beds and challenged all the most harmless of you,
piling up affidavits, summonses, depositions

till many jumped up in terror and went to the magistrate. (1037)
Produced in 422 B.C. The reference is to The Clouds *in its first version. Aristophanes seems to be making three points: (a) Socrates and his group are unhealthy invalids; (b) they are innovators rejecting the past; (c) by making the worse cause appear the better and the unjust argument strong they are behind the informers.*

4.1.3 The Birds (*414* B.C.)
4.1.3.1
HERALD:
Before your city was built
everyone was Sparta-mad,
long-haired, hungry, grubby, Socratic,
staff-in-handed. (1280)

4.1.3.2
CHORUS:
Near the Shadefoots lies a lake
where Socrates instead of washing
prefers to raise ghosts. (1553)

4.1.4 The Frogs (*405* B.C.)
CHORUS:
Nice to sit with Socrates
and say nothing
Nice to reject culture.
Nice to abandon the high skills
of tragedy
But to idle about
scratching at surfaces
with long words
is just crazy. (1491–9)

4.2 Other Comic Dramatists

4.2.1 *Cratinus*
. . . those whose greatest oath
for any statement was (*a*) a dog (*b*) a goose.

They never mentioned the gods. (*The Cheirons* 231 E, unknown date)

4.2.2 *Eupolis*
4.2.2.1
Yes and I loathe that poverty-stricken windbag Socrates
who *contemplates* everything in the world
but does not know where his next meal is coming from. (352 E, unknown date)

4.2.2.2
Socrates was next; he ran through a Stesichorus
Lieder recital – and went off with the decanter. (361 E, unknown date)
The scholiast to Aristophanes Clouds *96 says that though Eupolis does not often introduce Socrates he hits him off better than Aristophanes in the whole of* The Clouds.

4.2.3 *Ameipsias*
A: Socrates – shining in a small gathering, eclipsed in a large – have you come to join us as well? Tough, eh? Where *did* you get that coat?
⟨No shoes on your feet.⟩

You're bankrupting the cobblers with your insults!
B: Still he'd rather starve than flatter! (*Connus* 9 E, 423 B.C.)
This play was performed on the same occasion as the first performance of The Clouds. Connus *was a music-teacher associated with Socrates: the play had a chorus of intellectuals (the same root-word as 'contemplates' in Eupolis and 'Think-Tank' in Aristophanes).*

4.2.4 *Theopompus*
One is not really one.
Two is barely one, Plato says so. (*Sweet-Tooth* 15 E)
This seems to refer to Phaedo *96 E and suggests that contemporaries took* Phaedo *as representing Plato's thought not Socrates'.*

4.2.5 *Anon.*
The wretch who doomed double-natured Socrates
now lies with lips contorted in death. (386 E, unknown date: fourth century)
This refers to Meletus, who according to Diogenes Laertius 2, 43, 6 (**1.4**) *and Diodorus Siculus 14, 37, 7* (**7.1.2**), *was in his turn executed. Why is Socrates double-natured? Perhaps human and divine.*

PART FIVE

THE ATHENIAN ORATORS

Traditionally ten 'Attic Orators' survived, extending through the fourth century B.C. They were inevitably involved in politics and bear direct testimony to the political tone of the turn of the fifth century, and incidentally to the political impression made by Socrates.

5.1 Andocides

Andocides, like Socrates, was tried for impiety in 399. His offence was the fact that after sharing with Alcibiades in some blasphemous actions in 415 he had subsequently entered a temple in contravention of a law forbidding those guilty of impiety from doing so. Andocides' case is interesting because: (a) Meletus was for the prosecution but Anytus was for ·the defence; (b) he makes much of the amnesty law of 403. Unlike Socrates, he was acquitted.

5.1.1 When you established the Restoration from Piraeus the chance for revenge was in your hands. But you took the decision to let bygones be bygones. You thought your country's security more important than personal feuds. You resolved on a mutual obliteration of injuries from the memory. (*On the Mysteries* 81)

5.1.2 Well now, what of your oaths. The whole city took a common oath. There was general reconciliation and you all swore, 'I shall hold no memory of past wrong against any citizen except the Thirty and the Eleven, nor against any of them who is ready to face examination of his tenure of office.' (ibid. 90)

5.1.3 Here stands Meletus. As you all know, under the Thirty he arrested Leon, and Leon was put to death without a trial. (ibid. 94)
This was the arrest which Socrates refused to make.

5.1.4 I invite these gentlemen, who have given ample proof of their outstanding services to your democracy, to come forward and testify to you what they know of me. Anytus ... (ibid. 150)
Anytus was evidently a left-wing politician.

5.2 Isocrates

Isocrates (436–338 B.C.) is mentioned by Plato in Phaedrus. *He was a pupil of Gorgias, a stylist, and an educationalist of high merit. His speech* Busiris *is a showpiece written about 390 in rivalry with one Polycrates. Its importance here is his allusion to Polycrates' pamphlet against Socrates. It is significant that Socrates was stirring up pamphleteering ten years after his death: we may suspect that Plato's early work cannot be divorced from this context. Fictitious speeches for the prosecution and defence were a form of pamphlet.*

I notice that you take considerable pride in your *Defence of Busiris* and your *Prosecution of Socrates.* .... Your aim was to attack Socrates. One would have thought you were writing a panegyric of him when you gave him Alcibiades as a disciple. No one ever thought him a pupil of Socrates, though everyone would accept his outstanding qualities. (11, 4)

5.3 Aeschines

Aeschines (c. 390–315 B.C.) was Demosthenes' great rival. His speech against Timarchus dates from 345.

Gentlemen of Athens, you executed Socrates the sophist, because he was clearly responsible for the education of Critias, one of the Thirty anti-democratic leaders. .... (1, 173)
Cf. **9.1.1.34**; **9.11.2.6**; **10.2**[38]; **10.2**[52].

PART SIX

ARISTOTLE (384–322 B.C.)

Aristotle (384–322 B.C.) was a doctor's son from Macedon, who came to Athens in 367 and studied with Plato for twenty years. On Plato's death he struck out on his own. A superb biologist and an omnivorous collector of facts, he likes to survey the history of each subject he treats.

Aristotle's evidence has been much discussed. Fitzgerald found an important clue in suggesting that we can distinguish Socrates with the article in Greek as representing Socrates in Plato's dialogues and Socrates without the article as representing the historic Socrates. Taylor in *Varia Socratica I* exposed this theory to a withering fire of criticism, but Ross in his great edition of Aristotle's *Metaphysics* was able to rehabilitate it in a modified form, and probably most scholars today, though not all, would accept that some such distinction exists. I have rigorously eschewed all passages which seem to refer to Plato's dialogues – even more rigorously than T. Deman in his valuable *Le Témoignage d'Aristote sur Socrate* (Paris, 1942), who allows *Eudemian Ethics* 1247 B 11 despite its dependence on Plato's *Euthydemus* 271 D, and *Nicomachean Ethics* 1145 B 21 despite its dependence on Plato's *Protagoras* 352 B. Taylor suggested that as Aristotle's knowledge of Socrates must have depended on Plato, it was of no independent weight. Apart from the fact that Aristotle was not cloistered in the Academy, the conclusion is faulty. *If* Aristotle's knowledge of Socrates did depend on Plato, then it is the clearest possible testimony not merely that the Socrates of the dialogues is not the historical Socrates but that Plato knew that this was so.

I have, of course, ignored all passages where Socrates is used merely as a logical example.

6.1 Logical Works

This was why Socrates posed questions without answering them; he admitted his lack of knowledge. (*Sophistical Refutations* 34, 183 B 8)

6.2 Problems

Why have all the outstanding figures in philosophy, politics, creative art or the sciences been melancholic? . . . Empedocles, Plato, Socrates and many other famous names. (30, 953 A 10 and 27)

6.3 Metaphysics

6.3.1 Socrates rejected the study of science for ethics. In ethics he was looking for the universal; he was the first to concentrate on definitions. Plato received his instruction and through this approach came to the conclusion that the universal belonged to a different world from the world of sense-perception. (1, 6, 987 B 1)

A vital passage, identifying Socrates' contribution and distinguishing that of Plato. See the next passage.

6.3.2 Socrates was concerned with qualities of ethical character, and in this connection was the first to look for the essence: he was trying to use syllogistic reasoning, and syllogistic reasoning starts from the essence. . . . Two things

may properly be ascribed to Socrates, inductive reasoning and definition by universals – both belonging to the very fundamentals of science. But Socrates did not assign to the universal or the definitions an independent existence. It was the others who made them separate, and called these separate entities the Forms of everything that exists. (13, 4, 1078 B 17–32)

The key passage.

6.3.3 Socrates provided the starting-point for this theory [the Theory of Forms], as I remarked before, by his definitions, but he did not separate the definitions from the particular objects; and was right in refraining from doing so. (13, 9, 1086 B 2)

6.4 Nicomachean Ethics

6.4.1 Socrates thought courage a form of knowledge. (3, 11, 1116 B 4)

Cf. Eudemian Ethics *1229 A 12* (**6.6.2**); *1230 A 7.*

6.4.2 Self-depreciation is surely a grace of character; its aim is not advantage but the avoidance of ostentation. It is almost always favourable qualities which are denied, as by Socrates. (4, 13, 1127 B 22)

6.4.3 That is why some hold that all the virtues are forms of practical wisdom. In this Socrates was partly right and partly wrong. He was wrong in holding that all the virtues were forms of practical wisdom, right in holding that they could not exist without practical wisdom. . . . Socrates held that all the virtues were rational principles, all being forms of knowledge. (6, 13, 1144 B 18–30)

Cf. Eudemian Ethics *7, 1246 B 32* (**6.6.4**).

6.5 Magna Moralia

Probably not an authentic work of Aristotle, though the opposite view has been strongly argued recently.

6.5.1 Socrates succeeded Pythagoras. He discoursed more fully and fruitfully about the virtues, though even he was not on the right lines. He turned the virtues into pieces of knowledge. This is out of the question. All knowledge is associated with reason, and reason is in the intellectual part of the soul. So on his view all virtue is in the intellectual part of the soul. In equating virtue with knowledge he goes far to destroying the non-rational part of the soul. In so doing he does away with the passive and active aspects of moral character. So his treatment of the virtues is at fault. (1, 1, 1182 A 15)

6.5.2 Socrates was wrong in making the virtues pieces of knowledge. He took the view that nothing ought to be purposeless. By making the virtues pieces of knowledge he in fact made them purposeless. (1, 1, 1183 B 8)

6.5.3 Next we must consider whether or not virtue can be acquired. As Socrates put it, it is not in our power to be good or bad. If, he says, you ask anyone whether he wants to be righteous or unrighteous, no one votes for unrighteousness. So, too, with courage and cowardice and all the other virtues. It is clear that if there are

bad men it is not because they want to be. So too with the good. (1, 9, 1187 A 5)

6.5.4 So we ought not to use the word 'brave' of men whose courage comes from experience. Socrates was wrong in making courage a kind of knowledge. (1, 20, 1190 B 27)

6.5.5 Socrates was wrong in equating virtue with reason. He argued that there was no point in acting courageously or morally unless you had knowledge and made a rational choice. So he equated virtue with reason, wrongly. Modern views are better. (1, 34, 1198 A 10)

6.5.6 Socrates of old completely did away with incontinence, saying that it did not exist. No one, in his view, would choose evil, knowing it to be such. If a man is incontinent he must know that a thing is bad and still choose it under the power of his feelings. This was his argument against the existence of incontinence. (2, 6, 1200 B 75)

6.6 Eudemian Ethics

This work bears a close relation to the Nicomachean Ethics. *We may suppose that Aristotle's ethical thought was edited by different students at different periods.*

6.6.1 Socrates of old thought our object was knowledge of virtue. So he kept asking 'What is justice?' 'What is courage?' and so with every aspect of virtue. He had good reason for this. He thought that all the virtues were pieces of knowledge: it is the same thing to know righteousness and to be righteous. Once we have learned mathematics or the building trade we are mathematicians or builders. This is why he asked what virtue was rather than its origin or how to acquire it. (1, 5, 1216 B 2)

6.6.2 Military courage comes from experience and knowledge, not knowledge of objects of fear (as Socrates suggested) but knowledge of protection from them. (3, 1, 1229 A 14)
Cf. 1230 A 7; also **6.4.1**.

6.6.3 Some think that utility is the only basis for affection. The evidence is that everyone pursues it while rejecting what is useless. Socrates of old made this point, using as examples, spittle, hair and nails, and all the parts we discard as useless – including the body after death: the carcass is no use. Those who find it useful keep it, as in Egypt. (7, 1235 A 35)

6.6.4 So that it is clear that these dispositions of the rest of the soul combine goodness and practical wisdom. Socrates was right in saying that nothing is stronger than practical wisdom – wrong in equating it with knowledge. (7, 13, 1246 B 32)
Cf. Nicomachean Ethics *6, 1144 B 18* (**6.4.3**).

6.7 Politics

Self-discipline, courage, morality are different in a woman and in a man, as Socrates used to hold. Courage in the male is shown in authority, in the female in obedience: so with other virtues. (1, 13, 1260 A 21)
This is the only passage in Politics *not referable to Plato.*

6.8 Rhetoric

6.8.1 You must also consider before whom your panegyric is pronounced. As Socrates used to say, it's not difficult to sing Athenian praises before an Athenian audience. (1, 9, 1367 B 7)
Cf. also 3, 1415 B 30; Plato, Menexenus *235 D.*

6.8.2 Analogy was used by Socrates. For example, one might say, 'Public office should not be filled by lot. It's like choosing an athletics team by lot instead of the best athletes, or the captain of a ship by lot from the crew, instead of finding the expert.' (2, 10, 1393 B 3)

6.8.3 This was why Socrates refused to go to Archelaus. 'It's rather an outrage,' he said, 'not to be able to protect oneself from favours as much as from injuries.' (2, 23, 1398 A 24)

6.8.4 As Aristippus said to Plato when the latter was speaking somewhat too dogmatically in his view: 'How unlike our friend!' – meaning Socrates. (2, 23, 1398 B 29)

6.8.5 An example from Theodectus' *Socrates*: 'What temple did he dishonour? Which of the gods which the city recognises did he fail to honour?' (2, 23, 1399 A 7)
Theodectus, orator and writer of Tragedy, was a younger contemporary of Aristotle, author of a Defence of Socrates.

6.8.6 This is why mathematical treatises do not have ethical content. They do not deal with choice. They are not teleological. Socratic discourses are; this is their subject. (3, 16, 1417 A 18)

6.9 Poetics

The form of writing which uses either prose or verse, and verse in a single metre or a variety of metres, has up to the present no name. We have no common names for the mimes of Sophron or Xenarchus, or for Socratic dialogues. (1447 A 28)

Cf. **6.10**.

6.10 Fragments

So we shan't deny the title of dialogue to the works which Sophron called *Mimes* or the quality mimetic to the original Socratic dialogues, those of Alexamenus of Teos. (*Fr.* 72)

This (as Athenaeus points out, 505 C) is express evidence that there were Socratic dialogues before Plato.

PART SEVEN

LATER WRITERS:

HISTORICAL

7.1 Diodorus Siculus

Diodorus was born at Agyrium in Sicily and lived and worked in the first century B.C. *He set himself to write a* Universal History. *Unhappily he lacked the equipment to succeed in this almost impossible task, but he used good sources and used them sensibly. His general approach is moralising, and he is interested in 'great men'.*

7.1.1 The officers moved forward to arrest Theramenes. He took the disaster courageously; he had gone a long way in exploring philosophy with Socrates. In general, the crowd were distressed at Theramenes' fall, but did not venture to intervene in view of the force of armed attendants. Socrates the philosopher and two of his circle ran up to try to impede the officers. Theramenes urged them to do nothing of the kind; he applauded their loyalty and courage, but it would cause him great grief if he were to be responsible for the death of men who felt like that towards him. Socrates and his associates, in view of the lack of support from any of the others and the growing intransigence of the authorities, retired. (14, 5)

This event dates from 404 B.C. during the dictatorship of the Thirty.

7.1.2 At Athens Socrates the philosopher was prosecuted by Anytus and Meletus for impiety and corrupting the young. He was condemned to death and executed by a draught of hemlock. The prosecution was unjust, and the democracy subsequently regretted the action when they reflected on the quality of the man they had executed. So they became hostile to the prosecutors, and eventually put them to death without trial. (14, 37, 7)

This appears under the year 400 B.C. The statement about the counter-execution of the prosecutors is certainly untrue as it stands.

It is often repeated: it is in any case not directly relevant to the life of Socrates.

7.2 Appian

Appian lived in Alexandria in the second century A.D. and wrote a history of Rome in Greek.

In this way Scipio showed his scorn for an accusation which contrasted strongly with the way he lived, behaving in my view more wisely than Aristides (charged with theft) or Socrates, who, faced with a similar slander, made no reply to the charges – unless Socrates made the speech attributed to him by Plato. (11, 7, 41)

Cf. **8.14.3**; **9.16**.

7.3 Cornelius Nepos

C. *100–24* B.C., *Latin historian to whom Catullus dedicated a volume of verse. Most of his voluminous writings are lost. A few biographical writings remain, direct, straightforward and interesting enough to be admirable (and neglected) schoolbooks, but full of references to sources he has not read, and generally uncritical.*

He was brought up in Pericles' home (he was, it seems, his stepson) and educated by Socrates. . . . As a young adolescent he was the object of much homosexual love, among others from Socrates; reference will be found in Plato's *The Banquet.* Plato introduces Alcibiades, who recounts that he had spent a night with Socrates, and emerged as unscathed as a son should from his father. (*Life of Alcibiades* 2)

A straight reference to **2.5.2.2**. *References to Socrates in the historians are slight.*

PART EIGHT

LATER WRITERS:

PHILOSOPHICAL

8.1 Cicero

So also Brutus *87, 229*; Academics *2, 5, 15.*

Marcus Tullius Cicero (106–43 B.C.): greatest of Roman orators, statesman and man of letters. In his younger days he underwent a comprehensive education in philosophy; and philosophy gives weight and value to his speeches. During the period of Julius Caesar's monarchical power he went into philosophical retirement, and employed himself in providing the Romans with a philosophical encyclopedia: the effect was to provide western Europe with its basic philosophical vocabulary for two thousand years. He was not an original thinker: he described his work as 'mere transcripts: I simply provide the words, and I've plenty of those'. He himself inclined to the Academy (which was at the time sceptical) in epistemology, and to the Stoics in ethics.

8.1.1 Opposed to these [Gorgias, Thrasymachus, etc.] was Socrates. His practice was to refute their dogmatism by a subtle method of argument. From his copious conversations emerged leaders of learning, and from that time dates the discovery of a philosophy differing from the older form and concerned to discuss good, evil, human life and ethics. (*Brutus* 8, 31)

8.1.2 They say that the great Socrates used to declare that his work was done when his encouragement had fairly driven a man to an urge to understand and acquire virtue. When a man was convinced that his prime need was to become a good man the rest of philosophy followed easily. (*On the Orator* 1, 47, 204)
This seems to rest on a tradition independent of Plato and Xenophon.

8.1.3 In agreement with the best authorities I rank Socrates the supreme example of 'irony', that is mock-modesty, combined with charm and culture. (ibid. 2, 67, 270)

8.1.4 Socrates was the leading man in this class. On the evidence of all men of learning and the general judgement of Greece he was far and away the leading man in good sense, keen judgement, charm, subtlety, eloquence, range and wealth of argument in any field he chose. He took the general word 'philosophy' away from those who were handling practically and educationally the field of our present concern, although the one word was used, since the name 'philosophy' was given to theoretical learning and practical application in all that is good. In his discussions he separated the science of wise thinking from the science of elegant speaking, though they are naturally linked. Plato in his writings has given immortal currency to his character and varied discourse, though Socrates did not leave a single letter behind him. Hence the division of tongue from mind – damnable and damaging nonsense! – so that different people teach us what to say and how to say it. Most of them somehow are descendants of Socrates. Different people draw different conclusions from the all-embracing variety of his dialectic, so that he fathered families with conflicting views and widely divergent approaches; all philosophers think of themselves, and want others to think of them, as followers of Socrates. (ibid. 3, 16, 60)

8.1.5 Induction is a form of argument which produces in the interlocutor assent to assured conclusions. It uses this assent to induce acceptance of a doubtful proposition because of its similarity to the point assented to. In a dialogue by Aeschines the follower of Socrates, Socrates takes as an example a conversation between Aspasia and Xenophon and his wife. . . . Socrates made wide use of this conversational method because he did not want to introduce any persuasive arguments himself but preferred to reach conclusions on the basis offered by his interlocutor, a conclusion which the latter was bound to agree to on the basis of what he had already granted. (*On Invention* 31, 51–3)

Cf. *1, 35, 61* and Topics *10, 42*.

8.1.6 Socrates and all his followers . . . remained in the opinion of the philosophers of old. . . . (*On Divination* 1, 3, 5) *Cicero is speaking of divination. Xenophon's picture of Socrates emphasises this more than Plato's. But Plato has it (Apology 33 C (2.2); Crito 44 A (2.3); Phaedo 60 E (2.4.1)) and Xenophon issues certain caveats (Memoirs of Socrates 1, 1, 6 (3.2.1)).*

8.1.7 This is just what tradition says about Socrates, just what Socrates himself often says in the books of his followers. There is a divine power, which he calls *daimonion*. He always obeyed it; its instructions were always negative not positive. In fact, Socrates – and what better authority could we ask for? – answered Xenophon's request for advice about accompanying Cyrus by giving his views and adding, 'This is human advice; I consider that difficult problems should be referred to Apollo. . . .' There is a story that he noticed his friend Crito with his eye bandaged and asked what was the matter. Crito replied that he'd been walking in the country; he had pushed forward a branch which sprang back and hit him in the eye. Socrates said, 'You didn't listen to me when I called you back though I always use divine guidance.' It was Socrates too who, during the disaster at Delium under Laches' command, was retreating with Laches. They reached a crossroads and he refused to go the same way as the others. They asked why, and he replied that the god prevented him. Those who retreated by another route fell in with

a detachment of enemy cavalry. Antipater has collected a large number of stories of Socrates' miraculous divine guidance. I shall pass them over: you are familiar with them, and I do not need to remind you of them. (ibid. 1, 54, 122–4)

For the first story, see Xenophon, Anabasis 3, 1, (3.5.1) but Cicero takes the words perhaps from Posidonius. The Crito story is not otherwise known. The retreat from Delium is often narrated, but this story appears only here and in Pseudo-Socrates, Epistles 1, 9 (15.3.2). Antipater was a Stoic, successor of Diogenes of Babylon.

8.1.8 We've read how Zopyrus the physiognomer claimed to be able to identify a man's moral character from his external appearance, his eyes, looks and face, and how he identified Socrates as a dolt and dunderhead, describing those features as blocked up and clogged. He added that he was a womaniser – which is said to have made Alcibiades burst into a roar of laughter. (*Fate* 5, 10)

Cf. **8.1.14**; **8.11**; **12.18**.

8.1.9 This [Debate], as you know, is the old method Socrates used of arguing against the other man's views; Socrates thought that this was the easier method of approaching the truth. (*Talks at Tusculum* 1, 4, 8)

8.1.10 . . . the view that the Stoics took over from Socrates and clung to tenaciously, that a fool is a sick man. (ibid. 3, 5, 10)

8.1.11 . . . the unchanged expression which Xanthippe is said to have attributed to her husband Socrates: 'It's always the same when I see him leaving home and coming back.' (ibid. 3, 15, 31)

Cf. **8.1.23**; **8.2.10**; **8.4.2**; **9.5.1**; **9.7.15**; **11.2.18**; **12.15.9**.

8.1.12 What shall we say, when Socrates persuaded Alcibiades, as we have read, that he was not a human being at all, that there was no difference between the aristocratic Alcibiades and any manual worker, and Alcibiades was mortified and tearfully pleaded with Socrates to drive away his viciousness and grant him virtue . . .? (ibid. 3, 32, 77)

*From Aeschines, Fr. 10. See Augustine, City of God 14, 8 (***12.16.7***).*

8.1.13 When Euripides put on *Orestes* it is said that Socrates encored the first three lines:

There is no word so terrible to utter, no chance, no disaster brought by angry gods, that human nature cannot suffer and bear it. (ibid. 4, 29, 63)

8.1.14 Those who are said to be naturally hot-tempered, sentimental, grudging, etc., are endowed with a sickness of soul, but can be cured, as in the story of Socrates. Zopyrus claimed that he could identify a man's character from his face, and attributed to Socrates a whole agglomeration of vices. The audience, who could not discern these vices in Socrates, laughed at him, but Socrates rescued him, saying that he had the vices at birth but had overpowered them by reason. (ibid. 4, 37, 80)

Cf. **8.1.8** *n.*

8.1.15 Socrates was the first to call philosophy down from the sky and establish her in the towns and introduce her into homes and force her to investigate life, ethics, good and evil. (ibid. 5, 4, 10)

Cicero means that Socrates diverted philosophy from cosmology to ethics; in fact, this was the work of the sophists. Cf. **8.1.27**.

8.1.16 A great mass of gold and silver was being carried past in ceremonial procession. Socrates said, 'How many things I can do without!' (ibid. 5, 32, 91)

8.1.17 There is a story of Socrates. He was enjoying a walk which lasted into the evening. Someone asked, 'Why?' He replied that he was getting up an appetite for dinner. (ibid. 5, 34, 97)

8.1.18 Socrates was asked his nationality and replied, 'Universian'; he looked on himself as an inhabitant and citizen of the whole universe. (ibid. 5, 37, 108)

An unlikely story: Socrates seems to have been a loyal Athenian. Told with more plausibility of Diogenes. Cf. **8.4.1**; **8.19.1**; **9.1.1.24**; *contrast* **1.2**; **8.3.10**.

8.1.19 'First,' I said, 'please don't think that I'm about to deliver a formal philosophical lecture. . . . Socrates, who has some claim to be called the father of philosophy, never did anything of the sort.' (*On the Ends* 2, 1, 1)

8.1.20 I listen to Socrates, who gave pleasure no place, when he says that hunger is the best aperitif for food and thirst for drink (ibid. 2, 28, 90)

8.1.21 Why did Plato later visit Archytas at Tarentum? Why did he go to the rest of the Pythagoreans at Locri, Echecrates, Timaeus and Arion? His object was to add the learning of the Pythagoreans to his portrait of Socrates, and to extend his learning to studies which Socrates repudiated. (ibid. 5, 29, 87)

8.1.22 My philosophy is not much at variance with that of the Peripatetics; we both would like to be regarded as followers of Socrates and Plato. (*On Moral Obligation* 1, 1, 2)

8.1.23 It shows a lack of dignity to respond in an exaggerated form to prosperity or adversity. It is magnificent to

keep an even disposition, the same de-
meanour, the same expression, in all
circumstances, as Socrates and Gaius
Laelius are said to have done. (ibid. 1,
26, 90)

8.1.24 Among the Greeks we are told
that Socrates was a charming man,
witty, a delightful conversationalist,
and in all his works mock-modest, or, as
the Greeks put it, 'ironical'. (ibid. 1,
30, 108)

8.1.25 Socrates used to put it excellently: 'The nearest way to glory – a
kind of short-cut – is to act in such a
way that you are what you want to be
thought to be.' (ibid. 2, 12, 43)
    Cf. Xenophon, Memoirs of Socrates 2,
6, 39.

8.1.26 ... expediency can never conflict with morality. That is why the
tradition has it that Socrates re-
peatedly called down a curse on those
who first made the abstract distinction
between things naturally linked. (ibid.
3, 3, 11)
    Cf. Laws 1, 12, 33 (**8.1.32**); Plutarch,
Table-talk 662 B (**9.1.1.25**).

8.1.27 Then Varro began: 'My own
opinion accords with the general view:
Socrates was the first to call philosophy
away from mysteries hidden from us by
Nature, which were the concern of all
previous philosophers, and direct her
to the theme of ordinary life, the investigation of virtues and vices, and good
and evil generally. He judged that the
physical universe was either beyond our
knowledge or that even full knowledge
of it contributed nothing to goodness of
life. In almost all the conversations so
fully and variously recorded by his
hearers Socrates' approach was to avoid
positive assertions and to refute others;
he claimed to have no knowledge
except the fact that he had no knowledge, and his superiority to the rest lay

in their pretensions to knowledge where
they were ignorant, while his single
piece of knowledge lay in the recog-
nition of his ignorance; he imagined
that this was why Apollo named him
as the wisest of all men, since wisdom is
simply and solely not thinking that you
know what you do not know. He was
consistent in this assertion and steadfast in his views; yet all his words were
directed to the praise of virtue and encouraging his fellows to concern for
virtue, as we can gather from the works
of Socratic writers, Plato in particular.'
(Academics 1, 4, 15)

8.1.28 They [Platonists and Aristo-
telians] abandoned Socrates' practice of
being agnostic on all subjects and avoiding dogmatic assertions. So arose, in opposition to Socrates' position, a science
of philosophy with an organised curriculum and systematic doctrinal exposition. (ibid. 1, 4, 17)

8.1.29 Most of the startling arguments
of the Stoics, called paradoxes, derive
from Socrates. (ibid. 2, 44, 136)

8.1.30 Zeno [an Epicurean contro-
versialist] attacked with abuse not
merely his contemporaries like Apollodorus Silus and the rest but Socrates as
well, the very father of philosophy; he
said he was the buffoon of Athens. (The
Nature of the Gods 1, 34, 93)

8.1.31 Scipio said: '... I often think
that Socrates showed more wisdom in
having nothing to do with these matters
[astronomy and the like] and claiming
that questions of natural science were
either too large for human scholarship
to master or irrelevant to human life.'
    Tubero answered, 'Africanus, I don't
understand where the tradition arose
that Socrates completely rejected investigations in this field and concentrated on ethical questions. What better

authority can we approve on Socrates than Plato? . . .' (*Republic* 1, 10, 15)

8.1.32 Socrates was right in often cursing the man who first separated expediency from justice: he used to grumble that this was the source of all that is pernicious. (*Laws* 1, 12, 33)

The story comes from the Stoic Cleanthes. See Clement of Alexandria, Miscellanies *2, 22 (12.3.4).*

8.1.33 As if I needed a higher authority than Socrates, who never set foot out of doors during the dictatorship of the Thirty! (*Letters to Atticus* 8, 2)

8.2 Seneca

The younger Seneca was born about 4 B.C. in Spain, had a brilliant career, but in A.D. 41 was exiled in some jockeying for political power. Recalled in 49, he became tutor to young Nero, and later effectively regent. This position made him immensely rich and won him enemies. He was a figurehead in a conspiracy against the emperor in 65 and committed suicide. A Stoic, with an unusual knowledge of Epicureanism (perhaps from his brother Gallio), he wrote plays which influenced the Elizabethan stage, and ethical letters and dialogues with an over-sententious display of worthy sentiments.

8.2.1 Plato, Aristotle and the whole gang of philosophers who were about to go their several ways got more from Socrates' character than from his words. (*Letters* 6, 6)

8.2.2 Socrates in prison engaged in discussion. Although there were those who promised him a means of escape, he refused to leave; he stayed behind in order to free mankind of two oppressive fears, of death and imprisonment. (ibid. 24, 4)

Cf. Plato, Crito (**2.3**).

8.2.3 Socrates made the same point to a grumbler. 'Why are you surprised that travel does you no good? You always take yourself with you. The very cause which sent you off is on your track.' (ibid. 28, 2)

Cf. 104, 7.

8.2.4 Socrates was no aristocrat. (ibid. 44, 3)

8.2.5 Socrates recalled philosophy completely to ethics. He said that the height of wisdom lay in knowing the difference between good and evil. 'Follow men of that sort to be happy,' he said, 'if you listen to me; don't worry if some people think you silly. If anyone has a mind, let him insult and wrong you. You'll suffer no harm, provided that you have virtue. If you want to be happy,' he said, 'if you want in good faith to be a good man, don't worry if others look down on you.' (ibid. 71, 7)

8.2.6 Socrates used to say that virtue and truth were the same. (ibid. 71, 16)

8.2.7 If you need a model, take Socrates, a tough old man, tossed by every storm, unyielding to poverty (made worse by troubles at home) or hard work (including military service). He had trouble enough at home, whether we think of his wife with her brutality and sharp tongue or his undisciplined children, more like their mother than their father. Reflect on history: he lived in time of war, under a dictatorship, or an anarchy which was harsher than any war or dictatorship. The war lasted twenty-seven years. At the end of the fighting the country was under the disastrous rule of the Thirty Dictators, several of whom were his personal enemies. Finally condemnation came on the gravest charges: he was accused of offending against the religion and corrupting the youth, a crime against the gods, the parents and the State. Then prison and poison. All this did not stir Socrates to bat an eyelid. Wonderful! Glorious! Unique! To the last no one saw Socrates light-hearted or depressed. Fortune was strong: he was calm. (ibid. 104, 27)

8.2.8 Socrates . . . took in good part the witticisms levelled at him in word and action in comic drama, and laughed just as much when his wife Xanthippe threw dirty water over him. (*On Firmness* 18, 5)

Cf. **1.4**[17]; **8.4.11**; **12.15.3**.

8.2.9 That is why Socrates said to his slave, 'I would flog you if I were not angry.' He put off the correction of the slave to a sounder moment; at that moment the correction is for himself. (*On Anger* 1, 15, 3)

8.2.10 Shall the great Socrates lose the capacity to bring back home the same expression which he took from home? (ibid. 2, 7, 1)

8.2.11 There is a story about Socrates. Someone slapped his face. He merely said, 'It's a nuisance not knowing when to go out wearing a helmet.' (ibid. 3, 11, 2)

8.2.12 With Socrates it was an indication of anger if he lowered his voice and controlled his words. It was clear that he was engaged in an inner struggle. His friends would catch him at it and challenge him, but he was not sorry to be accused of suppressing his anger. (ibid. 3, 13, 3)

8.2.13 Socrates was there; he consoled the mourning fathers; he gave heart to those in political despair; he castigated the rich who were afraid of their wealth for a twelfth-hour repentance of the greed which brought them into danger; he presented a magnificent example to those prepared to imitate him, in moving like a free man despite the presence of thirty slave-drivers. Athens – Athens put him in prison and executed him. He had safely taunted an army of dictators, but Freedom could not tolerate freedom. (*On Tranquillity of Mind* 5, 2)

8.2.14 Socrates did not blush to play with kids. (ibid. 17, 4)

Cf. **9.4.7**; **9.7.19**.

8.2.15 Socrates was receiving gifts proportionate to the resources of the giver. Aeschines, a poor disciple, said: 'I have nothing worthy to give you: this is the only way in which I am conscious of my poverty. So I offer you all that I have – myself. Please look kindly on this gift, such as it is; remember that others may be giving you a lot, but have more left for themselves.' Socrates replied: 'A great gift indeed – unless you underestimate yourself! My job will be to return you better than when I received you.' (*On Benefits* 1, 8, 1)

8.2.16 It is Socrates who does not allow the name of Sophroniscus to die. (ibid. 3, 32, 3)

8.2.17 King Archelaus invited Socrates to visit him. Socrates, the story goes, was reluctant to go: he would not be able to make comparable return for the benefits he would receive. (ibid. 5, 6, 2)

8.2.18 Socrates in the hearing of his friends said, 'I would have bought a cloak if I had the money.' He made no request; it was a general admonition. Of course, there was a real to-do about who should give it to him. The gift was a minor matter, the question who should give it a major one. Could there have been a greater rebuke? 'I would have bought a cloak if I had the money.' Bustle as they might, they were too late; they had already let Socrates down. (ibid. 7, 24, 1)

8.3 Dio Chrysostom (c. A.D. 100)

Dio of Prusa, nicknamed Chrysostomus or 'Golden-mouthed', was a man of learning, eloquence and political renown. In A.D. 82 he fell from power and was sentenced to banishment. With this went conversion to Cynic philosophy. In Nerva's brief reign his sentence was annulled, and under Trajan he was a figure of some influence. As a Cynic he admired Socrates, whom he saw through the eyes of Antisthenes.

8.3.1 I do not accept pupils. I know that I should have nothing to teach them, since I know nothing myself. . . . I am pretty sure that you believe me when I speak of my inexperience and lack of knowledge . . . yes, and I think you would believe Socrates too; he was always making the same claim to everyone: 'I know nothing.' (12, 13–14)

8.3.2 When I was criticising everybody else and myself in particular in this way, finding myself at a loss I sometimes turned to an old argument used by one Socrates, one which he never stopped using, at the top of his voice, with all his powers, everywhere, to anyone and everyone, in the sports grounds and the Lyceum and the workshops and the city centre, like a god speaking from the stage-crane, as someone has put it. I never claimed originality for the argument: I acknowledged my source. I asked my hearers to bear with me if I was unable to recall every word precisely or the complete sequence of ideas, and not to withdraw their attention because my arguments were originally used many years before. 'It may be', I said, 'that this provides the greatest help possible for you. It's not likely that these old arguments have evaporated like drugs and lost their power.'

Whenever Socrates saw a group of people gathered together he did not hold back. He spoke out critically and courageously. 'Where are you off to?' he would say. 'Don't you realise that you're not doing any of the things you ought to be doing? You fix your minds and energies on making as much money as possible and on passing still more on to your children. You never bother about the actual children – or, even earlier, yourselves, their fathers. You have no education, no way of life fit for men – or even expedient – which might help you to use your money rightly and morally instead of dangerously and immorally, or to avoid damaging yourselves – you ought to have accounted yourselves more important than money – and your sons and daughters, your wives, your brothers, your friends: and to avoid them harming you too.

'Well. How do you think your country will be more prudently governed? By learning music, athletics and literature from your parents? By teaching them to your sons? Suppose we were to congregate all the best musicians, all the best athletics trainers and all the best school-teachers and make a single political community out of them, small or large – rather as you historically colonised Ionia – what sort of country would it be, do you suppose? What quality government? Wouldn't it be far worse than the business community in Egypt, where all the traders, male and female, settle? That's comical enough. Take the educators of your children, trainers, musicians, teachers: add in elocutionists and actors. Would they do better?

'People learn so as to apply their professional skill when the need arises. For example, a pilot uses the helm to control the ship once he is on board, and that was why he studied navigation. The doctor uses medicine or diet for healing once a patient comes under his care, and that was why he studied his profession. What about you? When a political decision has to be taken, and you take your places in the Assembly, do some of you stand up and play the fiddle? Do some of you give a demonstration of wrestling? Do some of you pick up a piece of Homer or Hesiod and read it out? This is your expertise. This is the thing you claim will make you good men, competent in politics and in the organisation of your private life. You rely on this in your own political position and in educating your children to be competent to handle their own affairs and the nation's interest – if only they are star players of 'Pallas, dread sacker of cities' or rush to the lyre enthusiastically. How are you to find out what is to your best advantage or your country's best advantage? How are you to practise politics with law, justice and unity, avoiding dishonesty and factiousness? You've never found the answer to that. You've never bothered your heads about it? Even today you don't *think* about it. Every year you watch the actors at the festival of Dionysus. You shed tears at the misfortunes which overtake the characters in the plays. Yet you've never considered that these disasters never happen to illiterates, to men without a note of music in them, to people who are hopeless at athletics. No one ever composed a tragedy about a man just because he was poor. No! Use your own eyes. All the tragedies deal with characters such as Atreus, Agamemnon, Oedipus, men with wealth in gold, silver, land and animals; there's a story that one of them possessed a golden sheep, and he was the most ill-starred of them all. Yes, and Thamyris, an expert on the lute who actually challenged the Muses to a musical competition, lost his sight as a consequence – and his capacity to play the lute into the bargain. Palamedes invented the alphabet, but that didn't save him from an unjust death by stoning at the hands of his pupils the Greeks. While they were illiterate and innumerate they let him live. When he'd taught them all to read and write, starting of course with Atreus' sons, and went on to beacons and an army-census – previously they didn't understand the application of arithmetic to large numbers of people, which shepherds use for their sheep – they became more clever and more efficient. They killed him.

'If you suppose that the political orators have any qualifications for decision-making, and that oratory produces better citizens, I am surprised that you don't turn over all political decisions to them instead of keeping them in your own hands. If you have such confidence in their integrity, why do you not put all financial control in their hands? It would be like promoting the A.B.s and bosuns to be captains and commodores!'

One of the political orators might answer: 'Anyway, this was Athenian education when the Persians came in their hordes to attack Athens – and, on the second successive occasion, the rest of Greece as well. The first time the king sent an army with generals; later Xerxes was there in person with all the massed troops of Asia. The Athenians beat them all; on every occasion they were their masters in planning and in the field. Their personal qualities must have been exceptional, or they couldn't have beaten such numbers and such armaments. And personal qualities don't come from a bad education. They must have had a first-class education.'

Socrates' answer was: 'The aggressors had no education, and no training in political planning. They were experts in archery, riding and hunting; they thought the supreme disgrace to appear naked, and to spit in public. That was no use to them. They had no commanding officer, no king; they were just endless masses of damned fools. Of course, there was one of them with a crown on his head and a golden throne under him. He was like an evil spirit forcing them on, into the sea, down the precipices, with whips behind them, crushed together in fear and trembling, driven to death. Think of a wrestling match between two inexperienced wrestlers. Sometimes one throws the other, but it's a matter of luck not skill. Often one will throw the other twice running. This happened between the Persians and the Athenians. At one moment the Athenians were on top, at the next the Persians, as later when they had the Spartans as their allies, and stripped Athens of her walls. Would you suggest that the Athenians of that generation were more illiterate or more ignorant of high art? And then again in Conon's day when they won the sea-battle off Cnidos, had they improved their singing and athletics?'

These were the arguments Socrates used to prove that their education was not all that it should be; and he applied this beyond the Athenians to almost all humanity, past and present.

Not only so. He claimed that to be alive and involved in major political decisions without education, essential knowledge or adequate preparation for life did not even satisfy the people concerned, who themselves reproach the uneducated and ignorant with their incapacity for right living. By ignorance he did not mean ignorance of weaving, cobbling or, for matter of that, dancing, but ignorance of the things which a man must know if he is to be a good man.

This was his method of directing his audience to pay close attention to themselves, that is to practise philosophy. He knew that if they made that their aim they would in fact be practising philosophy, since to make one's aim the acquisition of moral virtue is philosophy. But he did not usually use the word; he simply told his hearers to aim to be good men. (13, 14)

This is an interesting passage, probably borrowed from Antisthenes: there are echoes of Plato's Apology *(29 D), Clitopho, a work attributed to Plato (407 A), and Aristophanes'* The Clouds *(967, 985). There is one anachronism: the battle of Cnidos took place in 394 B.C., five years after Socrates' death. But in general it bears strong marks of authenticity – or at least of being a view of Socrates held by someone who knew him closely.*

8.3.3 The Athenians were used to being criticised. In fact, they met in the theatre for the very object of being targets for satire, establishing a competition and giving a prize to those who did it most effectively. They never thought this out for themselves; there was divine initiative. They would listen to Aristophanes, Cratinus or Plato without doing them any harm. But when Socrates, without stage or auditorium, without suggestive dancing or shrill music, did God's will, they could not take it. (33, 9)

Plato is not the philosopher but a dramatist of the same name.

8.3.4 But I'm not surprised at the troubles I am facing. The great Socrates, whom I am always talking about, defended the people in every possible way during the dictatorship of the Thirty; he refused to participate in their crimes; they tried to send him for Leon of Salamis, and he refused; he openly attacked the dictators, comparing them to wicked herdsmen, who took over many cows of high quality and reduced them in both quantity and quality. He had risked his life for the people; yet later when they came to power they executed him on false charges presented by informers. The prosecutor was a dreadful informer named Meletus. 'Socrates', he said, 'is guilty of corrupting the youth, and introducing new divinities instead of honouring the gods whom the state honours.' This is virtually the diametrical opposite of Socrates' practice; he was exceptional in the honour he paid the gods, even composing a hymn to Apollo and Artemis (which I still sing today). He tried by his criticisms and reproaches to stop the corruption of young and old alike, in cases of greed or intemperance, or political corruption, or bribery for legal acquittal, or blackmail, or extortionate practice against the wretched inhabitants of the islands under the guise of taxation or military conscription. . . . This is why they hated him and claimed that he was corrupting the young. (43, 11)

Much of this is based on Plato and Xenophon, e.g. Memoirs of Socrates *1, 2, 32; but there is independent matter as well.*

8.3.5 There was also at Athens Socrates, a poor man and a man of the people. He was not driven by poverty to exact fees. Yet he had a wife with no dislike for money, and sons needing maintenance, and tradition says that he was friendly with the richest young men of the day, some of whom literally would withhold nothing from him. He was generally friendly and accessible, open to anyone who wanted to get in touch with him and talk with him; he would spend a good deal of time round and about the city centre, he would wander into the sports grounds and sit down near the banks – rather like those who sell cheap goods in the market or take them round from door to door – in case anyone, old or young, should want to ask him a question and

hear his reply. The majority of the political establishment pretended not to see him; if any did come near it was like stubbing a toe – he beat a hurried retreat in some anguish.

The sophists made a great impression, but their words have vanished, leaving nothing but their names. Socrates' words, for some reason, survive and will survive for ever, although he wrote nothing and left behind no work and no testament. Socrates died intestate, economically and intellectually. He had no property to be impounded for the commonalty – as is usually done with condemned criminals; but his words have been presented to the commonalty, by his friends rather than his enemies. They are open for all; lip-service is paid to them; but only a few claim their share and grasp them. (54, 3)

8.3.6 'We have heard that Socrates in his younger days studied his father's profession. Can you please tell us clearly who taught him that glorious helpful wisdom?'

DIO: I should have thought that the answer was clear to a great many people who know both the men concerned. Socrates was not in fact a disciple of Archelaus (as some people suggest); he was a disciple of Homer. (55, 2)

The paradox is worked out in what follows: the chief points appear below.

8.3.7 'How do you mean that Socrates is like Homer?'

DIO: First and foremost in character. Neither of them was pompous or presumptuous, like the more ignorant of the sophists. Homer did not even bother to tell us his country, his parents or his very name. So far as he is concerned we would not know the name of the author of *The Iliad* and *The Odyssey*. Socrates couldn't keep his country dark because of the greatness, glory and dominating position of Athens at that period. But he never made extravagant statements about himself. He never professed wisdom, even though the oracle of Apollo proclaimed him wisest of all Greeks and foreigners. Finally, he left no writings of his own, in that being a stage ahead of Homer. We know Homer's name from others; we know Socrates' words because others have bequeathed them. In this way both of them were exceptionally modest and self-disciplined.

Next, Socrates and Homer were similarly not interested in acquiring money. Further, they were both concerned with the same subjects in their words, one in verse, one in prose – human virtue and vice, right and wrong in action, truth and falsehood, the errors of the man in the street and the understanding shown by the wise.

Yes, and both were expert in deploying similes and analogies.

'You amaze me. Are you really going to maintain that you can put Socrates' potters and cobblers alongside Homer's similes of fire, wind and sea, eagles, bulls, and lions and all the other figures he uses to beautify his verse?' (55, 7)

8.3.8 DIO: . . . Homer used myth and history to try to educate people – and a tough job it is! Socrates used the same method, sometimes admitting he was really serious, sometimes pretending to be joking – while aiming to help others; he perhaps trespassed on the preserves of historians and myth-writers.

Similarly, he deliberately introduced into his dialogues Gorgias, Polus, Thrasymachus, Prodicus, Meno, Euthyphro, Anytus, Alcibiades, Laches. He could have omitted their names. But he knew that this was a way of helping his hearers if they had any intelligence. It isn't easy for any but scholars and philosophers to understand words from

their speakers or speakers from their words. Plenty of people think this part of the dialogues a waste of time – tiresome nonsense. Socrates thought that in introducing a boastful character he was presenting a lecture on boastfulness. A presumptuous man offered a lesson against presumptuousness, a villain against wickedness, a callous man against callousness, a quick-tempered man against bad temper. Similarly with the rest – he displayed the nature of the weaknesses and afflictions in the persons of the men dominated by them more clearly than by the use of bare words. (55, 11)

An interesting passage. Dio has blurred and blended Socrates and Plato: yet he has suggested an account of the nature of Socratic dialogue, though not of course the only possible account.

8.3.9 DIO: . . . Socrates was deliberate in his use of analogies. With Anytus he would speak of tanners and cobblers, in conversation with Lysicles of lambs and fleeces, with Lycon of law-suits and information received, with Meno of Thessaly lovers and their beloved. (55, 22)

The true reading is quite uncertain, but the gist must be something like this. None of the references come from Plato or Xenophon.

8.3.10 Socrates used to congratulate himself on a variety of blessings – on being a rational being and on being an Athenian. (64, 17)

*This conflicts with the idea that he claimed to be a citizen of the universe (**8.1.18** n.); Cf **1.2**; **9.1.2.11**.*

8.3.11 They said that Socrates corrupted the young and was impious towards the divine. They went beyond words – that would not have been so bad – they executed him, exacting a penalty for his lack of shoes. (66, 25)

Most people don't like the man who is different.

8.4 Epictetus

The later schools made it a point of pride to trace their origins back to Socrates: the Stoics drew up a succession Socrates–Antisthenes–Diogenes–Zeno, and made of Socrates one of their ideal wise men, something between a sage and a saint, a guru.

Epictetus is the most lovable of the Stoics. Born in the middle of the first century A.D. in Phrygia, he was a slave at Rome, but able to attend the lectures of Musonius Rufus. At some point he was freed, and became a teacher himself. Towards the end of the century he emigrated to Nicopolis, where he became a noted figure in old age. His lectures were recorded by his student Arrian. They were full of references to Socrates, only a few of which appear below. Most of them are based on Plato and Xenophon, whom he quotes freely and from memory.

8.4.1 If what the philosophers have said about the unity of gods and men is true there is nothing left for humans except to follow Socrates, and, asked our nationality, never to reply 'Athenian' or 'Corinthian' but 'Universian'. (*Discourses* 1, 9. 1)

The story does not accord with other records of Socrates; it is also told, more plausibly, of Diogenes the Dog; cf. **8.1.18**.

8.4.2 Socrates practised this impassivity and always wore the same expression. (ibid. 1, 25, 31)
Cf. **8.1.11** n.

8.4.3 Well? Did not Socrates write? – Who wrote as much as he did? But how? He could not always have some to test his views and be tested in turn, so he tested and examined himself and was for ever profiting by exercising his initial ideas. (ibid. 2, 1, 32)

A very interesting passage. Most of our authorities suggest that Socrates did not write for publication (cf. **1.1**), but the idea may be that he wrote his thoughts down in order to scrutinise them himself.

8.4.4 How did Socrates set about it? He made his interlocutor into his own witness and never needed any other witness. (ibid. 2, 12, 5)
Cf. 2, 26, 6.

8.4.5 Socrates' primary personal trait was his refusal to get worked up in argument, his refusal to use abusive language, his rejection of intolerance. By putting up with abuse from others he prevented conflict. (ibid. 2, 12, 14)
Epictetus cites Xenophon's The Banquet as an example, cf. 4, 5, 1.

8.4.6 What does Socrates say? 'One man is proud of the development of his farm, another in the progress of his horse. My daily pride is following my own improvement'. (ibid. 3, 5, 14)
Not from Plato or Xenophon; perhaps from a lost dialogue by one of the other Socratic writers.

8.4.7 It takes cross-examination to get rid of self-satisfaction, and this is where Socrates starts. (ibid. 3, 14, 9)

8.4.8 Who ever heard Socrates saying, 'I know something and teach it'? He used to send people off in different directions. (ibid. 3, 23, 22)
Cf. 4, 8, 22; Handbook 46.

8.4.9 Did not Socrates love his own children? Yes, but he loved them like a man who was free, like a man who remembered that his first duty was to love the gods. So he never went outside the course appropriate for a good man in making his defence, or proposing the penalty, or in his previous experiences in office or in the army. (ibid. 3, 24, 60)

8.4.10 Take Socrates. Look at a man who valued his wife and children as if they were on loan, who valued his country in the right way and to the right extent, who subordinated his family, friends, etc., to the law and the obedience he owed the law. So when he was called to the forces he was the first to leave, and risked his life on active service unsparingly. When the dictators sent him for Leon he realised that it was dishonourable, and never hesitated, although he knew that he would have to die, if that was how it turned out. (ibid. 4, 1, 159)

The beginning of an extended passage based on Plato and Xenophon; cf. also 4, 7, 30 for Leon.

8.4.11 Socrates had this in mind in his home life. He put up with a shrewish wife and an unfeeling son. Why shrewish? Pouring water over his head ad lib and stamping on the cake. (ibid. 4, 5, 33)

See further **1.4**[17]; **8.2.8**; **9.2.14**; **9.7.18**; **12.15.3**.

8.4.12 Archelaus sent for Socrates to make a rich man of him. Socrates sent back the answer: 'In Athens four quarts of barley-meal are priced at an obol and there is running water available'. (Fr. 11)

Found in Stobaeus 4, 33, 28.

8.5 Marcus Aurelius

There are few more pathetic figures than Marcus Aurelius, the lonely, agnostic Stoic on the throne of a collapsing world. He ruled from A.D. 161 to 180 and left an intensely personal record in jottings during campaigns on the Danube in his last years. Epictetus was the greatest influence on him.

8.5.1 If you can see nothing higher than the deity enthroned within you,

putting your private inclinations under its own authority, scrutinising all that presents itself to your mind, having withdrawn itself (in Socrates' words) from the temptations of the flesh, putting itself under the authority of the gods and making mankind its concern. ... (3, 6)

There is no exact parallel to the words in other sources.

8.5.2 How do we know that Telauges was not a morally better man than Socrates? It is not enough that Socrates died more impressively, disputed more shrewdly with the sophists, showed more toughness in spending the whole night in the freezing cold, when ordered to arrest Leon of Salamis thought it more gallant to say No, 'held his head high as he walked the streets' (though the truth of this is controversial). We must rather consider what Socrates' soul was like. Was he satisfied with justice to men and piety to the gods? Was his opposition to vice controlled? Did he avoid subservience to ignorance in others? Did he never reject as alien anything the universe had to offer? Did he never put up with it, regarding it as intolerable? Did he keep the experiences of the flesh from swaying his intellect? (7, 66)

Telauges appeared in a Socratic dialogue by Aeschines of Sphettus: it is not clear whether as hero or villain. Marcus' questions are a mixture of Stoic presupposition and the traditions about Socrates: the quotation is from Aristophanes, Clouds *363 (**4.1.1.2**).*

8.5.3 Socrates used to call the beliefs of the man in the street 'bogies' – monsters to scare children. (11, 23)

8.5.4 Socrates used to say, 'What do you want? The souls of rational or irrational   creatures?'   'Rational.'

'What sort of rational creatures? Healthy or worthless?' 'Healthy.' 'Then why don't you try to secure them?' 'Because we have them already.' 'Then why all this fighting and contentiousness?' (11, 39)

This is doubtless excerpted from some anthology and not found elsewhere.

8.6 Apuleius

Apuleius lived in the second century A.D.*; he was born in Madaura in Algeria, where golden asses still stray among the ruins. He studied philosophy and rhetoric at Athens and became a popular lecturer. He was a Platonist by persuasion, but it did not run deep. His treatise* On the Guardian Spirit of Socrates *is of general rather than particular interest. His best known work is the novel* The Golden Ass.

8.6.1 Aristippus, the well-known founder of the Cyrenaic sect, and (as he preferred to be known) a disciple of Socrates. (*Florida* 23)

8.6.2 So it is not surprising that Socrates, a man of supreme perfection, attested wise on Apollo's evidence, recognised and honoured his personal god, and this god became his protector, I might almost say the spirit of his home, avoiding what had to be avoided, taking precautions where caution was needed and giving advance warning where advance warning was called for. When the services of wisdom were unavailing it was divine guidance not deliberation which he needed, so that, when uncertainty made him stumble, access to the divine might keep him firm. . . .

So with Socrates. When he needed other guidance on top of the services of wisdom he submitted to the foreseeing power of the Spirit, dutifully obeyed its advice and thereby was far more acceptable to his god. The Spirit acted entirely to stand in the path of some action Socrates had begun, never with positive direction, as I have explained. Socrates, a man of supreme perfection in himself, eager in all appropriate duties, did not need positive direction, but he did sometimes need someone to check him, if his enterprises involved some danger. With the warning he could take precautions and drop the course for the moment, to take it up later with greater safety or approach it by some other route.

On these occasions he said that he heard a voice of divine origin. So Plato: no one should think he picked up omens from all and sundry. With no one to consult, outside the city walls with Phaedrus, under the shade of a spreading tree, he recognised the sign telling him not to cross the little stream of the river Ilissus before giving a recantation to placate the anger of Love at being criticised. If he observed the omens sometimes he would have positive guidance; we see what happens to those who are superstitiously subservient to omens; they are governed by the words of others instead of their own reason; they crawl from street to street, gathering advice from others' words, and thinking with their ears instead of with their minds. However that may be, it is certain that the interpreters of omens pay attention to a voice which is heard through the ears; they have no hesitation: it comes from human lips. Socrates claimed to hear not a voice but a *particular* voice. From the addition you can realise that he is not talking about an ordinary human voice; if that were so, *particular* would be otiose: better 'a voice' or 'the voice of a particular person'. . . . When a person says he has heard a particular voice, either he does not know its origin, or he has some reservations about the voice, or he is shown that it contains something mysterious. So with Socrates and the voice which he claimed came from a divine source at the right moment. I hold that he grasped the signs of his guardian spirit with eyes as well as ears; he more often spoke of the presence not of a voice but of a divine sign. This sign could be the appearance of a divine spirit which only Socrates saw, as in Homer Achilles alone saw Minerva. (*On the Guardian Spirit of Socrates*)

8.7 Sextus Empiricus

Sextus Empiricus was a Sceptic, writing about A.D. *200 in criticism of dogmatic philosophy. His attitude to Socrates is coloured by his presuppositions. He was a doctor by profession.*

8.7.1 According to the rest of his associates, Socrates was interested only in ethics. (*Against the Logicians* 1, 8)
 '*The rest*' means all except Plato.

8.7.2 The school of Cyrene is agreed to be derived from Socrates' teaching, which was also the origin of the thought of Plato and his followers. (ibid. 1, 190)

8.7.3 Among those who investigated the concept [of Man] Socrates found no answer, and remained an inquirer, declaring himself ignorant of what he was and of his relation to the universe. (ibid. 1, 264)

8.8 Oenomaus
C. A.D. *1200. A Cynic writer.*

The great Socrates, being asked, 'Shall I marry or not?' did not answer Yes or No, but, 'Whatever you do, you will regret it.' When a man wanted children he said, 'You're acting wrongly. You are only considering how you can have children and not bothering at all to ensure how if children come you can give them the best treatment.' Another man decided to emigrate because things were so bad at home. Socrates said, 'It is a wrong decision. You are proposing to go away, leaving your country behind and taking your folly with you, and this will make you as discontented with your new environment as with your old one.' He did not wait to be questioned, but went voluntarily into such encounters. (Mullach, *Fragmenta Philosophorum Graecorum* 2, 372)

8.9 Aristocles of Messene

Second century A.D. *From Sicily, an Aristotelian, teacher of Alexander of Aphrodisias.*

8.9.1 Fire on fire, in the words of the proverb, applies not least to Socrates, as Plato says. He was naturally gifted, and skilled in producing an *impasse* on any subject. He introduced ethical and political subjects. He also introduced investigation into the Forms by being the first to essay definitions. He aroused interest in the whole field of philosophy and asked questions about everything, but died too early. (*On Plato's Philosophy* fr. 1, Mullach, *Fragmenta Philosophorum Graecorum* 3, 206)

This passage has been used to suggest that the Theory of Forms is authentically Socratic. It does not in fact support this view. It says what Aristotle says, that Socrates was concerned with definitions, and that this was the starting-point of the Theory.

8.9.2 Those who succeeded Socrates were many and various and held mutually contradictory views. Some praised cynicism with its attack on pride and mental disturbances; others embraced pleasures. Some gloried in their omniscience, others in their ignorance. Some stood in the public eye and mingled with all and sundry; others spent their lives in unapproachable unsociability. (ibid.)

8.9.3 Aristoxenus the musicologist tells this story about Indians. One of them met Socrates in Athens and asked him what was the character of his philosophy. He replied, 'An investigation into human life.' The Indian laughed and said, 'You cannot fix your gaze on human truth without a knowledge of the divine.' (ibid.)

8.10 Numenius

Latter part of second century A.D. *A syncretist who blended Plato with Pythagoras.*
The same thing happened long before to those who derived different points of view from Socrates: Aristippus, Antisthenes, the Megarians and Eretrians and others all took individual attitudes. The cause lay in Socrates. He posited three gods, and discussed philosophy with them in the pattern appropriate to each. His hearers did not realise this.

They thought that all his words were casual and depended on the breath of chance which won the day on any given occasion.

Plato followed Pythagoras: he realised that Socrates propounded the same views, which he derived from there or nowhere. (*On the disagreement of the Academics with Plato* fr. 1, Mullach, *Fragmenta Philosophorum Graecorum* 3, 154)

8.11 Alexander of Aphrodisias

Early third century A.D. *The ablest of Aristotelian commentators: his book on fate was dedicated to Septimius Severus. See further the next section.*
The physiognomer once said about the philosopher Socrates some surprising statements which were greatly at variance with the tenor of Socrates' life-commitment. Socrates' friends started laughing at Zopyrus. This was his natural character, had he not improved it by philosophical discipline. (*Fate* 6)
Cf. **8.1.8** *n.*

8.12 Commentators on Aristotle

The Aristotelian commentators range from Aspasius in the second century A.D. *to Sophonias in the fourteenth. The soundest of them is no doubt Alexander of Aphrodisias in the third century. Themistius belongs to later in the century. In the fifth century Syrianus writes from a Neo-Platonist view, Philoponus in the sixth century from a Christian.*

I have found nothing here which is not independently attested, but it seemed useful to show the sort of information possessed by these men of learning.

8.12.1 Socrates on all occasions insistently shows that he has no knowledge and does not act wisely either, although he always acts and speaks from the height of wisdom. (Alexander on *Sophistical Reflections* 165 A 19 (II iii 15))

8.12.2 Socrates' reply to the person who said, 'Socrates, you are being executed unjustly,' was 'Did you really want me to be executed justly?' (ibid. 180 B 17 (II iii 172))

Cf. **1.4**[16]; **3.1**; **9.4.5**; **9.19.3**; **12.4.5**. *The story is also told of Phocion.*

8.12.3 Why was it appropriate for Socrates to marry? Because it was appropriate for him to have children. (Themistius on *Posterior Analytics* 94 A–B (v i 52))

8.12.4 It is asserted that Socrates came to universals through definitions and did not grant them independent existence, and that Plato, in ignorance or deliberate misrepresentation of Socrates' use of universals, gave them independent existence. This seems to me an absolutely scandalous thing to say. Socrates did not confine universals to the subjects of definition: he made them patterns pre-existing in the soul, as Plato makes clear in *Phaedrus*, *Phaedo* and anywhere you care to look – Plato the most upright and reliable of all our writers about Socrates. He received his philosophy from Socrates. He would not have made a mistake in his master's instructions. He would not in error have attributed to him views which did not belong to him and which were diametrically opposed to his philosophical approach. (Syrianus on *Metaphysics* 1078 B 12 (VI i 104))

Unusual in its defence of the authen-ticity of Plato's Socrates: it will be noted that the fervour of Syrianus' advocacy implies that the other view was widespread. See also his comments on 1086 A 35 (VI i 160).

8.12.5 Socrates and Plato are the same in genus and species, both animals, both human beings. They are different individuals with several points of accidental difference. Socrates' parents were Sophroniscus and Phaenarete, Plato's Ariston and Perictione. Socrates was snub-nosed, pot-bellied and pop-eyed, Plato had a handsome nose, a body that did not bulge and beautiful eyes. Socrates was Plato's teacher, Plato Socrates' pupil. (Simplicius on *Physics* 224 A 2 (IX 772))

Cf. Olympiodorus on Categories 1 A 1; 6 B 13 (XII i 31; 106) where we have in addition Socrates as bald, a philosopher, an Athenian and grandson of Archimedes. Also Philoponus on Physics 185 B 5 (VI 2).

8.12.6 This is why Socrates at the battle of Delium stood through night and day without realising he was standing, because he was concentrating upon some thought. (Philoponus on *The Soul* 432 A 15 (XV 573))

There is some confusion between Delium and Potidaea.

8.12.7 This is why Socrates, a brilliant exponent of dialectic, asked questions without answering: he confessed his ignorance. (Anon. on *Sophistical Refutations* 183 A–B (XXIII iv 67))

8.13 Julian (A.D. 332–363)

Nephew of Constantine the Great, he rebelled against his Christian upbringing, and when he became emperor tried to restore the old paganism. In religion, a sun-worshipper; in philosophy, a Neo-Platonist.

8.13.1 You've heard of Socrates the Athenian: you know that the Delphic oracle publicly announced his reputation for wisdom. I have noticed that he had no praise for this sort of thing. He did not accept that a blissful happiness belonged to the rulers of large countries with many people under them, Greeks in large numbers and non-Greeks in still larger numbers, men who could cut a canal through Mt Athos and bridge continents when they wanted to cross from one to another, conquering nations, netting islands, offering thousands of pounds' worth of incense in sacrifice. He had no praise for Xerxes or for any king of Persia, Lydia or Macedon. He had no praise for military commanders in Greece, apart from a very few whom he knew to care about morality, to value courage and self-discipline, to honour wisdom and justice. When he saw a man to be sharp-witted, clever, a man of war, smart or a mob-orator with little disposition to moral virtue, he offered him no praise at all. (*Orations* 2, 79 A)

8.13.2 Socrates often offered panegyrics. (ibid. 3, 104 A)
Odd.

8.13.3 Socrates in his wisdom made an assumption of his own ignorance. (ibid. 6, 181 A)

8.13.4 Socrates, like many others, was prepared to indulge in speculation, but for practical ends. (ibid. 6, 190 A)

8.13.5 A divine voice accompanied Socrates too and prevented him from wrong action. (ibid. 8, 249 B)

8.13.6 It is recorded that Socrates discouraged from politics many who were not naturally that way endowed, including, according to Xenophon, Glaucon; he tried to stand in the way of Cleinias' son [Alcibiades], but the young man's drive forward was too much for him. (*Letter to Themistius* 255 C)

Xenophon, Memoirs of Socrates *3, 6, 1.*

8.13.7 Socrates dropped speculation for a life of practical action. He had no control over his wife or son. Did he have power over even two or three of his countrymen? He had no control over anyone: was he therefore impractical? No, I assert that Sophroniscus' son accomplished greater achievements than Alexander. I attribute to him Plato's wisdom, Xenophon's military prowess, Antisthenes' toughness, the philosophies of Eretria and Megara, Cebes, Simmias, Phaedo, thousands of others, not to mention the colonies from the same source – the Lyceum, Stoa and Academy. . . . All who today owe their salvation to philosophy owe their salvation to Socrates. (ibid. 264 B)

8.14 Maximus of Tyre

A second-century eclectic Platonist, who travelled widely and gave some forty lectures in Rome in the reign of Commodus.

8.14.1 Socrates was poor: the poor man will imitate Socrates. It is good that the snub-nosed and pot-bellied are not helpless in philosophy. But no one suggests that Socrates did not merely press on towards the poor but towards the rich, eminent aristocrats as well. I suppose Socrates thought that if Aeschines and Antisthenes became philosophers there would be some benefit to the state of Athens. (1, 9)

8.14.2 Socrates wore a coarse cloak . . . and specialised in proving people wrong. (1, 10)

8.14.3 Was Socrates Right in Making No Defence?
. . . To the point. Meletus indicted Socrates, Anytus prosecuted him, Lycon denounced him, the Athenians condemned him, the Eleven imprisoned him, the executioner took his life. He was superior to Meletus' indictment, scorned Anytus' prosecution, laughed at Lycon's words. The Athenians might vote; he gave a counter-vote. They proposed a penalty; he made a counter-proposal. The Eleven imprisoned him; he gave them his body, weaker than many, but not his soul, stronger than any. He showed no hostility to the executioner, no reluctance at the poison. The Athenians did not mean to take his life; he did mean to die. He showed the voluntary nature of his act; he could have offered a fine, he could have escaped from prison; he preferred to die. They showed the involuntary nature of theirs; they promptly regretted it, a ridiculous thing to happen to a jury.

Do you want to consider whether Socrates acted rightly or not? Suppose someone came and told you of an Athenian, elderly, a philosopher by profession, poor, outstanding in character, skilled in speaking, of mental acumen, alert and sober, not liable to hasty speech or action, long-lived, having won the praises of those of the Greeks who count, as well as of the god Apollo, for his qualities. He is assailed out of envy, hatred, hostility to his high qualities, by Aristophanes on behalf of the theatre, Anytus for the sophists, Meletus for the informers, Lycon for the political orators, pilloried on the stage, indicted, prosecuted, denounced, condemned. Suppose he began with anger against Aristophanes, and pilloried him in revenge at the dramatic

festival while his judges were still drunk. Then he went into court and countered the accusations with a long speech, a defence carefully composed to sway the jury, with an opening designed to charm the court, a persuasive exposition, overwhelming evidence of various kinds, supporting witnesses of wealth and renown to carry weight with an Athenian jury, and a peroration of eloquent and heart-rending pleading including appropriate tears, bringing in Xanthippe wailing at the end and his children blubbering. That by these devices he won the jury to take pity on him and acquit him. . . . Socrates kept silence; it was the safest course; he could not speak without loss of honour. He kept his integrity up and his anger down; he stained their reputations in that they condemned him without hearing him speak. . . . Socrates is dead and the Athenians are guilty; God, Truth is their judge. Socrates indicts the Athenians: 'The people of Athens are guilty of refusing to acknowledge the gods whom Socrates worships and introducing other new divinities. . . . The people are guilty of corrupting the youth. They corrupted Alcibiades, Hipponicus, Critias and countless others.' (3, 1–8)

Important testimony (though late) suggesting a tradition that Socrates made no defence.

8.14.4 'Ah, but Socrates went down to Piraeus to offer prayer to the goddess, and encouraged others to do the same. Socrates' life was full of prayer.' . . . Do you imagine that Socrates prayed for possessions or political power? Far from it! He prayed to the gods, and took from within himself, with their approval, virtue of character, tranquillity of living, a blameless life, hope in death, marvellous gifts, gifts of the gods. (5, 8)

8.14.5 On Socrates' Divine Spirit 1
Are you surprised that a divine spirit

accompanied Socrates, favouring him, prophetic, his constant companion, virtually a part of his own intelligence? . . . Socrates, by his intellectual association with the voices of the gods, gained a noble disposition through the company of the divine spirit; he showed no bitterness towards others or towards force of circumstances. . . . Socrates' divine spirit was single, simple, personal, public; it would call him back from crossing a river, dissuade him from the love of Alcibiades or from his desire to defend himself, encourage him to die by failing to prevent him. (8, 1–8)

Most of this is familiar. Maximus' general argument links Socrates' divine spirit with other divine spirits in Homer and elsewhere. It will be noticed that Maximus has the point that the spirit acted negatively.

8.14.6 A less clever person needs Socrates, not teaching but asking searching questions. (10, 9)

8.14.7 Socrates had no anger for Aristophanes, no grudge against Meletus, no desire for vengeance on Anytus. He shouted aloud: 'Anytus and Meletus can kill me; they cannot hurt me. It is not in the order of things for a good man to be hurt by a bad man.' (12, 8)

8.14.8 In What the Amatory Art of Socrates Consisted
But Socrates, who is so celebrated for his attachment to truth, is more dangerous in his enigmas through the credibility of his assertions, his power of imitation and the dissimilitude of his practice in amatory affairs to his theory. For in nothing is Socrates like himself, when he is in love, and when he speaks temperately; when he is agitated with a pleasing terror at the sight of beautiful forms, and when he confutes the unwise; when he opposes the amatory oration of Lysias, touches Critobulus, returns from hunting the

beauty of Alcibiades and is astonished at Charmides. For how do these things accord with a philosophic life? They are neither consistent with his freedom of speech to the people, nor his boldness towards tyrants, nor his strenuous contention at Delium, nor his contempt of his judges, nor his entering the prison, nor his preparation for death: they are very remote from all these particulars. For if these things are true we should predict that they have a good meaning; but if beautiful actions are enigmatically signified through base words the thing is dire and dangerous. For to place the beautiful under the base, and to indicate the profitable through the noxious, is not the employment of one who wishes to benefit (for the utility is unapparent) but of one who desires to injure, and which is easily accomplished. These things I am of opinion Thrasymachus would say, or Callias, or Polus, or some other enemy to the philosophy of Socrates. (18, tr. T. Taylor)

8.14.9 Socrates was glad to stay in prison in obedience to the law. Let us draw a comparison between the cups of Socrates and Alcibiades. Which suffered less from his drinking – Alcibiades from drinking wine or Socrates from drinking poison? (25, 7)

8.14.10 I am speaking of Socrates. Socrates, are you in love with Alcibiades? With Phaedrus? With Charmides? Socrates, are you in love? Have you an eye for beauty in an Athenian? Admit the reason. Don't be afraid of what people think. There is a love which is under control and gives pleasure, just as there is a love which is out of control and brings sorrow. If you love without seeking pleasure, if you're in love with souls not bodies, then fall in love with Theaetetus. But you don't: he's snub-nosed. Fall in love with Chaerephon. But you don't: he's sallow-complexioned. Fall in love with Aristodemus. But you don't: he's ugly. Whom do you fall in love with? You like them with fine hair, good complexion, graceful, handsome. I trust your integrity: your love is governed by principle. I don't distrust your soul in that you take pleasure in love. I don't even distrust your body when it's aflame with fire. . . . (32, 8)

8.14.11 Diogenes did not try marriage: he'd heard of Xanthippe. (32, 9)

8.14.12 Socrates, I often hear you expounding your preference for knowledge to all else, directing different young men to different teachers. You actually tell Callias to send his son to sit at the feet of Aspasia of Miletus, a man at a woman's feet. You yourself at your age seek out her company, and she's not good enough as a teacher for you, you collect contributions on love from Diotima, music from Connus, creative writing from Evenus, farming from Ischomachus, geometry from Theodorus. Whether this is mock-modesty or genuine, I approve, however one takes it. But when I hear you conversing with Phaedrus, Charmides, Theaetetus or Alcibiades I suspect that you are not giving everything to knowledge but think there is an older teacher for human beings – nature. (38, 4)

8.14.13 Do you think that Socrates achieved moral excellence by professional skill rather than divine dispensation? It was by professional skill that he became a sculptor rather than as a mere inheritance handed on from father to son. It was by divine election that he put his profession on one side and took up virtue. (38, 7)

8.14.14 Compare Socrates with his antagonists in the matter of possessions. You see Callias surpass him in wealth,

Alcibiades in beauty, Pericles in renown, Nicias in reputation, Aristophanes in the theatre, Meletus in a court of law. Did Apollo's approval and award of first place mean nothing? (39, 5)

8.15 Galen

Claudius Galenus (c. A.D. 129–199) was the greatest medical writer of antiquity: philosophy was his first interest.

8.15.1 This was Socrates' Muse: to mingle seriousness with a portion of lightheartedness. (*On the Use of the Parts of the Body* 1, 9 (Kühn 3, 25))
    Galen refers to Xenophon.

8.15.2 Some people have left no formal writing, like Socrates. (*On the Nature of Man* 1, 25 (Kühn 15, 68))

8.15.3 Intellections are called 'thoughts'. That is why Socrates was called 'Thinker' and his wise advice nicknamed 'thoughts'. You can find this in Aristophanes' *The Clouds*, where he brings Socrates on the comic stage and parodies him as a talker of nonsense. (*Commentary on Hippocrates' Epidemics* 5, 11 (Kühn 17 B 263))

8.15.4 The original philosophers concentrated on physical science and made this the end of philosophy so far as they were concerned. Socrates, belonging to a much later generation, regarded this as unattainable. He thought it one of the most difficult things in the world to achieve a firm knowledge of remote subjects, and far more useful to ask how a person can live a better life, turn from evil and share as far as possible in good things. Because he saw more use in this, he neglected physical science as not contributing to the improvement of life, and worked out an ethical classi-fication of good and evil things, morally right and morally wrong, choice-worthy and the opposite, thinking that those who gave these matters prior thought would readily avoid what is not in their best interest. So ethics entered philosophy, and Socrates used it to establish a principle of choice for those who would seek the finest life. He saw that the man who was going to put these views forward would need persuasive powers. This would come about if he were seen to make good use of dialectical arguments in meeting those who approached him, and to have thoroughly worked out the power of dialectic, which persuades us to aban-don harmful actions and turn to those which are naturally beneficial. So he invented dialectic. In this way Socrates was responsible for the division of philosophy into three parts; previously it had seemed to be confined to physical science. (*History of Philosophy* 1)

The three parts are logic, physics, ethics. This is probably not an authentic work of Galen.

8.15.5 Archelaus lectured to Socrates, who was in so many ways responsible for a genuine interest in philosophy on the part of his contemporaries and his successors. (ibid. 2)

The sort of dependence which Socrates showed to his tribe during their term of office is unworthy of divine characters who are naturally completely free and unattached. (*The Mysteries of Egypt* 1, 8)

An unexpected historical reference, tying up with the Arginusae incident.

8.17 Macrobius

Ambrosius Theodosius Macrobius (c. A.D. *400*), *statesman and Neo-Platonist. His* Saturnalia *is a fascinating miscellany, including an extended tribute to Vergil.*

8.17.1 Anachronism is justified on the evidence of Plato's dialogues. Parmen-ides was so much older than Socrates that the latter's youth could scarcely embrace the former's age; yet they argue on abstruse subjects. There is a notable dialogue between Socrates and Timaeus, but it is quite certain that they belong to different generations. (*Saturnalia* 1, 1, 5)

8.17.2 Socrates used to try to persuade people to avoid the sort of food and drink which goes beyond the allaying of hunger and thirst. (ibid. 7, 4, 32)

8.18 Philodemus

C. *110–30* B.C. *Poet and Epicurean philoso-pher. He came from the East, and acquired a villa at Herculaneum, from which a number of his works have been recovered in a frag-mentary state. There are several other*

8.16 Iamblichus

C. A.D. *250–325. Neo-Platonist, un-critical and superstitious, but historically a figure of some importance in the development of Neo-Platonism.*

references to Socrates in Philodemus, but they are mostly either trivial or closely based on Xenophon.

8.18.1 Socrates demonstrated that outstanding political skill cannot be taught from the fact that Themistocles, Aristides and Pericles were incapable of giving their sons their own qualities. (*Rhetoric*, ed. Sudhaus, 1, 262, 22)

8.18.2 Someone asked Aristippus how Socrates had helped him. He replied, 'He enabled me to find for myself satisfying fellow-students of philosophy.' (ibid. 1, 342, 13)

8.18.3 Socrates used dialogue. . . . (ibid. 2, 208, 30)

8.18.4 Socrates was expert in reconciling individuals; yet he did not seem to have the capacity for reconciling an individual to a group. (ibid. 2, 223, 12)

8.18.5 The orators [i.e. politicians] irreligiously accused Socrates, and as Plato records in his *Apology*, had him executed. (ibid. 2, 286, 2)

follow Socrates' excellent dictum that most men live to eat, he ate to live. (18 B)

Cf. **11.1.84**.

8.20 Demetrius of Phalerum

C. 350–280 B.C. *Peripatetic philosopher and statesman, who was for a period Macedonian governor of Athens, and later librarian at Alexandria.*

He wrote an Apology *or* Defence of Socrates *which survives only in minor citation. See Diogenes Laertius 2, 44 (**1.4**[44]); 9, 15; 9, 37; 9, 57; Plutarch,* Aristides *1 (**9.1.21**); 5; 37 (**9.1.2.2**). In general, the passages add little to our knowledge.*

8.20.1 = **1.4**[44]
8.20.2 = **9.1.2.1**
8.20.3 = **9.1.2.2**

8.19 Musonius Rufus

First century A.D. One of the saints of the ancient world; banished by Nero: teacher of Epictetus: a sane thinker who honoured manual work and family life.

8.19.1 Well? Is not the universe the common fatherland of all mankind, as Socrates held? (9)

8.19.2 We ought to eat for sustenance not for pleasure, if we are going to

8.21 Aristoxenus

Fourth century B.C. Musicologist and pupil of Aristotle. He wrote a Life of Socrates *containing scandalous anecdotes. The original is lost, but it was a quarry for later writers.*

8.21.1 fr. 55 = **9.1.1.29**
8.21.2 fr. 52a = **1.4**[19]
8.21.3 fr. 52b = **13.1.28**
8.21.4 fr. 53 = **8.9.3**
8.21.5 fr. 51 = **9.2.11**
8.21.6 fr. 60 = **14.2.6**
8.21.7 fr. 58 = **9.1.2.2**
8.21.8 fr. 56 = **9.15**

8.21.9 fr. 51 = **12.25.5**
8.21.10 fr. 54a = **12.25.2**
8.21.11 fr. 54b = **12.21.8**
8.21.12 fr. 59 = **1.4**[20]

8.22 Porphyry

C. A.D. *232–305. A Neo-Platonist from Tyre, and disciple of Plotinus, important not least because he cites his authorities.*

8.22.1 History of Philosophy: *lost, but quoted by Christian writers.*

8.22.1.1 = **12.17.2**
8.22.1.2 = **12.25.2**
8.22.1.3 = **12.25.5**
8.22.1.4 = **12.25.3**
8.22.1.5 = **12.21.2**
8.22.1.6 = **12.21.6**
8.22.1.7 = **12.21.8**
8.22.1.8 = **13.1.28**

8.22.2 Abstinence from Animal Food.

8.22.2.1 For this is no small indication that Pythagoras did not think sanely, that none of the wise men embraced his opinion; since neither any one of the seven wise men, nor any of the physiologists who lived after them, nor even the most wise Socrates, or his followers, adopted it. (1, 15, tr. T. Taylor)

8.22.2.2 Socrates therefore says, in opposition to those who contend that pleasure is the supreme good, that though all swine and goats should accord in this opinion, yet he should never be persuaded that our felicity was placed in the enjoyment of corporeal delight, as long as intellect has dominion over all things. (3, 1, tr. T. Taylor)

8.22.2.3 Nor was Socrates in jest when he swore by the dog and the goose; but in so doing, he swore conformably to the just son of Jupiter; nor did he sportfully say that swans were his fellow-servants. (3, 16, tr. T. Taylor)
 '*Just son of Jupiter*', *i.e. Rhadamanthys. Rather 'son of Zeus and Justice'. Swans: Plato, Phaedo 85 B (2.4.2).*

8.22.2.4 Socrates said that hunger is the sauce of food. (3, 26, tr. T. Taylor)

8.23 Aeschines of Sphettus

Aeschines was one of the closer associates of Socrates, though still quite young at the time of Socrates' death; Plato in Phaedo *records his presence in the prison. He wrote dialogues which were esteemed in his own day as 'noble disquisitions on justice and virtue' (as the orator Lysias puts it in a speech prosecuting him for non-payment of debts). Aelius Aristides (**9.11**) in the second century A.D. regards him as a more reliable historical source than Plato. We have seven titles:* Alcibiades, Axiochus, Aspasia, Callias, Miltiades, Rhinon, Telauges. *Socrates was probably the principal character in each: unfortunately the fragments are too scanty to help our picture. The passages which follow are all from* Alcibiades. *For further references, see **1.6**; **8.1.5**; **8.1.12**; **8.2.15**; **9.2.12**; **9.23**.*

8.23.1 'How would you like to have behaved to your parents as Themistocles is reputed to have behaved to his parents?' 'Hush, Socrates,' he said. 'Don't say such things.' 'Do you think that men are bound to be uneducated before they can become educated? To be unskilled with horses before they can become skilled with horses?' 'Yes,

I do.' (*Oxyrhynchus Papyri* 13, 1608 fr. 1)
Arguments of this nature are found in Plato too.

8.23.2 'Alcibiades,' I said, 'don't forget that even a man like Themistocles, for all his knowledge, lacked the capacity to avoid banishment and political dishonour; his skill failed him. What do you imagine it must be like for men of inferior gifts, who have never tried to make the best of themselves? It's not surprising if their achievements are insignificant. Alcibiades,' I said, 'don't charge me with irresponsible atheism over the ways of fortune and the work of the gods in attributing to Themistocles full knowledge of his achievements rather than giving the credit to fortune. I could much more readily demonstrate the atheism of those who take the opposite view than they could demonstrate mine, when they allege that fortune smiles on saints and crooks alike and that the gods shower no special blessings on men of reverence and virtue.' (fr. 1 K from Aelius Aristides 46)

8.23.3 'If I claimed to possess skill in helping others I should be exposing myself to a charge of stupidity. As it is, I thought that I had been endowed by divine Providence with a gift for Alcibiades: nothing surprising in that.' (fr. 3 K from Aelius Aristides 45)

8.23.4 'Through the love I felt for Alcibiades I experienced a kind of Bacchic inspiration. When the Bacchants are filled with the god's power they draw milk and honey from wells which do not yield even water to others. I have no learning to teach anyone and help him in that way; but I thought that through just being with him my love for him might make him

better.' (fr. 4 K from Aelius Aristides 45)
Notable for the expression of love for Alcibiades and the profession of ignorance.

8.24 Proclus

A.D. *412–485. Neo-Platonist, metaphysician and mystic.*
These points are established. From them one must accept that Socrates went beyond the concept of definitions, and had the concept of the separated Forms. Aristotle was wrong, he was not led to them by a concern for definitions; he came upon the Forms by a genuine divine direction. (On *Parmenides* 130 B)
One of the few passages contradicting Aristotle's testimony.

8.25 Olympiodorus

Early sixth century A.D. *The last of the great Neo-Platonists, a man of wide learning, who has left shrewd comments on Plato's dialogues.*

The characters are not completely historical. Plato was not concerned with the minutiae of historical research, e.g. Socrates flexing his leg. But the account of them is not a hundred per cent fictitious either, or there would have been no authenticity, merely a composition directed to establishing a single point. (*Prolegomena to Plato's Philosophy.*)

PART NINE

LATER WRITERS:

GENERAL

9.1 Plutarch

C. A.D. *46–125. A native of Chaeronea in Boeotia, who preferred his home town to the opportunities of larger centres, which he visited and stayed in briefly. A writer of clear and attractive Greek, an excellent recounter of anecdote, a man of deep piety with an interest in ethics. His* Parallel Lives of the Greeks and Romans *remains his best known work: North's translation provided Shakespeare with grist for his mill. In addition, there is the voluminous collection of essays on religion, ethics, literature and culture called* Moralia.

9.1.1 Moralia

9.1.1.1 Socrates once received a kick from a very impudent and gross young buffoon, but on seeing that his own friends were in such a violent state of indignation that they wanted to prosecute him, he remarked: 'If a donkey had kicked me, would you have condescended to kick him back?' ... When Aristophanes brought out *The Clouds*, and poured all manner of abuse upon Socrates, one of those present asked: 'Pray, are you not indignant at his ridiculing you in this manner?' 'Not I, indeed,' replied Socrates, 'this banter in the theatre is only in a big convivial party.' (*Education* 10 C, tr. T. G. Tucker)
   This may not be authentic Plutarch.

9.1.1.2 Socrates said the opposite: 'Bad men live to eat and drink, good men eat and drink to live.' (*Listening to Poetry* 21 E)
   See **9.2.3; 9.6.9; 11.1.84**.

9.1.1.3 Remember the case of Plato. Socrates having handled one of his associates somewhat vigorously in conversation at table, Plato remarked, 'Would it not have been better if this had been said in private?' 'And,'

retorted Socrates, 'would you not have done better if you had said that to *me* in private?' (*Flatterers and Friends* 70 F, tr. T. G. Tucker)

9.1.1.4 Socrates' way of quietly setting young men right. . . . (ibid. 72 A)

9.1.1.5 Socrates put up with Xanthippe's bad temper on the grounds that if he got used to standing her he would be reasonable company for others. (*Benefit from Enemies* 90 E)

9.1.1.6 At this point one might bring in Socrates' epigram, suggesting that if we all lumped our misfortunes in a single heap, and received an equal share, most of us would be glad to take our original misfortunes and clear away. (*Letter to Apollonius* 106 B)
   If Socrates said it, he borrowed it, for Herodotus quotes it (7, 152), and Valerius Maximus attributes it to Solon (7, 2 ext. 2).

9.1.1.7 To young men who are fond of looking at themselves in the mirror Socrates recommended that the ugly should correct their defects by virtue, while the handsome should avoid spoiling their beauty by vice. (*Advice to the Married* 141 D, tr. T. G. Tucker)
   Cf. **1.4**[33]. *Others attribute the* mot *to Bias of Priene.*

9.1.1.8 Someone was supporting the *bon mot* of Cleomenes, who in reply to the question 'How should the good king behave?' answered, 'Help his friends and harm his enemies.' Ariston commented, 'How much better, sir, to help one's friends and turn one's enemies into friends.' This *mot* is universally attributed to Socrates, but is also recorded of Ariston. (*Sayings of Spartans* 218 A)
   This passage shows how easily anecdotes pass from one well-known figure to another. The mot *does not appear in this form in our*

primary sources, but cf. *Plato*, Crito 49 *A*; (**2.3**); Gorgias *469 A*; Republic 1, *335 B*.

9.1.1.9 Socrates wrote nothing. (*Fortune of Alexander* 328 A)

9.1.1.10 Plato and Socrates had students of natural gifts from their own nation; if nothing else, they understood Greek! Yet they did not convert many. The Critiases, Alcibiadeses, Clitophons moved away from them, rejecting their philosophy as horses reject the bit. (ibid. 328 B)

9.1.1.11 Socrates was charged with introducing foreign deities and lost his case to the informers at Athens. (ibid. 328 D)

9.1.1.12 Socrates accepted Alcibiades as his bedfellow. (ibid. 333 A)
   Cf. **2.5.2.2**.

9.1.1.13 And so Socrates, as often as he perceived any anger rising in him against any of his friends, 'setting himself like some ocean promontory to break the violence of the waves', would lower his voice, and put on a smiling countenance, and give his eye a gentler expression, by inclining in the other direction and running counter to his passion, thus keeping himself from fall and defeat. (*Control of Temper* 455 A, tr. A. R. Shilleto)

9.1.1.14 And when Socrates once took Euthydemus home with him from the wrestling school Xanthippe was in a towering rage, and scolded, and at last upset the table, and Euthydemus rose and went away full of sorrow. But Socrates said to him, 'Did not a hen at your house the other day fly in and act in the very same way? And we did not put ourselves out about it.' (ibid. 461 D)

9.1.1.15 Socrates, when he heard one of his friends saying, 'How dear this city is! Chian wine costs one mina, a purple robe three, and half a pint of honey five drachmae,' took him to the meal market, and showed him half a peck of meal for an obol, then took him to the olive market, and showed him a peck of olives for two coppers, and lastly showed him that a sleeveless vest was only ten drachmae. At each place Socrates' friend exclaimed, 'How cheap this city is!' (*Content of Mind* 470 F, tr. A. R. Shilleto)

9.1.1.16 Socrates was apparently speaking to his accusers Anytus and Meletus, but was really speaking to the jury when he said, 'Anytus and Meletus can kill me, but they cannot hurt me.' (ibid. 475 E)

9.1.1.17 Socrates once said that he would rather have the sovereign than a sovereign for a friend. (*On Brotherly Love* 486 E)
   Better a man than money.

9.1.1.18 We often put a question to a person not because we need the information but by way of eliciting from him a few words of a friendly nature, or from a wish to lead him on to converse, as Socrates did with Theaetetus and Charmides. (*Garrulity* 512 B, tr. T. G. Tucker)

9.1.1.19 Remember how Socrates used to urge the avoidance of those foods and drinks which induce you to eat when you are not hungry and to drink when you are not thirsty. (ibid. 513 D)
   Cf. 521 F.

9.1.1.20 Socrates . . . went about inquiring, 'By what arguments did Pythagoras carry conviction?' So Aristippus, when he met Ischomachus at Olympia, proceeded to ask by what kind of conversation Socrates affected the Athenians as he did. When he had gleaned a few seeds or samples of his talk he was so moved that he suffered a physical collapse, and became quite pale and thin. In the end he set sail for Athens, and slaked his thirst with draughts from the fountain-head, studying the man, his discourses and his philosophy, of which the aim was to recognise one's own vices and get rid of them. (*Inquisitiveness* 516 C, tr. T. G. Tucker)

9.1.1.21 It is a smaller evil, as Socrates said, to drink dirty water when excessively thirsty than, when one's mind is disturbed and full of rage and fury, before it is settled and becomes pure, to glut our revenge on the person of a relation and kinsman. (*Delays in Divine Punishment* 550 F, tr. A. R. Shilleto)

9.1.1.22 IX. Then Galaxidorus spoke: 'Hercules! how hard it is to find a man quite free from vanity and superstition! Some are caught by these weaknesses against their will, owing to want of experience or of strength. Others, in order to appear singular and to be taken for friends of the Gods, bring the divine into all they do, making dreams and portents and such stuff a pretext for anything that enters their head. [580] Now, to men in public stations, who are compelled to adapt their lives to a self-willed and petulant multitude, this may have its advantage; superstition is a bit wherewith to check a populace, and direct it to what is expedient. But to Philosophy such posturing is unbecoming in itself, and, moreover, it contradicts her professions; she undertakes to teach all that is good and expedient by the reason, and then, as though in despite of reason, goes back upon the Gods and away from the first principles of action; and, dishonouring demonstration, in which her own excellence is supposed to lie, turns to prophecies and visions seen in dreams,

things in which the weakest often have as great success as the strongest. This, I think, Simmias, is why your Socrates embraced a system of intellectual training which bore a more philosophical stamp, choosing that simple artless type as being liberal and most friendly to truth; and casting to the winds for the sophists, as a mere smoke from Philosophy, all pretentious nonsense.' Theocritus broke in: 'What, Galaxidorus, and has Meletus persuaded even you too that Socrates despised what was divine, for that was the charge which he actually brought before the Athenians?' 'What was divine – no,' he said, 'but he received Philosophy from Pythagoras and Empedocles full of visions and myths and superstitions, and deeply dipped in mysteries; and trained her to look at facts, and be sensible, and pursue truth in soberness of reason.'

X. 'Granted,' said Theocritus, 'but as to the Divine Sign of Socrates, good friend, are we to call it a falsity or what? To me, nothing recorded about Pythagoras seems to go so far towards the prophetic and divine. For, in plain words, as Homer has drawn Athena to Odysseus

> In all his toils a presence and a stay,

even so, apparently, did the spirit attach to Socrates, from the first, a sort of vision to go before and guide his steps in life, which alone

> Passing before him shed a light around

in matters of uncertainty, too hard for the wit of man to solve; upon these the spirit used often to converse with him, adding a divine touch to his own resolutions. For more, and more important, instances you must ask Simmias and the other companions of Socrates. But I was myself present, having come to stay with Euthyphron the prophet, when Socrates, as you remember, Simmias, was going up to the Symbolum and the house of Andocides, asking some question as he walked and playfully cross-examining Euthyphron. Suddenly he stopped and closed his lips tightly and was wrapt in thought for some time. Then he turned back and took the way through the Trunk-makers' Street, and tried to recall those of our friends who were already in advance, saying that the Sign was upon him. Most of them turned in a body, among whom was I, keeping close to Euthyphron. But some young members of the party no doubt to put the Sign of Socrates to the test, held on and drew into their number Charillus the flute-player, who had come to Athens with myself, staying with Cebes. Now as they were going through the street of the Statuaries near the Law Courts they were met by a whole herd of swine loaded with mud and hustling one another by press of numbers. There was no getting out of the way; on they charged, up-setting some, bespattering others. At any rate, Charillus came home with his clothes full of mud and his legs too, so that we always laugh when we remember Socrates and his Sign, and wonder that this divine presence of his should never fail him or forget.'

XI. Then Galaxidorus said: 'Do you think then, Theocritus, that the Sign of Socrates possessed a special and extraordinary power, not that some fragment of the ready wit which we all share determined him by an empiric process, turning the scale of his reasoning in cases which were uncertain and incalculable? For as a single weight does not by itself incline the balance, but, if added to one scale when the weights are even, sinks the whole of that one on its own side, [581] so a cry, or any such feather-weight sign, will fit a mind already weighted, and draw it into action; and when two trains of thought are in conflict it reinforces one, and solves the difficulty by removing

the equality, so that there is a movement and an inclination.' My father broke in: 'Well, but I have myself heard, Galaxidorus, from a certain Megarian, who had it from Terpsion, that the Sign of Socrates was a sneeze, proceeding either from himself or from other persons; if someone else sneezed on his right, whether behind or in front, it encouraged him to the action; if on the left, it warned him off it. Of his own sneezings there was one kind which confirmed his purpose when he was still intending to act; another stopped him when he was already acting and checked his impulse. The wonder to me is that if he made use of a sneeze he did not so call it to his companions, but was in the habit of saying that what checked or commanded him was a Divine Sign. For that would be like vanity and idle boasting, not like truth and simplicity, in which lay, as we suppose, his greatness and his superiority to men in general, to be disturbed by a sound from outside or a casual sneeze, and so be diverted from acting, and give up what he had resolved. Now the impulses of Socrates, on the other hand, show firmness and intensity in every direction, as though issuing from a right and power-ful judgement and principle. Thus for a man to remain in voluntary poverty all his life, when he might have had plenty, and the givers would have been pleased and thankful, and never to swerve from Philosophy in the face of all those hindrances; and at last, when the zeal and ingenuity of his friends had made his way easy to safety and retreat, not to be bent by their entreaties. nor yield to the near approach of death – all this is not like a man whose judgement might be changed by random voices or sneezings; it is like one led to what is noble by some greater and more sov-ereign authority. I hear also that he foretold to some of his friends the disaster which befell the power of Athens in

Sicily. At a still earlier time Pyrilampes, the son of Antiphon, when taken prisoner in the pursuit near Delium, after having received from us a javelin wound, as soon as he had heard from those who had arrived from Athens to arrange the truce that Socrates had returned home in safety by The Gullies with Alcibiades and Laches, often called upon him by name, and often on friends and comrades of his own who had fled with him by way of Parnes, and been slain by our cavalry; they had dis-obeyed the Sign of Socrates, he said, in turning from the battle by a different way instead of following his lead. This, I think, Simmias too must have heard.' 'Often,' said Simmias, 'and from many persons. For there was no little noise at Athens about the Sign of Socrates in consequence.'

XII. 'Well, then, Simmias,' said Pheidolaus, 'are we to allow Galaxi-dorus in his jesting way to bring down this great fact of divination to sneezings and cries, which plenty of common ignorant persons apply to trifles in mere sport, whereas, when grave dangers overtake them, or more serious business, we may quote Euripides:

These follies have a truce when steel is near?

Galaxidorus said: 'I am quite ready to listen to Simmias on this subject, Pheidolaus, if he has himself heard Socrates speak about it, and to join you in believing; but as for all that you and Polymnis have mentioned, it is not hard to refute it. For as in medicine a throb or a pimple is a small matter, but is the indication of what is not small; and as to a pilot the cry of a bird from the open sea, [582] or the scudding of a thin film of cloud, sig-nifies wind and rougher seas, so to a prophetic soul a sneeze or a voice is nothing great in itself, but is the sign of a great conjuncture. There is no art in which it is thought contemptible to forecast great things by small, many things through few. Suppose a man ignorant of the meaning of letters were to see a few insignificant-looking characters, and to refuse to believe that one who knew grammar could, by their help, repeat the story of great wars between old-world peoples, and found-ings of cities, and what kings did or suffered, and then were to say that a voice, or something like a voice, revealed and repeated each of these things to that historian, a pleasant laugh would come over your face, my friend, at the ignorance of that man. Now, consider, may it not be so with us? In our ignorance of the meaning of different things by which the prophetic art hits the coming event, are we simple enough to rebel if a man of intellect uses them to reveal something not yet evident, and says, moreover, that a Divine Sign, not a sneeze or a voice, directs him to the facts? For now I turn to you, Polymnis, who wonder that Socrates, a man who did so very much to make Philosophy human by simplicity and absence of cant, should have named his Sign, not a sneeze or a voice, but, in full tragic phrase, his Divine Sign. I, on the contrary, should be surprised if a man so excellent in Dialectic and mastery of terms had said that the sneeze and not the Divine Sign gave him the intimation. As if a man were to say that he had been wounded 'by the javelin', not 'by the thrower with his javelin', or, again, that the weight had been measured 'by the balance', not 'by the weigher with his balance'. For the work is not the work of the tool but of the owner of the tool which he uses for the work; and the Sign is a kind of tool used by the signifying power. But, as I said, if Simmias should have anything to tell us we must listen, for his knowledge is more exact.' (*On the Genius of Socrates* 579 F–582 C, tr. T. G. Tucker)

9.1.1.23 However, they were far on in an inquiry of no mean import, Heaven knows, but one which Galaxidorus and Pheidolaus had started a little earlier, the problem of the real nature and potency of the Divine Sign of Socrates, so called. What Simmias said in reply to the argument of Galaxidorus we did not hear; but he went on to say that he had himself once asked Socrates on the subject, and failed to get an answer, and so had never asked again; but that he had often been with him when he gave his opinion that those who claim intercourse with the divine by way of vision are impostors, whereas he attended to those who professed to hear a voice, and put serious questions to them. Hence it began to occur to us, as we were discussing the matter among ourselves, to suspect that the Divine Sign of Socrates might possibly be no vision but a special sense for sounds or words, with which he had contact in some strange manner; just as in sleep there is no voice heard, but fancies and notions as to particular words reach the sleepers, who then think that they hear people talking. Only sleepers receive such conceptions in a real dream because of the tranquillity and calm of the body in sleep, whereas in waking moments the soul can hardly attend to greater powers, being so choked by thronging emotions and distracting needs that they are unable to listen and to give their attention to clear revelations. But the mind of Socrates, pure and passionless, and intermingling itself but little with the body for necessary purposes, was fine and light of touch, and quickly changed under any impression. The impression we may conjecture to have been no voice, but the utterance of a spirit, which without vocal sound reached the perceiving mind by the revelation itself. For voice is like a blow upon the soul, which perforce admits its utterance by way of the ears, whenever we converse with one another. But the mind of a stronger being leads the gifted soul, touching it with the thing thought, and no blow is needed. To such a being the soul yields as it relaxes or tightens the impulses, which are never violent, as when there are passions to resist, but supple and pliant like reins which give. There is nothing wonderful in this; as we see great cargo-vessels turned about by little helms, and, again, potters' wheels whirling round in even revolution at the light touch of a hand. These are things without a soul no doubt, yet so constructed as to run swiftly and smoothly, and therefore to yield to a motive force when a touch is given. But the soul of a man, being strained by countless impulses, as by cords, is far the easiest of all machines to turn, if it be touched rationally; it accepts the touch of thought, and moves as thought directs. [589] For here the passions and impulses are stretched towards the thinking principle and end in it; if that principle be stirred they receive a pull and in turn draw and strain the man. And thus we are allowed to learn how great is the power of a thought. For bones, which have no sensation, and nerves and fleshy parts charged with humours, and the whole resultant mass in its ponderous quiescence, do yet, as soon as the soul sets something a-going in thought and directs its impulse towards it, rise up, alert and tense, a whole which moves to action in all its members, as though it had wings. But it is hard, nay, perhaps altogether beyond our powers, to take in at one glance the system of excitation, complex strain and divine prompting whereby the soul, after conceiving a thought, draws on the mass of the body by the impulses which it gives. Yet whereas a word thus intellectually apprehended excites the soul, while no sort of voice is heard and no action takes place, even so we need not, I think, find it hard to believe that mind may be led by a stronger mind and a more divine soul external to itself, having contact with it after its kind, as word with word or light with reflection. For in actual fact we recognise the thoughts of one another by groping as it were in darkness with the assistance of voice; whereas the thoughts of spirits have light, they shine upon men capable of receiving them, they need not verbs or nouns, those symbols whereby men in their intercourse with men see resemblances and images of the things thought, yet never apprehend the things themselves, save only those upon whom, as we have said, there shines from within a peculiar and spiritual light. And yet what we see happen in the case of the voice may partly reassure the incredulous. The air is impressed with articulate sounds, it becomes all word and voice, and brings the meaning home to the soul of the hearer. Therefore we need not wonder if, in regard to this special mode of thought also, the air is sensitive to the touch of higher beings, and is so modified as to convey to the mind of godlike and extraordinary men the thought of him who thought it. For as the strokes of miners are caught on brazen shields because of the reverberation, when they rise from below ground and fall upon them, whereas falling on any other surface they are indistinct and pass to nothing, even so the words of spirits pass through all Nature, but only sound for those who possess the soul in untroubled calm, holy and spiritual men as we emphatically call them. The view of most people is that spiritual visitations come to men in sleep; that they should be similarly stirred when awake and in their full faculties they think marvellous and beyond belief. As though a musician were thought to use his lyre when the strings are let down, and not to touch or use it when it is strung up and tuned! They do not see the cause, their own inner tune-

lessness and discord, from which Socrates our friend had been set free, as the oracle given to his father when he was yet a boy declared. For it bade him allow his son to do whatever came into his mind; not to force nor direct his goings, but to let his impulse have free play, only to pray for him to Zeus Agoraios and to the Muses, but for all else not to meddle with Socrates; meaning no doubt that he had within him a guide for his life who was better than ten thousand teachers and directors.

XXI. This, Pheidolaus, is what has occurred to me to think about the Divine Sign of Socrates, in his lifetime and since his death, dismissing with contempt those who have suggested voices or sneezings or anything of that sort. (*On the Genius of Socrates* 588 B–589 F, tr. T. G. Tucker)

9.1.1.24 Socrates' *bon mot* was even better: 'There is no Athenian and no Greek – only Universians.' (*Exile* 600 F)

9.1.1.25 Marcion said that he thought Socrates' damnation applied not merely to those who separated expediency from honour but to those who differentiated between pleasure and health, suggesting that they were hostile and in conflict instead of working together. (*Table-talk* 662 B)
Cf. **8.1.26**.

9.1.1.26 On the sixth of Thargelion we celebrated the birthday of Socrates. (*Table-talk* 717 B)
This is a date in May: remember that this is nearly 600 years later. Cf. **9.7.4.**

9.1.1.27 Socrates didn't organise a lecture-room, sit in a lecturer's chair, announce a fixed hour for a seminar or class with his students. He relaxed casually with them, had a drink with them, served in the forces with some of them or met them in the city centre.

In the end he was imprisoned and executed by poison. And it was philosophy all the time. He was the first person to demonstrate that life is open to philosophy at all times, in every part, in every experience and every activity. (*Old Men in Public Life* 796 D)

9.1.1.28 Lysias also wrote *A Defence of Socrates* directed to the jury. (*Lysias* 836 B)

Cf. **1.2** [20]; **9.4.4**; **9.12.9**; **11.1.70**; *also Cicero*, On the Orator *1, 231. The speech Plutarch knew was probably a pamphlet.*

9.1.1.29 Aristoxenus described Socrates as an ignorant uneducated sensualist, adding, 'But there wasn't much wrong with him.' (*The Malice of Herodotus* 856 C)

Aristoxenus was a musicologist and philosopher of Aristotle's school, born about thirty years after Socrates' death (**8.21**).

9.1.1.30 'Why did the god tell Socrates to act as a midwife to others and bar him from giving birth himself, as is said in *Theaetetus*?' There would be no mock-modesty or flippancy in the god's name. . . . Socrates used his negative critique as a kind of purgative medicine. His criticisms of others were more persuasive because he did not make positive assertions himself. His grasp was firmer because he seemed to be sharing in a common search for truth rather than coming to the rescue with some dogma of his own. . . . Socrates' medical skill was not applied to the body; it was an antiseptic for a diseased and festering soul. . . .

Take a close look. The compositions and treatises and discourses of orators and the dogmatic expositions of sophists are worthless. It is these which the divine spirit prevented Socrates from producing. Socrates thought the only wisdom worth having lay in the field of the divine, the intellectual. He called it the science of love. Its origin did not

lie with men. It was a recollection, not an original discovery. This is why Socrates did not teach. He implanted in the young the first seeds of doubt, like pains of childbirth. He awakened their innate thoughts, stirred them into motion, brought them together. This was the skill he called midwifery. It did not consist in implanting intelligence from outside in those whom he encountered, as others professed to do, but in revealing an intelligence already naturally there, but immature and chaotic and needing someone to nurse it and strengthen it. (*Questions about Plato* 999 C)

9.1.1.31 In the third volume of his *Dialectic* he [Chrysippus] comments, 'Plato, Aristotle and their successors up to Polemo and Strato laid especial stress on dialectic, and Socrates more than any.' (*Contradictions in Stoicism* 1045)

9.1.1.32 Colotes prepared his defence from the start. He recounts how Chaerephon brought back from Delphi the oracle about Socrates which we all know, and adds, 'We will pass over the Chaerephon stuff, a tale of banality and verbal jugglery.' (*Against Colotes* 1116 E)

Colotes was a younger contemporary, friend and follower of Epicurus; he came from Lampsacus and attacked the work of Plato and his followers, polemically: Plutarch wrote an extended refutation.

9.1.1.33 Colotes puts forward these splendid maxims about the senses: 'We eat food, not grass. When rivers are swollen we cross them by ferry; when fordable, on foot.' He goes on: 'Your arguments were inflated, Socrates. You discussed one point of view with the people you met, you acted on another.' Of course Socrates' arguments were inflated. He admitted his ignorance: he was always learning and looking for the truth. . . . As for the discrepancy between Socrates' words and actions, you have marvellous evidence in the events at Delium, at Potidaea, during the dictatorship, before Archelaus, before the commons, his poverty, his death. None of this really compared with his words. My dear man, the only tenable charge of inconsistency in Socrates would have lain in a life of this quality contrasted with a profession of the pursuit of pleasure. (ibid. 1117 D)

9.1.1.34 He attacks Socrates quite scurrilously for his investigation what man is while 'flaunting' (Colotes' word) his failure in self-knowledge . . . . Socrates that 'inflated sophist' . . . Socrates was not stupid in seeking self-knowledge. (ibid. 1118 C)

9.1.1.35 I am no worse, says Socrates, if a man hits me in the face without provocation. (*Fr.* 32)
Cf. *Plato*, Gorgias *508 D*.

9.1.1.36 . . . the dictum of Socrates that every bad man is bad against his will. (*Fr.* 40)

9.1.1.37 Socrates said that the student should pray to become a scholar and the husband to become a father. (*Fr.* 67)

9.1.1.38 Poverty is a short cut to self-control. (*Fr.* 151)
Attributed by Stobaeus (**11.1.121**) *to Socrates, though not by Plutarch.*

9.1.2 Lives

9.1.2.1 Demetrius is obviously anxious to rescue Aristides from poverty, a great evil. Socrates too; he says that Socrates owned a house and had seventy minas on loan at interest to Crito. (*Aristides* 1, 9, 319)
Demetrius of Phalerum wrote a book on Socrates about a century after Socrates' death (**8.20**).

9.1.2.2 Demetrius of Phalerum, Hieronymus of Rhodes, Aristoxenus the musician and Aristotle (if the work *On High Birth* is to be classified as genuine Aristotle) record that Aristides' daughter Myrto married the philosopher Socrates. He had another wife, but took Myrto, who was badly off and unable to remarry because of her poverty. Panaetius has given an adequate answer to these gentlemen in his work on Socrates. (ibid. 37, 2, 335)
Panaetius of Rhodes: Stoic philosopher of the second century B.C. *See Athenaeus 13, 555 D* (**9.2.11**).

9.1.2.3 Cato thought that there was nothing to admire in old Socrates except his continual patience with a difficult wife and idiotic sons. (*Marcus Cato* 20, 2, 347)

9.1.2.4 He called Socrates a powerful windbag who did his best to become a political dictator by subverting tradition and enticing the citizens away to illegal attitudes. (ibid. 23, 1, 350)

9.1.2.5 Socrates the philosopher was warned by his divine sign through its usual indications that the expedition [against Sicily] was working for the destruction of Athens. He told his friends and associates, and the story got around to a lot of people. (*Nicias* 13, 6, 532)
This was the expedition of 415–413 in which Athens lost two armies. Cf. Alcibiades *17, 4, 199.*

9.1.2.6 It is said with some justification that the good graces of Socrates contributed considerably to his reputation. (*Alcibiades* 1, 2, 191)

9.1.2.7 The love Socrates showed him was strong evidence of the lad's innate quality. Socrates saw it gleaming brightly in his looks, and was afraid of his wealth and position and the gang of Athenians, allies and foreigners who were using flattery and service to try to get hold of him. So he went to his defence rather than stand by and watch his flower let its natural fruit fall to destruction. . . . Alcibiades . . . in the end had the natural sense to recognise Socrates for what he was, and to stick to him and reject his wealthy and famous lovers. Things moved fast. He was close to Socrates. He had a lover who was not pursuing effeminate lust or pleading for kisses and physical union, but one who challenged the rotten part of his personality and pressed heavily on his foolish, worthless pride. He listened.

He crouched, a cock, like a slave, with folded wings. He thought Socrates' action a real divine service to help and rescue the young. He began to criticise himself, to admire Socrates, to listen patiently to his loving care, to respect his moral quality. He did not realise that he was acquiring (in Plato's words) an image of love in response to love. Everyone was astonished to see him taking his meals with Socrates, taking his exercise with Socrates, sharing a tent with Socrates, while being difficult and harsh with his other lovers. (ibid. 4, 1, 193)

9.1.2.8 The love of Socrates had many powerful rivals, but somehow it conquered Alcibiades. He was a man of good natural quality, and Socrates' words gripped him, turned his heart inside out and brought tears to his eyes. Sometimes he surrendered himself to the flatterers who offered many enticements and slipped away from Soc-

rates; he had to be hounded down just like a runaway slave. Yet he really thought nothing of the others; Socrates alone won his awe and respect. (ibid. 6, 1, 194)

9.1.2.9 Just as iron is made pliable in the furnace and toughened again by cold water, with its particles solidly united, so Socrates would find Alcibiades full of idle folly and debauchery, and would hammer him with words, force him to collect himself and make him humble and circumspect till he learned the size of his defects and his failure to achieve real excellence. (ibid. 6, 4, 194)

9.1.2.10 When he was still a youngster he served in the campaign against Potidaea; he had Socrates to bivouac with him and to stand at his side in action. There was fierce fighting. Both distinguished themselves, but when Alcibiades fell from a wound it was Socrates who stood over him and protected him and patiently saved his arms and his life. Socrates deserved the prize for valour by any just reckoning, but the commanding officers were obviously anxious to give Alcibiades the honour because of his influence. Socrates was ready to encourage Alcibiades' honourable ambitions and led the way in testifying to his behaviour and calling on them to give him the crown and suit of armour.

On another occasion the battle took place at Delium and the Athenians were in flight. Socrates with a few others was retreating on foot. Alcibiades had a horse. He saw Socrates and refused to ride on, but kept at his side and protected him from the deadly assaults of the enemy. This was later. (ibid. 7, 2, 194)

9.1.2.11 Plato at the point of death used to offer a prayer of thanks to Fortune and his guardian spirit, first, because he was a human being, not an irrational animal, second, because he was a Greek, not a foreigner, third, because he lived in the age of Socrates. (*Marius* 46, 1, 433)

Cf. **1.2**; **8.3.10**.

9.2 Athenaeus

We know little of Athenaeus. He came from Egypt and was writing about A.D. *200. His vast sprawling work* The Professors at Dinner *is often dull, occasionally entertaining, but always incidentally important for clarifying points about Greek life and preserving hundreds of extracts from a miscellany of earlier writers.*

9.2.1 Even Socrates in his wisdom enjoyed the Memphis-dance and was often caught dancing it. (So Xenophon.) He used to tell his friends that dancing exercised every limb. (1, 20 F)

The reference is to Xenophon, The Banquet *2, 19.*

9.2.2 Socrates was often caught walking up and down in front of his house just before dark. When they asked, 'What are you up to now?' he would reply, 'Collecting an aperitif for dinner.' (4, 157 E)

9.2.3 Socrates used to say, 'I am different from the rest. They live to eat; I eat to live.' (4, 158 F)

See **11.1.84** *n.*

9.2.4 Socrates saw a man helping himself liberally to the dressing. 'Gentlemen,' he said, 'which of you is it who helps himself to bread as if it were dressing and dressing as if it were bread?' (5, 186 D)

9.2.5 So much for philosopher-soldiers. Demochares says of them, 'No one could possibly make a spear out of savory. No one could possibly make a useful soldier out of Socrates.' Actually, Plato says that Socrates fought in three campaigns, against Potidaea, Amphipolis and the Boeotians (when the battle of Delium was fought). It does not appear in the history books, but Socrates tells us that in the general rout and massacre of the Athenians he won an award for valour. It is all untrue. The expedition against Amphipolis took place when Alcaeus was archon. Cleon was the commanding officer, and the soldiers were carefully picked; Thucydides says so. Socrates must have been one of these picked men – Socrates with nothing in the world but a cloak and a staff! What historian, what poet records it? Where has Thucydides even mentioned in passing Plato's soldier Socrates? 'What has a shield to do with a staff?' And when did he campaign against Potidaea, as Plato suggests in *Charmides*, claiming that at that time he also won the award for valour and stood down in favour of Alcibiades? Thucydides does not mention it – nor even Isocrates in his speech *On the Team of Horses*. What sort of battle was there for Socrates to win the award? What was his outstanding feat? There wasn't a battle at all in Thucydides' record. Plato, not content with this miracle-story, introduces the battle of Delium as well – or rather an adventure-story. Even if Socrates had captured Delium (as Herodicus, Crates' pupil, records in his work *Against Idolatry of Socrates*) he would have been unceremoniously routed with the rest, when Pagondas made a surprise attack round the hill with two cavalry detachments. On that occasion the Athenians were routed in several directions, to Delium or the sea or Oropus or Mt Parnes. The Boeotians in hot pursuit with their own Locrian cavalry were cutting them down. With the Athenians in all this panic and confusion, did Socrates stand alone 'with chin up and eyes rolling' and throw back the cavalry of Boeotia and Locris? Thucydides does not record his valour. No poet records it. How could he stand down in favour of Alcibiades when Alcibiades had no part at all in this expedition? In *Crito* Plato, that worshipper of the goddess of Memory, says that Socrates never travelled abroad except for one visit to the Isthmus. Antisthenes, Socrates' associate, tells the same story about the award for valour as Plato. 'This is no true tale.' The dog-philosopher is very obliging to Socrates. No one who has Thucydides as standard ought to trust either of them. As a matter of fact, Antisthenes adds to the legend in the words: 'We hear that you actually won the award for valour in the battle with the Boeotians. – Sh, sir. Alcibiades, not I, has that privilege. – Yes, by your gift, we understand.' Plato's Socrates says that he was present at Potidaea and resigned the award for valour to Alcibiades. All the historians say that the expedition to Potidaea, with Phormio in command, preceded the expedition against Delium. (5, 215 C)

9.2.6 In another passage Plato says that Chaerephon asked the Delphic oracle if anyone was wiser than Socrates. The priestess replied, 'No one.' This is another point where Xenophon differs. He says: 'Chaerephon once consulted the oracle at Delphi on my behalf. Apollo answered that no one excelled me in justice or good sense; there were many witnesses.' On what grounds is it likely or plausible that Socrates, who admitted his own ignorance, should be acclaimed by the omniscient god the wisest of all men? If ignorance is wisdom omniscience must be folly! What was the point of Chaerephon's bothering the god with a question about Socrates? Socrates spoke credibly enough about himself in disowning wisdom for himself. 'A man who asks the god such questions is a "fool" – it's like asking "What wool's softer than Athenian?" "Are there camels tougher than the Bactrian?" "Is anyone more snub-nosed than Socrates?" Anyone who puts that sort of question gets what he deserves from the god. It's like the man (the fabulist Aesop or some other) who asked:

Son of Zeus and Leto, how should I get rich?

The sarcastic reply:

By acquiring the territory between Corinth and Sicyon.

More. None of the comic dramatists presents Plato's picture of Socrates – the son of a fat midwife, married to a difficult wife Xanthippe, who emptied the slop-bucket over him, bedfellow to Alcibiades. Aristophanes (whom Plato depicted at the banquet) would have made a fanfare of this. He made Socrates out to be a corrupter of young men; he would never have passed this over. The brilliant Aspasia, Socrates' instructor in rhetoric, says in lines attributed to her and recorded by Crates' pupil Herodicus:

Socrates, I have not missed your passion
for Deinomache and Cleinias' son. Listen
  to me
if you want your love to prosper. Don't
  ignore
what I say; pay attention. It will be better
  for you.
When I heard, my body was aglow with
  beads
of joy, and welcome tears fell from my
  eyes.
Furl your sails; fill your heart with the
  Muse's inspiration,
She'll help you get him; let her loose on
  his ears till they yearn.
She is the first point of love for both. She'll
  help you
hold him, if you offer to his hearing gifts
  to unveil his heart.

So our good Socrates goes hunting with the woman of Miletus as his instructor in love. Huntsman, not, as Plato says, quarry to the snares of Alcibiades. Yes, and he doesn't stop crying, for his lack of success I suppose. Aspasia sees what a state he's in and says:

Socrates dear, why these tears? are you struck
by some thunderflash of desire, with its home in your heart, bursting
from the eyes of that invulnerable lad whom I undertook
to make pliable for you?

Plato, in *Protagoras*, makes it clear that Socrates really did lose his heart to Alcibiades, though Alcibiades was almost thirty. . . . (5, 218 E)

There are references to Plato, Apology *21 A* (**2.2**)*;* Theaetetus *149 A* (**2.5.4.1**)*;* Banquet *219 B* (**2.5.2.2**)*;* Protagoras *309 A*; Xenophon, Apology *14* (**3.1**)*.*

9.2.7 *Gurgling-cup*: a cup from Rhodes designed by Therides. Socrates comments on its shape: 'Those who drink all they want from a bowl will stop first; those who drink from a gurgling-cup which lets in a trickle at a time . . . .' (11, 784 D)

From Antisthenes, Protrepticus *(the full text of Athenaeus is missing for some pages: this is supplied from a summary: hence the odd numbering).*

9.2.8 The matter of years would not easily allow Plato's Socrates to come together with Parmenides for a conversation of that sort. (11, 505 F)

Part of an attack on Plato's reliability.

9.2.9 Hegesander of Delphi, in his *Memoirs*, speaks of Plato's hostility to all and sundry, adding: 'After Socrates' death his closest friends were gathered in a mood of considerable depression. Plato was there: he took up a cup and cried, "Don't be downhearted: I am quite competent to lead the School," and

toasted Apollodorus. Apollodorus said, "I'd rather have taken the cup of poison from Socrates than this toast of wine from you."' (11, 507 A)

The story can hardly be true. Hegesander (second century B.C.*) was very unreliable.*

9.2.10 In general, Plato seemed naturally disposed to act like a stepmother to all Socrates' disciples. Hence Socrates' witty shot in recounting a dream in company. 'I thought,' he said, 'that Plato turned into a crow, alighted on my head, pecked at my bald spot, looked round and croaked. Plato, I deduce that you are going to tell many lies over my head.' (11, 507 C)

Evidently a parody of the swan story: **1.11.1**; **9.10.2**; **12.6.4**.

9.2.11 On this basis one may criticise those authors who attribute two wives to Socrates, Xanthippe and Myrto, daughter of Aristides – not Aristides the 'Just' (the chronology is wrong) but his grandson. These are Callisthenes, Demetrius of Phalerum, Satyrus the Peripatetic and Aristoxenus; Aristotle gave them the note in his account in *On High Birth*. The story is doubtful – unless bigamy was permissible at the time by decree because of the shortage of males. This would account for the fact that the writers of comedy, who often mention Socrates, say nothing about it. Hieronymus of Rhodes cites a decree about women; I will send you a copy when I get hold of the volume. But Panaetius of Rhodes published a refutation of those who attribute two wives to Socrates. (13, 555 D)

The work On High Birth *(lost) is doubtfully authentic, but the story seems to have been strong in Peripatetic circles within a century of Socrates' death. The suggestion that the alleged bigamy was a misunderstanding of some comic innuendo is contradicted by this passage. Panaetius' refutation was probably to attribute the bigamy to another man of the same name. See Plutarch,* Aristides *37, 2, 335* (**9.1.2.2**).

9.2.12 Who expected Socrates' disciple Aeschines to turn out the sort of character described by the orator Lysias in his speech *On Contracts*? From the dialogues attributed to him we admire him as a good, honest man – unless these are really works of Socrates the philosopher, presented to Aeschines by Socrates' wife Xanthippe after Socrates' death, as Idomeneus and others maintain. (13, 611 D)

9.2.13 In his poetry, Socrates says that the best dancers make the best soldiers.

Those who best honour the gods with their dancing are best in battle. Dancing has affinity with military drill: it is a display of physical training as well as general organisation. (14, 628 E)

9.2.14 Alcibiades sent Socrates a cake. Xanthippe stamped on it. Socrates laughed and said, 'Well you won't get any of it either!' The story comes from Antipater, *Anger*, volume I. (14, 643 F)
Cf. **8.4.11**; **9.7.18**.

9.3 Lucian

Lucian, the wittiest of all Greek prose-writers, lived in the second century A.D. *He was not a philosopher, though influenced by Cynics and Epicureans, and by Plato's writings. He gives a satirical picture of the philosophers of his day: it is a disappointment that he tells us nothing new about Socrates: it is interesting that he notes the political motive behind the execution. For other pictures of Socrates (adding nothing) see* Dialogues of the Dead.

9.3.1 Why should I mention Socrates, who was unjustly slandered to the Athenians as a godless traitor? (*Slander* 29)

9.3.2 ZEUS: Cheer up! At last they've been completely persuaded to choose you over Injustice by the philosophers, above all by Sophroniscus' son with his generous praise of just action and his assertion that it was the greatest good of all.

JUSTICE: Yes, and look what he got out of speaking about me! Handed over to the Eleven, thrown into prison, condemned to drink poison, poor fellow, without even offering that cock to Asclepius first. His accusers won easily with their philosophy of injustice opposed to his.

ZEUS: At that time the man in the street knew nothing of philosophy and its work. Of course, the jury leaned to Anytus and Meletus. (*Double Indictment* 5)

9.3.3 Yes, and Socrates was brought up by Sculpture here, but as soon as he knew good from bad he took to his heels and deserted her for my camp – and you know his praises are sung on all sides. (*Dream* 12)

9.3.4 Socrates . . . used to proclaim to all and sundry that so far from knowing absolutely everything he knew absolutely nothing – or nothing except the fact that he knew nothing. (*Hermotimus* 48)

9.3.5 ZEUS: Put up another.

HERMES: How about that windbag from Athens?

ZEUS: Splendid.

HERMES: Here, you. (*Announcing*) FOR SALE: One way of life with intelligence and morality thrown in. What am I offered for sainthood?

BUYER: Now, what's your special expertise?

SOCRATES: Homosexuality. I'm a specialist in love-affairs.

BUYER: Then you're no use to me. I'm looking for a tutor for my boy, and he's good-looking.

SOCRATES: A good-looking boy? I'm just your man. My passion isn't for bodies. I look for beauty of mind and spirit. They can sleep under the same blanket as me; they'll tell you they come to no harm.

BUYER: Not very likely. You'd be a queer queer if you only interfered with the soul when you had all the openings of sleeping in the same bed!

SOCRATES: By the dog, by the plane tree, I swear it's true.

BUYER: Heracles! What odd gods!

SOCRATES: Do you think so? Do you imagine that the dog isn't divine? Have you never seen Anubis' standing in Egypt? What about Sirius in heaven and Cerberus in the underworld?

BUYER: You're right; I was quite wrong. Now what is your particular way of life?

SOCRATES: I live in a city which I've invented for myself. It has an unusual constitution and laws of my own.

BUYER: I should be interested to hear one of your rules.

SOCRATES: Let me tell you the most important of them: my decision about women. No woman belongs to one man only. Anyone who wants can have a share in the marriage.

BUYER: You mean that you've abolished all legislation about adultery?

SOCRATES: Yes, and all the petty bickering it causes.

BUYER: What have you enacted about pretty boys?

SOCRATES: Their kisses shall be a reward for valour and outstanding service.

BUYER: There's generosity for you! Now what is the cardinal point in your philosophy?

SOCRATES: My 'ideas' – the patterns of the universe. All that you see – sea, sky, earth and everything on earth – have invisible likenesses outside the material world.

BUYER: Where are they?

SOCRATES: Nowhere: if they existed in space they wouldn't exist.

BUYER: I can't see these patterns of yours.

SOCRATES: Of course not. You're suffering from intellectual blindness. Now I can see all these images, an invisible you, a second me; in fact, two of everything.

BUYER: I must buy you. You combine sharp eyes and a sharp mind. (*Ways of Life for Sale* 15)

This, though amusing, tells us little. It is based entirely on Plato. It can't even be taken as implying that Lucian held the Platonic Socrates to be an authentic portrait, as the ways of life concerned are those current in Lucian's day. Socrates therefore is not intended to represent the historic Socrates, but the general tradition of the Academy. In fact, there are really three points: homosexuality with reference to The Banquet (**2.5.2.2**)*; community of wives from* The Republic*; and the Theory of Forms.*

9.3.6 One's love for young men should be like that of Socrates for Alcibiades; he slept with him under a single blanket like a father. (*Types of Love* 49) *Cf. Plato,* The Banquet *219 C* (**2.5.2.2**).

9.3.7 Socrates was as much a devotee of love as anyone, and Alcibiades did not arise unscathed after lying with him under the same blanket. (ibid. 54)

The work is not by Lucian: it perhaps dates from the late third or early fourth century A.D. *The two passages are contradictory.*

9.3.8 SOCRATES: . . . I shall often sing your praises to my wives, Xanthippe and Myrto . . . (*Halcyon* 8)

Halcyon *is a pleasant Socratic dialogue mentioned as attributed to Plato by Athenaeus* (*506 C*) *and found in manuscripts of Lucian and Plato. Diogenes Laertius* (*3, 62*) *says that Favorinus assigned it to an author named Leon, a little earlier than Lucian: this is probably right. There is nothing relevant to our understanding of Socrates except the mention of the two wives.*

9.4 Valerius Maximus

Valerius Maximus compiled an uncritical collection of extracts for orators, which he dedicated to the Emperor Tiberius. It was immensely popular later.

9.4.1 The Athenians . . . condemned Socrates because he appeared to be introducing a new religion. (1, 1, ext. 7)

9.4.2 Socrates, adjudged the wisest man in the world by the consent of his fellows, and by Apollo's oracle, had a midwife named Phaenarete for a mother and a stone-mason named Sophroniscus for a father, and reached the highest pinnacle of glory. (3, 4 ext. 1)

9.4.3 The state of Athens, imbued with an error as cruel as it was criminal, unanimously carried a grim resolution to execute the ten commanders who had annihilated the Spartan fleet at Argi-nusae. Socrates happened to bear the legal responsibility for ratifying the resolutions of the commons at that moment. He thought it unjust that so many men of high quality should be eliminated through an outburst of jealousy without real cause. He confronted the impetuosity of the mob with his own firmness of purpose. The deafening howls of the assembly and the pressure of their threats could not compel him to assent to the general madness. They insisted on staining their hands unjustly with the commanders'

blood; his opposition prevented them from doing it legally. Socrates was not afraid that his own death might be an eleventh example of the madness of his distracted country. (3, 8, 3)

9.4.4 Socrates, the outstanding figure in Greek scholarship, was on trial. Lysias declaimed to him a speech he had composed for him to use in court, a humble, supplicatory speech, tailored to the threatening storm. 'Please take it away,' said Socrates. 'If I could be brought to declaim that stuff out of earshot in the wilds of Russia I would gladly hand myself over to capital punishment.' He had no interest in life if it meant loss of dignity. Socrates was keener to die than Lysias to survive! (6, 4, ext. 2)
  Cf. **9.1.1.28** *n.*

9.4.5 Socrates, a kind of earthly oracle of human wisdom, thought that the only gift to be asked of the gods was blessings. They knew the needs of each individual; we usually offer prayers which are better unfulfilled! . . .

He used to say that the ready way to glory is to be what you want to appear to be. It was a sermon, a direct challenge to drain the cup of virtue instead of chasing its shadow.

He was asked to advise a young man whether to marry or remain celibate. His answer was: 'Whichever you do, you will regret it. You have a choice between loneliness, loss, the extinction of your line and an alien heir, or continual trouble, a web of grumbling, the dowry thrown in your face, the frowns of your in-laws, the incessant talking of your father-in-law, the man who lays siege to other people's marriages, not knowing how your children will turn out.' He didn't allow the young man to make his choice of evils as if they were joys.

The Athenians showed the criminal insanity of condemning him to death.

He took the cup of poison from the executioner's hand with unchanged expression and resolution. The cup was at his lip when his wife Xanthippe with an outburst of tears cried out, 'You are going to die innocent!' 'Well,' he said, 'do you think it better for me to die guilty?' What philosophy – remembering its own principles at the very moment of death! (7, 2, ext. 1)

Cf. Gnomologium Vaticanum *478*; **8.12.2** *n. It will be noticed that in Plato Xanthippe is not present at the moment of death. The story is, however, told of Phocion and others. Similarly the first story is also told of Pythagoras; it comes in the pseudo-Platonic 2 Alcibiades.*

9.4.6 It is generally agreed that Socrates, at an advanced age, began to study the lyre, on the principle 'better late than never'. What little advantage he was going to gain from it! But his industry and tenacity wanted to add the basic principles of music to the bank-balance of his learning. So while he always insisted that he was a poor learner he made himself a rich teacher. (8, 7, ext. 8)

9.4.7 Socrates saw this [the need for relaxation]; he missed no part of wisdom. This is why he did not blush when he was seen by Alcibiades playing with some small children with a stick between his legs. (8, 8 ext. 1)

Cf. **8.2.14**; **9.7.19.**

9.5 The Elder Pliny

Gaius Plinius Secundus (A.D. *23–79*), *a soldier, lawyer, administrator and encyclopedist.*

9.5.1 Tradition says that . . . the renowned philosopher Socrates was always seen with the same expression, never more cheerful or more *distrait.* (7, 19, 79)

Cf. **8.1.11** *n.*

9.5.2 Equally highly considered are the Graces in the propylaeum at Athens. These are the work of Socrates – not the painter, though some people identify them. (36, 4, 32)

One of the few records of Socrates as a sculptor: it is strange that Pliny does not seem to recognise him as the philosopher. Cf. Pausanias 9, 35, 7 (**9.10.3**). *Also* **13.1.28**; **14.1.1.12.**

9.6 Aulus Gellius

C. A.D. *125–165. Roman lawyer, author of an interesting miscellany entitled* Attic Nights.

9.6.1 Xanthippe was married to the philosopher Socrates. Tradition has it that she was pretty gloomy and quarrelsome. Night and day she poured out a flood of bad temper and tantrums. Just like a woman! Alcibiades took a poor view of her impossible behaviour towards her husband and asked Socrates why on earth he didn't throw the shrew out. 'Well,' said Socrates, 'you see, putting up with a woman like that at home is good practice for putting up with arrogance and injustice from others away from home.' (1, 17)

9.6.2 Among hard work freely undertaken and physical exercise designed to strengthen the body for whatever suffering it may have to undergo the story goes that Socrates had one peculiar practice. It is recorded that

Socrates used to stand in a constant attitude all day and all night from early morning till dawn next day, unblinking, immobile, on the exact spot, eyes and face fixed in one direction, meditating, just as if his intellect and spirit had migrated from his body. Favorinus touches the point in his full discussion of the great man's courage and says, 'He often stood from one day to the next, more rigid than a tree-trunk.'

Our records show that he practised such moderation that he lived virtually his whole life without suffering ill-health. In the devastation caused by the plague which ravaged the state of Athens with a fatal affliction towards the beginning of the war with the Peloponnesians, the story goes that he used the practice of moderation to avoid the after-effects of indulgence and maintain his physical well-being. Consequently the general disaster did not touch him. (2, 1)

9.6.3 Phaedo was a slave, but his looks and intelligence were those of a free man. According to some accounts, in his youth his owner, a pander, forced him to prostitution. The story goes that Cebes, an associate of Socrates, bought him at Socrates' request, and opened the door of philosophy to him. Later he became a famous philosopher, and wrote some stylish works about Socrates which are still in circulation. (2, 18)

9.6.4 The Athenians passed a decree providing that any citizen of Megara caught setting foot in Athens should be executed. . . . Euclides came from Megara. Before the decree he was regularly at Athens listening to Socrates. After the promulgation of the decree, when evening fell, under cover of darkness he put on a woman's long dress, wrapped a coloured cloak round him, put a veil on his head and made his way from Megara to Socrates in Athens, to enjoy his words and wisdom for some part of the night. Towards daybreak he returned more than twenty miles in the same clothes. (7, 10)

9.6.5 An additional point: Xenophon in his volume recording the life and words of Socrates says that Socrates never discussed physical science or natural philosophy or touched – or approved of others touching – any of the disciplines which the Greeks classify as 'subjects' unless they were relevant to ethics and the goal of life; he implies that those who attribute discourses of this kind to Socrates are crooks and liars. Those who make the point say, 'Xenophon in writing this is stigmatising Plato; in Plato's works Socrates does discuss physics, the arts and mathematics.' (14, 3)

The reference is to Xenophon, Memoirs of Socrates *1, 1, 11* (**3.2.1**).

9.6.6 . . . the verse of Homer which Socrates claimed as his favourite:

> All good and bad which you have met *at home*. (14, 6)

The reference is Homer, Odyssey *4, 392. Cf.* **1.4**[6]; **12.11.3**.

9.6.7 Euripides turned from physical training to intellectual discipline, and studied with the scientist Anaxagoras and the orator Prodicus, and (for ethics) with Socrates. (15, 20)

9.6.8 At this time Sophocles and later Euripides were prominent as tragic dramatists, Hippocrates in medicine and Democritus in philosophy. Socrates at Athens was a younger contemporary of these. (17, 18)

9.6.9 Socrates used to say that many people wanted to live in order to eat and drink; he preferred to eat and drink in order to live. (19, 2)

Cf. **9.1.1.2** *n.*

9.6.10 Let me cover my head with my cloak, as they say Socrates did when his words were a little risqué. (19, 9)

9.7 Aelian

Claudius Aelianus (c. 170–235) came from Praeneste, taught rhetoric at Rome and went into retirement to write. A fluent and popular writer, who is important for his use of sources from the Hellenistic Age and early Empire.

9.7.1 When the ship returned from *Delus*, and *Socrates* was now to die, *Apollodorus* (a friend of *Socrates*) coming to him in Prison brought him a vest of fine cloth and rich, with a Gown of the same, desiring him that he would put on that Vest and Gown when he was to drink the poison; since he should not fail of handsome Funeral-Robes if he dies in them. 'For it is not unfit that a dead body should be covered with decent ornaments. Thus *Apollodorus* to *Socrates*. But he would not permit it, saying to *Crito, Simmias* and *Phaedo*, "How high an opinion hath *Apollodorus* of us, if he believe that after I have pledged the *Athenians*, and taken the potion, he shall see *Socrates* any more? For if he thinks that he which shall shortly lie at your feet extended on the ground is *Socrates*, it is certain he knows me not."' (*Varia Historia* 1, 16, tr. T. Stanley)

9.7.2 *Socrates* discoursed thus to *Alcibiades*. The young man was much perplexed and abashed, being to appear before a public Assembly. But *Socrates* encouraging and exciting him, Do you not despise (saith he) that Shoe-maker? (naming him). *Alcibiades* assenting: and so likewise (continueth *Socrates*) that publick Crier? and that Tent-maker? [*Alcibiades*] the son of *Cleinias* granting this; And doth not, said *Socrates*, the *Athenian* Commonwealth consist of these? If you condemn theme single, fear them not in an Assembly. Thus [*Socrates*] son of *Sophroniscus* and *Phaenarete* prudently instructed [*Alcibiades*] son of *Cleinias* and *Deinomache*. (2, 1, tr. T. Stanley)

9.7.3 *Anytus* and his Companions studied to do *Socrates* a mischief, for those reasons which are related by many; but feared the *Athenians*, doubting, if they should accuse *Socrates*, how they would take it, his name being in high esteem for many respects, but chiefly for opposing the Sophists, who neither taught nor knew any solid learning. Wherefore they began, by making trial in less things, to sound how the *Athenians* would entertain a Charge against his life: for to have accused him upon the very first, he conceived unsafe as well for the reason already mentioned, as lest the friends and followers of *Socrates* should divert the anger of the Judges upon them, for falsely accusing a person so farre from being guilty of any wrong to the State, that he was the onely Ornament of *Athens*. What, then, do they contrive? They suborn *Aristophanes* a Comick Poet, whose only business was to raise mirth, to bring *Socrates* upon the Stage, taxing him with crimes which most men knew him free from; Impertinent discourse, making an ill cause by argument seem good, introducing new and strange Deities, whilst himself believed and reverenced none: hereby to insinuate an ill opinion of him even into those who most frequented him. *Aristophanes* taking this theme, interweaves it with much abusive mirth and pleasant verses; taking for his subject the best man of the *Grecians*. The argument of his play was not against

Cleon; he did not abuse the *Lacedae-monians*, the *Thebans* or *Pericles* himself; but a person dear to all the Gods, especially to *Apollo*. At first (by reason of the novelty of the thing, the unusual personating of *Socrates* upon the stage) the *Athenians*, who expected nothing less, were struck with wonder. Then (being naturally envious, apt to detract from the best persons, not onely such as bore office in the Commonwealth, but any that were eminent for learning or vertue) they begun to be taken with the *CLOUDS* (so was the Play named) and cried up the Poet with more applause than ever any before, giving him with many shouts the victory, and sending word to the judges to set the name of *Aristophanes* in the highest place. *Socrates* came seldome to the Theatre, unless when *Euripides* the Tragick Poet contested with any new Tragedian, there he used to go. . . . *Socrates* being personated on the Stage, and often named, (nor was it much the Players should represent him, for the Potters frequently did it upon their stone Juggs) the strangers that were present (not knowing whom the Comedy abused) raised a humme and whisper, every one asking who that *Socrates* was. Which he observing (for he came not thither by chance, but because he knew himself should be abused in the Play, had chosen the most conspicuous Seat in the Theatre) to put the strangers out of doubt, he rose up, and all the while the Play lasted continued in that posture. So much did *Socrates* despise the Comedy and the *Athenians* themselves. (2, 13 tr. T. Stanley)

This is a curious farrago, worth printing as a warning about these later anecdotes. Aelian does not realise that nearly a quarter of a century separated The Clouds *from the accusations of Anytus and Meletus. Further, we know from more reliable sources that* The Clouds *was a disastrous flop, not a resounding success. It is, I suppose, just possible that Anytus sponsored a re-*vival *as part of his campaign; more likely that there is a faulty deduction from a careless reading of Plato's* Apology. *The story of Socrates standing up in the theatre could be grounded in fact.*

9.7.4 It is observed, that on the sixth day of the month *Thargelion* many good fortunes have befallen not onely the *Athenians* but divers others. *Socrates* was born on this day . . . . (2, 25, tr. T. Stanley)

A date in May. Cf. **9.1.1.26**.

9.7.5 *Plato* . . . betook himself to writing Tragedies, composing a Tetralogy; which Poems he gave to the Players, intending to contest at the Games. But before the *Bacchanalian* Feast he heard *Socrates* discourse, and was so much taken with that Siren, that he not onely forbore his design of contending, but from thence forward wholly gave off writing Tragedies, and addicted himself to Philosophy. (2, 30, tr. T. Stanley)

'Bacchanalian Feast', i.e. Festival of Dionysus. 'That Siren': rather 'his Siren'.

9.7.6 *Socrates* being very old fell sick; and one asking him how he did, 'Well, said he, both waies: for if I live longer, I shall have more Emulators; if I die, more Praisers.' (2, 36, tr. T. Stanley)

9.7.7 There were most excellent persons among the *Grecians* who lived in extreme poverty. . . . *Socrates* son of *Sophroniscus* . . . (2, 43, tr. T. Stanley)

9.7.8 *Socrates* would not meddle with the *Athenian* State, because the Democracy of the *Athenians* did at that time more resemble a Thyrannical and Monarchick Government. Neither would he joyn in sentencing the ten Commanders to death, nor partake of the injustices committed by the thirty Tyrants. But when occasion called him forth, he was a Souldier. He fought at *Delium*, and at *Amphipolis* and *Potidaea*. (3, 17, tr. T. Stanley)

9.7.9 This also I have had, but whether it be true or not I know not: They say that *Plato* son of *Aristo* was driven by Poverty to betake himself to the Warres; but intercepted by *Socrates*, while he was buying his Arms, and instructed in that which concerns mankind, he through his persuasion addicted himself to Philosophy. (3, 27, tr. T. Stanley)
  Highly implausible! Not recorded elsewhere.

9.7.10 *Socrates* perceiving *Alcibiades* to be exceeding proud of his riches and lands, he shewed him a Map of the World, and bid him find *Attica* therein; which done, he desired that he would shew him his own lands. He answered, 'They were not there.' – 'Do you boast,' replies *Socrates*, 'of that which you see is no (considerable) part of the Earth?' (3, 28, tr. T. Stanley)

9.7.11 *Diogenes* said that *Socrates* himself was luxurious: for he was too curious in [concerned about] his little House, and in his little Bed, and in the Sandals which he used to wear. (4, 11, tr. T. Stanley)

9.7.12 *Alcibiades* was beloved of *Socrates*, *Dio* of *Plato*. But *Dio* received advantage by the love of his friend. (4, 21, tr. T. Stanley)

9.7.13 *Xanthippe*, wife of *Socrates*, refusing to put on his Vest [cloak], so to goe to a publick Spectacle, he said, 'Do you not perceive that you are not to see, but rather to be seen?' (7, 10, tr. T. Stanley)

9.7.14 *Socrates* said of his Daemon to *Theages*, *Demodocus*, and many others, that he many times perceived a voice warning him by Divine instinct, which saith he, when it comes, signifieth a dissuasion from that which I am going

to doe, but never persuades me to doe any thing. And when any of my friends (saith he) impart their business to me, if this voice happens, it dissuades also, giving me the like counsel: Whereupon I dehort him who adviseth with me, and suffer him not to proceed in what he was about, following the Divine admonition. He alledged as witness hereof *Charmides* son of Glaucon, who asking his advice, whether he should exercise at the *Nemean* Games; as soon as he began to speak, the voice gave the accustomed sigh. Whereupon *Socrates* endeavoured to divert *Charmides* from this purpose, telling him the reason: But he not following the advice, it succeeded ill with him. (8, 1, tr. T. Stanley)
  ('*Sigh*': sic, *but surely it should be* '*sign*'. *The account of the effect of the sign is drawn from* Theages (**2.8.2**).

9.7.15 *Xanthippe* used to say, that when the State was oppressed with a thousand miseries, yet *Socrates* alwaies went abroad and came home with the same look. For he bore a mind smooth and chearful upon all occasions, farre remote from Grief, and above all Fear. (9, 7, tr. T. Stanley)
  Cf. **8.1.11** *n.*

9.7.16 *Socrates* coming home one night from a Feast, some wilde young men knowing of his return, lay in wait for him, attired like Furies, with Vizardes and Torches, whereby they used to fright such as they met. *Socrates* as soon as he saw them, nothing troubled, made a stand, and fell to question them, as he used to doe to others, in the *Lyceum* or *Academy*.
  Alcibiades ambitiously munificent, sent many Presents to *Socrates*. *Xanthippe* admiring their value, desired him to accept them. 'We (answered *Socrates*) will contest in liberality with *Alcibiades*, not accepting by a kind of munificence what he hath sent us.'
  Also when one said to him 'It is a

great thing to enjoy what we desire.' He answeres, 'But a greater not to desire at all.' (9, 28, tr. T. Stanley)

The first story does not seem to be elsewhere recorded. The last is told of Menedemus.

9.7.17 *Socrates* seeing that *Antisthenes* alwaies exposed to view the torn part of his Cloak 'Will you not (saith he) lay aside Ostentation amongst us?' (9, 35, tr. T. Stanley)

Cf. **1.12.2.**

9.7.18 *Alcibiades* sent to *Socrates* a large Marchpane fairly wrought. *Xanthippe* angry hereat, after her manner, threw it out of the Basket, and trod upon it: whereat *Socrates* laughing said 'And you then will have no share in it your self.' (11, 12, tr. T. Stanley)

Marchpane: the same as marzipan, a kind of cake. Cf. **8.4.11**; **9.2.14.**

9.7.19 *Socrates* was on a time surprised by *Alcibiades* playing with *Lamprocles*, as yet a Child. (12, 15, tr. T. Stanley)

A sudden insight into Greek life: fathers were not expected to play with children. Cf. **8.2.14**; **9.4.7.**

9.7.20 *Xenophon* relates that *Socrates* disputed with Theodota a Curtizan, a Woman of extraordinary beauty. He also argued with *Calisto*, who said, 'I (o Son of Sophroniscus) exccel you, for you cannot draw away any of my followers, but I can whensoever I please draw away all yours. He answered, 'Very likely, for you draw them down a precipice, but I drive them to vertue, which is a steep and difficult ascent.' (13, 32, tr. T. Stanley)

9.7.21 It is a saying that the Discourses of *Socrates* are like the Pictures of *Pauson*. for *Pauson* the Painter being desired to make the Picture of a Horse tumbling on its back, drew him running. And when he who had bespoke the Picture, was angry that he had not drawn it according to his directions, the Painter said, 'Turn it the other way, and the Horse which now runneth, will then roll upon his back.' So *Socrates* did not discourse downright, but if his discourses were turned, they appeared very right. For he was unwilling to gain the hatred of those to whom he discoursed, and for that reason delivered things enigmatically and obliquely. (14, 15, tr. T. Stanley)

9.8 Fronto

M. Cornelius Fronto came from Africa; he was the leading orator in Latin of the second century A.D. *and the chief figure in the introduction of the new style called* elocutio novella, *an elaborate, hot-house rhetoric, which may have owed something to Africa and certainly revived the old 'Asianic' style. Fronto was tutor to Marcus Aurelius, and some of his correspondence is preserved.*

What do you think of that prince of wisdom and eloquence, Socrates? I've subpoenaed him as chief witness before you. Did he use a style of oratory completely free from slant and completely open? How did he trip and trap Protagoras, Polus, Thrasymachus and the other sophists? When did he show his hand? When did he fail to set ambushes? Who do you think was father of that inverted language which the Greeks called 'irony'? What was his method of approach to Alcibiades and the other young men who were aggressively aristocratic, rich, or handsome? Quarrelsome or cultivated? Bitter reprobation of their faults or gentle persuasion? Yet Socrates had all the weight and force that Diogenes the Cynic showed in his ferocity. But he made a point of realising that the characters of human beings, and young men in particular, are more easily won by courteous conversation than overwhelmed by sharp and angry words. He did not try to storm the young man's errors by battering-rams and siege-engines but to undermine them by sapping. When his audience left him they might have been teased but they were not torn limb from limb. (*Letters to Marcus* 3, 15, 2)

Written in A.D. *143.*

9.9 Strabo

C. *63* B.C.–A.D. *25. Historian and geographer.*

9.9.1 At Delium the Athenians were worsted in battle and fleeing pell-mell. In the rout Xenophon, Gryllus' son, fell from his horse. Socrates the philosopher was fighting in the infantry. He saw him lying there. His horse was gone. Socrates took Xenophon on his shoulders and carried him some miles to safety till the rout came to an end. (9, 403)

9.9.2 Pythagoras warned people to give up meat. So did Socrates and Diogenes. (15, 716)

9.10 Pausanias

Greek traveller and geographer of the second century A.D.; *T. R. Glover in a charming essay styled him 'Prince of Digressors'.*

9.10.1 At the very entrance to the acropolis stands a Hermes called 'Hermes of the Propylaea', and tradition has it that Sophroniscus' son Socrates sculpted the Graces – the man whom the Delphic oracle declared to be the wisest of humans. . . . (1, 22, 8)

9.10.2 Socrates, on the night before Plato was to come and join him as a student, had a dream of a swan flying into his lap. (1, 30, 3)

Cf. **1.11.1**; **12.6.4.**

9.10.3 Socrates, son of Sophroniscus, made statues of Graces for the Athenians for the entrance to the acropolis. These are all alike clothed. Later sculptors for some reason or other have changed the method of portrayal. My contemporaries, whether in painting or sculpture, represent the Graces as naked. (9, 35, 7)

Cf. Pliny the Elder 36, 432 (**9.5.2**).

9.11 Aelius Aristides

C. A.D. *129–89. A Greek orator who shared in the revival of the style of the great period of Athenian oratory: he wrote eloquently of Athens and of Rome: a chronic invalid, he showed notable attachment to the healing god Asclepius. He was critical towards the philosophers.*

9.11.1 Rhetoric: *mainly based on Plato, but with some knowledge of Aeschines too.*

9.11.1.1 There is a false report of some who hold that these writings are actually by Socrates. Unless it is right to swallow all they say, as I would be the first to deny, yet their error is not utterly irrational: these works were adjudged so characteristic of Socrates that there is in fact room for that view. But I think that even if we have no actual words of Socrates preserved in writing, he remains a witness no less strong than Plato in his grandeur and Aeschines in his subtlety, a finer one in fact, and genuinely open to all. It is unanimously agreed that he claimed to know nothing: all his associates say so. It is also agreed that the Delphic oracle declared that Socrates was the wisest man in the world. How is that? It would be blasphemous to suggest that the god attributed full wisdom to a man in complete error. He said, it seems, that he was not interested in science, and that is correct: he clearly had no respect for the work of his teacher Anaxagoras. Socrates attests one fact: there is no shame in the lack of scientific skill, since he has no sense of shame in what he says about himself. Another point follows. Everyone agrees that Socrates said that a divine spirit gave him guidance. It is impossible for anyone guided by a divine spirit to be ignorant where knowledge is essential. Yet he asserted his ignorance and was not wrong in doing so – if the god was not wrong either in declaring him the wisest man in the world. It remains to ask what is this assertion of ignorance. It is an assertion of scientific ignorance, I fancy. And yet if he were the wisest man in the world on neither count, neither speaking falsely about himself (which would be a matter for shame) nor telling the truth, if the absence of scientific knowledge were among supremely shameful traits, Socrates attests the statement on both grounds, in his denial and his admission, and through Socrates the god bears witness on both counts, proclaiming him the wisest man in the world, strengthening Socrates' double evidence with his own decisive statement. (*Rhetoric* 22)

Parts of the argument are somewhat obscure.

9.11.1.2 And yet a person could say of Archelaus that he invited Socrates rather than any of the politicians to join him. (ibid. 56)

9.11.1.3 Think of Socrates in action at Potidaea, or retreating in the general rout at Delium. It was clear to everyone, even from a considerable distance, that anyone who laid a finger on him would meet a desperate resistance. His witness is equally clear that those who practise injustice are not to be trusted. (ibid. 71)

9.11.1.4 There is a problem which concerns me. Alcibiades and Critias were associates of Socrates. They were utterly condemned alike by the commons and by men of moderate and sound judgement; in fact, it is not easy to think of a more damnable villain than Critias, leader of the Thirty, the most despicable dictatorship Greece knew. How can we defend the fact that they claim it wrong to adduce these men as evidence that Socrates used to corrupt the youth; they claim that their offences do not touch Socrates (who never denied conversing with the young men). (ibid. 83)

9.11.2 In Defence of the Four. *The Four are Miltiades, Themistocles, Pericles, Cimon, and the reference is to Plato's Gorgias. There are many other references besides those below; nearly all are based on Plato.*

9.11.2.1 I fancy that Pericles gained more from his association with Anaxagoras than Plato suggests, whereas Alcibiades gained little or nothing from his association with Socrates. (124) *Cf. 247.*

9.11.2.2 I should not say that Socrates either turned the Athenians into contentious interminable talkers. (134)

9.11.2.3 Socrates was not expert in astronomy either, and that although he is recorded as an associate of Anaxagoras. For all that, he was not Anaxagoras' inferior. (176)

9.11.2.4 Socrates fought at Delium, at Amphipolis and at Potidaea. You applaud his courage in the retreat from Delium: it is clear that if anyone had laid a finger on him he would have met a spirited resistance. (198)

9.11.2.5 Socrates and Pythagoras did not write out the actual discourses in which they spent their lives. (298)

9.11.2.6 Did not Androtion speak of the seven sophists (meaning the Sages) – and again call Socrates a sophist? (311)
Androtion: an Athenian statesman of the fourth century B.C. *Cf.* **5.3.**

9.11.3 On Qualifying Statements
Consider another defence of a man of wisdom who was so far from boastfulness that he went round showing up the sophists for their self-assertiveness. He threatens the Athenians, saying that if they kill him they will be hard put to replace him. He refers this to the authority of the god at Delphi. He says, 'I believe you have never had a greater blessing in the State than my service of the god.' I quote approximately from *The Defence of Socrates.* And yet, you may say, that is why he was arrested. His supporters would answer that those who condemned him repented later. *Socrates never spoke those words.* Let that be. If he didn't but another of equal authority attributed them appropriately to him it comes to the same thing. I assert that Socrates shows his arrogance in his life, even if most people failed to realise it. What do you think of his colossal mock-modesty? I think that he was treating the ordinary citizens like children, playing with them, treating them as simpletons. But if he never took

himself seriously, and thought of himself as worthless, yet used this language, it might be supposed that the only possibility was that he was treating them as unworthy of his company.

9.11.4 On Rhetorical Technique. *The two treatises on rhetorical technique, which are of doubtful authenticity, contain several references to Socrates, most of which are taken straight from Xenophon. Even if they are not by Aelius Aristides, they belong to the same period.*

9.11.4.1 It is an excellent Socratic practice to lead people from an open position to an assured conclusion. (47)

9.11.4.2 The method of self-depreciation produces results, as with Socrates conversing with the youth and educating them as if he did not know himself but was rather investigating. (48)

9.11.4.3 It was characteristic of Socrates to use examples. (79)

9.12 Quintilian

M. Fabius Quintilianus, the greatest educationalist of ancient Rome, was active in the second half of the first century A.D.*; he was one of those immigrants from Spain who so deeply affected Roman culture at this period. His great work* The Education of the Orator *is a storehouse of good sense and wide learning: his quotations and comments must always be seen in relation to his theme.*

9.12.1 Why need I speak of the philosophers when Socrates, their fountain-head, was not ashamed to learn the lyre even in old age? (1, 10, 13)

9.12.2 The principle of gesture ... was approved by the outstanding leaders of Greece including Socrates. (1, 11, 17)

9.12.3 All these views appear in the book *Gorgias* in the mouth of Socrates, who seems to be a mask for Plato's own views. (2, 15, 26)

9.12.4 Even Socrates is taunted by the comic dramatists with making the worse cause appear the better. (2, 16, 3)

9.12.5 More than one charge may be combined, as when Socrates was accused of corrupting the young and of introducing new superstitions. (4, 4, 5)

9.12.6 Socrates usually used this method of procedure. He asked a number of questions to which his opponent had to say Yes; he then inferred a conclusion about the subject under discussion by analogy with the points granted. This is induction. (5, 11, 3)

9.12.7 Some include under this head divine authority derived from oracular responses, e.g. 'Socrates is the wisest man in the world.' (5, 11, 42)

9.12.8 A man's whole life may seem an embodiment of 'irony', as with Socrates. He was called 'ironical' because he played the part of an ignoramus who revered others as sages. (9, 2, 46)

9.12.9 Everyone knows that nothing would have contributed more to Socrates' acquittal than if he had used familiar forensic defence advocacy, conciliated the minds of the jury by speaking with humility and been at pains to rebuke the actual charge. But it would not have been like him. So he made his defence like a man who was going to reckon his sentence a supreme honour. The wisest man in the world preferred to lose his future rather than

his past. His own generation failed to understand him. He kept himself for the verdict of posterity. He gave up the short period of old age remaining to him for an immortality of fame. Lysias, the outstanding advocate of the day, offered him the manuscript of a defence plea. He refused: it was good, but not 'him'. This is enough to show that the aim the orator must hold in view is speaking well, not winning his case; sometimes one can only win dishonourably. What Socrates did could not touch his acquittal. More important – it touched his humanity. (11, 1, 9)

9.13 Josephus

Josephus was born in A.D. 37; he took part in the Jewish revolt of A.D. 66, and was subsequently accused both of inciting the rebellion and of betraying it. He was captured by the Romans at Jotapata, and later honoured by them, and spent the rest of his life in writing about his people: the work Against Apion *is an answer to criticism of his* Antiquities *and a general defence of Judaism. He died about A.D. 100.*

On what grounds was Socrates executed? He never betrayed his country to the enemy. He never robbed a temple. He was accused of swearing strange oaths and of claiming, as a joke of course, in some views, that some sort of spirit instructed him; on these grounds he was condemned to death and executed by a draught of hemlock. Another charge of the prosecutor was that he corrupted the young by encouraging them to disregard their national laws and constitution. So Socrates, citizen of Athens as he was, met this penalty. (*Against Apion* 2, 263)

9.14 Philo

C. *30 B.C.–A.D. 45, an Alexandrian Jew who blended Judaism with Greek philosophy.*

9.14.1 The story runs that someone in a former generation saw an opulently ornate procession, turned aside to some of his students and said, 'Friends, see how many things I can do without.' (*The Immutability of God* 31, 146)

See **1.4**[25]; **8.1.16**; also Philo, Noah as Planter *16, 65*.

9.14.2 The Hebrews call this approach Terah, the Greeks Socrates. They say that Socrates grew old in the meticulous consideration of 'know yourself', and never practised philosophy on anything that was not concerned with himself. But he was a human being. Terah is the actual way of self-knowledge, standing before us like a spreading tree. . . . (*Dreams* 1, 58)

9.15 Synesius

C. *A.D. 370–414. He came from Cyrene, was educated in Alexandria and interested in Neo-Platonism. His writings are miscellaneous. In Praise of Baldness is satirical. Later he became a Christian and a bishop, but his writings date from before his conversion.*

Aristoxenus says the same about Socrates: he was naturally irascible, and when he succumbed to the emotion he would walk about in an absolutely disgraceful state. Socrates wasn't even bald at the time, being only twenty-five when Parmenides and Zeno came to Athens, as Plato says, to view the Panathenaea. But if anyone later talked about Socrates as difficult – or as with a fine head of hair – I should think he owed a debt of laughter to those who really know. (*In Praise of Baldness* 17)

9.16 Philostratus

C. *A.D. 170–245. Philostratus was a courtier of Julia Domna, who wrote at her instance a fictional biography of a first-century shaman, Apollonius of Tyana, as a counterblast to the magnetism exercised by Jesus over a growing section of the Roman world.*

'Apollonius to Musonius the philosopher: greetings. Socrates the Athenian did not want to be rescued by his friends. He presented himself in court and was executed. Best wishes.'

'Musonius to Apollonius the philosopher: greetings. Socrates was executed because he was not prepared to defend himself. I propose to defend myself. Best wishes.' (*Life of Apollonius of Tyana* 4, 46)

*Musonius was a well-known Stoic of the first century A.D. There was evidently a tradition later that Socrates did not defend himself (***7.2.1***). It could be that all the Defences are fictitious.*

9.17 Petronius

Gaius Petronius, arbiter of elegance in Nero's court, as Tacitus styles him, wrote a racy, bawdy novel called The Satyricon, *ancestor of the work of Fielding, Smollett and Sterne, and a few poems. He committed suicide in* A.D. *66.*

9.17.1 So I'm grateful for your love. Very Socratic. Alcibiades never lay so virginally in his professor's bed. (*Satyricon* 128)

    Cf. **2.5.2.2.**

9.17.2 Socrates, friend of all the gods and all mankind, used to pride himself that he had never glanced into a public house, never trusted his eyes with a gathering larger than usual. There's nothing handier than always having wisdom to talk to. (ibid. 140)

    Very odd. The word for 'friend' is missing in the Latin.

9.18 Demetrius

The author of a treatise On Style, *of uncertain date, but probably in the first century of the Empire.*

What has been called the peculiar Socratic pattern, which Aeschines and Plato seem particularly to emulate, changes the stated subject to a question. For example, 'My boy, how much property did your father leave? A large amount? Not easily to be estimated?' 'A large amount, Socrates.' 'And did he leave you the knowledge to use it?' At the same moment he has brought the boy imperceptibly to resourcelessness, reminded him of his ignorance and given him the impulse to seek education. (*On Style* 217)

9.19 Theon

Aelius Theon lived in Alexandria in the second century A.D. *and wrote a popular handbook of rhetorical exercises.*

9.19.1 The best examples of characterisation will be found in Homer's poetry, the dialogues of Plato and the other writers about Socrates, and the plays of Menander. (*Rhetorical Exercises* 164)

9.19.2 Socrates, being asked if he thought the king of Persia happy, replied, 'I can't answer; I don't even know the state of his education.' (ibid. 204)

9.19.3 Apollodorus, a man of some prominence, said to the philosopher Socrates, 'The Athenians are executing you unjustly.' Socrates' reply was syllogistic. He laughed and said, 'Would you rather they executed me justly?' (ibid. 208)

    Cf. **8.12.2.**

9.19.4 It is especially commendable to achieve greatness from humble beginnings: Socrates, for example, the son of Phaenarete the midwife and Sophroniscus the sculptor. (ibid. 230)

9.20 Eustathius

His name is uncertain: it may be Eumathius. His home-town is ambiguous: it may be Constantinople, or Parembole in Egypt. His date is unknown: it could be as late as the twelfth century A.D. *He seems to have held* a responsible post as keeper of the archives. He has left us a rather dull love-story.

They are all round me. It's magnificent the way they dance attendance on me – just as Socrates was surrounded by his disciples. (*Hysmine and Hysminias* 1, 3, 2)

9.21 Polemo

A Greek writer on physiognomy whose work is preserved in Latin and Arabic.

If you see a watery eye, which is neither deep-set nor protruding, but which is shining and brilliant, give it your approval. You may be sure that it signifies intelligence, a capacity to learn, an enthusiasm for company and for humane studies. I have been told that Socrates the philosopher's eye was of this kind, and Apollo said that Socrates' knowledge surpassed all others; he would not have been killed if men had not seen and envied his immense knowledge. (13)

9.22 Plautus

T. Maccius Plautus, c. 250–184 B.C., greatest of Roman comic dramatists; he drew extensively on Greek models.

He'll knock you into a cocked hat with
    words, till you think
it's Socrates not Pseudolus talking to you.
                (*Pseudolus* 464)

9.23 Victorinus

Fourth century A.D. *Commentator on Cicero.*
Aeschines was a Socratic, i.e. a pupil of Socrates. He wrote a great deal. It was the practice of pupils to attribute their own discoveries to their teachers as if they were their teachers' views. (On Cicero's *Rhetoric* 1, 31, Halm, *Rhetores Latini Minores* 240)

For Aeschines, see **8.23.**

PART TEN

LIBANIUS

Libanius was born in Antioch in A.D. 314, went to university in Athens and enjoyed a brilliant success as professor of rhetoric at Constantinople, Nicomedeia and Antioch. He was a vigorous champion of paganism and supported the Emperor Julian's revival. He was evidently a man of real commitment, a magnetic teacher and a real professional in his field; at the same time touchy and opinionated. We last hear of him in A.D. 392.

10.1 On the Silence of Socrates

[1] It is difficult in your presence to say anything, even of what's wholly just, in behalf of Socrates, for you have condemned him out of prejudice and have believed the original slanderous attacks made on him. Nevertheless, since the informers have gone to extremes and have treated unjustly not only Socrates but also a law which applies to all unlucky men, it is necessary to say this much to you, that although many men were condemned by you in the past and were executed unjustly or justly, none died in silence.

[2] You ordered Socrates to die and he obeys quite meekly, but these men have imposed on him a second penalty, namely to keep silent before his death and to converse with no one, thus killing him even before the hemlock does. Now this is easy for Socrates, for just as he can speak, so he can be quiet; but you must beware lest you be blamed by gods and men for taking away from Socrates a good shared by all who are still alive and depriving him at once of his body and, before that, of his voice.

[3] I am one of those who go to Socrates regularly for instruction and listen to him. For indeed it is wonderful how he philosophizes in prison and dies joyfully; and I stood up to oppose the man who spoke this harsh judgement, believing that it would be not his loss but ours if we were not to have some small benefit from the last days of Socrates.

[4] In truth, contrary to all that is just, Socrates has been falsely accused and has been pressed with charges which are untrue and most unworthy of his philosophy. He will die who was the most godfearing of all men, of all men the most helpful to the young, who was always obedient to the laws of the city both as a citizen and as a soldier, but opposed himself to the tyrants and the oligarchies, who alone did not require the payment of fees from those who came to him for instruction, who to the best of his ability not only was master of his own evil inclinations but also made many others into good men, and has caused his city to be renowned and to be admired by Greece, both through the visitors who gather around him and through his words, which issue forth from him in all directions.

[5] Indeed, I believe that time and the gods will show that Socrates is such a man and has been falsely accused, and that the jury brought in its verdict sooner than was right; and I pray that this will happen without divine retribution and without public harm to the city. And this I know well, that those who judged Socrates would have repented of their decision if they had been afforded the opportunity of pronouncing a second time, just as you once did regarding Mytilene.

[6] But after those prevailed who bore Socrates ill-will because he might yet refute their arguments, you heard him discussing philosophy even in court; for he did not weep nor beg nor devise an escape, a shameful thing and unworthy of philosophy; but he obeyed the god who has led him to this end, and he happily followed the Eleven and went to prison as joyfully as he would the Lyceum, the Academy, the Ilissus or his other resorts; and there he was ready to engage in conversation. Could it be otherwise with a man who still lived and breathed? And eagerly he joined with his friends in the pursuit of wisdom, for he is Socrates; and though he was imprisoned he was not dismayed by mere physical misfortune, and his conversation was so godly and beautiful that if you had all heard it you would undoubtedly have released him.

[7] Socrates is to be congratulated

that, with death standing beside him, he rejoices and ungrudgingly talks and discusses philosophy with those who listen to him and are able to gain some profit to serve them throughout their lives. But Anytus and Meletus were harsher even than the jailer. He has allowed Socrates visitors, but they have rendered his time of grace useless to us and have contrived these new bonds for him; not only are Socrates' hands and feet bound before his death, but also his tongue.

[8] O what malice! What stupidity! What ignorant wickedness! Shall Socrates not speak, Apollo, even though he is still alive and possesses the faculty of speech? But this present day Solon is writing a statute 'against a man', a thing expressly and distinctly forbidden by the laws – 'Nor to write a law or statute against a man, unless it apply in common to all Athenians.'

[9] 'He is wicked and has been condemned.' Granted 'he is wicked'. Let no word of the indictment or of the clamoring of Anytus and Meletus be disbelieved. I know well that there will be a time in which you will revere Socrates, as the Ephesians do Heraclitus, and the Samians Pythagoras, and the Lacedaemonians Chilon, and the Milesians Thales, and the Lesbians Pittacus, and the Corinthians Periander, and you yourselves once Solon. For while they are alive, wise men are opposed by the ill-will of those near them; but, when they have died, their wisdom is judged solely from impressions formed without prejudice.

[10] Very well, then, let the decision which has been reached stand. In that case it is fitting that judgement be given in accordance with the decision of the court. It was decided that Socrates should drink hemlock just like any of the others who had been condemned before him. Socrates does not refuse to do this nor would he at any time flee the penalty you have imposed upon him, nor leave the city even if, among his friends, some wish to carry him off to Boeotia, others to the Peloponnesus, and others to Thessaly, and all the cities of Greece call him; nor would he permit a stolen deliverance. Quite the reverse; somehow or other he desires his death more than you do, and he thirsts after the hemlock.

[11] Is it not illegal and reprehensible after the verdict to pass in a decree an additional sentence, which was not passed by the jury and is not specified in the laws dealing with the condemned? It is not necessary for everyone to bestow on the condemned more kindness than is required by law, nor, on the other hand, to be harsher than is customary. For each of these things, both to inflict additional penalties on the condemned and to take away what is suitable to those in such a situation, is against the law. Moreover, the court herald did not announce that the Eleven were to take charge of Socrates and order him to be quiet until his death, and not to speak, but only to die.

[12] And you, accusers of Socrates, when you determined upon the penalty of death for him, did not add also that of silence. For in that case there would be two penalties. Furthermore, that additional penalty which you did not impose at the very height of the jury's rage of delusion, you now devise in excess of all previous laws.

[13] Now if Socrates is guilty of some newer crime and you are bringing charges against him after the verdict of the jury, over and above what was previously noted in the indictment, tell us so; explain. If your complaint is that he talks and chats, who in the world was ever punished for that? Was silence ever one of the prohibitions imposed on a condemned man? Who was brought before the people for talking?

Did anyone of those condemned to die at Athens ever have his tongue cut off? You are making us Thracians instead of Athenians and instead of Greeks, barbarians.

[14] Once Miltiades also was imprisoned among you; but though imprisoned he was not silent. Once you condemned nine generals who were innocent against the will of Socrates and without his participating in that lawless action (on the contrary he thought that the law was more important than anger). You condemned them, but you did not order even them to be silent.

[15] This is indeed a sorry situation: murderers and robbers of temples and traitors and men who have dared to commit the greatest crimes pay the penalty, but are ordered by no one to be silent and not to converse. Some give solemn instructions to those dearest to them, some converse with their immediate family, some with friends and relatives, some call upon the gods, some bemoan their fate; but in this one case alone out of all history will it occur that a man condemned to die, but most worthy of talking, was ordered not to talk.

[16] Critias alone, when he was one of the tyrants, gave Socrates orders to refrain from conversation; Critias, who, proving to be an unsatisfactory pupil, condemned Socrates. And so the democracy has become an imitator of the tyranny and in making this judgment Athenians are enacting laws equal to the edicts of the tyrants.

[17] And yet Critias forbade Socrates conversation only with young men, but not altogether, so long as he avoided analogies involving shepherds and herdsmen, being angry with the Socratic analogy that it was the part of bad shepherds to reduce the flock, a statement which Socrates really did make in denunciation of the tyrants. But you refuse Socrates all conversation, either with the jailer or with Xanthippe or with his little children. But if Lamprocles or Sophroniscus asks his father a question, will Socrates make no answer, but only await the hemlock with a bit in his mouth, deprived of the common freedom of all men, even the unlucky and the wicked?

[18] Man is by nature a talkative creature, and the people of Athens are especially talkative and in love with talk. And when death is near they are gripped by a certain garrulousness and a desire to say and hear many things, since in a short time their powers to do so will be at an end. For it is no reproach to say as much as you like when soon you will keep a long silence.

[19] 'Let Socrates await the hemlock in silence,' he says, 'for Theramenes also died in silence.' But before he died Theramenes said many things at the council hearth. And when some 1500 men drank the hemlock under the oligarchy, not one of whom died because of Socrates, he was ordered to go to Leon the Salaminian; but he would not obey nor bring the man to the tyrants to be executed. Although those who perished at that time were so many, none is said to have drunk the potion in silence. Not a man was ordered to keep back a single word or protest before his death, not by Dracontides, or Pison, or Charicles, or any of the others.

[20] But you are giving Socrates here an order much crueller than the actions of the harshest tyranny. Men must cry out when they are under the surgeon's knife, and in prison a man will weep. But shall he, who will soon lose his very life, die without echoing a single word to a single person and will he be even before his death a lifeless corpse? You are causing Socrates to die many times.

[21] The philosophers say that ghosts have voices and that this property is

left even to shades, and Homer too seems to indicate this. For when he describes the appearance of the shade of Patroclus, he says that it is altogether the same as before both in body and in voice. But you are cutting the voice out of Socrates while he is still alive. All other men are unusually talkative in time of misfortune. It is said that the son of Croesus the Lydian, though dumb before, broke into speech at a time of danger for his father. Shall Socrates alone in his present circumstance neither weep nor call upon the gods?

[22] Now this is not Socratic behavior. Even he should be guaranteed his common rights. But everyone else who is in prison talks and chats, and each, when he is near death, even if he is an unschooled layman, philosophizes on the subject of death itself. Shall not Socrates then be allowed to end his life and his philosophy together?

[23] 'He says things which are neither meet nor just.' This is their contention. Is it not indeed for this reason that he is to be put to death? Since you have no further charge to add to the one on which he was convicted, do not inflict on him a penalty greater than what was prescribed. 'But he corrupts the young.' But what young boy has entered the prison? Apollodorus and Crito and Phaedo and Simmias and Cebes, Hermogenes, old men, are the disciples of Socrates. If Socrates' conversation is evil and harmful, surely these men were corrupted long ago. But if it is good and profitable, it is not just at this time to deprive them of it.

[24] Therefore leave him alone and do not stand in his way. Is it not disgraceful that Gorgias and Protagoras speak and Polus and Prodicus the quack, and Hippias, sophists, wordpeddlers, and that Greeks pay money to listen to them publicly and privately, men who are Eleans and Ceans and Abderites and Leontines, but that the Athenian Socrates must even before his death remain silent?

[25] You will have your fill of silence from Socrates, you slanderers. Not only will the Lyceum be dumb but also the Academy, and the wrestling grounds will be mute. Rudeness and silence will choke the conversations of the noble. Not in the gymnasiums will Socrates speak, not in the colonnades, not in the Royal Stoa will he converse with people, not in the Painted Hall, not at the money-changers' tables, not in the courts, not in the house of Agathon, not in the house of Callias, not in the house of Damon, not in the city, not in the Piraeus, not by the Ilissus under the beautiful plane tree, but there the cicades will sing, not at Potidaea, not at Delium, not on justice with Thrasymachus, not on moderation with Charmides, not on courage with Laches, not on brotherly love with Chaerephon, not on virtue with Meno, not on the beautiful with Hippias, not on rhetoric with Gorgias, not with Protagoras on the practice of virtue, not on piety with Euthyphro, not with Xenophon on not kissing the beautiful boy. You will have your fill of the absence of Socrates. He will keep a long silence for you.

[26] Now, while he is still with us, give him these one or two days to talk. Now especially is the wisdom of Socrates put to the test, if in bonds he is not pained and though about to die he does not wail, and philosophizes with death upon him. Let him speak though he be in bonds. I praised Xenophon too, because, when imprisoned in Thebes, he did not neglect the discourses of Prodicus but posted bail and went to hear him. Do you think that the pupil should be a better philosopher than the teacher, and do you force Socrates to be silent when he will cease so soon? Why do you make him resemble a man in grief? Surely, let him

speak before the end, since he is all the nearer to the truth.

[27] Let him now discuss philosophy. I also ask you to let him make a prophecy. Swans sing before their death and let go their lives in song, and musical is the death of a musical bird. Allow to sing both the Attic nightingale and the swan. Socrates is a fellow slave along with them and he is blessed of Apollo. Once you announced, O Pythian One, 'Of all men Socrates is wisest.' But the wisest of men is now ordered to die as a wise man should not.

[28] At times in the past also there were unjust judgments. Once it was unjustly decided that Palamedes, the wisest of the Greeks of his time, should be put to death; for there were also at Ilium certain Anytuses and Meletuses. He, however, was not ordered to be silent before his death, but was permitted both to speak and to write, and writing his fate on an oarblade he sent to his father, Nauplius, a letter bearing the news of his death.

[29] Socrates, however, does not write one malicious or bitter thing, nor does he bear the jury a grudge, but he dies rejoicing and goes away obediently to the gods. Just as he was when speaking during his life, so is he now in conversation. Do not be surprised. This is the nature of wise men. Their wisdom does not leave them, not even in times of bad fortune.

[30] Music did not leave Orpheus after his death. The Thracian women tore him to pieces, just as the false accusers have Socrates. But though torn apart he still sang. The head of Orpheus went down the river Strymon singing its songs. A Phrygian fluteplayer Marsyas, who had been punished, wished to exchange his gifts and could not do this. But he heard another man playing and came to life again at the song. So it is with Socrates also.

[31] Now do not hate nor mistrust philosophy. Can it be that you fear he will pray to the gods against you if he converses? But when he was speaking he did no such thing. Besides, a man could do this even in silence. Do you shrink from bringing him the hemlock when he is engaged in conversation? But when he is silent he is not Socrates. Allow him to speak as at a banquet. Let him drink a health to the deity.

[32] Just now when he was seen to be joyous and glad in his misfortune, and said what he said, I was certain that Socrates' accusers had been refuted. What did he say that caused you to order him to be silent? What attack did he make on the government, the laws, the civil authorities or the traditions handed down by our ancestors? Now as always he philosophizes most piously on behalf of the laws, and he says that he will never flee these his masters or be a metic among Megarians or Boeotians or a guest of Peloponnesians or Thessalians, but that he will remain here and obey the decision of Athenians.

[33] O Socrates, you who are most law-abiding and of all the men I know most in love with Athens to the very end, not even now do you wish to be away from Athens. No, he composes and plays songs and, though imprisoned, hymns the gods and now sings odes to Apollo. For at the end of his life Socrates became a poet. But you do not allow Socrates to speak even in prose.

[34] Your orders are contrary to the wishes of the god. O Apollo, on purpose you keep back the Delian ship as a hostage for Socrates and you do not send the holy vessel to Athens, thus giving your servant more days to live; and you order the winds not to carry the ship to Athens, so that Socrates may continue to philosophize. But these men are making your favor profitless.

[35] 'Socrates is not to talk,' he says,

'not even if there are hearers present or Socrates himself wishes it.' When in pain from his fetters he lifts up his legs to go to sleep, shall he say nothing about this? Shall he not philosophize on the relation of pleasure and pain? Simmias and Cebes ask him a question about the soul. Shall he not speak on this subject? While Thebans philosophize shall an Athenian remain silent? He is about to die and he is joyful. This is what especially excites the wonder of his friends. Is he not to converse – how can it be? Not even if there is anyone who believes that the soul is immortal? If he owes a sacrifice to the gods shall he not bid one of his friends offer it? Even though he is about to drink the hemlock, shall he not make his customary drink offerings and prayers?

[36] For what does he say that is troublesome or untimely? Another man at the time of his death gives instructions regarding his property or his children or on the handling and burial of his body. But Socrates sits quietly, saying that there is no need to weep or moan or to think that the present life will prove to be the only one, but that another life waits to receive us longer than our bodily one; and when we are released from bones and flesh and all this prison, whether it is to be called a body or a tomb, we each shall go away to a just dispensation; that while we are alive we must pursue wisdom and think of life as a training for death, remembering the great number of the ancient lessons surrounded by which we remain here, as we believe; but when our allotted destiny comes, we must be borne light and through the air to our masters the gods and the spirits who judge souls and assign to those who live with purity and justice and who with true philosophy have held themselves aloof from earthly things, attendance upon the gods and the course above the heavens and a vision of justice itself and of the Beautiful and of Immortality and of blessed Souls. But for those who have lived lawlessly and immorally, their souls filled with many impieties, there are Tartaruses and Cocytuses and Pyriphlegethons as receptions and terrible chastisements and eternal punishments in fire and darkness and weird rivers driven in an unending course.

[37] These are the words of Socrates, these his instructions, this is the will of Socrates. Who will begrudge us a share in the immortality of Socrates? Allow us to hear him again and to confirm these hopes of happiness. It is no matter to Socrates; for even if he does not speak, a long life awaits him and many conversations and the gods will be his hearers. To them he will speak, being set free he will philosophize, with them he will discuss all things. But for us, who will be left orphaned of Socrates, it is a terrible thing if no one of us will ask him any questions on any of our disputes or on these matters in particular, and if no one of us gains any benefits from the last hours of Socrates.

[38] Apollo, please stay the ship yet longer; let the festival at Delos continue to move slowly. I have questions to ask Socrates about speech and silence and salvation. And you, false accusers, permit us to benefit from Socrates while he is still alive. Alas, perhaps the ship will come today. This was foretold Socrates in a dream. Do not begrudge us one day. And perhaps even now, while I am busy here, Socrates converses with his friends. Words such as these one can hear from the friends of Socrates who have listened to him speak, but not such words as one can hear from Socrates himself.

[39] I ask you, Socrates, the opposite of what these men order, to speak not only while you are alive nor with mortal tongue alone, but also to speak after you drink the hemlock. And do not stop speaking even when you die.

I believe you: the soul is completely immortal, especially your soul. If any of the spirits of the wise visit the souls of their friends, do not be silent, but speak to us in dreams, Socrates, as now do the gods. (tr. M. Crosby)

A brilliant note by Professor W. M. Calder III attached to the original publication of this suggests that Socrates is used to represent the pagans of Libanius' own day, and the accusers to represent the Christians.

10.2 Defence of Socrates

[1] Men of Athens, even if someone were to bring even more charges than the present ones against Socrates, trying to persuade you that if Socrates fails to pay the penalty the city will inevitably suffer disaster, I would not think it right not to have stood with him and used every moment to defend him to you. Unjust slanders are now being levelled against him. It would not be an upright act to let these outweigh the righteousness of his every word and deed which I well know. I used to associate with him and to consult him on all my affairs. It would be an act of great cowardice to desert him now that he has fallen upon evil times.

[2] Since this is what I think, it would be right if I invoked the gods, who best know the quality of his life, to come to the help of Socrates in this present case, and it would perhaps be right too to show openly my support in words and leave nothing undone which I might think it right to do. Anytus has brought forward his lying charges, and then Meletus stood up with a speech of interminable abuse, and in addition Lycon used every means in his power against Socrates

to secure the death of one of you: it would therefore be strange indeed if we stood voiceless, as if we were quite unmoved, and behaved even more basely than the accusers hoped we might, particularly when it is a matter of fulfilling the obligations of friendship and rescuing you, the jurymen, from the risk of perjury. Anyone who prevents those who make violent attacks on others from deceiving you, and gaining the day, is making the jurymen into vigilant guards. Therefore I have come forward to speak with your interests at heart just as much as the defence of the prisoner at the bar.

[3] Socrates, gentlemen of the jury, said little about death, for in those investigations in which he spent his time he found death no more harsh than life, and that the man who had conquered physical pleasures, for which most of us are eager in life, could, of course, easily bear the passing from this world. There are those, not a few indeed, who are quite plainly malefactors, who have found a means of saving themselves by playing on your sympathy, weeping themselves and getting their children to act as supplicants; but Socrates was so far removed from employing such methods as these that I have already noticed that some of you have been more harshly disposed towards him because he did not deign to employ such methods. [4] It was not because Socrates had but a little time left and in any case did not fear death that I dissociated myself from his defence; rather I thought that it was right that a man of such character ought not to suffer unjustly in any way at your hands, and at the same time such wickedness should not be perpetrated in the city nor the jurymen forced into any irreligious act so that all of Athens together should be dishonoured, [5] and therefore I determined to prove Anytus' libellous charges

wrong. I hope that you will listen with sympathy to what I have to say. If Socrates himself were experienced in making speeches in a court of law and could have defended himself sufficiently against these present charges, then perhaps you would have been satisfied by his words, and persuaded to vote correctly in the present case. But since he has made the sort of speech to you that he would have made in the workshops, which did not at all fit the needs of his present circumstances, he has at least confounded one of the slanders against him – that of being a clever speaker. And if you will bear with me, gentlemen, although I may not be able to equal Anytus in speech-making, yet I may be able to contribute something and say something nearer the truth than what these men have said.

[6] I know that certain slanders have been spread against Socrates by those who could not endure his dialectic when they met him, and who, when they would more justly have taken themselves to task for not paying attention to the cultivation of their own intellects, rather hated the man who would not let them ignore the more important things in human life, and who spurred on some people to say such things as this: 'Socrates is tainted, an abomination, a plague of the young.' These [7] were the reasons that gave them the confidence to bring the charges. The day before yesterday someone visited them and said that he was not in full sympathy with the prosecution; he did not even see that their feet were on the path of victory. They replied that the enmity of the jurors towards the prisoner at the bar would be greatly to their advantage. For a long time they have wanted to convict Socrates by process of law, so that this should seem to be sufficient retaliation for them. This is what Anytus would have done if he had been one of the jury, and those of his party,

and he expects you to act similarly; but he is deluded in his hopes. And why? First, I have seen many of you often delighted when Socrates put the sophists to the test, and, by Zeus, they were much improved in virtue by his efforts. [8] Secondly, even if you were all as ill-disposed towards him as could be, and the whole of the court was equally hostile to him, it would not be possible for you to gratify your ill-feeling there. The law-court is not the place, gentlemen, for enmity or for partisanship, nor have you come here to avenge yourselves on someone who has wronged you on some other account, nor to show favour to one who has done you a good turn before – the judgement is to be made on the facts before you; on them rests the decision whether you should acquit or punish the prisoner. [9] Doubtless it was because he knew this that Solon, thinking that some who were brought to trial would be pleading their case before their friends and others would be facing their enemies, so that justice should not be influenced one way or the other, laid down an oath that neither favour nor enmity nor any other consideration should pervert the course of justice. And in this case there may be someone who hates Socrates, but he has sworn that he will in no way give vent to his own anger, and the gods are witnesses of how he votes. The man who votes unjustly exposes himself and his children and household and family to their wrath, and will have perverted the mighty matter of justice to bring himself a little pleasure.

[10] Let no one consider this alone, that by condemning Socrates to death he would on leaving the court be freed from Socrates' blunt criticisms. Let him consider also what a reputation and what future expectations will now be his. When in the theatre, to laugh at the comic drama one is hearing, and to join in attacking the man who is the

object of attack and to show favour to the poet, may not be the best way to behave, but it would not seem to be absolutely out of place at the festival of Dionysus, and the laughter is without risk. But in a court of law the man who gives himself over completely to the prosecutor, who thinks all that he is told must be true, who puts nothing to the test and no obstacles in the prosecutor's way, who changes his position to align himself with the accusers rather than keeping to his own duty, punishes himself more than the man he thinks he is punishing, and leaves the court having suffered more ill than he has inflicted. The man in the theatre does not draw his children into the risk he runs, but the unjust juror brings disaster on all his family in turn.

[11] And indeed it would not be reasonable if those who were claiming to be angry in the cause of reverent behaviour were themselves guilty of impious behaviour and were themselves convicted of incredible wickedness when they thought that they were themselves exacting just punishment in more important cases demanding justice.

[12] If anyone of you has come here angered by any of the arguments used previously by Socrates against some people, he must not combine that with what he hears in this present case. He must remember his duty to the gods to whom you have sworn an oath before coming here. To have a full and fair hearing and a decision. I could say more on this subject, but I think that men of judgement need nothing more.

[13] I shall show you for what reason Anytus attacked Socrates, and demonstrate that it was not from any well-wishing towards you, nor, on the other hand, was he giving any thought to the virtue of your sons, but for quite different reasons. Gentlemen of Athens, I am quite as keen on proving my point as he is. And if I show that Socrates never

taught any man the crime of stealing, or to indulge in deceit or sacrilege or to swear false oaths, or laziness, or disregard for the laws, or the destruction of the State, but that he always led them in the path of wisdom and justice, and that he was and still is of all men the best disposed towards you, I call on you to make Anytus hide his face in shame.

[14] Consider this then. Socrates, gentlemen of the jury, was born of an Athenian father and brought up among your laws and customs: it may be that he took greater thought for the well-being of his own affairs, but he always paid due attention to the affairs and reputation of the city. I agree that he differed from the majority in not following a downward path and being persuaded to become evil, as these men allege, but of all the courses which were proposed to him, he reached out after virtue and considered this the possession he ought most to covet. [15] To spend one's life working as a craftsman or tilling the land or sailing the sea to make a living, to work metals, or canvass for a command, or to compose speeches against private citizens and by this means to enjoy gain at the expense of those who like a quiet life, all this he knew brought power to those who took part in it, and advantages that are admired by the commons, and make them to be feared among the ranks of those who enjoy wealth, but all the same, Socrates could not think that any of those things was important or brought happiness. He considered that of all men's possessions the most godly was the soul, and that the man who kept his soul free from evil was the only one who was in truth happy. He thought that the pursuit of wisdom was able to free the soul from evil, and that this would be found to be its greatest remedy. He left to others those things from which wealth and power come, and applied himself to that which,

although it does not gratify the body, makes the soul better in every way.

[16] He avoided spending his time in examining the nature of the heavens or the character of the sun, or calculating the movements of the moon or the provenance of lightning or the cause of thunder, for he thought that all knowledge was vain if it brought no real profit to people once they had understood it. But he set himself to seeking what was right, whom it was just to call courageous and who might rightly be termed wise, which is the greatest blessing among all people in private and public life. He remained devoted to these pursuits and never set himself up as anyone's teacher, nor did he receive money for it, as would any miserable sophist, but he spends his life in examining among his disciples the nature of every deed.

[17] He has done this although he had not inherited any great fortune, nor did his private means afford him the leisure for such activities. When his father died he left Socrates eighty minas, but when a contemporary took the money for a job he was to do, and then suffered financial disaster over the commission, Socrates bore the misfortune in silence. In fact, those who had nothing to do with the money would more readily have mentioned it than the man who lost it! [18] But he was left to live in unspeakable poverty. So what did he do? Because he was left with no income he did not change his calling, nor did he think he ought to change his character to match his circumstances. He kept his mind unmoved throughout, although he had a wife and children. Instead of seeking a livelihood that he did not consider good (although from it he might get money for his daily expenses to replace the sum he had lost), he let all this go and schooled himself so effectively not to feel want that he did not look for any means of earning a living. He wore one old cloak for many years and drank water, finding it sweeter than others do Thasian wine: he enjoyed the diet of a pauper, preferring it to Eastern delicacies. Since this was all he required in the way of subsistence, his friends saw to its provision, and Socrates troubled himself not at all!

[19] Such a man he is, and spends his life in such a way, like some common father to all, and a benefactor to the whole city. He went round the palaestra and the gymnasia, the Lyceum and the Academy and the market-place, wherever he was likely to meet the most people, and performed as it were a sacred service on your behalf, unlike any you have seen at the Panathenaic festival or the festival of Dionysus, for a man gains credit from the performance of these; but he gave his mind to this in particular, how he might best drive out evil, and persuade you to consider virtue something good to have. [20] He never stopped trying to convince some of you who wished to be leaders either in military or public affairs, and to direct the nation's business, that they were bending all their energies to getting into office before learning how to act in your interests, and to ascertain how the city might become prosperous. He said all this, not, by Zeus, wishing to make them feel ashamed but so that they should know that here was a man who would blame those who were negligent, and who would examine them and call them to account: so that either, if they were insufficiently prepared to be of service to you, they would stand down, or if they did come forward in the public service they would show themselves fitting rulers for you.

[21] For reasons such as these, Athenians, Socrates became the object of hatred of many; but if one were to examine your affairs without prejudice one would find that in many ways they were better served by Socrates' nagging

reproaches. He said that all the attention of the Athenians is directed towards making money, and that they have striven after this, but they have given no thought at all to how their souls and those of their children might be made as good as possible. Since Socrates repeated such things daily and brought forward such teaching unceasingly, one can only think that although those who were set in their evil ways were benefited in no way at all, those that understood were ashamed, converted and improved.

[22] Whenever he met those sophists who enchant everyone, Protagoras, Gorgias, Prodicus and Thrasymachus, and all those others who are drawn by the prospect of gain to every place like donkeys drawn by a carrot, and showed by his arguments how much they were his inferiors in wisdom, and that they gave no thought at all, one might say, to those things which they claimed to be able to teach others, at one and the same time he was protecting the young men from an association that was doing them little good, and spreading among all men the Athenians' reputation for wisdom. For he showed that those men who were venerated everywhere for the arguments which they composed to earn money were bringing forward an empty collection of phrases, and that they were, for the most part, ignorant and without any knowledge of the nature of those things about which they tried to speak, and that they would do better to spend money on learning something than to take money on the pretext that they can teach anything that matters.

[23] Because you realised all this you crowded around Socrates whenever he chanced to be questioning such men as these. You saw those men who were supposed to know about wisdom being overwhelmed and being made dizzier and more at a loss than any slave, and you laughed at them as they looked round for a means of escape. At the same time you turned your attention to true learning and bade your sons pay heed to the man who could do all this, thinking that it would be a great advantage to them if they had even a small share in these good things, rather than all the gold in the world.

[24] Anytus, at present Socrates' bitter prosecutor, was one of these. His sons, too, followed and enjoyed the company of the man who now stands accused in this court. He did not turn them away from Socrates. He did not blame them; you did not fault your sons, either. Naturally, you understood that the man who talked with Socrates might feel wonder, and that if he felt wonder he would grow enthusiastic, and by the frequency of his intercourse with Socrates conceive a longing to be like him. You knew that those who were eager to share in the pursuits of Socrates would immediately become superior to the majority and rise above gluttony and drunkenness and ill-gotten gain, burning anger or enslaving flattery and other similar evils. But you knew that in enduring heat and cold as if their bodies were made of steel, and being oppressed by neither hunger nor thirst, they would become men fit to strike terror into the enemy if they were to serve as soldiers, and would be good men and see what was fitting in giving counsel.

[25] What was it, then, that drove the good Anytus off balance? Why did he conceive this desire to kill the man whom he had often hoped would be the close companion of his sons? In those discussions, gentlemen, by which he sought the truth, Socrates needed to use certain examples to show clearly what he had in mind, as we are all accustomed to do: even the man who wishes to avoid it cannot do so altogether. [26] Socrates used to talk of shoemakers and tanners and those

who dye wool, and those engaged in other crafts, and said that each man would know the particular skill from which he got his livelihood better than any other, and that he would more easily detect lack of skill in it and the opposite. In pursuing such discussions he came up against the subject of Anytus, who did not think it wrong to earn a living from shoemaking, but who grew angry at an argument involving craftsmanship, and although he did not avoid the work itself, he dislikes talk about it. [27] Each of you often talks of his own craft, and is thankful for the income that it affords him; and Socrates himself often when speaking would add the example of his father Sophroniscus, and the craft of being a stonemason, nor did he conceal the calling his mother had followed. [28] So it is clear that he did not cite the examples of others offensively, but so that each discussion should be given the examples appropriate to it, and that nothing that ought to be mentioned was omitted. Because of this, Apollodorus was content to listen quietly, and Xenocleides did not issue a writ, but Socrates is only running a risk when he mentions Anytus as if he were some dictator or other, and that no one was allowed to say what Anytus had decided to do.

[29] But, as I said, let no one think that Anytus brought this charge out of any good intentions towards you, or because he wanted to remove the evil influence that was corrupting your children. If Socrates had gone beyond the bounds of truth and magnified Anytus' importance by maintaining that he had inherited all his wealth from his forebears, then you would not have been injured, nor would a sacrilegious act have been done nor would the young men have been corrupted. But now Anytus is not helping you; he is hurt by the insult done to him. He is not taking vengeance on behalf of the city, but he is angry if he is going to be seen to be just what he is, and is inventing charges and making lying accusations, and buying the services of Meletus, who would do anything for a drachma. [30] I shall give you ample proof that it was from quite different motives that he brought forward your interests as a front. For when the writ against Socrates had already been issued and the charges announced, he sent a message to Socrates as if for a truce, asking him to stop talking about crafts and skills, and in return he would cancel the indictment. When Socrates replied that as long as he lived he would never stop telling the truth, but would go on using the same words on the same subjects, and that the accusation was not so powerful that he would be silent in the face of it about those things of which he had thought it right to talk before, then Anytus delivered up to you this man who never betrayed through fear anything that he thought was right.

[31] Socrates is now on trial, and to tell the plain truth, the responsibility lies not with Anytus or Meletus but with Socrates himself. For if he had accepted the offer made by his accusers and so overruled his conscience that he either dropped the subject of Anytus once and for all or still talked about him but gave him unmerited credit, he would now be in the Lyceum conversing as he used to do. [32] But it was not in the nature of this brave man to play the coward and be frightened by the indictment, and be silent about Anytus as the price of gaining his own safety. He thought it right that he should be saved by his previous record, and that he should stand his trial and be acquitted by your votes because of the truth, but not through the disgraceful reconciliation offered by his accusers.

[33] I think I have shown you clearly from what I have said that Anytus was not protecting the young men from destruction, and did not

think he was personally injured if someone was going to corrupt your children,
and so he persuaded Meletus to indict
Socrates; further that though it was
possible for Socrates to escape from his
present danger, he cheerfully came to
court with nothing base or worthy of
retribution on his conscience. And I
was made glad by what I heard some
of you saying when you were summoned
to serve as jurymen. For it was a source
of wonder to some people that if Socrates had been living so wicked a life
for so long and pursuing interests that
would corrupt the young, Anytus
should have been seen to be angry only
after such a long period had elapsed
and that he was seeking a reason for
bringing his case from other causes.

[34] So this is the point from which
I shall begin my examination, and you
will know better for what reason Anytus
recently came forward as a prosecutor.
I shall in your presence question that
patriot: 'Tell me this, by the gods. This
old man is seventy years old, was it
yesterday or the day before yesterday
that he became a teacher of evil? This
year? or last year? For all the rest of
his life was he a good citizen harming
the city in no way whatever? Ought he
not to be praised for all that time in
which he was a good man? Should he
be hated for the change which has come
about? [35] What do you say, Anytus?
Why are you silent? Was he from of old
a wicked man or was it as he approached
old age that he praised evil? Indeed,
you have given me an answer by your
silence. For when you mentioned men
that were dead and said that the city
had suffered at their hands, you were
asserting that Socrates had not just
started on his career of corruption, but
that it dated from the time when he
took up philosophy.

[36] 'Well, then, O benefactor of
the young, if the wickedness is of such
long standing, why was your indictment
so slow in coming, and when you saw

a long time ago that we were being
wronged, why have you only just now
come to our aid? Have you not lived in
the city all your adult life – even
longer? Did you not notice that the
young men were devoted to him? Have
you not listened to their conversations?
You will not be able to withdraw from
that by saying that Socrates would lurk
in a corner or close the door on his
conversations, or that he would draw
his followers together under oath that
they would keep their discussions secret.
Nor can you say that he escaped notice
because he taught his wicked words
after offering sacrifices as part of un-
mentionable rites, and that it only
afterwards happened to come to light
when someone with a wagging tongue
blurted it out. [37] But you know that
he loved those places where crowds
were gathered together, and so much
did he abhor solitude that one might
more easily make the charge against
him of seeking the crowd than of
speaking with the young men when
no one else was present. And you
were one of those who listened to him
and who knew the penalty, and who
knew quite well the stage to which the
affair had progressed. [38] What, then,
should the well-wishers have done?
Grow angry, cry out, not allow the
malefactor to walk the streets, say,
"O men of Athens, Socrates is giving
instruction to the young contrary to
the law, the State is at risk. This sophist
is creating for us men who are too
bold, insufferable, tyrants who over-
look what is right. Shall we not stop
him? shall we not put an end to it?
Shall we not exile him before those
whom he is nurturing overthrow the
force of law?"' Ought Anytus to have
said this? What ought he to have done
in addition? To set someone to make
a charge, even if he was unwilling to do
so himself.

[39] 'We had once a king to rule us,
Anytus, and all the rest of the time

there was the priestly tribe of the Eumolpidae: there was the whole machinery for safeguarding the observance of what was holy. Tell these men the reason for your tardiness. Was it that you were helpless? Well, all this present preparation and the making of every effort to secure the conviction of Socrates proclaim the opposite. But you never really loved the common people, and because of this you did not think it was necessary even to consider the possibility that some would show themselves men and would free Socrates from all the wicked imputations they had heard about him.

[40] 'It is, then, a question of whether you should prosecute and Socrates die, or whether rather he should pay for his wickedness, and you for allowing him to do wrong, although you would have been able to prosecute. For if a man is able to restrain a criminal, and refuses to do so, he should be set alongside the criminal. Therefore either Socrates did nothing wrong, and your silence about that is a present proof that your prosecution is unjust, or else by allowing him to act evilly you shared in the wrong to the people by overlooking crimes that it was within your power to prevent.'

[41] But Socrates never did anything wrong, Athenians: Anytus does not need to pay you any penalty for having allowed him to get away with so much. He is now making false accusations against a man who is innocent. It was not that he closed his eyes to a malefactor before but that he is now judging a man who is incapable of evil. When we see thieves stealing goods from private houses or having evil designs on another's property we do not let them get away with their loot and wait until they are old men before we bring them to justice; no, we punish them immediately with fetters and whips and the treadmill, torturing them as soon as they are caught. Does it seem at all

likely to you that Anytus would have allowed all this time to elapse while Socrates undermined your democracy and prepared citizens to destroy you?

[42] But I will let this pass. Let us suppose that Anytus was prevented from seeing all this because he had his mind on other things. Even this, Athenians, should not be forgiven. Let no one be so zealous in his own affairs that when he considers the course of public events he overlooks danger that is looming. Nevertheless, I will not be the one to blame him if he paid no attention to public affairs because he was intent on his private business. [43] Since he is silent, one can only suppose that the charge and the case have arisen from some other root-cause. Is not the rostrum in the assembly thronged with speakers, and the law-courts full of those bringing cases, some in retaliation for real wrongs they have suffered, others activated by hatred and malice, and in some cases by desire to cause trouble and fill their purses? Are we not sick and tired of cases advertised before the magistrates 'A charges B with being guilty of C'? But you never find 'A charges Socrates of the deme Alopece with being guilty of C', whether it is of disrespect to the gods or corrupting the young or of criminal violence or anything else.

[44] Those who love honour and who expend their wealth on your behalf, those who wish to be called the leaders of the city and who pride themselves on having the interest of all at heart, and who receive honours from you in return – these men are more than ready to bring charges and make accusations of theft for relatively small sums, for they believe that there is certain safety in the zealousness of the greater in their prosecution of the weaker. If such men as these saw another sapping the strength of the city and showing such insolence in the face of the laws that in their very midst he was leaving no stone unturned in

aiming at the disruption of the State, would they really think that they should allow him to continue, ignore him, condone his activities, almost go as far as rewarding him for them? Who would believe that?

[45] There is assuredly not one of you who does not know that some citizens who, empowered by the rest, were leaders while the city enjoyed prosperity and great power directed the State and while preserving the name of democracy, in fact brought everything under their single command and who, having incited all the Spartans to envy, then conquered them at sea and secured the islands, yet did not evade standing to account in this lawcourt. The high reputation of the defendants did not deter those who wished to bring a charge; on the contrary they were indicted, stood their trial and made their defence. [46] Perhaps they feared Socrates' poverty and his lack of experience in legal debate, these men who have sat in judgement on the most sparkling of orators, on the man who has made important decisions in matters of war and peace and the State in general. Then what was the cause of their silence? Not the fact that there was a dearth of witnesses who saw Socrates' misdeed but the fact that Anytus is now making false charges. If it is true that the prisoner is often judged on the evidence of the prosecutors, and when in this case no one has brought forward these or any other reasons for prosecution, how can Socrates, more than anyone else, fail to be acquitted of Anytus' charges?

[47] There are many things that I might say, but perhaps the strangest of all is that this man who spent all his time in the Lyceum and squandered the whole of his life in argument and inquiry should be calling for the writs from the orators. For you know, I suppose, that involvement with that sort of thing is generally for those who

engage in public affairs, who mount the rostrum, make known their opinions and cast their votes. It is these men who have the power to harm the State; power which they have in fact been given at the hands of the people. But if a man merely philosophised about events, talking against the sophists in the palaestra or with any others of those who are always to be found there, how could he change the nature of the State?

[48] I will leave this subject, having said so much, gentlemen, and I shall put this question: 'Tell me, Anytus, did Socrates hate democracy, and would he have been glad to see a dictator set up in the city? If so, whom? Surely not himself, by Zeus. He would more readily have paid a corps of lancers or raised a band of mercenaries or armed a private army!'

[49] Your answer is: 'He did not want outward show himself: he implanted the desire in others instead.' Just as Anytus was wrong in not bringing Socrates to judgement long ago, so he is now wrong in bringing him and him alone to judgement. If all those who consorted with him have been corrupted and taught to despise the laws, why has Anytus not handed them all over to you? Why has he not brought charges against them all? For it is not generally thought right that the man who incites to evil is worthy of punishment but one ought to stop short of punishing those through whom the deed is accomplished. In our homicide laws we do not see it laid down that charges are not brought against the murderer but against the man who causes his crime. To name the murderer is to involve the man behind him as an accessory. The man who commits the crime is regarded as more abominable than he who persuades him. [50] Socrates is on trial charged with persuading others to overthrow the law, but no one demands any account from those who were so

zealous for this revolution. Anyone who had the laws really at heart ought to have moved against all those who threatened democracy, not allow that they should all escape and he should fight one man alone. It is clear that even if Socrates suffers the death penalty, all those who have been corrupted by him will be evil men surrounding you. Who would accept as a doctor one who watched a disease grow ever greater when he ought to have been treating the body as a whole?

[51] If Anytus here knew that Socrates was evil, but did not think he was teaching wickedness, he would have been right to attack him alone. But if now, as he says, your young men are corrupted and made revolutionaries by Socrates' arguments, then the charges ought to be brought against them all together. In that case you might really hope that he would make an end to the affair, which he will not do by making the disciples even more difficult because of their master's death. [52] So how is it that Socrates is being charged alone? His accuser was hot with anger because he could never catch Socrates or any other of his associates through their deeds or the truth they told, and what he had against Socrates would not be sufficient to convict the others. And what is the charge against Socrates? He is called a sophist. He got across many people. He was made a butt on the comic stage. He is not liable to property-tax. Anytus could not have used these charges against the young men too. He was afraid to bring into court those against whom slanders would not stand up, and he was trusting only in slander in prosecuting Socrates, not in real proof.

[53] Examine this then. They say, 'Socrates hates the State and urges his followers to belittle democracy.' By god, Anytus, by doing what? Does he compose speeches against democracy and read them to his companions? He never did any such thing. Or did he say in words that the city should be overthrown? Has anyone heard him say that the city is diminished by living under the rule of law and that it would be great if ruled by the authority of a dictator? Have you ever heard him expounding such ideas in the Lyceum or the palaestra or the shops? [54] What was to prevent him turning openly to favour monarchy and to leave nothing unsaid which it would be right for a revolutionary to say? If he foresaw danger from his ideas, then he would have been altogether silent on those things for which he now stands trial. If, however, he thought that he was speaking to sympathetic listeners he would have praised openly people like Peisistratus, marvelled at Hippias and looked longingly back to Hipparchus, and called Athens happy indeed in those days gone by.

[55] It is the habit of plotters for everyone to speak out clearly what he has in mind, to give voice to all his ideas, to bring forward all arguments calculated to persuade, to be pleased at having carried the day and to take it ill if he misses his opportunity. And whoever asserts that Socrates was plotting with the young men to seek the overthrow of the State would not be able to demonstrate that Socrates had done any of these things. [56] It is likely, gentlemen, that, even if at first Socrates had been afraid of clearly showing his plans, and therefore spoke in such secrecy that he would have nothing to fear if he failed to persuade, as time went by and the young men paid attention to what he said he would have dared to speak out openly. Or do you suppose that the young men were not deterred from speaking in public because of the great disturbance that the changes they wanted would create but put up with anything to get their views established, but that

Socrates, although he could have carried his listeners with him, with no one to gainsay him, betrayed his own enthusiasms for no good reason because he wanted to keep quiet?

[57] But the most important point is this: twice our constitutional pattern changed when Socrates was living at home and was in fact in Athens, first, after the Sicilian débâcle, and secondly, after the disaster at Aegospotami. Could one say, then, that this man took part in the oligarchy of the Four Hundred or the illegal rule of the Thirty? Did he follow the example of Peisander? Was he found in the ranks of Theramenes? Was he seen doing the same things as Phrynichus?

[58] Or was it that he did not show himself in their midst but rather prepared his plans secretly, as a man would who was not accustomed to manipulating the mob but who had the same object as those others? This was the way of another, one of the Four Hundred, who has paid the penalty for those things in which he was deemed to have done wrong. But Socrates had nothing to do with this state of affairs when it was coming to pass, nor did he take part in it when it was at its peak, nor was he condemned when it came to an end.

[59] Nor was he ever seen rejoicing in the change of government or joining in the hopes of those who had the power, as a man might who avoided everyday intercourse through cowardice and because of his baseness rejoiced in seeing the citizen body suffer. He was not one of the Thirty, either, nor was he an admirer of them, but rather they so displeased one another that he condemned what they were doing, and Critias, his disciple and friend, condemned his master to silence. Is it possible that a man who favours dictatorship should work for its establishment when it is absent but hate its presence, that he would pray to see the people eliminated from political power but would be grieved when it happened?

[60] Where is he, this teacher of dictators? Show him forth. Did he take his young followers to Dracontides, Charicles, Melobius and the others and bid them consider these men as examples of the best kind of life; and ask them to summon the young men to them, and urge the young men to gaze on them and observe how they proposed to pass dictatorial power down the line of succession?

[61] If Anytus could show that any of this was so now, then he is just in bringing his accusation, and is benefiting the city, even if he is slow in doing so. But if, on the other hand, when he has all these opportunities to show the man's unconstitutional nature he is unable to secure a prosecution, and having collected a lot of evidence that does not exist exasperates the jurymen, then let him not escape those whom he has wronged in his dealings with Socrates by making them swear oaths under false pretences.

[62] What is it that has encouraged him to have the effrontery to bring such charges and to prefer the indictment? He says, 'He takes the poems of Hesiod and Theognis, Homer and Pindar, and those poets who receive honour and respect from us and others, and he shows that many of their sayings are despicable.'

[63] Then he was doing something, Anytus, which he had every right to do, for it is legally granted to me and you, to every citizen, to foreigners, to young and old, to anyone who wishes, to speak of the poets according to his own point of view. A praised them, B did not wish to. But neither was brought to judgement, even if one or the other missed the truth. In the same way as it is possible for men to look at a statue and some to admire it and others not, and for someone to find

fault with one of its parts, if he wishes, or with it as a whole, so when considering poetry and prose some give it a good opinion, and others the opposite. And, by Zeus, you will even find that the man who recently thought things splendid will afterwards consider them quite differently. For frequent examination better shows their true nature to the man who looks at them. But it would be a laughable matter if a man were brought into court to give an explanation of why he finds fault with what he praised before.

[64] But what should one do? Help with argument those who are brought into court because of their disputatiousness about literature, and convict the man who finds fault of being a fool. This is the sort of cause for philosophers to deal with, but giving judgement and passing the death-sentence are set down for other matters. And you would know even more the strangeness of Anytus' procedure.

[65] Hesiod once contested with Homer, and Hesiod himself, eager for praise, tells us this in an epigram and says that he beat Homer. Well, then, if Hesiod won on every count, everyone must have thought that Homer was only a poetaster. But if some thought that Homer was better, but the poems of Hesiod found favour with the majority, then each had some who did not favour him, and it is clear that when the assembly broke up there were some who preferred Homer and maligned Hesiod, and vice versa. This was the effect of their support.

[66] Does any of the historians tell us that anyone was brought to court in Chalcis for criticising Hesiod or Homer? No. And surely it is strange that it was possible for men of old who actually heard the poets reciting in person to censure them, but that men in after times, when they see something that is not good in their works, must either be silent or perish.

[67] Now, by Zeus, do you not think that Sophocles and Euripides and Aeschylus would rightly be numbered among the wise? And who would not join with his children in hoping that they would be performed to the Greeks at the Dionysia? But does none of the audience ever come away criticising the iambics? Some criticise them in countless numbers, and it matters little to them if they deal sharply with the poets. And comedy, too, brings the greatest part of its enjoyment when it mocks tragedy.

[68] If a man then says that those of the Athenians who seem outstanding in education are wrong in what they do he is not responsible at law, but if he says the same things about the older generation he will be brought to trial. And is it all right for Aristophanes to make jokes at Socrates' expense, jokes which will last for all time because they are written down, and there will be no one to blue-pencil the script; but we don't allow Socrates, on the other hand, to criticise Homer or any other poet although his criticisms are not preserved in books or writings? If only that had been laid down by the law of the Dionysia! If only it were proclaimed by the common law of all men, according to which poets and authors are to be examined by all who meet them.

[69] Socrates only takes Pindar to task, as you do Socrates; or rather, no. For he does so justly and you unjustly: he finds fault with a man who is a threat to him, but you wish to do so with someone who is your benefactor, but you both have the same right to do so. And how is it not an anomaly that Anytus thinks it all right to censure the words of the citizens, but that he should forbid any of the citizens to examine the works of others, as if it were laid down by some law of nature that the men from Boeotia or I don't know where should excel in wisdom, but that the nurselings of Athens should all live together in

ignorance? The opposite was true in time past; but, Anytus, you do not allow that.

[70] And, to be sure, if finding fault with words was a crime there would be a law about this too, just as there is about the other crimes so that one says 'Do not take bribes', another 'Do not commit assault and battery', another 'Do not commit highway robbery', and there are penalties laid down for all the others to deter us. But there is no law to say 'If a man find fault with the poets of old, he shall die', nor in the decrees which were passed to honour them did they ask as a favour that all the Athenians should hold their tongues about all their writings. In what, then, has the prisoner now before us done wrong, if he is in law not prevented from showing that some of Hesiod is harmful, nor threatened by the death-sentence if he says that Pindar did not always say the best things?

[71] It is agreed that those two poets, I mean Hesiod and Homer, were more ancient than Solon. If Solon thought that it was undesirable for all and sundry to assail their poetic sentiments, then surely he would have laid down a law preventing the Athenians from making trial of those poetic passages, and if not Solon, then someone else, just as in the matter of the names of Harmodius and Aristogeiton we took the decision that no slave should be named after the tyrannicides, and we observe it.

[72] Why was it that we did not think that poetry was worth the same providential care? Because the one would do violence to our benefactors because of the slaves, the other would give poets the same power as dictators, whom their subjects have to praise, even if they excel all other men in their stupidity and wickedness. But Socrates did not recognise Homer or Theognis as a dictator of the Athenians, and if he had seen them as dictators he would not allow himself to flatter them, that is, if he drew on analogy with political authority he would have felt himself to be the subject of dictatorship when he came to examine the poems, just as when he examined the works of the Thirty. But you in a democracy and amid freedom of speech have set up the poets of old as absolute masters over those who concern themselves with the words and you block up the mouths of abler men and bring silence down upon the Athenians.

[73] Even Peisistratus, that eager zealot for the poetry of Homer, never took and executed a citizen for criticising a poem, and it is likely that many such occasions took place when the works of Homer were being collected together; but you, Anytus, in a democracy, are acting more harshly than any dictator, and that while praising Theseus for renouncing the power he held. For he did not place the freedom of the people higher than the poems in order that Anytus and Meletus might prevent the man who wanted to conversing in Athens, but so that, freed from all fear, we might exercise our spirits by learning and our bodies by physical exercises.

[74] It is for this reason that Athens is a fair and delightful sight, and men come here from all quarters by land and sea: some stay and others go away reluctantly, and it is not because we excel Sybaris in the excellence of our tables, nor that our land is particularly rich in wheat. Quite the opposite, for we owe our sustenance to imported goods. It is because the city is a factory of words. One man asks questions, another answers. One is content to learn, another teaches. You might see one praising something in what has just been said, another finding fault with it, another showing the faults in an incorrect supposition.

[75] All this is worthy of the goddess on the Acropolis, and of those educated by the gods, and of Theseus, and of our

democratic constitution. This makes the city more pleasant than Sparta. Because of this those who revere wisdom are held in higher esteem than those who are dreadful in battle. This is what makes the great difference [76] between us and non-Greek peoples. And he who is now taking away our freedom of speech is also destroying the customs of democracy just as surely as if he were gouging the eyes out of the body or cutting out the tongue. And I would gladly ask him whether he is depriving diners-out also of their familiar conversation. These more often talk of the poets, admiring some felicity of expression, or suggesting that some other point needs correction.

[77] And if he is laying down a law of silence, bidding them eat and drink without speaking, then he is making the dinners of free men like those of slaves, bidding them measure their companionship by their appetites; and who would come to dinner when invited if he were unlikely to find there the most delightful of pleasures? But if he is not taking away from these people the power to talk about such things, but is depriving the palaestra of conversation, and particularly if he is allowing everyone else to speak everywhere but Socrates to speak nowhere, then you, gentlemen of the jury, must be convinced that this is a miscarriage of justice.

[78] How ought we to speak about the poets? When Zeus sends us no rain, or again when he sends us too much, we cry out that we are being wronged and we say what it would be just for him to send us it with respect to the land. Theognis of Megara was aware of these complaints. So we take to task the year and the seasons and Zeus himself, and no one brings an indictment: and if anyone should say to either the young or the old that something that would have been better left unsaid escaped from the lips of Pindar, is it just that

he should immediately be condemned to drink hemlock, and that the man who does not cast his vote against him is destroying the city?

[79] What man in his right mind would say so? And even if they were held in excessive honour by our forefathers, this is a reward for their praise of our city, however brief, not a clear proof that poets have always spoken with good sense. But because one man says that Menestheus was a good strategist, and another maintains that the city is the prop and stay of Greece, they turned from actions to words, and with the natural generosity attested by their actions they thought it right to show gratitude to those poets who had offered them praise, and so they honoured the poets in their turn. But in doing so they were not tying their city's hands. They came to no agreement with the poets that Socrates afterwards must die if he does not praise them. But nothing, Athenians, prevents the same men from singing the truth about our city and not being wise counsellors in all things.

[80] My argument to you, he says, is the same about his finding fault with some of our customs. For if Socrates goes through all these arguments against the city, and teaches that it is more expedient for the city to be governed by the wishes of one stupid man rather than the force of law, a situation where gangs get out of hand, where violence is done to marriage, property stolen, maidens are at the mercy of drunkards and boys outraged, where there is fright and murder, wailing and continuous lamentation, if these are what he loved and this is what he taught, then I am surprised, Athenians, that he has lived so long when he long ago deserved death at the hands of the Athenians. But if he would want you to live under democratic rule but there are things in our custom which he thinks are not right, and says so, then he

does this, Athenians, in accordance with the laws of our democracy.

[81] For which of you does not know that it is granted by the laws themselves that any laws which are harmful may be repealed? For the man who laid down the laws did so thinking that they were right, but the man who finds that they are not so can repeal the law by working through the law itself.

'If I do not help those who use the laws in what I have written, and if I do not in fact fulfil the promise, then expunge the words, condemn them, do not hold back.'

[82] And, Athenians, we have never forgotten this remedy at any time in conducting the affairs of the city, putting new laws in the place of old. From that time we have repealed some laws and written new ones, and the older ones have given place to better ones. How many of the laws of Dracon, Solon or Cleisthenes have we left? For the better gains power instead of the worst, and the correct law is set up to take the place of another.

[83] I would have told you and identified individually for you all those which have been expunged and those which have been written in their stead, if there had not been a sufficient witness in the council of the Areopagus which does not now have all the power it once had. And the council would not disagree that it considers it necessary to yield to new and better laws. And if a man talks in the workshops of those things which can be raised in the Assembly, and concerning which a man may bring a prosecution in a court of law and gather votes there, and asks for the constitution to be sharpened, is this man therefore displeased with the democracy?

[84] Gentlemen, if the right to have said such things was open to Socrates, but any harm had come from this opportunity, I myself would be the first to condemn him by the vote. And yet because everyone has an equal share in this right certain persons have already been brought to trial and acquitted; nevertheless, such a means of gaining his acquittal would not be fitting in the case of Socrates. How, then, ought one to defend properly a man who, in my opinion, is a true patriot?

[85] I am telling you the truth, by Pythian Apollo, when I say that Socrates often did speak of the poets, but not always to censure them. Whenever they make the listener a better man he calls them wise, noble and godly, and other such epithets. But whenever he perceives that they are doing damage and influencing the hearer and leading him to great evil, then he opposes them and shows where the pitfalls are, since he will not allow young minds to fall into the trap and be carried away to destruction. [86] In his conversations he follows some such method as this, and it is this that Anytus had seized upon to make his lying accusations. Socrates asks the man with whom he is whether Hesiod is not a wise man. Of course, the man involved in the argument agrees. 'Well, then,' says Socrates, 'does he not praise all work, maintaining that no work is a disgrace?' When Socrates repeats the question the other cannot deny it. 'So the man who digs his way through the wall of a house or tent to rob it, has a wise man, Hesiod himself, to bear witness that he does no wrong?' Whereupon the man being questioned is confused and bystanders laugh, but no one is inspired by these words to rush off and commit a robbery – exactly the opposite. For often Socrates has shown up the poet and they have laughed at him, they know that they do not have to try to do everything in their turn. [87] And he spoke thus about Pindar, fearing his teaching and worried lest one of the young men, on

hearing that 'Justice yields to the force of a powerful hand', may think nothing of the laws and start getting his hands in practice! Here Socrates was quite naturally suspicious that our clever Anytus had dared to alter part of Pindar's poetry in which he might be talking to the Scythians, so that men did not know which bit was Pindar and which Anytus. But his evil deed turned out for the best. For in altering Pindar's work he brought him into disrepute and praise to Socrates.

[88] And examine this too: was Theognis correct in thinking that everything possible ought to be done for gain, since poverty forces a man to be silent, or Socrates, who believes that the poor man is often more capable of expressing himself than those in better circumstances? It will suffice if I take two examples from Anytus' speech to use in my defence, Lamprus and Pheidias – one would be better than Ischomachus in any discussion of statues, the other would be superior to Hipponicus when it came to the consideration of music. And if I must provide additional evidence, who does not know that in the Assembly many of those who have made a lot of money sit silent with nothing to say, and that many of those who are in need say what befits the occasion? So when we are speaking of the comparative intellectual power of those who have great wealth and those who have only a little money the former seem to think but little, the latter to advocate the best policies. So Socrates was right in maintaining his assertion that the power of self-expression belongs to the educated but not necessarily to the wealthy. [89] Indeed, there are not many wealthy Athenians, but many poor ones. Therefore according to Socrates the majority of you have the power to speak, but according to Theognis it would be dishonourable for the majority of the people. Athenians, I ask you,

which gives the better counsel for public man and private citizen alike – the man who burns with a frenzied desire for money and persuades you to consider as good any hardships or dangers, deeds of daring or loss of life which it may involve, or the man who advocates wise reflection rather than wealth? [90] This is what Socrates was taught by you and by the customs of the city, and either both he and you were mistaken or both he and you are free from any blame.

During the Persian wars you had the opportunity, men of Athens, to throw in your lot with that of a king who had very great wealth, and have become partakers in his prosperity. When he was defeated in the great sea battle round that island near by he bade farewell to any hopes of gaining the city by force of arms and came to gain it by his wealth instead. He sent a message promising untold wealth as well as his favour in all time to come. But those men who had been dispossessed of their land and who had taken to the ships did not remember the words of Theognis or take the money. Rather they punished the man who said that they ought to take the money. They did not consider their flight for that wealth. They could not bear to grow rich under the yoke of slavery which they would have had to endure in a city ruled by the Persian king.

[91] So Socrates was echoing the feeling of all the citizens when he thought that Theognis was advocating policies that were dangerous for the city. If those who now speak before you and conduct public affairs in personal poverty were to turn to trade and leave the business of the Assembly to those who had money but no sense of public responsibility, think how low the fortunes of our city would have sunk.

[93] So that you may learn even more clearly that these men are bringing false

charges against Socrates, who always did what was best for the people in his meetings and conversations, I shall pass over the rest of this matter of which I have been speaking in silence. Let Socrates speak through my mouth to your sons – and let Anytus show what harm has been done, and if he manages to persuade even one of you, then subject me to the same punishment as Socrates.

[93] 'Young men, Homer did not do right when he says in *The Iliad* that some who were common folk were beaten by Odysseus when they tried to sail away, but that others who held high positions were simply restrained by his words, and gentle words at that. Justice ought not to be circumscribed by circumstances. If the attempted launching of ships was a crime that ought to have been punished by flogging, then everyone ought to have had the same treatment. If it was a misdemeanour that simply needed a rebuke it was not right to rebuke some but flog the others – words would have sufficed for both parties. A man may not judge those who have authority over the people to be better by nature, and so alter the standard of justice to fit in with their excellence in outward appearance. It is possible for a man who lives and dies as one of the people to be good, and for another who enjoys better fortune than others to be weighed down with wickedness. [94] The man who dishonoured Cassandra before the eyes of Athens, and who was thereby the cause of much misfortune to the army, was not one of the common people, but one of their generals. If Odysseus did not realise that all this was so, he was not a wise man – so why should he be praised? If, on the other hand, he flogged no one, but the poet merely said he did, then Odysseus is wronged and all the rest are harmed by the poet's lies. [95] Do not let me hear you calling the wicked thefts carried out by Auto-

lycus, and his false oaths, gifts of Hermes or a reward won by the many sacrifices that pleased the gods. If it is the practice of the gods to exact punishment, how can it be granted to men that they should be able to change things?'

[96] What do you say, Anytus? Have I made those who have listened to my words worse men? Of course not, and nor did Socrates, but very much better for not allowing them to believe all of Homer indiscriminately. It would not be right for me, and so not for Socrates either, to be punished because, not being a poet himself, he points out in what ways they are harming those who listen to their poetry. He does it, rather, so that those who come across the poets, and whose interest he has at heart, should not be destroyed, and therefore he removes any notions that they might be entertaining about the wisdom of poets by pointing out that they cannot consider them wise and untrustworthy at one and the same time.

[97] But Anytus, as if set upon being contrary, grows angry if any Athenian stands out as being cleverer than the men born elsewhere, and maintains that he must be handed over to the authorities, although we must consider him the saviour of our young men when it comes to arguing about the poets. Look, I will ask you again, has Socrates ever praised the flogging that Odysseus gave the people and said to any man 'So be sure to keep your hands off those who are powerful and famous, and persecute the poorer sections of society'? Has he ever said that any man was not convinced by what he taught if he has not acted like this?

[98] If you say 'It was because he thought that his own opinions carried no weight that Socrates used the opinions of the poets to persuade people', I shall pass that by, for you are contradicting yourself in traducing Socrates at one moment for criticising the poets and at the next for applauding

these same poets. [99] I shall bring a much more weighty argument to bear against you. Tell me, to what god is it that we have recourse when we are uncertain, and from whom do we learn the truth on each occasion? Is it not from him who has his oracle at the centre of the earth, Pythian Apollo, by whose oracles we have been guided when we accomplished our greatest deeds? [100] It was this god, the ancestral god of our country, who passed over all the others and pronounced that the man who is now standing trial was the wisest of all men; not in the way that most men admire (he put many others before Socrates on that count) but in that he spends his life in a concern for truth and the pursuit of truth. And from that day Socrates has been an enviable man, more so than any other. He has not given himself airs any more than he did before, nor has he been puffed up with pride by the god's testimony; but his enemies yield to him in his wisdom on every subject.

[101] So in his conversations with the young what need had he of Pindar, Simonides and the other poets, after the pronouncement from Delphi? If a man had jurymen to act as his witness, would he think it right to set them aside and employ instead some rascal who would do anything for money? It would have been possible for Socrates to call those who would not submit to him and say: 'Consider what the priestess of Apollo has told you; this is the oracle that the god has delivered on Mount Parnassus. He called me the wisest of men. If anyone crosses me he is wronging Apollo also.' But no one ever heard him speak in any such way, and Anytus will not dare to spread that lie about, although he is behaving too boldly against those who have the greatest reputation for wisdom. Socrates stands fast in his reputation; what need had he of any round-

about method when he had the greatest means to persuade people – his reputation of wisdom?

[102] If the young men had paid greater attention to Socrates than to their own fathers, as you say, and had been heedless of the advice of their elder brothers and been drawn by Socrates' magic, what more would they have wanted than the fellow's fall? Anytus would not have needed the poets to persuade you; the fathers who had been insulted and the brothers who had been slighted would have had every cause for feeling hurt and would have been angry, they would have come to the law-court and forced their sons to come to their senses, and stopped Socrates from corrupting the young. [103] What father, then, has disinherited his son on the grounds that he has been corrupted by Socrates? Who has confined his son indoors so that he should never hear this corrupting talk? No one. For they were well aware of all those other things which I have just recounted to you, and about all these things which I shall deal with now – the charges of stealing and sacrilege and deceit. He did not consider that these things were necessarily always wicked and contrary to the law – the need for them does arise in time of war. The general who acts by stealth is better than the one who is afraid of winning victory by stealth. If you employ deceit as a device against the enemy you have done what the law allows. [104] The famous Themistocles acted deceitfully twice – once when he built the city's fortifications, and again when he saved Greece. We see, too, that the doctors give their patients false encouragement when they are in great distress. Indeed, we sometimes do the same even to those who are well when it is better for them to be deceived than to hear the truth.

[105] In what way, then, did Socrates or Melanthus do wrong in winning a victory through words? Deceit is

permissible in war. When your life is in danger stealthy methods are justified. Is it wrong to say that Odysseus was honoured for the theft of the Palladium? For he stole from the Trojans their most prized possession, whereas they had previously stolen his most prized possession from Menelaus. [106] But do you think that Socrates, if he were bidding the young men act in defiance of the citizens and their friends, would have brought forward as an example the deeds done by one enemy against another, enemies clashing by the laws of war? Of course he would be told by those who were listening to him that the examples he was using were discordant with what he was trying to say. But, I think, he showed when he mentioned the theft of what was most important from Troy that he was saying nothing new. He was merely showing what you yourselves do in time of war, and the Spartans and everyone else who brings about the fall of an enemy city. They do not keep off the wealth in the shrines, but think rather that anything that the vanquished hold sacred is all gain to them.

[107] Anytus in his wickedness has thrown in Thyestes and the deceiving of the Greeks by your fathers, for he knew that Socrates would not seem to be making his audience wicked from his talk about the Trojans and the kings of the Boeotians, but from the examples that he himself brought forward. But Socrates knew well, Anytus, that he would be using examples that conflicted with one another if he talked in the same breath of Odysseus, Thyestes, Melanthus and our forefathers as all having been guilty of deceiving the Greeks. [108] If Socrates had behaved in this way through simplicity, then he would have been a long way from expertise in evil, from cunning and from the easy deceit of others. But if he were really clever he would have taken great care not to use examples that harmed his

argument, and would have omitted one of the two groups. The man who is trying to make others good would not find it appropriate to speak of those who harmed their family; and if he were trying to make others evil it would hardly serve his purpose to talk of enemies harming one another.

[109] But why do I spend all this time on this subject and leave aside the charge which might more justifiably be pressed? 'Socrates,' they say, 'teaches men to perjure themselves.' Is it that he does not generally swear by the gods when he makes an oath but falls back on something else and substitutes gods of his own in his oaths, so that he should not lightly approach the names of the gods? It would be as if someone were to use the example of a man who dare not even look at the sea from the land to persuade others to take to the water and voyaging.

[110] So, sir, show us first that Socrates often did swear false oaths and break his word and only then dare to maintain that others were taught by him to despise the gods. And I say the same about the other remaining charges. Show us that he has been guilty of sacrilege, theft and violence, and only then allege that many were kept in his company by constraint. If you say that his words are wicked – you do not prove even that – and yet you cannot find fault with his deeds, then these, which are the essential test of the way a man lives, show that your accusations against his words are malicious. [111] We do not see the man who advocates theft or adultery abstaining from the goods of others: no, we see him breaking up marriages or worming his way through walls, and in such situations his acts conform exactly with his words. If a man safeguards himself as much as he can from the things which he says it is right that others should do, the opinion he sets forth in words is destroyed by the evidence of his actions;

the encouragement is of weaker quality than the deterrent. For example, if a man were to advocate the giving of money to the State but kept his own wealth jealously he would prevent the contribution of others by the concern he showed for his own money. Or if a man in battle gave the order to attack the enemy and then on top of those words left the battle-line he would make all the others cowards, inspiring them with fear by his actions, rather than encouraging them by what he said. In all such situations the man whose advice is the most persuasive is the one who practises what he preaches.

[112] So if Socrates taught others to swear false oaths, steal and use violence and all the rest which Anytus alleges, while he himself thought the opposite was really right and reverenced the gods, despised wealth, was moderate, disciplined and reasonable in his behaviour, then he would seem to have just been joking in what he said, since his deeds showed him to be a different kind of man, and it would appear that he thought the things that were truly good were not those that he maintained in his arguments, but the principles according to which he so obviously lived. So men would have paid no attention to his words, but rather emulated his deeds. They would not suppose that Socrates urged one course of action on everyone else but avoided it himself: or that he showed those to whom he talked the way to better things but himself followed the path that leads to something inferior. [113] He never in word or deed encouraged the young to do evil; it is those who in no way resemble him who write false indictments and prosecute on false charges. And if they can drag one of the citizens into the law-court they think it is a wonderful thing, asking what they would have suffered if they had just talked about him in private. Nothing evil of course, if indeed they

were dealing with an evil man, for Socrates did not use wicked arguments, and it is to his credit that he did not conduct his discussions in secret! Evildoers and wicked men may do such things in secret when they hope to go undetected, but when men choose to live simply and justly they do all things in the open under the eyes of their fellows.

[114] So some of you may be rather surprised that Anytus urges you to consider what is hidden as more dangerous than what is open to view. He says, 'If what Socrates does not trouble to hide would be so harmful, what sort of man would he show himself, and what advice would he give, when he had his admirers to himself?' Where? When? Why do you make these impudent charges, Anytus? Where did Socrates ever meet people apart from the well-known places? Whom did he ever meet at his home, or in the country, or anywhere else? [115] But so that you shall not get away with making these assertions and putting them forward as crimes, answer me this: Are these things which you allege, the ones that have been done openly and of which many men are witnesses – are they the work of someone out to harm us and acting lawlessly or not? If there is nothing evil which could arise, or has arisen, from them you have admitted that these charges are all a libel. But if things really are as you alleged, then you attribute to Socrates courage to the point of lunacy. [116] What was his object in bringing some things into the open and concealing others? If he were afraid of danger he would have kept everything dark. If he enjoyed living dangerously there would have been nothing in the whole business to cause him alarm. I assume that you will not allege that there were more serious criminal activities than his overt acts: what could be more scandalous than corrupting the young,

scorning the laws and destroying the constitution?

[117] When Anytus states that Socrates conversed with the young but was unwilling to argue with their elders he is lying. He is so shameless that even though he can see among you those who are standing around the court here who enjoyed conversing and associating with Socrates and to whom he used to speak while they listened attentively, he can nevertheless say that he avoided full-grown men and only sought out the young. He thinks that you will consider what you now hear more persuasive than what you yourselves have always known to be true. [118] Apart from this, if anyone could show that Socrates has turned himself into a teacher and some building into a college, and built a porter's room so that he could allow some to come in and keep others out, and that he had made it a rule to allow the young to enter but not older men, then a man might well be suspicious of his associations. But if, as is the case, he undertook to teach not the young men alone but anyone who said he wanted to train, and if, wherever he came across someone to talk to, that became the lecture-room for anyone who wanted to learn and a flock of those who wanted to hear surrounded him in a circle there, then how can it be said that some were allowed in and others excluded? Socrates did not drive away those who wanted to hear him, but those who did not want to hear his words did not frequent Socrates. You are acting like one who brings a charge against the winds on behalf of those who do not wish to sail, or, by Zeus, against springs of water for those who do not wish to draw any. [119] If one must find a reason why it was young men rather than old who took part in his arguments I shall not have to find a subtle one. Whatever it is that makes young men more than others go to those who teach

music or literature or anything else is the same in this case. And what is this? It is only those who are of the right age for learning who can devote their minds exclusively to this and ignore everything else. I imagine that your thoughts, gentlemen, are taken up with all sorts of other concerns, about your wives and children, your household and your old age, and affairs of government – in short, consideration of affairs of others as well as your own, and all this would be an impediment, even to those who wanted very much to do so, to engaging in such pursuits as do the young. [120] So let no one say that the young consorted with Socrates but if any older man wished to meet him he was prevented from doing so. That would be the sort of thing that a man would say out of jealousy about what they were getting or, if they really had leisure, out of malice towards Socrates, if business pressures really were not responsible for keeping them away. So far was Socrates from avoiding those who pursued him that he rather pursued some who were trying to avoid him. If he found anyone who did not care for his own intellectual welfare he would not praise him, but would cause him pain with his rebukes. So that if it had befallen all of the Athenians to pass the day in Socrates' company with no one and nothing to drag them away they would have heard exactly the same things as the young men did: that is, to learn what the poets really said and to follow the example of those who steer a ship, keeping close watch for any rotten place in the words they read as a helmsman looks out for holes below the water-line.

[121] Why is it, gentlemen of Athens, that you want your sons to believe immediately (from what the poets say) that Athene assumed the guise of a man and roused Pandarus to break all his oaths, or that Hera was hung up in the

stocks by Zeus when he was angry? Do you want them to believe that Aphrodite acted as a bawd for Paris, or that she and Ares were wounded by Diomedes? Do you think the account of the servitude of Apollo and Poseidon is going to be of any benefit to the young? Or the story that Zeus made a request for a little help from the gods that were sitting in judgement on him? Or the account of the battles of all the gods against one another? What about the story of the castration inflicted by Cronus, or the penalty which he himself suffered for executing the most extreme vengeance on his own father, and the no less terrible punishment which he suffered at the hands of his own son?

[122] In considering this is Socrates corrupting the young or stopping them being corrupted? Is it fair that Homer should blaspheme the gods so much and yet receive honour, and that Socrates, because he praised some of what Homer said but was not able to praise it all, must die – and that when the prosecutor has maligned Homer when he states that although all others must give an account of themselves for doing the same thing, it is not necessary for Homer to give any account at all?

[123] So that both he and you may both see what a slander it is upon Homer, let me recall a short episode from what he said. When he maintained that Odysseus suffered this and that because of his desecration of the shrines of Troy – in his travels by sea and land, in his return home and at his home itself – in all these cases he is driving Homer hard. What do I mean? Everyone would agree, I think, that *The Odyssey* was written in praise of that wandering sufferer, Odysseus, and that Homer lavished on Odysseus alone as much attention as he gives all the others together. He wrote *The Iliad* as a work in praise of all the heroes, but Odysseus alone is honoured in the other

work. [124] Because of this he makes Athene share concern for the safety of his hero, and not just looking after everything else but even busying herself with Odysseus' appearance, giving him either ugliness or beauty when it was needed. He even made the cause of Poseidon's anger an unjust one; for Poseidon was angry because the Cyclops had been blinded, whereas Odysseus had done the deed in self-defence and to save himself. So Odysseus is represented as having suffered wrong in all his wanderings and having won through to virtue when he overcame all the great ills that beset him. [125] So Homer took the opportunity to praise Odysseus as a wonderful man, but Anytus maintains that the hero whom Homer thought noble in every way, and who alone brought an end to the Trojan war, was in fact the most miserable of men and unholy – an evil-doer into the bargain. What greater way is there of condemning Homer than by saying that he chose as his hero and lavished all his attention on the man who was the most wicked of those who fought at Troy? [126] So is Anytus acting justly in exacting justice on Homer's behalf – or ought he rather to be paying the penalty? In criticising others for a few words he has completely uprooted the argument he himself put forward. If it would be right to punish the man who mutilates a hand, surely the murderer ought to suffer some greater punishment. But in fact neither Anytus nor Socrates are doing anything wrong if they find fault with some of the words of the poets.

[127] 'But,' they say, 'Socrates used to make men lazy.' How? Has he said that it is better for a man to sit doing nothing than to take part in some work? Has he ever bidden craftsmen abstain from their work, or farmers hate the land? Has he ever advised merchants to leave seafaring, or sailors to sleep or shipwrights to stop preparing vessels?

Has he ever bidden all men leave their employment and gaze at the heavens, as if sustenance will come to them from there? Let one Athenian come forward and bear witness that this is so and I will hold my tongue. But if Socrates did not praise laziness, but if he thought that they were strange men who showed more zeal in the gaining of money than in the gaining of greater virtue for their souls, since he said that the sou was the possession men ought to honour most while the body was of secondary importance and money took last place – then how was this persuading people to be lazy? [128] He did not say that it was wicked to pay attention to work, but he did not think it was right to consider those things that were by nature of secondary importance before those that were better. For when he saw that many men brought up their sons as if they were no better than slaves and neither educated their souls nor exercised their bodies but gathered wealth from every source as if this was the one means of bringing happiness, so that he might show those who were mistaken the error of their ways he took them to task and tried to change them and to re-educate them, advising them not to shut their minds to what they ought to do about these things, not to be lazy about those affairs which demand a greater degree of forethought while troubling themselves unduly about what was of less importance. This was charac- teristic of a man who wanted the same people to prosper and to show intelli- gence.

[129] Apart from this, if Socrates had taken away from their homes those who earned their living by manual work, so that they were forced to beg their bread, then perhaps he would have been doing wrong. But if it was those who had many to work for them – and you agreed with me on this, Anytus, when you said that it was not the poorer sections of society that consorted with Socrates –

then how was he making the land un- sown or denuding the countryside of farmers, as long as it was possible for those who owned the fields and profits to give thought both to the conditions of their souls and to the land as well?

[130] So he did not turn the others away from their work, and he himself had no land inherited from his father, nor any ship, and what money he did have, as I have told you, he lost, so that he had to endure poverty lightly. No man ever managed to overcome the pangs of hunger as he did – indeed, if it were possible to raise an army com- posed of men like Socrates there would be none harder for the enemy to overcome. For such men thirst and heat alike would have no terrors; they would cross desert as if it were well- watered land.

[131] You have been able to make trial of Socrates' laziness, Athenians, at Delium and at Amphipolis. On those occasions he drew the other soldiers to him by his endurance in the face of everything, night and day alike. He was like a man of iron. He laughed at the Thracian winter. Surely laziness always brings softness after it, and soft- ness makes a man unable to bear such privations as these. Socrates showed himself master of the extremes of climate. In the action at Delium, when he fled with the others he was the only one who still struck fear into the enemy as he retreated. This was how his body and soul were corrupted by laziness!

[132] Perhaps Anytus thinks that only slanderers are hard workers, while those who pay attention to education and the improvement of their minds are doing nothing. He does not abuse athletes, even though their work brings no advantage to anyone else. But he calls those who exercise their minds instead of their bodies useless, even though others may receive some benefit, from their activity; and he does not

consider what a great achievement it is if, by the reproaches of Socrates, those who are involved in politics pay attention to virtue.

[133] Another charge is that he does not speak out in public. Together with many Athenians (and even Solon confessed to this), he has the nature which makes it impossible for him to speak in public, a thing which has kept many others from participation in public life. But if he saw young men mounting the rostrum before they were ready for it he would pounce on them and hold them back and not allow them to practise on public issues. This was Socrates' own way of saving the city from inexperienced government. Has this man really spent his life in idleness at Athens? He has performed a most useful service to everyone, has he not, by removing the plethora of orators who did not know what they were doing. I consider that whoever pits himself against those who would be harmful has been a benefactor to those who have avoided having to experience that harm. And when we can call a man a benefactor, then how could anyone also call him lazy?

[134] It is true he is no banker: perhaps if he had been he would have been a better leader for the young. He can do nothing right. You blame him, Anytus, because he is not wealthy, but you show no admiration for the patient way he had borne poverty. You think that Sparta is an admirable state, for it is barren ground for sophists there, but when Socrates, like the Spartans, lives in poverty you maintain that he is wrong in doing what they are right to do. [135] Is that it? There was never a charge like this brought in the courts before, that of not being wealthy or having accumulated gold or invested in land. Generally it is quite the other way about: 'This man inherited a small amount of money from his father, but he has amassed a great fortune and has suddenly become superior to the majority. What is this change and why has it come about?' Socrates alone seems to be in danger of being punished for being content with his circumstances.

[136] Anytus has stated that Socrates taught evil practices and maintains that your young men were corrupted by him, but has only mentioned Alcibiades and Critias. It is easy enough to speak in their defence, but I would be ashamed if I were to consign Alcibiades to a similar reputation to that enjoyed by Critias, who harmed our common interests by his counsels, while Alcibiades did many good things and was prevented in all his designs and therefore forced to cause us grief. But after saying a few things in defence of Alcibiades, I would agree that they both did wrong but that Socrates had no part in their misdeeds.

[137] What is it that people charge Alcibiades with? Was it that he heard the tales of Alcmaeon and Hipponicus, their noble deeds and their rivalry, and of Cleinias and his battles and noble death, and was filled with an ambition to be worthy of those two noble houses [from which he was descended]? Or was it that he was born beautiful, a marvel to look upon? Or that he accepted in turn the duty laid upon him by his forefathers and began to devote himself to the public service? Was it that he made Sparta's neighbours hostile to her, and saved Attica from destruction by substituting theirs? Was it that he considered the present state of affairs in Athens to be less than she deserved, and set his sights on what the city lacked? [138] If you hate those who deprive you of what you have, you must surely praise the additional benefits you receive. Alcibiades turned his eyes towards Ionia, he saw a great island, he stretched out his hand towards Sicily, he wanted Italy and he hoped to gain Libya; he knew that he could bring

about the destruction of the Peloponnese if he held Magna Graecia, and he was eager to bring about a fair end to the war and to fall upon the Spartans only after he had increased the strength of Athens. But those who envied him and tried to stop him were not able to thwart him by what they said, and so they themselves committed sacrilege and mutilated the Hermae. They then brought forward their own outrageous acts and laid them at Alcibiades' door. They blamed him too for the troubles with the metics and the Mysteries, and accused him of all kinds of knavery and deceit.

[139] Consider this, gentlemen. Alcibiades wanted to give an account of himself, but they ordered him to set sail. He sailed across the Adriatic, and his enemies roused the Athenians to anger. He brought over the island to his side, while his enemies called for his destruction. So what did he do? He did what any man in his right mind would do. He saved his own skin and guarded himself from destruction. He thought then that he heard those words from the Salaminia: 'Flee as quickly as you can, Alcibiades, flee! Seek safety which you cannot find in Athens. It may seem that you are being summoned to judgement, but it is to your death. Slanders are believed and accusations levelled against you all the time.' [140] It is not surprising that he did not want to die unjustly. It is no wonder that he sailed to the place from which he expected to find safety. He was in Sparta, but he dreamed of Athens. But he did not go further than the trust that had been placed in him: his heart was always with Athens, and because of this he tried to involve the might of the Persian king on the city's behalf; he broke up the Spartan navy because of a shortage of money to pay them, and he deprived them of the triremes that they had been expecting. He did not stop waging war against them, Anytus,

although he was an exile and knew that the people were ill-disposed towards him, until you were ashamed of all the battles by land and sea, the victories and cities which had fallen to you, and voted for his return from exile and lifted the curses pronounced against him. And this man who was so wicked over the Mysteries gave you back the Ancient Way. [141] I do not mention the large number of chariots and the great expenditure which he made at the Olympic games in your name, from which you gained a reputation for strength which is to the common good. And yet it will become clear that he paid the penalty not of his wickedness but of his hastiness in government in the later periods, and although he has shown himself master of affairs abroad, he has been beaten by the slanders circulating among you, although he was in fact far more useful to the city than those who procured his exile.

[142] I have gone through the recital of all this not for the sake of Alcibiades and Socrates, gentlemen, but rather for the sake of your reputation. Your duty is clear. It is not a matter of apparent complicity in impiety, but rather of receiving back the man who has done nothing wrong. But so that you may better learn what righteous qualities there are still outstanding in the man now standing before us, let us grant that Alcibiades is no better than Critias; let us also grant that Socrates never offered himself as a teacher to anyone of such things as those. I ask that this too should be given your consideration – if a man claims to be a teacher, is he legally responsible for the crimes of those who are unwilling or unable to learn? For if he taught things which would be to the advantage of those who performed them but they paid no attention because other things pleased them more, then why should you hate Socrates instead of them? Is it as if a man were

to think that a farmer who worked as hard as he could on the land, working with his hands and equipment and using oxen and good seed and every practice of good husbandry, but who got nothing out of the land because it was barren, was himself the cause of the disaster, even though the farmer might be ready to explain his craft and show the man the land. [143] We see in other crafts too that some apprentices outstrip their master, some equal him eventually in skill, others fall rather below his standards and others learn nothing at all. So one shoemaker may turn out better than another, one joiner than another and so on with all the other crafts, though they are apprenticed to the same master. Nature is a stronger and more potent force than education, Athenians: when it is poor it drags a man down to its own level and makes all instruction a vain exercise. If this were not so, everyone engaged in the same craft would reach the same degree of expertise. It is the nature of the pupil which plays the biggest part; if men failed to realise this but instead punished the teachers for the lack of skill displayed by those who received instruction from them, then all crafts would come to an end, since no one would care to teach because he was afraid he might suffer for it. But, I think, gratitude is universally felt towards teachers, and failure to learn in pupils is a matter for rebuke.

[144] Indeed, men consider the law-givers as nothing other than teachers, and their pupils embrace those in the city of every age and nationality, young and old alike, men and women, citizen and stranger, slave or free. It is for that reason that the law-givers are honoured first after the gods, for from them we have learnt what we ought to do and what to leave alone. And we hear not only this but also the privileges and punishments that are laid down, the latter which will follow those who do not obey, and the former which will reward those who live a peaceable life. Even so, the thought of punishment or reward is not sufficient to eradicate wickedness. The law-givers may provide deterrents, but Anytus does wrong; they may proclaim their rewards, but Meletus thinks nothing of honour, but chooses rather to bring false charges for financial reward than to be an object of admiration by being included among the good.

[145] And so, since all kinds of crimes are committed despite the laws, and the punishments do not have the effect one would hope, has anyone reviled Solon or spoken ill of Dracon, making a fuss because they died before they could be called to account for it: has anyone told us that they are to be considered useless or harmful men? Of course not. We consider them our saviours and we punish those who act contrary to the laws they laid down. [146] And what should one say, Athenians, about those who are the most awe-inspiring teachers of all – you, the jurymen? You do not just take counsel together verbally to enforce the law, you act too, you confiscate property and exile people, you commit criminals to the Eleven for execution. This does not stop the wicked from doing wrong nor you from condemning them: some suffer the death-penalty straight away, others are caught later for their misdeeds. No law-giver will ever find a penalty so terrible that it will make all men good. [147] So since the penalties of the law-courts are shown to be ineffective, and criminality still knows how to challenge society, is Socrates really at fault if he failed to make all those whom he taught sincerely good through his conversations with them in the Lyceum? In the case of slaves, with whom we do not have to deal by the processes of law, it is possible for a master to use the treadmill, fetters, whips, to brand them or put them to the rack. But if they are evil

you may not be able to change them even by such tortures as these. Do you not think, then, that when Socrates was dealing with free-born men whose very high birth gave them intelligence he was not a more exacting master than you are of the slaves you have merely purchased?

[148] 'Critias harmed the State' is another complaint. He hurt Socrates too! 'He took away your freedom of speech.' He deprived Socrates too of the converse to which he was accustomed. Do you think that if he had been a devoted disciple of Socrates and really eager to follow his words and mode of living he would have rewarded his master in such a way and stopped the way of life in which Socrates had lived for so long? Was it likely that Socrates should have deplored the rule imposed by Critias, and that Critias should have ordered about those whom he grieved most? Was it not rather likely that Socrates should have admired his pupil's cruelty, since this is what he had taught him, and that Critias should have rewarded those who had fitted him for the position he held? [149] When athletes win prizes we see that their coaches are not filled with envy towards them – or violently suppressed by them; they rejoice with each other in the victory: Socrates was not so peculiar that when he saw all his efforts brought to an end, the laws powerless and democracy vanished under the dictatorship of Critias, he then censured the form of government that he had sought when it was absent and chose to put his neck into a noose rather than to stick by what seemed right to him.

[150] You have talked of Alcibiades and Critias, but you have not mentioned many men who are useful. Even if they take no part in public affairs, we can still admire their way of life, for a man has the opportunity to display virtue in the conduct of his private affairs.

What charge could you make against Plato? Or against Crito, Aeschines or Chaerephon? Or countless others? Have these men ever betrayed their friends, helped the enemy or disregarded the laws? What dictators have they set up? Have you made a collection of sayings by which you hoped to deceive us, while rushing by the things which Socrates said in contradiction of the poets? Was he not arguing on behalf of self-control when he urged Aristippus not to be the slave of his belly? When he taught Lamprocles, who paid no attention to his mother, was he not teaching him what regard we ought to pay to our parents? What could be juster than the advice he gave Chaerecrates and his brother about reconciliation? What could be better than what he taught Antisthenes about his conduct to his friends? [151] He made useful citizens both out of Glaucon, the son of Ariston, and out of Charmides, the son of Glaucon, by rousing the former to take part in public affairs when he was lazy, and by directing the latter when it seemed he was incapable of doing anything worthwhile. Pericles (Pericles' son) too listened to his speeches encouraging men to take command. Why should I number all these separately? If I wanted to call witness to his power of inculcating justice, self-discipline, bravery, gentleness, prophecy and all the other wonderful things which they heard I should have to summon the whole city apart from those who resemble these men here; not that they had not heard Socrates' teaching but that I think they would lie and say the opposite.

[152] I am sure that none of you, Athenians, would deny what was true or be persuaded to condemn Socrates because Theseus united the city and replaced the form of government that it had then, and Solon added Salamis and introduced the cancellation of debts – and this although he was owed

five talents. What I mean is this. It would surely be right to honour the men who did such things as this, but it would not be right to execute all the others. If it were necessary to execute those who did not unite the city when this had already been done, or failed to gain possession of Salamis when it was already ours, or those who never wrote laws or acted as generals, your supply of hemlock would run out! Theseus has the honours he deserves, as the temple in his honour shows, Solon's statue in bronze stands in the market-place, but I do not see what honour it would be doing either of them to exe-cute other Athenians because they had already done all these good deeds.

[153] Let him speak of your anger towards the sophists – Anaxagoras, Protagoras and Diagoras. He will enable you to ask this question: 'If Socrates was like the others with whom the people were angry, why was he not also a target for their anger?' If he was engaged in the same pursuits he ought to have been punished in the same way. If no sophist was punished this would have been apathy on the part of the city towards the gods, and a man could say that Socrates, too, had escaped because of this. But by your harsh behaviour towards them those of you who had not engaged in such things have showed yourselves free of the guilt which contaminated them. [154] It was right that Anaxagoras should be called to account for his irreligious reflections on the nature of the sun and moon. You acted justly in prosecuting Pro-tagoras for his researches on whether the gods exist or not. You were wise in offering a reward for the murder of Diagoras, for he joked about the Eleu-sinian Mysteries and the secret rites. But who can quote a book of Socrates or a saying about the gods which is contrary to the law? There is no evi-dence you can produce, Anytus, and however many sophists you cite who

have been put to death, you do not thereby convict Socrates. The ven-geance executed upon evil-doers cannot be constituted as the wickedness of the innocent!

[155] You have explained that those who have not associated with the sophists have become good men, citing Miltiades, Themistocles and Aristides, but you have forgotten that Miltiades died in prison, that the mighty Themis-tocles fled in a sea-battle. What virtue or nobility of character did that show, Anytus? Of course that is not why they were punished, but for evil and wicked-ness. Where is the profit in not associat-ing with the sophists: or is it that these men were really very good and it was the people that were base? By what sophist had they been corrupted? [156] So we see that those who never asso-ciated with the sophists came to such a pitch of evil, but that Pericles, the son of Xanthippus, who was a pupil of Anaxagoras and apart from having great power in the city was dignified by the title 'Son of Zeus' and enjoyed honours, when his old teacher met with harsh treatment from the citizens and was brought to trial by the people and imprisoned so that he should mind his ways, gained his release and saved him. Pericles is considered to have succeeded in all that he undertook. The law does not reward the base with such privileges as these, but those to whom is entrusted the guardianship of the commonwealth. Did the citizens not consider Pericles an excellent man, this man who ad-mitted that he had associated with a sophist and who helped him just because he was an old associate?

[157] When we consider the case of Damon, if he indeed did wrong, then it was just that he was exiled; if, however, he was the victim of slander it was no better that he should have suffered for it than that Socrates should be suffering now. Anytus says that Damon was exiled on lesser charges,

for he was never charged with trying to ruin the State by his enemies, as is the prisoner now before us. That very fact is proof that his opponents were less intransigent than Socrates'. There was nothing to stop them levelling lighter charges against him with justice and graver charges unjustly as well.

[158] Who would not complain if he heard evil of Bias, the companion of Solon, beloved by Pythian Apollo, who gave advice to all mankind in accordance with the precepts of Delphi, or many others through whom with Bias Ionia became great? It was not through the doing of Melissus, Thales and Pythagoras that those who occupied the cities suffered dissension and alien rule – dissension is a disease epidemic among mankind – and their subjection came about because the mighty kingdom of Persia blockaded them, and it was not Pythagoras or Melissus that made Persia mighty, but Cyrus by his destruction of Croesus, and after him Darius.

[159] As proof that the sophists do not play a part in revolt, or enjoy it if it does happen, I make the Spartans your witness. They came out in revolt at a time when no one else did, and changed their form of government. This was not because at that time they made sophists welcome at Sparta but because Pausanias was an insolent and overbearing man, whom the Greeks found unendurable, and he had never set eyes on a sophist! [160] Perhaps Thrasybulus and Conon might have been the better for concerning themselves a little with philosophical argument, while Critias and Alcibiades might have been made much worse if they had never touched it. The latter might perhaps have lacked a restraining influence, and the former might have been more pleasant men.

[161] I have spoken at sufficient length about these matters. You acted like good men when you grew angry that Meletus and Anytus should be teaching Socrates what was right and wrong. Perhaps one hardly need speak against men who had set out to do such a thing, but nevertheless I will say something about this too.

[162] What did you want the man to do to please you? To show the same reverence to the gods as does the rest of the city? So he has done, for everyone to see. To benefit parents? He made the others do so too. To wrong no one? He has been just in his dealings with everyone. To pay attention to the rulers? When has he ever failed to do so? To obey the laws? He has never broken one of them. To take thought for his family? He has done that and paid attention to the needs of strangers too. [163] He has grown old doing all this and entreating others to do so too, and yet you are trying to teach him as if he were ignorant of it all. It is as if someone were trying to teach Meletus the science of bringing false charges. On what do you base your charges, you shameless man, when you dare to charge Socrates with being a supporter of dictatorship? From what source do you hope to convince your listeners? From Socrates' madness? His boldness? His love of money? The rich banquets he gives or his costly clothes? From his followers? If a man came from elsewhere and having spent a short time among us judging the opinions of all was led to the assembled people and forced to say on the evidence of what he had seen who he thought was the most democratic man, do you not think he would give his vote to Socrates, whom he had seen as being superior to wealth and pleasures, and who would not immediately agree that the Lord of Asia was a happy man? What would a man who thought that such an exalted position as that was not happy consider to be the advantages of any smaller autocratic power? How could he want the sort of state where it was unprofitable

for a man to pay attention to education? [164] There is no need of a lengthy speech when I can show by clear and indisputable signs that he does not consider hereditary kingship praiseworthy either. I tell you, men of Athens, that many dictators wanted to see this man, because many of their courtiers had been struck by Socrates' virtue, and they thought it would befit their kingly state that they should see him too. [165] Accordingly, Eurylochus of Larissa sent for him, as did Scopas of Cranon and, greatest of all, Archelaus of Macedon. They begged him to come, they sent envoys to bring him and messages, and made him promises. How could he who used to teach the young act against the laws? We need the letters in which you might best see the man — but still, why do we need letters when the action he took cries aloud? He laughed at the three dictators, men of Athens, and their offers of presents and sustenance and luxuries. He reverenced the soil of Athens and the laws under which he had been born to his father and had in turn begotten children, and he did not consider it was his nature to serve any autocrat or receive favours from one. [166] They were not completely out of their minds in summoning him, for such a man was quite beyond their experience, but as they made their offers to him as he sat at home they heard that it was quite impossible to win him over by offers of money. Socrates himself, since he considered that it was no more fitting for him to enjoy wealth from there than to walk there to get it, rejected their offers, and although he could have enjoyed wealth greater than that brought by the fruits of slander, he remained in poverty gladly, and would not have taken the whole of Thessaly if it had been offered to him.

[167] Are you going to kill a man of this character, forgetting the oaths you have taken because of Anytus' words? Do you not fear the anger of the gods? Forget these false charges: look at his acts. Will you not prosecute the poets rather than those who put them to the test? Socrates himself does not consider it a terrible thing to die. Philosophy has taught him that in the other world he will enjoy the rewards of virtue; that there the gods will be his masters; that there he will meet the poets face to face and be able to question them. But it is not for you to consider what Socrates thinks important or not, but what is in accordance with the laws. You have not taken an oath to vote in accordance with Socrates' wishes, but in accordance with the laws that are laid down — none of which prevents a man from talking about the poets.

[168] So for Socrates there waits in Hades the great reward for a disciplined and well-ordered life: let him receive from you, men of Athens, the rewards which you owe him, for he is a poor man with a wife to support and children to rear. He never paid attention to the earning of money and the things from which he might have procured sustenance, but taught his family to endure what fortune brought. He himself went, as a guardian to all men, round the citizens making inquiries and ascertaining if anyone's son was being destroyed by drink or dicing or any other vice, and he would then take to task their thoughtless fathers. He roused generals who were sunk in lethargy and he made the political orators think seriously. He caused grief and pain if that were necessary. I have seen doctors doing the same thing, [169] and in this way Socrates copied them except that his work was even nobler. Doctors look after the needs of the body, he corrected men's souls. You are grateful to doctors for doing a lesser service — and you are right to do so — but will you put to death the man who has laboured in a yet worthier cause? Will this be his

reward for wanting to make all the Athenians into upright men? To many sons he showed more care than their own fathers; will you make his children orphans, and even dishonour them? Where will they be able to show themselves, talk or speak freely, unable to forget the tragedy that befell their father? [170] Weep unhappy children. Weep, wretched Xanthippe. Socrates will never do that, for he is confident in the face of death and he does not fear exile. The place that is prepared for the just, as the saying goes, is far sweeter than any spot here. So he will not seek safety in any way he considers disgraceful, nor will he abandon in the law-court the courage he has always practised, thinking that to be a suppliant is a disgrace both to himself and the city, if a man with a reputation for wisdom shrinks from death like any foreigner. But you can plead with the jury, entreat them and weep. [171] I shall not be afraid to join with you. Men of Athens, save and have pity on one who is a true friend, a good man and just counsellor, a righteous citizen, who may have caused grief to some but has done what befitted men of good will. He may not have been able to lead an army, but he knows how to control himself. He may not have been able to lead an expedition by sea, but he would not allow many young men to sail out into intemperate behaviour. The laws are an important matter for you to consider, and so is the vote of the jurymen, but it is not unimportant that Socrates, in criticising those who were going astray and blaming those who were acting unjustly, performed, as I have said before, a kind of continuous sacred service for the city.

[172] How many fathers who were heedless of their sons do you think began to consider their welfare through Socrates' investigation? How many men who would have fought with their brothers did not dare to do so? How many who would have treated their parents despitefully were moved to show them honour? They feared the reproaches of Socrates more than judgement in a court of law, for they knew that there they could buy off their accuser but that it was quite impossible to escape from such reasoning as Socrates', the watchdog of the just who cannot protect themselves, or persuade him to be silent. Must he die and pay the penalty because he made men better when he touched them most painfully? [173] You want to free yourselves from his arguments, and you do not fear the story that will go about concerning this. 'The Athenians want anything rather than to pay attention to their souls, and want to grow rich in ignorance. They have put to death one of their citizens who did not pay attention to such things, but who put them to shame and hurt their feelings, and who went around giving them good advice and acting with the interests of everyone at heart, treating him as if he were one of the enemies who had often ravaged the land. They showed no respect for his life and works, his words or his old age.' Do you think that this will be but a small hurt to you? Do you think the city will be able to act with moderation towards others when it treats so cruelly its best citizens? [174] There are perhaps some now who look upon him living and would like to see him dead; but if he does die and is deprived of his spirit, when the deed is seen in the light of reason, I think that everyone will be very regretful and blame Socrates' accusers and the way the votes were cast; indeed, blame everyone including themselves. They will grieve when they remember Socrates' voice and his discourses, when his companions think about him and his friends weep for him; when strangers sail to Athens hoping to see him and finding him dead will search for his tomb, and when one man will say to

another, pointing out the place, 'There he once spoke about self-control; there about bravery; there about justice. That was the place where he got the better of Prodicus in argument, there Protagoras. That was where he overwhelmed the man from Elis, and over there the man from Leontini.' [175] How will anyone be able to remember his triumphs without tears coming to his eyes? How will we be able to look at one another after Socrates has drunk the hemlock? There are many things, Athenians, which offend you by their presence, but when they have disappeared you long for them. Do not make wealth the only subject of conversation for those who frequent the palaestra; do not show that the acquisition of wisdom is a risky business liable to prosecution in Athens. Do not let the world witness a terrible spectacle, quite out of keeping with the spirit of the city, by only bringing Socrates out of prison for burial and depriving the city of his voice as if of a nightingale's. Do not allow his comrades to curse you from their silence of the tomb and then flee far and wide to Megara, Corinth, Elis and Euboea, bearing away the flower of Attica and saying wherever they go: 'Gentlemen, receive us as exiles from Athens; we are not traitors or deserters, we have not given away any opportunities, we have done nothing wicked for which the laws could punish: we are accused merely of love of intellectual discussion and education. This is what Lycon persuaded the jury; this is what Meletus accused us of, and it is for those reasons that Anytus has prosecuted us. We saw Socrates tried, condemned, imprisoned and executed. All this warned us that we should flee, that we should avoid such a fate ourselves.'

[176] Will other cities not receive them gladly and console them and give them encouragement? And as each of them establishes himself and shares the knowledge that he has, they will first of all show that many cities are more estimable than Athens with regard to wisdom, and they will also protect themselves from the murderers of Socrates by their words, and not just these men who are prosecuting, Athenians, but you too and the rest of the city, for they will say that you had a part in it by not preventing what was done. It will not be possible to escape from their reproaches, and time will not eradicate the story. There may be disagreement over oral tradition. But when men commit an account of actions, whether good or bad, to writing there they must remain immortalised. [177] Do you not see Minos suffering on the stage, his house brought to shame because of the love of Pasiphae? But this story would never have been known to many men if the tragedians had not spread the story everywhere. And now in return for the harsh treatment he meted out to our city when he held power by sea, Minos is punished by the poets even after his death. So do not now make the tongues of many wag about you, nor make those who attack what is happening here into enemies of the city.

[178] Why should I try to persuade you not to appear in an unfavourable light in the histories that will be written about you? Fear the power of the Delphic oracle, Athenians. Show reverence for the oracle and the testimony from Delphi and do not vote for the death of the man who was honoured by the pronouncement from the tripod. Do not copy the outrageous example of Idas, who, so they say, took up his bow against the god. This is to make war on Apollo, war arising from an Attic lawcourt against the centre of the earth. From there the god pronounced, 'Socrates is the wisest of all men,' while you shout from here, 'Put Socrates to death.' [179] How will you be able to send embassies to Delphi? How will you

be able to go and make sacrifices? How pray to the god? How will you consult the sacred tripod when you have condemned its pronouncements as so much nonsense? And yet who should with more justice than you sustain the oracle's reputation? You sent out your colonies through his advice; through him you destroyed the Persians and found relief from many other evils; through him you celebrate the harvest festival for the whole of Greece. [180] Come now – if you want to go to the god seeking release from an enemy who was pressing you hard (may it never come to pass) as you have done before and he were to drive you out of the shrine of the Muses as he did the murderer of Archilochus, asserting that you actually killed his minister, then we would have a fine reputation throughout Greece. Archilochus' murderer could fall back on the laws of war, but what excuse will be found for your behaviour? [181] The god himself once, angered by the treatment given to Aesopus, brought evil on his own priests. Surely no one would dispute that Aesopus the Physician is of less importance to the god than your own Socrates? Then how do you think he would lightly bear the death of Socrates when he thought that previous death a grievous crime? A fine reputation we will have among the Greeks without having to suffer punishment as well! If Socrates is put to death by your votes and there has been the appearance of a trial the blame will be even greater than if the deed had been perpetrated in a fit of anger. Does not the fact that the sacred ship has already been garlanded to take the sacred choir

to Delos show that the god is opposed to Socrates' death and is bearing the ship away so that he shall be saved?

[182] To show care for those who love the arts is right for good men, Athenians. To demonstrate the truth of this, consider how the Lebethrii paid the penalty for the murder of Orpheus by being deprived of music and having this land plunged into the darkness of ignorance. Surely it is the worst of all evils, the most harmful of deprivations, that the intellect should be blinded and that men should have to live in ignorance of what is beautiful, no different from the beasts? Do not make such a mistake or suffer such a fate yourselves!

[183] Crito, you are a contemporary of Socrates and from the same deme. Tell these men what you owe to your friend. Where are the sons of Leon of Salamis? Socrates was sent to their father by the Thirty, but went home instead. Will his demesman come and tell of his character? And I call too upon the families of those who were associates of Thrasyllus and Pericles, and who did not die without a fair trial through the intervention of Socrates.

[184] Stop interrupting, Anytus. Fear what is coming. Do not wish for a Cadmean victory. Take care lest you rejoice today but find pain tomorrow. Callixenus may have taken generals captive, but in doing so he destroyed himself. Keep his example in mind and cease your complaints. Phaedo is expiating his wickedness by becoming a philosopher after an evil life. This is how Socrates is accustomed to corrupt the young! (tr. G. Salway)

PART ELEVEN

GNOMOLOGIA

Collections of aphorisms, technically known as *gnomologia*, were a feature of the Byzantine age, and a number have come down to us, of which that of Stobaeus is the best known. In a brilliant article in *Classical Quarterly* 44 (1950), 126–37, and n.s. 1 (1951), 1–19, entitled 'A New Gnomologium: With Some Remarks on Gnomic Anthologies', J. Barns argued that these collections can be traced back not merely to the early Ptolemaic period in Egypt (say, the third century B.C.) but to Athens in the fourth century, where they were fostered by Isocrates, the greatest educationalist of the age.

It follows that aphorisms attributed to Socrates *may* be of respectable antiquity, but we cannot be sure that they are. The Cynics, as we have seen, adopted Socrates as a kind of patron saint, and themselves espoused an aphoristic moralism which they tended to foist on to him. The matter is controversial, and the individual must make up his own mind, but it seems useful to print the bulk of the aphorisms from the two main collections.

11.1 Stobaeus

John Stobaeus collected a commonplace book for his son Septimius, drawing on earlier writers, and indeed earlier anthologies, and classifying his extracts under subject-headings. The work is a complete miscellany; we know nothing about the editor except that he may be tentatively placed in the fifth century A.D.

What follows comprises most of the extracts dealing with Socrates. The principal omissions are direct citations from Plato and Xenophon (which may not, however, appear elsewhere in the present volume), and a longish allegorical explanation of the horn of Amalthea, which is so clearly from a Cynic source that it would be perverse to include it.

Some of the sayings are aphorisms attributed directly to Socrates: these appear in inverted commas.

11.1.1 Socrates, being asked 'What is god?', replied, 'The immortal and eternal.' (1, 1, 29a W)

11.1.2 Philosophy is a hunt for truth – also an aspiration to it. Some philosophers define it as catching the quarry: so Epicurus and the Stoics. Some say that the climax is the search, as the goal is with the gods, and wisdom is not a human possession. So Socrates and Pyrrho. (2, 1, 18)

11.1.3 When did anyone ever hear Socrates discoursing on astronomy or recommending the ethical value of studying mathematics? We know that he had a grasp of music – ear-deep! He was always asking what is beauty, or courage, or justice or one of the other virtues. He would call these 'goods within man's scope'. The rest he described as outside human grasp, or a kind of myth, winning the hostility of the sophists who expounded such trivialities. But Socrates practised what

he preached. (2, 1, 29 (from 'Xenophon's' letters))
Cf. **15.5**.

11.1.4 Socrates said that the most powerful authority lay in monarchical rule, the finest in self-rule. (2, 8, 29)

11.1.5 Socrates, when asked whose words carried the greatest weight, answered: 'Those whose actions echo their words.' (2, 15, 37)

11.1.6 'Education is a festival for the mind; there is so much for it to see and hear.' (2, 31, 44)
Some editors attribute this to Isocrates: cf. Panegyric *43*.

11.1.7 'For runners who reach the winning post there is ready the winner's trophy, for those who persevere in their labours to old age the first prize of wisdom.' (2, 31, 45)

11.1.8 He saw an illiterate millionaire and said, 'Look! a gilded slave!' (2, 31, 46)
Cf. 3, 4, 84 and note Gnomologium Vaticanum *484* (**11.2.7**).

11.1.9 'Adorn cities with votive offerings and minds with learning.' (2, 31, 53)
Also attributed to Demonax.

11.1.10 Socrates, being asked the best way to bring up one's own family, replied: 'Educate them when young: when they are grown up teach them to adapt themselves to circumstances; give them resources in such a way as not to make enemies of them.' (2, 31, 54)

11.1.11 Socrates, being asked, 'What is knowledge?', replied, 'Care of the mind.' Being asked, 'What is the chief reason for people turning out badly?', he replied, 'Bad training and bad company.' (2, 31, 79).

11.1.12 Socrates used to encourage young men to look in the mirror frequently. The handsome were to match their looks with their character; the less handsome to cover over ugly looks with loveliness of character. (2, 31, 98).

11.1.13 Socrates, being asked, 'What is the most delightful thing in life?', replied, 'Education: virtue: finding out what one does not know.' (2, 31, 99)
Cf. Gnom. Vat. *470.*

11.1.14 Socrates saw Xenophon, a well-endowed young man, and asked him if he knew where in the market the fish were. 'Yes,' he replied. Next Socrates asked about the vegetables, and he said Yes to them and all the other things. Now Socrates asked, 'Do you know where the good men live?' He had nothing to say, and Socrates left him with a rebuke. Xenophon, confounded by Socrates, began to philosophise. (2, 31, 101)
Cf. **1.5.**

11.1.15 On the way to the Academy Socrates happened to fall in with a man who claimed omniscience, and promised information on any subject. He stopped by a piece of cultivated ground and said, 'Don't you think the farmer negligent for not planting every inch of ground and leaving intervals between the trees?' He replied, 'Well, if he did that, none of them would survive; they would destroy one another. Socrates answered, 'Then what about you? You don't leave an inch of your mind, but pack in one piece of knowledge on another. Do you expect to reap any harvest from them?' (2, 31, 102)

11.1.16 'Education like a fertile field produces blessings everywhere.' (2, 31, 103)

11.1.17 Socrates recommended making the least – or the most – of the company of princes. (3, 1, 23)
Attributed to Aesop and Xenophanes.

11.1.18 'Reason is the only sober trustee for life and youth.' (3, 1, 73)

11.1.19 'It's less trouble when your shoes – and your life – fit.' (3, 1, 74)

11.1.20 'You don't judge a good horse by its rich saddle but by its natural quality. You don't judge a good man by his rich possessions but by his quality of mind and character.' (3, 1, 84)

11.1.21 'When the mouth of a wise man opens it is like a temple. Beauties of mind and character appear like statues.' (3, 1, 85)

11.1.22 'In sailing trust the captain, in life the man with the best judgement.' (3, 1, 86)

11.1.23 'There's no fun in a party without company or in money without virtue.' (3, 1, 87)

11.1.24 'It is not good to choose the smoothest road or the easiest life.' (3, 1, 88)

11.1.25 'Life is like a statue; every part should be beautiful.' (3, 1, 89)

11.1.26 'A statue ought to stand firm on its plinth and a good man firm on his profession of goodness.' (3, 1, 90)

11.1.27 'Don't secure your ship on a single anchor or your life on a single hope.' (3, 1, 104)

11.1.28 'In life as in a play the primary role should belong to the wisest character, not the richest.' (3, 1, 180)

11.1.29 'It is good to see a bright fire in a grate, and intelligence in prosperity.' (3, 1, 181)

11.1.30 'Disruptive influences should be banished from a well-ordered city; and inclinations to evil from the soul that seeks salvation.' (3, 1, 182)

11.1.31 'You're not safe in using a horse without a bit or money without intelligent thought.' (3, 1, 185)

11.1.32 'Life is like a musical instrument – more attractive when tuned by tautening and relaxation.' (3, 1, 186)

11.1.33 'Give incense to the gods and praise to the virtuous.' (3, 1, 187)

11.1.34 'To get money from wrong-doing and use it on good works is like robbing a temple and then worshipping in it.' (3, 1, 188)

11.1.35 'Defend those who are unjustly accused of injustice; praise those who stand apart from others for a good cause.' (3, 1, 189)

11.1.36 'Give credit to anything which is done scientifically.' (3, 1, 190)

11.1.37 'Staking the future on an ill-formed judgement is the same as mooring your boat with a weak anchor.' (3, 2, 45)

11.1.38 Socrates, being asked, 'What is wisdom?', replied, 'Harmony in the mind.' Being asked, 'Who are wise?', he replied, 'Those who have difficulty in going astray.' (3, 3, 44)

11.1.39 Socrates the philosopher was offered many presents by his friends. He refused them all, and was told off by his wife Xanthippe. He answered, 'If we are too ready to take them all when they are given freely we shall never have anything when we ask for it.' (3, 3, 50)

Cf. Gnom. Vat. *486*

11.1.40 'Men sailing in fair weather keep their storm equipment at the ready. Intelligent people in prosperity have ready rescue equipment against misfortune.' (3, 3, 56)

11.1.41 'Put on board ballast from wisdom as on an empty ship.' (3, 3, 61)

11.1.42 'The wise man treats life as a journey and takes as luggage useful rather than expensive possessions.' (3, 3, 62)

In these last three sayings the words for 'intelligent', 'wisdom', 'wise' are all connected with the phron-*root of the 'think-tank' in Aristophanes.*

11.1.43 'The coward betrays his fatherland, the man obsessed with reputation betrays his hereditary substance.' (3, 4, 55)

A curious saying: the point is not wholly clear.

11.1.44 'Runaway slaves are scared even if there is no pursuit; fools lose their tranquillity without doing anything immoral.' (3, 4, 56)

11.1.45 'Unintelligent people misuse wine at drinking-parties and misuse their minds in times of prosperity.' (3, 4, 57)

11.1.46 'Unmusical people cannot get in tune with their instruments; uneducated people cannot get in tune with their circumstances.' (3, 4, 58)

11.1.47 'Uneducated people change their attitude to life as often as an actor changes his costume.' (3, 4, 59)

Seemingly the only appearance of the noun for 'change of costume' (metekduma).

11.1.48 'Fools are like children; it doesn't take much provocation to make them cry.' (3, 4, 60)

11.1.49 'Strangers lose their way in the streets. Uneducated people lose their way in life.' (3, 4, 61)

11.1.50 'You might as well make a sick man carry a load as to make an uneducated man carry prosperity.' (3, 4, 62)

11.1.51 'There is no safety on a voyage in mooring without regard to the lie of the land; there is no security in life in living without regard to the law.' (3, 4, 63)

11.1.52 'Proteus is for ever changing his appearance: the man without education is for ever changing his inner disposition.' (3, 4, 64)
Proteus: a mythical divinity with the power of changing his shape.

11.1.53 'It is the extent of burdens which oppresses men off-colour and men who have had a stroke of luck.' (3, 4, 65)

11.1.54 'The physically weak are difficult to cure in illness, the spiritually weak in disaster.' (3, 4, 107)

11.1.55 'The coward keeps his weapons for himself, the fool his property.' (3, 4, 114)

11.1.56 'Rough wine makes bad drinking and rough manners bad company.' (3, 4, 115)

11.1.57 'Achilles' weapons don't fit Thersites, nor the blessings of fortune a fool.' (3, 4, 118)
Achilles: hero of the Trojan war. Thersites: a man of the people, depicted as fool, boor and coward.

11.1.58 'Sick men can't take rich food or fools good fortune.' (3, 4, 119)

11.1.59 'Peals of thunder scare off boys, threats scare fools.' (3, 4, 120)

11.1.60 'The man who is serious-minded ought to speed by pleasures like Sirens and look on virtue as his native land.' (3, 5, 30)

11.1.61 Socrates was asked, 'Who is the richest man of all?', and replied, 'The man who is satisfied with least. Self-sufficiency is natural wealth.' (3, 5, 31)
Cf. Gnom. Vat. 476. It is not clear whether the last words are attributed to Socrates or an editorial comment. Also attributed (with more probability) to Epicurus.

11.1.62 Socrates, being asked what to avoid, answered, 'Pleasures which involve shame and injustice.' (3, 5, 32)

11.1.63 Socrates said that it was a mark of a god to need nothing and that he who needs least is closest to god. (3, 5, 33)

11.1.64 'Self-sufficiency is a pleasant short-cut involving little trouble and much delight.' (3, 5, 34)
Not quite certainly attributed to Socrates even in the MSS. of Stobaeus.

11.1.65 Socrates used to say that pleasures ought to be pursued inside oneself, not just from outside sources, by right physical predispositions. (3, 5, 35)

11.1.66 'You can't wrap up fire under a cloak or a disgraceful act under the passage of time.' (3, 6, 14)

11.1.67 'Wind feeds fire and intercourse feeds love.' (3, 6, 15)

11.1.68 Socrates said that adulterers were men who refused to drink from a flowing stream but insisted on the inferior static water from the bottom. (3, 6, 16)

11.1.69 Socrates, being asked, 'What is strength?', replied, 'A movement of mind and body together.' (3, 7, 15)

11.1.70 Socrates was put on trial. Lysias composed a speech for him, brought it along and told him to use it, adding, 'It's very lovely.' 'So are roses,' said Socrates, 'but no garland for me, thank you.' 'You'll be doomed to death,' said Lysias, 'if you don't make your defence along these lines.' 'Well,' said Socrates, 'if I don't die now, I shall be doomed to death sooner or later.' (3, 7, 56)
Cf. **9.1.1.28** *n.*

11.1.71 Socrates, being asked who are the avaricious, replied, 'Those who pursue sordid profit and neglect the needs of their friends.' (3, 10, 46)

11.1.72 'Sediment: lees in wine, illiberality in a miser.' (3, 10, 54)

11.1.73 'No use looking for company from a corpse or a present from a miser.' (3, 10, 55)

11.1.74 'Frank comment is like personal beauty – entrancing at the right moment.' (3, 13, 61)

11.1.75 'The right of speech without action is like a dagger without an edge.' (3, 13, 62)

11.1.76 'To deny frank comment its place in education is to deny the sun its place in the sky.' (3, 13, 63)

11.1.77 'Free speech combined with poverty is like wealth wearing old clothes.' (3, 13, 64)

11.1.78 'The support of flatterers runs away from misfortune as if there'd been a military disaster.' (3, 14, 21)

11.1.79 'Hunters chase hares with hounds; the average man chases fools with praise.' (3, 14, 22)

11.1.80 'Wolves are like dogs, but their objects are different. So with flatterers and their friends.' (3, 14, 23)

11.1.81 'Flattery is like weapons in a picture, pretty but useless.' (3, 14, 24)

11.1.82 'The life of businessmen is like a dead man's feast. It has everything except someone to enjoy it.' (3, 16, 27)

11.1.83 'The wealth of businessmen is like the sun after sunset; it doesn't shine on the living.' (3, 16, 28)

11.1.84 Socrates, being asked in what way he differed from the rest of mankind, answered, 'The rest live to eat, I eat to live.' (3, 17, 21)
See also (*from Musonius*) *Stobaeus 3, 18, 37*; Gnom. Vat. *479*; **8.19.2**; **9.1.1.2**; **9.2.3**; **9.6.9**.

11.1.85 Socrates said that self-control was stronger than physical pleasure. (3, 17, 27)
There is a slight pun in the Greek.

11.1.86 Socrates, being asked how a man might become rich, answered, 'If he is poor in desires.' (3, 17, 30)
A saying attributed to Pythagoras, Democritus, Epicurus, Cleanthes and others.

11.1.87 Socrates, being asked why he didn't write, answered, 'Because I notice that paper costs more before it's written on.' (3, 21, 9)
A free translation of slightly strained Greek. The meaning is clear. Cf. Gnom. Vat. *499.*

11.1.88 'Arrogance is like a bad sculptor; you can see the distortions in its picture of reality.' (3, 22, 35)

11.1.89 'Superstition obeys arrogance like a father.' (3, 22, 36)
Point obscure.

11.1.90 'Air distends empty wine-skins, self-conceit distends men without wisdom.' (3, 22, 37)

11.1.91 Socrates, being asked the meaning of vulgarity, said, 'Looking down on your equals.' (3, 22, 38)

11.1.92 Socrates used to say that if in the theatre there were an announcement asking for the shoemakers to stand up, they and only they would do so. So with the bronze-smiths, the weavers and all the other professional groups. But if the announcement were 'Will the intelligent, or the honest, people present stand up?' the whole theatre would rise. The greatest damage is done by the fact that the majority think that they are intelligent and are not. (3, 23, 8)

11.1.93 Socrates, being asked what is tranquillity, answered, 'Living in the knowledge that nothing in your life is out of place.' (3, 24, 13)

11.1.94 Socrates in old age studied the lyre with Connus, the musician. Someone said, 'Learning music at your age!' Socrates answered, 'With learning, better late than never.' (3, 29, 68)

11.1.95 'Use laughter like salt – sparingly.' (3, 34, 18)

11.1.96 'Clothes may cloak a want of proportion; a smiling face may mask a life gone wrong.' (3, 37, 26)
The original words of the Greek and their purport are quite uncertain.

11.1.97 'Beauty of reputation quickly fades before envy as before a disease.' (3, 38, 34)

11.1.98 'Envy attends those who make their way by reputation as surely as shadow attends travellers in the sunlight.' (3, 38, 35)

11.1.99 Socrates said that envy was a wound in the soul. (3, 38, 48)
See Gnom. Vat. *485* (**11.2.8**).

11.1.100 Socrates used to say that it was easier for a man to hold a blazing coal on his tongue than a secret of the Mysteries. (3, 41, 5)
Cf. Gnom. Vat. *475.*

11.1.101 'Enjoyment of prosperity, like political power, should be shared among the meritorious.' (4, 1, 47)

11.1.102 Socrates, being asked which city was best governed, answered, 'The one which lives by law and prosecutes its crooks.' (4, 1, 82)

11.1.103 Socrates, being asked which city was badly governed, answered, 'The one where the rulers depend on political cliques for their power.' (4, 1, 83)

11.1.104 Socrates, being asked which city was strongest, answered, 'The one which has good men.' (4, 1, 84)

11.1.105 Socrates, being asked who ought to be elected to political office, answered, 'Those who have been well educated and reach manhood without betraying their upbringing for money.' (4, 1, 85)
A guess at the meaning behind some impossible Greek.

11.1.106 Socrates used to say that the best king was the one who could rule his own emotions. (4, 7, 26)
Cf. Gnom. Vat. *472* ('only *king*').

II.I.107 Socrates, being asked what human beings have regrets, answered, 'Those who marry.' (4, 22b, 59)

II.I.108 'Men ought to obey the laws of the state, and women the dispositions of their husbands.' (4, 23, 58)
Attributed by Dindorf to Dio of Prusa.

II.I.109 'Put up with an ununderstanding father as with a harsh law.' (4, 25, 42)

II.I.110 'A father's rebuke is pleasant medicine: the benefit outweighs the sting.' (4, 26, 22)

II.I.111 A man said to Socrates, 'I shall die if I don't get even with you'; he answered, 'I shall die if I don't get friends with you.' (4, 27, 20 (from Hierocles))

II.I.112 Socrates, asked, 'What is good breeding?', answered, 'A good balance of soul and body.' (4, 29a, 20)

II.I.113 'We don't rank as the best grain the one which comes from the best soil, but the one which produces the best food. We don't rank as the best man or best friend the one who comes from the best family, but the one who has the best character.' (4, 29a, 23)

II.I.114 Socrates, being taunted with his low birth by a vulgar aristocrat, said, 'My family is a reproach to me, you to your family.' (4, 30, 12)
Similar stories are told of Themistocles and others.

II.I.115 'Ankle-long robes trip you up physically; excess of possessions trips you up spiritually.' (4, 31c, 83)

II.I.116 Socrates said: 'Wealth would be of major importance if enjoyment went with it. As it is, the two are separate. Those who want to use their wealth are distraught by luxury, those who want to keep it, by anxiety, those who want to acquire it, by avarice.' (4, 31c, 90)
See Gnom. Vat. *497* (**II.2.16**).

II.I.117 'Wine changes with its container, and wealth changes with the character of its owner.' (4, 31d, 107)

II.I.118 'A gold bed is of no help to a man who is ill, nor outstanding fortune to a man who is unwise.' (4, 31d, 108)
Wrongly classified by Stobaeus under wealth.

II.I.119 'Sweat is seemliest when it comes from physical exercise, wealth when it comes from a man's own efforts.' (4, 31d, 129)

II.I.120 'See that your wealth is like a friend and comes unhesitating and eager with you on honourable occasions.' (4, 31d, 130)

II.I.121 Socrates described poverty as a minor form of self-discipline. (4, 32a, 18)
See **9.1.1.38**.

II.I.122 Socrates used to say that he thought the gods must be for ever laughing at the spectacle of human beings' petty enthusiasms; the enthusiasm is not commensurate with the pettiness of all human objects. (4, 34, 69)

II.I.123 Socrates, being asked, 'How can a man live his life without trouble?' answered, 'Impossible. Anyone who lives in a house or state in company with others is bound to meet trouble.' (4, 35, 35)

II.I.124 Socrates, being asked, 'What is illness?', answered, 'A disturbance of the body.' (4, 36, 9)

11.1.125 Socrates, being asked, 'What is happiness?', answered, 'A pleasure you do not later regret.' (4, 39, 18)

11.1.126 Socrates, being asked, 'Who are happy?', answered, 'Those who combine reasoning power with good wits.' (4, 39, 19)

11.1.127 Socrates was in the middle of a chain of reasoning. The news came that his son was dead. He brought his argument to a conclusion, and then said, 'Let us be going to perform the customary rites over Sophroniscus.' (4, 44, 74)
A doubtless apocryphal story, also told of Cleobulus.

11.1.128 'In life to be worsted by fortune and rail at her is rather like being worsted in athletics and prosecuting your opponent for foul play; you are not acknowledging the rules of the contest of life.' (4, 45, 9)

11.1.129 'Evil ambitions are like bad guides and lead you to lose your way.' (4, 46, 21 (from Aristonymus))

11.1.130 'A woman never produces offspring without a man and hopefulness never produces anything useful without hard work.' (4, 46, 26)

11.1.131 'Commend doctors to those who are ill, friends to those in misfortune.' (4, 48b, 31)

11.1.132 'Shelter is called for in a storm, and tranquillity in old age.' (4, 50c, 93)

11.1.133 'Don't grieve the soul and trouble it with tears and lamentation. A good man knows how to take what comes.' (4, 51, 23)
The Greek is quite uncertain.

11.1.134 'In life, as in a theatre, wait for the moment when the spectacle of what is happening gives you pleasure.' (4, 53, 39)

11.1.135 'Life is like a game of backgammon; what happens in life is a move in the game. You can't change a move once made or withdraw your piece.' (4, 56, 39)
This appears to be derived from a saying of Antiphon (fr. 106).

11.2 Gnomologium Vaticanum

A fourteenth-century codex in the Vatican library at Rome, Codex Vaticanus Graecus 743, contains a collection of 577 aphorisms, arranged not by subject but by the person to whom they are attributed. These were brilliantly edited by Leo Sternbach (Gnomologium Vaticanum, Berlin, 1963). Thirty-one are attributed to Socrates, but some of these overlap with Stobaeus, or other sources: in addition, there is one under the name of Xanthippe.

11.2.1 Socrates, being asked what is the most advantageous possession, said, 'A firm friend.' (471)
See Xenophon, Memoirs of Socrates 2, 4, 7; but this is not derived from there.

11.2.2 Socrates saw a man grumbling at poverty, encountering him at a time when the Thirty Dictators were doing away with the rich. 'You never repent poverty, do you?' he said. (473)
*A similar but not identical story in Diogenes Laertius 2, 34 (**1.4**).*

11.2.3 Someone said to Socrates, 'I love you.' 'That's not my fault,' he replied. (474)

11.2.4 Socrates said that it was the same mistake to give to the wrong people and to refuse to give to the right people. (477)

11.2.5 Someone asked Socrates how he could argue without making mistakes; Socrates answered, 'If you never say anything you're not absolutely certain of.' (482)

11.2.6 Someone was talking nonsense. Socrates said: 'It's better to make a slip with your foot than your tongue. The first makes your clothes dirty; the second leaves a permanent mark. Water can remedy the first, but a word once spoken can never be unspoken.' (483)

11.2.7 Socrates saw an uneducated millionaire and said, 'Look: a gilded sheep!' (484)
Cf. Stobaeus 2, 31, 46 (**11.1.8**).

11.2.8 Socrates said that envy was a wound for truth. (485)
See Stobaeus 3, 38, 48 (**11.1.99**).

11.2.9 Socrates was at a party and was criticised for spilling the wine as he poured it. 'Yes,' he said, 'and if I drink it it gets spilled down my throat and spills me into the bargain.' (488)
Also attributed to Diogenes. Unlikely to be authentic.

11.2.10 Socrates was asked whether the world was spherical, and replied, 'I don't know: I've never been in a position to see.' (489)
Also told of Diogenes.

11.2.11 He also said that everything belonged to those who could use it. (490)

11.2.12 He also saw a man gratifying all comers with his favours. 'Damn and blast you!' he said. 'You've turned the virgin Graces into whores.' (492)

11.2.13 He also saw Aristippus extravagantly dressed, and crapped on the seat on which he was about to sit. Aristippus sat down in the clear, and Socrates said, 'I thought that you owned a suit; I didn't think the suit owned you.' (493)

11.2.14 He also saw a man in a pool eager to be admired for his swimming, and said that he was amazed that he made such an excellent porpoise and such a poor human being. (494)
Also of Aristippus.

11.2.15 Socrates, being asked, 'How is King Archelaus off for happiness?', answered, 'I don't know. I don't know how he's off for education.' (496)
This comes from Plato, Gorgias 470 D–E, but it is not quoted from there; most likely it was filched somewhere along the line as a freely remembered anecdote, but just possibly Plato was incorporating an anecdote into his dialogue.

11.2.16 He also said: 'If enjoyment went along with wealth, it would be worth a lot. As it is, the two are separate. Menelaus in Homer says, "I take no enjoyment in being lord over these riches."' (497)
See Stobaeus 4, 31c, 90 (**11.1.116**) *with a different elaboration: Homer, Odyssey 4, 93.*

11.2.17 He also learned that one of the young men was neglecting everything else in his enthusiasm for hunting, and said to him, 'What is the price of a good hunter?' He replied, 'A thousand drachmas.' Socrates said, 'Remember he won't be worth more even if everything turns out as you want.' (498)

11.2.18 Xanthippe, being asked what was the greatest thing about Socrates, replied, 'The fact that he doesn't change his expression in prosperity or adversity.' (573)
Cf. 8.1.11 n.

PART TWELVE

CHRISTIAN WRITERS

Christian writers tend to be polemical and selective in what they record. The whole attitude to pagan culture was a matter for controversy. 'What has Athens to do with Jerusalem?' cried Tertullian, but Justin, Clement and others were treating this as a serious question, not as a rhetorical rejection. Even with a basic rejection of pagan culture, it was possible to take different attitudes to Socrates. He might be seen as a typical embodiment of paganism and criticised and rejected as such. Or he might be seen as himself a critic of pagan society, rejected and executed by the pagans, a man of true wisdom, a man groping towards the Christian enlightenment.

I have in general not included passages which are directly based on Plato and Xenophon, except where they are integrated into a total picture. But the Christian writers had access to other traditions, and Hippolytus and Epiphanius in particular were used by Hermann Diels to establish the 'doxographic traditions' about the philosophers. Mostly the Christian polemists take a few stock themes and repeat them *ad nauseam* from one author to the next, but occasionally we encounter a *mot* not recorded elsewhere, or a refreshingly original treatment.

There is one problem of translation in the Greek writers. The word *logos* means 'reason' and also 'word', and is used by John at the beginning of his gospel as a title for Jesus, the Word. This creates a barely translatable pun, with which Clement (for instance) makes rich play. Another word-play occurs because *daemon*, originally a divinity, has taken on the connotation of 'demon'.

12.1 Justin Martyr

C. A.D. *100–165. Well educated in philosophy, converted to Christianity at the age of about 30, author of two defences of Christianity or 'Apologies' in Greek, martyred under Marcus Aurelius for refusing to sacrifice.*

12.1.1 When Socrates tried by criticism and by the word of truth to bring these things to light and to draw men away from daemonic spirits, these very spirits used men who take pleasure in evil to get him executed as an impious denier of the gods, accusing him of introducing new divinities. (*First Apology* 5, 3)

12.1.2 Those who have lived in conformity with reason [or the Word] are Christians, even if they have been accounted atheists: among the Greeks, for example, Socrates, Heraclitus and others. (ibid. 46)

12.1.3 In this the most energetic of them all was Socrates, and he was accused on the same charges as we are. They said that he introduced new divinities and did not acknowledge the gods the State honoured. He in fact expelled the evil spirits from the community, those whom the poets described, and taught men to reject Homer and the other poets, and directed them to use reason [or the Word] to seek knowledge of the god unknown to them, saying, 'It is not easy to find the father and creator of all, or having found him it is not safe to declare him publicly.' (*Second Apology* 10, 5)
Justin (who is favourable to Socrates) seems to think that Plato's Republic *represents legislation essayed by Socrates. The quotation (not word-perfect) is from Plato,* Timaeus *28 C – where the speaker is Timaeus not Socrates.*

12.2 Theophilus of Antioch

Bishop of Antioch in the second century A.D. and the author of an apologia for Christianity directed to one Autolycus.

What was the point of Socrates swearing by Dog and Goose and Plane and Asclepius blasted by lightning and the divine spirits he invoked? What was the point of his acceptance of death? What sort of reward did he expect to gain beyond death? (*To Autolycus* 3, 2)

12.3 Clement of Alexandria

C. A.D. *150–215. Clement is the great example of the Greek scholar who sought a synthesis between pagan and Christian wisdom. He was head of the Church college in the cosmopolitan centre of Alexandria.*

12.3.1 Archelaus succeeded Anaxagoras, and lectured to Socrates.

> From these dropped off the stone-mason
>   prating about Law,
> the wizard of the Greeks

said Timon in his *Silli* because he transferred his attention from physics to ethics. Antisthenes and Plato were pupils of Socrates: Antisthenes founded the Cynic school, Plato seceded to the Academy. (*Miscellanies* 1, 14)
Timon: satirist and sceptic of the third century B.C. *Cf.* **1.4** [19].

12.3.2 Socrates' divine spirit was responsible, not by not preventing him but by encouraging him, even if it never actually encouraged him. (ibid. 1, 17)

12.3.3 So Socrates tells people to avoid all temptations to eat when we are not hungry and to drink when we are not thirsty, all gazing on and kissing handsome boys, as containing a more vicious poison than scorpions and tarantulas. (ibid. 2, 20)

Cf. The Tutor 1, 1; 3, 11.

12.3.4 Cleanthes, in his second volume on *Pleasure*, says that Socrates taught by individual instances that justice and happiness go together, and damned the man who first distinguished morality from expediency as a blasphemer. (ibid. 2, 22)

Cleanthes: Stoic philosopher of the third century B.C. Cf. 8.1.32.

12.3.5 Socrates thought that law would not have come into being for good men. (ibid. 4, 3)

Not found elsewhere.

12.4 Tertullian

C. A.D. 160–220. Q. Septimius Florens Tertullianus, most eloquent of Christian Latin writers, came from Africa, was trained as a lawyer and converted to Christianity by the faith of the martyrs. For part of his life he was a Montanist, believing in the present outpouring of the Holy Spirit. His Apology *for Christianity, written in 197, remains deservedly his best-known work.*

12.4.1 I say nothing of the philosophers. Socrates is quite enough. He swore by Oak, Goat and Dog to derogate the gods. They condemned him, for annihilating the gods. (*Apology* 14, 7)

Cf. To the Nations 1, 4; 1, 10; 2, 2.

12.4.2 The philosophers know all about spirits. Socrates waits for his divine spirit to advise him. Naturally. The spirit is said to have stuck to him from

boyhood, dissuading him – from good, of course. (ibid. 22, 1)

Cf. also 46, 5; On the Soul 1. The word for spirit is the hostile word 'demon'.

12.4.3 Socrates in Greece and Cato at Rome shared with their friends' wives they had taken to produce children for themselves – and others. Did the wives care? Why should they bother about chastity when their husbands gave them away so easily? (ibid. 39, 12)

Perhaps from the community of wives in The Republic, *or from the story of Socrates' two marriages. Valueless as evidence. Cf. Salvian,* On the Governance of God, 7, 101–3; Clement, Recogn. 10, 5.

12.4.4 Let us challenge you on chastity. I read in evidence part of the indictment from Athens directed against Socrates for corrupting boys. (ibid. 4, 6, 10)

12.4.5 When Socrates was in prison there was a skirmish over the nature of the soul. I don't know whether it was the first, or an appropriate *moment* for the master; the *place* does not matter. . . . After the sentence his wife met him and, being a woman, cried, 'Socrates, you've been unjustly condemned.' He cheerfully answered, 'Did you want me to be justly condemned?' . . . Of course Socrates was easily led by a different sort of spirit [from the Holy Spirit], since he is said to have had a daemonic power attached to him from childhood, the most disreputable sort of attendant in truth. . . . Socrates was voted the wisest man in the world by the Delphic spirit in support of his fellow spirit. . . . The wisdom of the college of heaven is freer to deny the gods of this world. It doesn't give lying orders for a cock to be sacrificed to Aesculapius; it doesn't introduce new divinities. . . . (*On the Soul 1*, 2–6)

Parts of an extended passage whose purpose is that Christ has delivered man from all 'demons', including the 'demon' of Socrates: there is a new wisdom. *Tertullian's knowledge of Socrates consists of commonplaces, but it is not all from Plato. For the Delphic 'spirit', see Salvian,* On the Governance of God *7, 101. For the anecdote, see above* **8.12.2** *n.*

12.4.6 Mind was to Socrates a god. (ibid. 12, 1)

A fascinating statement. Is it a false memory of the reference to Anaxagoras in Plato Phaedo *97 B? Does it come from* Philebus *28 B–C? Or does it refer to his divine spirit, as later philosophical writers do sometimes refer to mind in these terms? Or is it an independent testimony to something Socrates believed?*

12.4.7 For instance, Socrates was condemned for trying the truth too closely in undermining your gods. . . . And you won't refuse him the name of 'wise': your own Delphic oracle gave its testimony: 'Socrates is the wisest of all men.' (*To the Nations* 1, 4, 6)

12.4.8 So Socrates started an offensive against the gods, swearing by oak, dog and goat. He was condemned for it, but the Athenians regretted their verdict and condemned his accusers. . . . (ibid. 1, 10, 42)

12.4.9 Socrates repudiated those gods firmly: he equally firmly ordered a cock to be sacrificed to Asclepius. (ibid. 2, 2, 12)

12.5 Hippolytus

C. A.D. *170–236. A theologian from Rome who wrote in Greek. His principal work,* Refutation of all Heresies, *is of particular importance as preserving some of the traditions about the Greek philosophers, as well as for its positive teaching.*

Socrates was a student of the scientist Archelaus. He had a high regard for the maxim 'Know yourself' and gathered together a large school. Among these was Plato, by far the ablest of his students. Socrates left no writing. Plato took notes of all his philosophy and built up a school, combining science, ethics and logic. (*Refutation of Heresies* 1, 15)

12.6 Origen

C. A.D. *185–254. One of the most brilliant minds in the history of Christianity, and a supreme biblical scholar, he studied under Clement at Alexandria, and wrote voluminously in Greek himself. For our purpose his main work is his defence of Christianity against a philosopher named Celsus. Other references will be found at 6, 4 and 6, 56.*

12.6.1 Celsus compares the dangers faced by Christians with those faced by men like Socrates for the sake of philosophy. . . . My answer to that is that the Athenians regretted their action over Socrates. (*Against Celsus* 1, 3)

12.6.2 If we are going to bring reproaches on the grounds of their former life against men who have been converted we are bound to lay a charge against Phaedo even after he became a philosopher. The story goes that

Socrates converted him to a philosopher's life from a brothel. (ibid. 1, 64)

12.6.3 A man who criticises Christianity because of its sects should bring the same charge against the teaching of Socrates also: from his system some schools emerged with different tenets. (ibid. 3, 13)

12.6.4 Anyone who wants to bring accusations of recording supernatural occurrences will find a subject in the story of Plato and Socrates, and the swan which came to Socrates in his sleep, and the master's words on encountering the young man 'Here's my swan....' Some will attack Socrates' divine spirit as a figment. (ibid. 6, 8)

Cf. **1.11.1**; **9.10.2**.

12.6.5 If the oracle called Socrates the wisest of all men it detracted from the value of its commendation by what it said about Euripides and Sophocles. Here are the words:

> Sophocles is wise, Euripides is wiser,
> of all mankind Socrates is wisest.

If the tragedians are termed 'wise' Socrates is not being honoured for his philosophy or his love of truth and virtue.... Perhaps it was not for his philosophy that Socrates was termed 'wise' but for the victims he sacrificed to Apollo and the other daemons. (ibid. 7, 6)

12.6.6 Socrates knew that the draught of hemlock would cause his death. If he had let Crito persuade him he could perfectly well have escaped from prison and avoided this disaster. But he took the decision to follow right reason and die in a spirit appropriate to a philosopher rather than live in a spirit inappropriate to one. (ibid. 9, 7)

12.7 Minucius Felix

M. Minucius Felix, author of the attractive Octavius, *appears to have come from Africa to Rome, and to have been a lawyer by profession. We cannot date him precisely, but the early third century may not be far wrong. For a Christian apology his work has curiously little reference to Christ!*

12.7.1 If any of you has a passion for philosophising he should try to imitate, if he can, the original man of wisdom, Socrates – if he's up to it. That great man was asked about astronomy and cosmology and gave his famous reply, 'What is over our heads is nothing to do with us.' So he thoroughly deserved the oracle's testimony to his unique good sense. He clearly saw the oracle's meaning: he had been preferred to all other men not because he had discovered all there was to know but because he had learned his own ignorance: the height of wisdom is the admission of ignorance. (13, 1)

The 'famous reply' is also attributed to Epicurus. *It is not found in our early sources on Socrates; but cf.* **3.2.1**; **3.2.23** (*Xenophon,* Memoirs of Socrates *1, 1, 11; 4, 7, 6). See further* **12.10.3**; **12.12.1**; **12.15.6**.

12.7.2 These spirits are recognised as 'daemons' by the poets; the philosophers discuss them; Socrates was familiar with them. He used to refuse or initiate a course of action at the judgement and encouragement of his attendant daemon. (26, 9)

It will be noted that in Minucius' tradition Socrates' divine sign was positive as well as negative.

12.7.3 Then let Socrates, 'the buffoon of Athens', look to his laurels, professing to know nothing – and boasting the support of a lying demon. (38, 5)

The phrase 'buffoon of Athens' comes from an Epicurean named Zeno via Cicero, The Nature of the Gods *1, 34, 93* (**8.1.30**). *Minucius passes from 'daemon' to 'demon'.*

12.8 Cyprian

Thascius Caecilianus Cyprianus was like Tertullian a lawyer, an African and a Latin writer. He became bishop of Carthage soon after his conversion, and was martyred ten years later in A.D. *258.*

The poets knew these spirits, and Socrates asserted that he was directed and controlled at the will of a spirit. (*Idols Are Not Gods* 6)

The only reference to Socrates in Cyprian.

12.9 Arnobius

Another Christian African Latin writer, who was converted to Christianity after having been at one time an Epicurean, and who in the early fourth century wrote an essay on the integration of Christian and pagan thoughts entitled Against the Nations. *Arnobius is muddle-headed but full of curious learning.*

Similarly, Socrates was executed by verdict of the state court. Are his ethical discussions made valueless because he was unjustly eliminated from life? (1, 40)

12.10 Lactantius

C. A.D. *240–320. L. Caecilius Firmianus Lactantius was professor of rhetoric at Nicomedia before his conversion to Christianity: later he received Constantine's favour. A fine Latin writer, he has been nicknamed 'the Christian Cicero'. He was a pupil of Arnobius.*

12.10.1 Socrates and the Academics after him were right to eliminate knowledge. (*Divine Institutes* 3, 3)

Cf. Anger of God *1.*

12.10.2 So Plato gave thanks to nature: first, that he was born a human being rather than a dumb animal; second, that he was a man rather than a woman; then that he was a Greek not a foreigner; finally, that he was an Athenian born in the time of Socrates. . . . What was the use of congratulating himself that he was born in the time of Socrates? Was Socrates able to implant ability in his disciples? It did not occur to Plato that Alcibiades and Critias were also continually associating with Socrates; one became his own country's most energetic opponent, the other a ruthless dictator. (3, 19)

Cf. **1.2** *n.*

12.10.3 Socrates had a measure of wisdom. He realised that these questions were incapable of resolution and withdrew from them. I am afraid that this is his only claim to wisdom. Many of his actions merit criticism rather than approval . . . . Socrates coined the familiar phrase 'What is above us is nothing to us' . . . But the same man swore by dog and goose. Buffoon (as Zeno the Epicurean calls him)! Senseless, abandoned, desperate, if he wanted to make a mockery of religion! Mad, if he seriously reckoned a filthy animal as god! (3, 20)

Cf. Epitome *37. See further* **8.1.30**; **12.7.1**; **12.7.3**.

12.10.4 Socrates tried to overthrow the old religions, and was thrown into jail for his pains. (5, 15)

12.11 Eusebius

C. A.D. 260–340. Bishop of Caesarea, adviser to Constantine and author of the standard history of the early church.

12.11.1 Socrates, proud of his dialectical skill, making the worse cause appear the better, all the time playing with hair-splitting arguments, fell victim to the false accusations of his own countrymen and fellow-citizens. (*Oration of Constantine* 9)

12.11.2 Socrates puts it correctly and very elegantly, in saying that parts of reality are over our heads and parts are nothing to us. The nature of the universe is over our heads; what happens after death is nothing to us; we are concerned only with man and his works. So he said goodbye to the physical science of Anaxagoras and Archelaus and concentrated on investigating

the good and evil in our own homes.

(*Preparation for the Gospel* 15, 62, 10)
    Homer, Odyssey 4, 392. Cf. **1.4**[6]; **9.6.6.**

12.12 Epiphanius

C. A.D. 315–403. Bishop of Salamis in Cyprus and (like Hippolytus) author of a refutation of all heresies, called Panarion,

which similarly draws on the doxographic traditions.

12.12.1 Socrates was son of Sophroniscus the sculptor and Phaenarete the midwife. He was an ethical philosopher. He said that human beings ought to concentrate on what concerns them and not go beyond. (*Panarion* 3, 6)
    Cf. **12.7.1** *n.*

12.12.2 Socrates, the son of Elmaglus or Sophroniscus and Phaenarete the midwife. . . . (*On Faith* P 1087)
    Otherwise as **12.12.1**. *Elmaglus is unaccounted for.*

12.13 Nemesius of Emesa

Nothing is known of him except that he was bishop of Emesa in Syria in the late fourth century A.D. and tried to harmonise Platonic and Christian thought.

A man's death would be expedient if Providence foresaw that he would commit some crime, and that it would be better for his life to end before the fatal situation arrived (this may have been so with Socrates, or with the martyred saints). (*The Nature of Man* 70)
    A strange thought, neither Greek nor Christian.

12.14 John Chrysostom

C. A.D. 347–407. The eloquent bishop of Constantinople, nicknamed 'Golden-mouthed' – Chrysostomos: a great expositor of scripture, and a man of tactless honesty in his public dealings. Except for **12.14.5** the passages are based on Plato.

12.14.1 Socrates shows them that public opinion is not to be despised, for all his interminable moralising on the subject. He had an eye to his reputation in everything he did. If you were familiar with the dialogues I might have enlarged on this topic, showing his colossal mock-modesty in them – at least if we may believe what his disciple says of him – and the basis of arrogance to all his writings. (*Homily on Acts* 36)

12.14.2 Plato's master has a foolish respect for these idols: he actually tells them to sacrifice a cock to Asclepius. (*Homily on Romans* 3, 23)

12.14.3 But you will find many to scorn death among them too, it is suggested. Whom? The one who drank hemlock? I can find you thousands such from within the Church. If the law had permitted those facing prosecution to take their departure by drinking hemlock they would all have surpassed him in fame. Further, he drank when he had no choice in the matter; he had to, willy-nilly. No courage there! Duress – and nothing else. . . . So there is nothing admirable in his drinking the hemlock. It was no longer in his power to refuse. In any case he had reached extreme old age. When he showed that he was above life he was, according to his own words, seventy. Is that being above life? (*Homily on 1 Corinthians* 4)

12.14.4 The great Socrates, who towered above his contemporaries in philosophy, was given a draught of hemlock because he was suspected of introducing some minor amendment in theology. (ibid. 4, 5)

12.14.5 One of the heathen philosophers is said to have had a difficult, talkative, tipsy wife. When they asked why he put up with her he answered, 'To have a practice-ground for philosophy at home.' 'I shall,' he said, 'be more patient with the others if I have a daily education in the subject.' (ibid. 26, 8)

12.15 Jerome

C. A.D. *342–420. The greatest of Latin biblical scholars, who settled to a monastic life at Bethlehem, and issued a stream of scholarly, personal, aggressive writings.*

12.15.1 In this field a certain creative writer has been carrying off all the prizes. He has written a book entitled *Banquets of Poets and Philosophers*. In it he depicts Euripides conversing with Menander and Socrates with Epicurus, though we know them to have been separated not by years but by generations. (*Letters* 52)

Socrates was a favourite figure of fiction as late as the fifth century A.D., *which makes it the harder to disentangle fact from fancy.*

12.15.2 I wish we could grasp that saying of Socrates, 'I know that I am ignorant.' (*Letters* 57)

12.15.3 Socrates had two wives, Xanthippe, and Aristides' granddaughter Myrto. They were always quarrelling, and he used to laugh at them for falling out over him with all his ugliness, snub nose, bald head, hairy shoulders and bow-legs. In the end they turned their aggression on him. When he ran away badly mauled they chased him. Once Xanthippe had been heaping interminable abuse on him from higher ground. He stood his ground and she poured some dirty water over him. He simply dried his head, saying, 'I always knew that there would be rain after all that thunder.' (*Against Jovinianus* 1, 48)

Cf. **1.4**[17]; **8.2.8**; **8.4.11**.

12.15.4 I would here mention – to our shame – the asceticism of Pythagoras, Socrates, Antisthenes and the others, only it is a long story and not wholly relevant. But the story of Antisthenes is certainly relevant. He had been an outstanding teacher of rhetoric. The story goes that he heard Socrates discussing poverty and said to his students, 'Leave me and look for a real teacher; I've already found one.' (ibid. 2, 14)

12.15.5 . . . the saying of Socrates 'I know what I don't know.' (*Defence against Rufinus* 17)

See above **12.15.2**, *but the text may be faulty.*

12.15.6 . . . you put in my path the whole of physical nature, so that Socrates failed in his move to ethics, saying, 'What is above our heads is nothing to us.' (ibid. 28)

Cf. **12.7.1** *n.*

12.15.7 Socrates' elegant charm. . . . (ibid. 40)

12.15.8 This sort of eloquence is very common: so to say, I thought true the views which I read in Socrates. Not that Socrates wrote any books: the things attributed to him by Plato and other followers. (ibid. 40)

12.15.9 We cannot always keep the same expression, a false claim the philosophers make for Socrates. (*Against the Pelagians* 3, 1)

Cf. *also* Commentary on Isaiah *12, 42*; **8.1.11** *n.*

12.16 Augustine

A.D. *354–430. The greatest of all Latin-speaking Christian leaders, he was influenced by Cicero's lost* Hortensius, *by the Manichaeans and by the Neo-Platonists, before his final conversion to Christianity.*

12.16.1 This view, of the limitations of perceptions, may properly be attributed to the Old Academy, though it was not at the time controversial. It is possible to prove this on the authority of Socrates himself, Plato and others of the old school: they believed that they could defend themselves from error by being chary of committing themselves to positive statements. (*Against the Academics* 2, 6, 14)

12.16.2 Plato is said to have learned a great deal from the Pythagoreans after the death of his beloved master Socrates. . . . Plato added to Socrates' acute and subtle ethics scientific and metaphysical knowledge. (ibid. 3, 17, 37)

12.16.3 Socrates is said to have been bolder than the rest. He swore by any old dog and any old stone and anything to hand and on the spot when he wanted to swear. (*True Religion* 2, 2, 4)

12.16.4 Socrates is said to have been a disciple of Archelaus, and Plato's teacher. (*The City of God* 8, 2)

12.16.5 History records Socrates as the first person to redirect philosophy to the correction and direction of moral behaviour; before him they all concentrated on physics, that is the investigation of natural phenomena. It cannot in my view be clearly established whether Socrates did this because he was induced by boredom with these obscure and inconclusive matters to direct his mind to some immediate and conclusive discovery essential for a life of blessedness (and this is the single object of the wakeful and energetic labours of all the philosophers), or whether, as his supporters suggest, he was unwilling for minds defiled by worldly desires to reach up towards things divine. He saw that they were investigating the causes of things, causes which in a primary and ultimate sense he believed were reducible to the will of the single supreme God. So he thought that they needed an immaculate mind to grasp them, and reckoned for that reason it was urgent to purify one's life by right behaviour, so that the mind might be freed from oppressive lusts and use its natural vigour to lift itself to things eternal, and with purified understanding might look on the real being of immaterial and unchanging light in which the causes of all created things live eternally. However, it is clear that he assailed, to their discomfiture, the folly of ignorant men who imagined themselves to possess some knowledge; he showed remarkable charm in discussion; his shafts were barbed, he was unruffled; even in those very questions of morality on which he seems to have concentrated his whole attention he either professed ignorance or concealed his knowledge. All this aroused hostility. He was condemned on a trumped-up charge and executed. . . . This illustrious life and death enabled Socrates to leave many disciples his philosophy. Their earnest concern was to participate in ethical discussions dealing with the ultimate good which brings bliss to human beings. Socrates in his conversations was always raising questions on all subjects, setting up propositions and knocking them down. The ultimate good does not obviously appear. So each took from Socrates what suited his own taste, and made up his own mind where to locate the ultimate good. (By the ultimate good we mean the thing which makes its possessor perfectly happy.) Socrates' followers held different views about this ultimate good. It scarcely seems credible that the followers of a single teacher should act in this way, but some, like Aristippus, placed it in pleasure, others, like Antisthenes, in virtue. Each held a different view, and it would be a lengthy business to record them all. (ibid. 8, 3)

12.16.6 Among Socrates' disciples, the most brilliant – and deservedly – outshining all the others was Plato . . . he thought that his own genius and what he learned from Socrates were inadequate for a complete philosopher. . . . Because he loved his master Socrates above all others, he made him the chief speaker in almost all his work, leavening the things which he had learned from others or derived from his own outstanding intelligence with Socrates' charm in ethical discourse. Socrates is said to have been outstanding in practical philosophy, Pythagoras in abstract thought. . . . His master Socrates (whom he makes an interlocutor in his books) had the practice, as is well known, of concealing his knowledge or his views. Plato endeavoured to maintain this. (ibid. 8, 4)

12.16.7 There is a story of Alcibiades (if I remember the man's name aright). He thought he was happy, but when Socrates proved to him in discussion how wretched his folly made him he burst into tears. (ibid. 14, 8)

12.17 Socrates Scholasticus

C. A.D. *380–450. Church historian, clear but unexciting.*

12.17.1 Socrates, the topmost philosopher among the Greeks, rejected the myths and was condemned for trying to put their divinities out of circulation. (3, 16)

12.17.2 Porphyry, in his *History of Philosophy*, maligned the life of Socrates, the greatest philosopher of them all. He bequeathed us an account of Socrates of a kind that Socrates' prosecutors, Meletus and Anytus, never thought to produce. Yes – of Socrates, a man admired among the Greeks for his self-discipline, morality and general virtue, a man honoured for his piety by Plato (the eminent Greek philosopher), Xenophon and the rest of the company of philosophers, and regarded as endowed with superhuman wisdom. (3, 23)

12.18 John Cassian

C. A.D. *360–435. A monk from the East, who deeply influenced monasticism in the West, where he settled, bridging the two cultures. He was a ' semi-pelagian', accepting some but not all of the orthodox criticisms of Pelagius.*

For instance, Socrates, the most famous of them all, was not ashamed, as they themselves record, to make the following admission about himself. A 'physiognomer' looked closely at him and said, 'You've a pederast's eyes.' Socrates' disciples rushed at him and were for avenging the insult to their master, but Socrates apparently checked their indignation by saying, 'Hold it, friends, I am, but I control myself.' (*Conferences* 13, 5, 3)

Cassian uses Greek sources, and tells his story partly in Greek: we do not have the identical story elsewhere, but compare **8.1.8** *n.*

12.19 Orosius

A friend of Augustine and a vigorous (and unfair) controversialist. He lived in the early fifth century.

Scarcely two years had intervened [after the amnesty] when the great philosopher Socrates was driven by the disasters to end his own life among them with poison. (*Against the Pagans* 2, 17, 16)

A highly tendentious account.

12.20 Isidore of Pelusium

An ascetic monk of Egypt, author of a voluminous correspondence. Early fifth century.

12.20.1 If Socrates, the chief authority in Athenian philosophy, did not protect himself from physical assault, why are you put out, when, as you write, you have merely been insulted? (*Letters*, 1, 11)

12.20.2 And Socrates – I shall record their sayings too, since they tend to self-discipline – seeing someone kissing a handsome boy, said, 'The man who dares to light such a fire in himself by a kiss would as easily dive on to sword-points or leap into a furnace.' (ibid. 3, 66)

12.20.3 Why did Socrates, condemned to drink the hemlock, not think that any wrong was being done to him? (ibid. 3, 154)

Cf. 4, 205.

12.21 Theodoretus

C. A.D. *393–458. Bishop of Cyrrhus in Syria. A wise pastor and administrator. His* Cure for the Diseases of the Greeks *is one of the finest of all Christian 'apologies'. He frequently quotes Plato and Xenophon.*

12.21.1 Socrates, son of Sophroniscus, the best of philosophers, saw nothing unworthy of philosophy in accepting useful knowledge from women. He did not blush to call Diotima his teacher and spent much time in Aspasia's company. (*Cure for the Greeks* 1, 17)

12.21.2 Even you admit that Sophroniscus' son Socrates was the best of all Greek philosophers. But his father was a stone-mason and for a long period he followed his father's profession. Many writers record the fact, including Porphyry in volume III of his *History of Philosophy*. He writes: 'Let us record of Socrates what the other writers have thought worth preserving, distinguishing for the moment those facts in his life recorded for praise or censure by scholars, and leaving on one side without examination the question whether he practised stone-cutting with his father or whether it was only his father. If he practised it only briefly it made no contribution to his wisdom. But if he was a sculptor, so much the better; it is an honourable profession.' It goes on in the same vein, introducing authors who claim that Socrates practised sculpture. Well, perhaps he spent his younger days as a sculptor, and later fell in love with poetry and rhetoric and went in for education. No, we cannot say that either. Porphyry explicitly states the contrary. He writes: 'He did not lack natural endowment, but was more or less completely uneducated. He was practically illiterate and made himself conspicuous by stammering like a child when called on to read or write. . . . Yet this uneducated, unlearned man was more worthy of respect than all the others, including Plato, the most eloquent of all the Greeks. Ariston's son could not deny it. How could he, when he attributes to Socrates all the dialogues which he himself brings to birth, and presents them as the offspring of Socrates' thought.' (1, 26–31)

Cf. 1, 53.

12.21.3 The ideas are Socrates', the words Plato's. (2, 16)

12.21.4 Socrates, the wisest of all men according to the Delphic oracle. (2, 19)

12.21.5 Socrates, a contemporary of Anaxagoras and Archelaus, learned from them what he taught about reality. (2, 51)

12.21.6 Porphyry says that Socrates, Sophroniscus' son, was inclined to intemperance in his younger days, but eliminated that character by effort and discipline and stamped himself with the lineaments of philosophy. (4, 2)

12.21.7 His interlocutor thought about this. Socrates said, 'Don't you think my conclusion inescapable?' He replied, 'Inescapable, not like mathematics but like love, which is stronger than mathematics in its persuasive compulsion over ordinary men.' (9, 47)

The conversation is on community of families, as in The Republic, *but this is not in Plato.*

12.21.8 Porphyry, in writing the *History of Philosophy*, said that Socrates was originally irascible and quick-tempered, taking Aristoxenus' *Life of Socrates* as his evidence; he said he had never come across a more reliable witness. His voice, his face, his characteristic appearance suggested it, and apart from his words, his peculiar looks. This was true when he was not in a temper. When he was caught up in the emotion he became terribly contorted. There was no word or act from which he would refrain. Porphyry goes through similar evidence and shows that Socrates was also a slave to pleasure. He says: 'He was passionate for sex, though he kept this from proving injurious by confining himself to his legitimate wives or to prostitutes. He had two wives at the same time: Xanthippe, a freewoman, but rather common, and Myrto, daughter of Aristides and granddaughter of Lysimachus. He took Xanthippe as his concubine and had Lamprocles by her, and Myrto in formal marriage, and had Sophroniscus and Menexenus by her. They were in conflict with one another. When they came to a truce they made for Socrates because he never stopped them fighting but laughed when he saw them fighting one another and himself. He adds that in personal encounter Socrates was sometimes malicious, abusive and arrogant.' So much for Porphyry on Socrates. (12, 174)

Cf. **12.25.3.**

promulgates on chastity and what those of whom we are speaking proposed. Let no one have his own wife, said Socrates; marriages must be communal for everyone: there will be greater political unity if all the men are indiscriminately united with all the women, and of course if all the women submit without distinction to all the men, and in this way all the men become husbands to all the women and all the women wives to all the men.... Socrates carried the day: he wrote books on the subject and handed down these shameful views to posterity. ... It is said that his legal condemnation was unjust. It is true: mankind would more rightly condemn him for preaching of this sort, just as it did condemn him on dubious grounds. (*On the Governance of God* 7, 23, 101)

Mainly from Plato's The Republic: *the historical knowledge is confused, and subserves the controversy.*

12.22 Salvian

C. A.D. *400–80. Born near Cologne, associated with Lerins and Marseilles. His work* On the Governance of God *is a critical view of Roman civilisation.*

If anyone is indignant at my words he should tell me: 'Has not Socrates always been accepted as the wisest of all men – certainly on the evidence of the spirit at Delphi, the head spirit as Socrates was the head philosopher?' Let us, then, see what laws Socrates

12.23 Sidonius Apollinaris

C. A.D. *432–80. Bishop of Clermont, aristocratic and well educated, he bridges the gap in the West between pagan and Christian culture. A Latinist who read Greek, he held high office in Church and State.*

12.23.1 ... he divides like Socrates. ... (*Letters* 4, 3, 6)

In a long list of one-word accounts of the contributions of different philosophers.

12.23.2 ... Socrates with his hair diminishing. ... (ibid. 9, 9, 14)

Again in a list of single-phrase descriptions of philosophers.

12.23.3

Next shone the School
of Socrates, passing from the heaviness of
nature,
turning to sharpen the characters of men.

(*Poems* 15, 96)

12.24 Epiphanius Scholasticus

*Epiphanius composed under the guidance of
Cassiodorus (to whom the work is sometimes
attributed) a Church history, based mainly on
Socrates Scholasticus, Theodoretus and Sozo-
men. He belongs to the sixth century* A.D.

Porphyry, in his own *History of Philosophy*, tore to shreds the life of Socrates,
giving an account which might be expected of a hostile critic – this about
that Socrates who was accounted
among the Greeks exceptional for his
self-control, justice and other virtues,
whom Plato, their outstanding philosopher, and Xenophon and the rest of
the philosophic band honour as beloved
of God and proclaim to have been endowed with superhuman wisdom. (7,
2, 10)

12.25 Cyril of Alexandria

*Bishop of Alexandria in the early fifth cen-
tury* A.D. *and in all perhaps the most un-
lovable of the saints. A crude but forceful
writer, a powerful preacher, an acute
theologian and a bigoted opponent, he was
responsible for the murder of the Platonist
blue-stocking Hypatia.*

12.25.1 The story goes that the prophetic spirit of Pytho – or else Apollo –
answered from the tripod with an
oracular response that Socrates was the
wisest of all human beings. The man
certainly won extensive admiration
among the Greeks – yet he was imprisoned and ended his human life with
a dose of hemlock. (*Against Julian* 5, 170)

12.25.2 Now let us look at the quality
of the man with the highest reputation
of them all – Socrates. He was admired for his worldly wisdom, and
accorded considerable renown, but if
you look at his character and behaviour
you could see that he was no better
than those who live an ordinary average
life. There may be those who find this
incredible, but they will not go on to
contradict the writings of Porphyry,
who carefully sets out the biography of
each of the older thinkers. This was his
explicit aim, and he thought it demanded a good deal of trouble. He
writes as follows about Socrates: 'Aristoxenus in narrating Socrates' life says
that he learned about Socrates from
Spintharus, who knew him personally,
and Spintharus said that his voice,
speech and the character they revealed
were such that he did not meet many
more persuasive characters – and in
addition to all he said there was his
peculiar appearance. This was true
when he was free from anger; when he
was inflamed by this passion his dis-
composure was startling, and he lost all
control of language and action.' (ibid.
6, 185)

12.25.3 Again Porphyry wrote in the
following vein about him. 'In his
general life he was easy-going; he did
not require much to satisfy his daily
needs. But he was passionate for sex,
though he kept this from proving injurious by confining himself to his
legitimate wives or to prostitutes. He
had two wives at the same time,

Xanthippe, a freewoman but rather common, and Myrto, daughter of Aristides and granddaughter of Lysimachus. He took Xanthippe as his concubine and had Lamprocles by her, and Myrto in formal marriage, and had Sophroniscus and Menexenus by her.' What will Socrates' admirers say to this? (ibid. 6, 186)

Cf. **12.21.8**.

12.25.4 I pass over Socrates, who said that a divine spirit used to give him oracular pronouncements, and actually swore by Oak and Dog; this, as I have already said, is why he was prosecuted successfully. (ibid. 6, 190)

12.25.5 I come to Sophroniscus' son Socrates, who had a midwife for a mother and a stone-mason for a father. They say he went to the top in his profession without any sense of shame. Porphyry writes of him in the third volume of his *History of Philosophy:* 'Now that this is clear, let us speak about Socrates, touching lightly on the things which others have thought it important to record, and omitting such questions as whether he practised stone-masonry along with his father, or whether it was only his father without him. The fact that he was professionally employed for a short while has nothing to do with his wisdom. If he was a sculptor the more commendation to him; it is a worthy profession. Aristoxenus adds, 'Socrates was a workman, who practised his father's profession of stonecutting.' Timaeus, in volume IX, also states that Socrates learned stonemasonry. If Aristoxenus is a hostile witness and Timaeus an immature one, we must use Menedemus of Pyrrha, a student of Plato's and older than Aristoxenus. He says in his *Life of Philocrates* that Socrates never stopped defending his father for being a sculptor, or his mother for being a midwife. Tell me, did it stand in Socrates' way that he was a sculptor, or that his father was a sculptor? Did it prevent his doing what he thought was right? Did his mother's position as a wage-earner make philosophy unapproachable for him? (ibid. 6, 207)

There is some textual emendation in the middle: the general sense is clear.

12.25.6 Sophroniscus' son Socrates, who had philosophy for his schoolfellow, a man of few possessions who began life as a manual worker and was used to simple living and was (in Homeric terms) 'under duress, oppressed by extreme poverty, close to the ground', made love to his wives Myrto and Xanthippe, and went with prostitutes, finding his base and obscene passions ungovernable. All right – are we to say of Socrates, 'What colossal virtue! What wealth of wisdom!'? He couldn't even conquer pleasure. (ibid. 7, 226)

PART THIRTEEN

LEXICOGRAPHERS

13.1 The Suda

Until recently reference books spoke of a Byzantine lexicographer named Suidas. In fact, the word is a title, not an author, and means 'The Fortress'. The compiler is unknown, but he drew on available texts and commentaries and earlier handbooks, with greater industry than scholarship. In consequence, The Suda preserves nonsense and fact in a curious amalgam. It seems useful to append here all the entries relative to Socrates. It will be noticed that some of the historical information is clearly wrong, e.g. Plato was not associated with Socrates for anything like twenty years.

13.1.1 Alcibiades . . . was a pupil first of Sophilus, then of Socrates, whose lover he was according to some accounts . . . .

13.1.2 Aristippus: son of Aristades, from Cyrene, philosopher, student of Socrates, founder of the so-called Cyrenaic School. . . .

13.1.3 Aristippus: friend of Socrates, always fond of pleasure and enjoying life. . . .

13.1.4 Archelaus . . . was a pupil of Anaxagoras of Clazomenae; Socrates was a pupil of his, some would add Euripides.

13.1.5 *Diakeknaismene*, 'seduced' (of a woman). Also *diakeknaismenos*, 'washed out': if I were to be pallid, like Socrates' follower, and go barefoot and un-washed.

13.1.6 *Epitaktoi* . . . Socrates was president and refused to vote or to pass sentence.

13.1.7 *Epresbeuen*, 'fostered'. Socrates 'fostered' ethical philosophy.

13.1.8 Euclides . . . a pupil of Socrates.

13.1.9 Euripides . . . originally a painter, he studied with Prodicus for rhetoric and Socrates for ethics and philosophy.

13.1.10 Zeno: son of Musaeus, from Sidon, Stoic philosopher . . . he wrote *A Defence of Socrates.*

13.1.11 Hierocles . . . Theosebius said that Hierocles once in a lecture compared Socrates' words to dice: they always stand firmly where they fall. . . .

13.1.12 Theaetetus . . . a pupil of Socrates. . . .

13.1.13 Theon: from Smyrna, philosopher. Also Theon from Antioch (Daphne), Stoic philosopher. He wrote *A Defence of Socrates.*

13.1.14 *Theoris:* an Athenian ship sent annually to Delos. . . . It was not possible, once it was dispatched, to execute any sentence till it returned. This is why Socrates was imprisoned for a long period till the ship's return.

13.1.15 Cebes: from Thebes, philosopher, pupil of Socrates. . . .

13.1.16 Crito: Athenian, philosopher, pupil of Socrates. A close friend of Socrates who looked after all his needs. He wrote *A Defence of Socrates.*

13.1.17 Xenophon: disciple of Socrates . . .

13.1.18 Plato . . . renounced literature and practised philosophy with Socrates over twenty years. There is a legend that on the very day Plato was presented to him Socrates saw a swan settle at his feet. . . .

13.1.19 Polydeuces: from Naucratis . . . Works . . . *Against Socrates* . . .

13.1.20 Polycrates: from Athens, orator. An expert who wrote two speeches against Socrates for Anytus and Meletus.

13.1.21 Rhadamanthys' oath: swearing by the goose, dog, plane, ram, etc. . . . Socrates' oaths were of this kind.

13.1.22 Simmias: from Thebes, philosopher, pupil of Socrates. . . .

13.1.23 Sophocles . . . seventeen years older than Socrates.

13.1.24 Favorinus: polymath from Arles . . . Works . . . *Socrates and his Science of Love* . . .

13.1.25 Phaedo: from Elis, philosopher, who studied with Socrates. He founded the School of Elis, which was named after him; it was later called the School of Eretria after Menedemus of Eretria. Phaedo was captured by Indians, sold to a brothel-keeper and advertised by him along with whores at Athens. He met Socrates lecturing, fell in love with his words and asked him to release him. Socrates persuaded Alcibiades to buy him. From this point he took to philosophy.

13.1.26 Chaerephon: from Athens, of the deme Sphettus, philosopher, student of Socrates.

13.1.27 To swear by the goose: Rhadamanthys gave orders for oaths to be by the goose and ram instead of naming the gods on every occasion. Not, as some say, Socrates.

13.1.28 Socrates was son of a stonemason named Sophroniscus: his mother Phaenarete was a midwife. He began as a stone-mason and is said to have been responsible for 'The Draped Graces' at Athens. Later he turned to philosophy through a succession of teachers – Anaxagoras of Clazomenae, Damon and Archelaus. Aristoxenus says that Archelaus was his first teacher and his lover as well, and that Socrates had violent sexual drives but exercised them innocently, as Porphyry says in his *History of Philosophy*. As an adult he campaigned against Amphipolis and Potidaea and fought in the battle of Delium. He had two wives, Xanthippe, by whom he had a son named Lamprocles, and the second, Myrto, daughter of Aristides the Just: she bore Sophroniscus and Menedemus – or in some versions Menexenus. In round figures he was born at the time of the Peloponnesian War in the 77th Olympiad and lived to the age of 80. Then the Athenians in a fit of irrationality, or rather insanity, executed him by hemlock-poisoning. He left no writing behind, except (in some versions) a hymn to Apollo and Artemis and a fable of Aesop in hexameters. He produced a number of philosophers: Plato, who abandoned the Lyceum (a place in Athens) and moved his college to a suburb called Academia – hence the name Academics applied to his successors down to Aristotle (Aristotle was a student of Plato, and lectured in a garden by the city and called his followers Peripatetics from the walks in the garden); Aristippus of Cyrene, who introduced his own doctrines and established the school known as Cyrenaic; Phaedo of Elis, who also established a school of his own known as Elean after him (later called Eretrian from Menedemus, who taught at Eretria: Pyrrho also came from that school); Antisthenes, who introduced the Cynic sect; Euclides of Megara, who also established a school of his own, called Megarian after him, or Dialectical after his pupil Clinomachus; Xenophon, Gryllus' son; Aeschines of Sphettus, Lysanias' son; Cebes of Thebes; Glaucon of Athens; Bryson of Heraclea, who introduced eristical dialectic after Euclides (Clinomachus advanced it, attracted many students who came for it and then went over to Zeno of Citium; the latter called his school

Stoic after the place where they met; he was born in the 125th Olympiad. Some writers assert that Bryson was a student of Euclides, not Socrates; Pyrrho, from whom the Pyrrhonians are named, was one of his students); Alcibiades, Critobulus, Xenomedes and Apollodorus, all from Athens; Crito and Simon in addition; Eumares from Phliasus; Simmias from Thebes; Terpsion from Megara; Chaerephon. Theodorus, nicknamed 'Atheist', was a student of his; he made a dogma of logical indistinguishability, and formed a school of his own for posterity, called the Theodorian. So much for Socrates.

When Socrates in later life became a philosopher he studied with Archelaus, the natural scientist, but his main interest lay in ethics. He had notable disciples: from Athens, Plato, Xenophon, Critias, Antisthenes; from Thebes, Simmias and Cebes; from Cyrene, Aristippus; Phaedo; from Megara, Euclides. He used to say that he was accompanied by a divine spirit. He began to take music lessons with Connus when already of advanced years. He laughed at Solon's dictum, saying, 'In learning, better late than never.' By Xanthippe he had two sons, Sophroniscus and Lamprocles. The passion with which most of the youth of the day regarded him aroused jealousy. Aristophanes in *The Clouds* was the first to make a butt of him, portraying him as corrupting the youth by his religious scepticism, simply because he used to swear by Dog and Plane tree out of an excess of piety. Later Anytus and Meletus secured his conviction on these very charges. In the assessment of punishment he proposed free meals in the City Hall; they proposed death. He suffered a long period of imprisonment until the sacred ship arrived from Delos; once it had put to sea, all legal executions were postponed till its return. Crito encouraged him to escape, but he refused, on the grounds that it

was wrong to break the laws. He drank the hemlock, not forgetting to pray, with the words, 'Offer a sacrifice to Asclepius.' A man named Cyrsas from Chios had come to be with Socrates. He slept near the grave and saw Socrates in a dream; so he had his company. He left by boat without delay, although this was the only way in which he had enjoyed the philosopher's company.

These are plainly two separate entries from different sources, as the repetition of the list of disciples shows; so too the discrepancy over wives and sons. The history is somewhat vague. The 77th Olympiad is 472–468 B.C. Socrates was born in 469 B.C., but the Peloponnesian War did not begin till 431 B.C. However, unless we are professional historians we might well be a little vague about dates in the Dark Ages, and say 'about the time of Alfred' for an event in the same century. I do not know any other source for the story of Cyrsas.

13.1.29 'Socrates the Melian and Chaerephon who has studied fleas' footprints.' – A skit on the language of the Mysteries. It is unhistorical, since Socrates was an Athenian. But in view of the fact that Diagoras, who was a Melian, was attacked as an opponent of religion, he is attacking Socrates in the same way as an atheist. All because of his investigating how many feet a flea has to jump. Or possibly, as some have held, Melian means someone who sharpens the minds of beginners, who were savage before they embarked – a metaphor from irrational animals: *mela* are sheep and cattle. Some refer it to a kind of rough shagginess, taking it as a metaphor. Diagoras of Melos had originally been a devout man, but he was cheated out of a deposit and turned to atheism: the Athenians were furious at this and sacked Melos for it. There was also a poet from Melos named Aristagoras who was condemned for impiety for letting out the Mysteries of

Eleusis. From him the comic dramatists pillory the Melians for impiety. He is ranked with the blasphemers too.

Compare **4.1.1.6**; **14.1.1.13**. *The Athenians did indeed sack Melos in 416* B.C., *but as a piece of* Machtpolitik. *The central section is interesting: some supporters of Socrates have tried to find a favourable explanation of the nickname.*

13.2 Photius

Photius, patriarch of Constantinople in the ninth century A.D., *was the finest of the Byzantine scholars.* The Lexicon *is an early work.*

Dog: Socrates seems to have been the first to swear by the dog. (*Lexicon*)

PART FOURTEEN

COMMENTATORS ON CLASSICAL AUTHORS

14.1 Scholia on Aristophanes

The Byzantine notes to Aristophanes add little or nothing to our knowledge of Socrates from other sources. They are naturally chiefly from The Clouds.

14.1.1 The Clouds

14.1.1.1 The play is a deliberate attack on the philosopher Socrates for misleading the young men of Athens by his teaching. There was hostility between the writers of comedy and the philosophers. It was not, as some have suggested, due to Archelaus, king of Macedon, for preferring him to Aristophanes. (*Argument* 1)

14.1.1.2 They say that Aristophanes wrote *The Clouds* under pressure from Anytus and Meletus, who wanted a foretaste of Athenian reaction to an attack on Socrates. They were cautious, because he had many lovers, in particular Alcibiades and his circle, who in fact prevented the author from winning first prize with his play. . . . (*Argument* 2)
Cf. Arguments 8, 10.

14.1.1.3 'Think-tank' . . . Socrates and his associates were called 'Thinkers', because they thought about one another, and because they never stopped thinking. (94)

14.1.1.4 . . . No one paid fees to Socrates, since he claimed no knowledge. That is why the Delphic oracle judged him wise. He thought acknowledgement of one's own ignorance the first evidence of wisdom. (98)

14.1.1.5 'Miscarriage' . . . Socrates said, 'I practise the profession of midwife and use it to induce young men to bring to birth the thoughts in their minds.' Aristophanes is parodying this in the word 'miscarriage'. (137)

14.1.1.6 'Chaerephon' . . . It was, it appears, to him that the Delphic priestess pronounced the oracle about Socrates:

Sophocles is wise, Euripides is wiser,
of all mankind Socrates is wisest.

14.1.1.7 . . . Chaerephon had heavy eyebrows, Socrates was bald. (146)

14.1.1.8 . . . Socrates used to compare his own appearance with Silenus: he was snub-nosed and bald. (223)

14.1.1.9 'What gods?' This is a riddling allusion to the slander brought against Socrates by some; they said he was irreligious because he swore by the cock and honoured the plane tree (etc.: see Xenophon's *Memoirs of Socrates*). (247)

14.1.1.10 . . . He is cramped by Socrates' questions. (403)

14.1.1.11 'Floored': When you're floored, she says, leap hurriedly to a fresh idea. 'Floored': where there's no solution or way out. It's an attack on Socrates: he followed the same practice in his investigations. When he was floored or in a corner he would change the subject. (703).

14.1.1.12 'By the Graces': Socrates uses yet another oath. – Not only so. He was not content to swear by the graces. Behind Athene on the wall were some Graces, carved, it is said, by Socrates. He was originally by profession a sculptor. It's an allusion to Socrates' own original profession. (773)

14.1.1.13 'The Melian': contrary to fact. Socrates was an Athenian. But since Diagoras, who *was* a Melian, was attacked as hostile to religion, and he is attacking Socrates as an atheist, he calls him a Melian.

Or: Aristagoras was a Melian poet who betrayed the Eleusinian Mysteries in dance and word, and had a reputation for impiety. 'Melian' is a comic equivalent for 'impious' through him.

Some say that Melian is used of him because his teaching brought peace to the minds of his disciples, others that it means long-haired or shaggy.

Or: 'Melian': some explain that he sharpened the minds of those who came to him, minds untamed before they came. It is a metaphor from irrational animals: sheep (*mela*) are domestic animals. . . . (830)

Cf. **13.1.29.**

14.1.2 The Frogs

'Diagoras': Diagoras was a lyric poet and an atheist, who also introduced new divinities as did Socrates.

14.2 Scholia on Plato

14.2.1 Socrates makes himself out to be confused by Gorgias so as to challenge him to a confrontation in dialogue. (On *Gorgias* 455 B)

14.2.2 There are two kinds of confrontation:

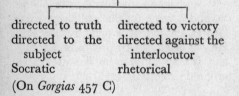

directed to truth	directed to victory
directed to the subject	directed against the interlocutor
Socratic	rhetorical

(On *Gorgias* 457 C)

14.2.3 Aspasia, from Miletus, daughter of Axiochus, wife of Pericles, studied philosophy with Socrates, as Diodorus says in his work on Miletus. . . . (On *Menexenus* 235 E)

The last word has been challenged by Wilamowitz (Aristoteles und Athen 1, 236 n. 7).

14.2.4 'Irony' is the pretence not to be able to do something you can do. (On *The Republic* 1, 337 A)

14.2.5 'Smart' is applied to Eubulus. He was asked by Socrates, 'Eubulus, would you rather be wise or rich?' 'Rich', he said. 'I see the wise sleeping at the doors of the rich.' Socrates answered shrewdly: 'Eubulus, the wise know what they need, provision for the necessities of life, which the rich can provide if they are willing. But these same rich don't know what they need. They need virtue, and that is accessible through the teaching of the wise for all who are willing.' (On *The Republic* 6, 489 B)

14.2.6 This Anytus was son of Anthemion, an Athenian by birth, lover of Alcibiades, and made a fortune out of tanning. Socrates ribbed him on this, and that was why be bribed Meletus to bring a writ of impiety against Socrates. Lysias records this in his *Defence of Socrates*, Xenophon too, and Aristoxenus in his *Life of Socrates*. (On *Apology* 18 B)

The reference to Xenophon is Apology *29–31* (**3.1**).

14.3 Scholia on Hermogenes

Hermogenes was a teacher of rhetoric in the second century A.D.*; his discussion* On Rhetorical Standpoints *was of considerable influence, and his work was the subject of extended discussion later. Syrianus and Sopater belong to the fifth century* A.D.*, John of Sicily perhaps to the tenth.*

14.3.1 If any alleged that Socrates led a loose life sexually he would never be believed. (Marcellinus 55)
  Cf. 61.

14.3.2 A man's actions appear in his face as Socrates proclaims: 'His philosophy depends on his way of life, and his actions depend on his philosophy.' (Syrianus 33)
  Cf. John of Sicily, Scholia on Hermogenes, Forms of Rhetoric 2, 4, 5; 2, 4, 8.

14.3.3 Socrates and Pericles, the most democratic of the citizens. (Syrianus and Sopater 138)

PART FIFTEEN

FICTITIOUS LETTERS

There are genuine letters surviving from the ancient world, some by well-known authors, such as Plato (**2.7**), Cicero (**8.1**), Seneca (**8.2**), Julian (**8.13**), Fronto (**9.8**) and the Younger Pliny. These might be written up for publication, but they are in every other sense genuine.

But fictitious letters were also found: mostly they may be dated between about 200 B.C. and A.D. 200: it is hard to be more precise. These are of four kinds. Some are forgeries, to stock the libraries at Alexandria and Pergamum. Some are works of fiction in the modern sense, a substitute for the short story or novel. Some are school exercises. Some are serious attempts at the presentation of philosophical or ethical truth conveniently and vividly.

References to Socrates are historically almost completely valueless, because we can never be certain whether a new slant (rare enough) represents an actual tradition or a bright idea. The most that can be said is that they offer an impression of how Socrates might appear four or five hundred years later.

15.1 Alciphro

Alciphro was an Athenian of the second century A.D. *who wrote fictitious letters attributed to Athenians five or six centuries previously.*

Thais to Euthydemus
. . . We are no worse educators. Compare if you like Aspasia the courtesan and Socrates the sophist, and ask yourself which was the better educator. You will notice that Pericles sat at Aspasia's feet, Critias at Socrates'. (1, 34, 7)

Thais was a courtesan herself.

15.2 'Diogenes'

Diogenes 'The Dog', founder of the Cynics, was a leading personality of the fourth century. The letters are fictitious.

15.2.1 To Metrocles
. . . Socrates used to say that he did not beg from good men, he demanded his due. All things were theirs, as all things were the gods'. In this he was trying to bring together the thoughts that the gods are lords of all things, that friends hold all things in common and that the good man is a friend of God. So you will ask for what is your own. (10)

15.2.2 . . . If you have any sense (you haven't), if you get drunk you'll have a general meeting of the youth and listen to some joint advice from Socrates in his wisdom and from myself – learn to control yourselves or go to the devil. (28, 7)

15.2.3 To Aristippus
. . . My friend, I am astonished that you are critical of the poverty of those who set their mind on higher things, and you a follower of Socrates, when he wore the same cloak winter, summer and all seasons, shared it with women and didn't look for his dinner in an orchard or a café but on the athletics field. (32, 1)

'Women'; perhaps 'his wives'; this is probably a reference to the anecdote about Xanthippe's refusal to wear his cloak.

15.2.4 To Monimus
Practise your departure from this life. You will do so if you practise death, that is the detachment of soul from body while you are still alive. This, I fancy, is what Socrates and his circle used to call death. (39, 1)

This is based on Plato, Phaedo *80 E.*

15.3 'Socrates and his Circle'

The Socratic letters ought to be the most interesting, but on the whole they are dull and uninspired. 'Xenophon's' letters appear separately at **15.5.**

15.3.1 From Socrates
You don't appear to have grasped my principle, or you wouldn't have written a second time and promised a larger sum. You seem to imagine that Socrates, like the sophists, is a retailer of educational merchandise. . . . (1, 1)

An imaginary answer to a monarch, presumably Archelaus, who courts his services. The first part is an exercise on this theme.

15.3.2 I should not be surprised if you were sceptical about my divine sign; you would not be the only one. There were many sceptics at the battle of

Delium. I was there in the army. My country had marched out in full force, and I was in their ranks. There was a rout, and a mass of us in retreat. We reached a ford: my familiar sign came to me. I halted and called, 'Not this way, men: I've just had my divine voice.' Most of them were furious; they thought that I was having them on at a most unsuitable moment; they marched straight on. Some few listened, and joined me along another route. We arrived home safely, and a runner brought the news that all the others were killed, falling in with a detachment of enemy cavalry who were returning from the pursuit. . . . I made several personal predictions of the future to a number of individuals on information received from the god. (1, 8)

15.3.3 From Socrates
. . . A frugal diet is enough for me. I wear the same clothes winter and summer. I don't wear shoes at all. I am not interested in political repute, apart from a reputation for justice and self-discipline. (6, 2)
    An exercise on this theme.

15.3.4 In my view there is only one basic principle of happiness, and that is thinking straight. (6, 5)

15.3.5 So I shall not leave my sons any money. I shall leave them a more precious possession than money – good friends. (6, 8)

15.3.6 From Socrates
The content of your letter does not surprise me. You report that the Thirty hold the same attitude towards us that they did before you went away. Immediately after your departure I came under their suspicion. The word was circulating among them that their actions needed Socrates. A few days later they summoned me to the council-chamber and brought these charges against me. I defended myself. They ordered me to Piraeus to arrest Leon; they proposed to execute him, confiscate his money and make me accessory to their crime. I refused, saying that I would never willingly be a party to injustice, or something of that sort. Charicles was there; he has a personal grudge against me. 'Socrates,' he said, 'you talk freely; do you imagine that you are incapable of suffering evil for it?' 'Zeus!' I exclaimed. 'Of course not, Charicles. But nothing comparable to the evil of committing a crime.' Not one of them had anything to say to that. I fancy that from that moment they were differently disposed towards me. (7, 1)

15.3.7 From Aeschines to Xenophon
Gryllus and his friends have sent your son Geta with all the news about Socrates' trial and death. However, fortune prevents you from being in Athens instead of Sparta. Oh, Xenophon, how can I write of the villainy of Anytus the leather-worker, the brazenness of Meletus, the outrageous conduct of them both? They are both villains and persisted in their villainy to the bitter end. When we thought that they were ashamed of their practices they went even further in their attacks on us. Meletus is merely ill-starred; he had no personal contribution in the court. Anytus was the root of the prosecution, because of Socrates saying that the leather industry was an abomination in all his conversations in the presence of the young men and his insistence on experts sticking to the field in which they are expert.

The reading is very uncertain. Xenophon was, of course, in Asia Minor, not Sparta, at the time of Socrates' death. I do not know of any other suggestion that he had a son named Geta: there is some confusion.

15.3.8 After he was condemned he went out with a laugh. He seemed happier talking with us during his period in prison than before Meletus' indictment and his own incarceration. He used to say that the prison and the chains forced him to philosophise. 'Out there in the city centre,' he would say, 'people never gave me any peace.' (14, 5)

This does not accord with our general picture: it might be a genuine ironical remark; more likely a foolish invention.

15.3.9 His chief aim in view of his imminent death was to get us to laugh with him. He buttonholed Crito. 'You idiot,' he said, 'it's the Olympic games and the like that are dead. I'm going to travel to a much better place beyond death – to truth.' (14, 6)

15.4 Theophylact

Theophylact is a much later writer who lived at Constantinople in the early seventh century A.D.; the letters are an attempt to present serious problems seriously. Other letters signed 'Socrates' will be found at 52; 64; 82; they are mere ethical clichés.

15.4.1 Socrates to Plato
No one suffers wrong; everyone commits wrong, and commits wrong freely against himself. We are masters of virtue and vice in ourselves. . . . (40)

15.4.2 Diogenes to Demonicus
. . . If a donkey kicks us we don't take him to court. I owe this excellent illustration to Sophroniscus' son. (43)
Cf. **1.4**[21]; **9.1.1.1.**

15.5 'Xenophon'

For Xenophon, see **3**. *The letters are fictitious. One other passage will be found at* **11.1.3**.

15.5.1 To Crito
I would have you know that Socrates often told us that those who take thought to pile up plenty of possessions for their sons but do not trouble about their moral development are like trainers of horses who feed up their horses without training them for war. (2)

15.5.2 To Lamprocles
You should begin by learning a splendid dictum of Socrates, 'Measure wealth in terms of use.' (4)